The Abbé Grégoire and the French Revolution

THE S. MARK TAPER FOUNDATION

IMPRINT IN JEWISH STUDIES

BY THIS ENDOWMENT

THE S. MARK TAPER FOUNDATION SUPPORTS

THE APPRECIATION AND UNDERSTANDING

OF THE RICHNESS AND DIVERSITY OF

JEWISH LIFE AND CULTURE

The Abbé Grégoire and the French Revolution

The Making of Modern Universalism

Alyssa Goldstein Sepinwall

UNIVERSITY OF CALIFORNIA PRESS
Berkeley • *Los Angeles* • *London*

An earlier version of chapter eight appeared as
"Exporting the Revolution: Grégoire, Haiti, and the
Colonial Laboratory," in Richard Popkin and Jeremy
Popkin, eds., *The Abbe Grégoire and His World,* pp.
41–69. Kluwer Academic Publishers, 2000. It appears
here with kind permission of Kluwer Academic
Publishers.

University of California Press
Berkeley and Los Angeles, California

University of California Press, Ltd.
London, England

First paperback Printing 2021

Library of Congress Cataloging-in-Publication Data

Sepinwall, Alyssa Goldstein, 1970–.
    The Abbé Grégoire and the French Revolution : The
making of modern universalism / Alyssa Goldstein
Sepinwall.
        p.   cm.
    Includes bibliographical references and index.
    ISBN 978-0-520-38306-7 (cloth : alk. paper)
    1. Grégoire, Henri, 1750–1831—Political and social
views.   2. Grégoire, Henri, 1750–1831—Influence.
3. Revolutionaries—France—Biography.   4. Bishops—
France—Biography.   5. France—Politics and
government—1789–1799.   I. Title.
DC146.G84S47   2004
282'.092—dc22   2004055308

29   28   27   26   25   24   23   22   21

10   9   8   7   6   5   4   3   2   1

In loving memory of my father,
Dr. Jerry Sepinwall

The publisher gratefully acknowledges the generous contribution to this book provided by the Jewish Studies Endowment Fund of the University of California Press Associates, which is supported by a major gift from the S. Mark Taper Foundation.

O you, the idol of France,
Zealous defender of its rights . . .
                    —Ignace Kolly, 1790

The name of the abbé Grégoire will be the indignation of all centuries. God has already effaced him
from the book of life. In the great day of celestial
vengeance, his name will be joined to the list of the
greatest villains.
                    —Abbé Jean Siffrein Maury, c. 1818

This great citizen . . . was the apostle of the liberty of
peoples.
                    —Ho Chi Minh, 1946

Whatever may be the merits of the abbé Grégoire,
he was the instigator of a veritable cultural genocide
which France must not appear to support at this
time. . . .
                    —Sénateur Jean-Claude Gaudin, 1989

[Grégoire's] message—a passionate appeal for the
unity of mankind—is still as profoundly relevant
today as it was two hundred years ago, and it will
remain so for as long as racism exists in the world.
                    —T. Cassirer/J.-F. Brière, 1996

Abbé Grégoire, wake up!
                    —Chief Rabbi Gilles Bernheim, 2002

Contents

Illustrations

Prologue

Regenerating Biography,
or In Search of Universalism

The history of the world is but the biography of great men.
Thomas Carlyle (1841)

The biographies of the great men of the past are generally useless. They are idle and incredible panegyrics, with the features drawn without shadows, false, conventional and worthless.
James Anthony Froude (1882)

I never planned to become a biographer, particularly of Henri Grégoire. Though biography has long been popular among general readers, the genre had fallen under suspicion in academic history by the time I entered graduate school at Stanford University in the early 1990s.[1] Although nineteenth-century writers like Froude had occasionally challenged *how* biographies were written, the genre suffered a more profound attack in the early twentieth century, when scholars of the French *Annales* school argued that historical change occurred because of structural forces, not the actions of individuals. Biography was further hampered by the rise in the United States and Britain of social history, which regarded studies of political leaders as elitist and old-fashioned; and by poststructuralists, who were skeptical about the idea of a coherent self and about whether individuals could transcend the dominant thinking of their eras.

A second factor made it unlikely that I would look to spend years studying a particular elite male. As an undergraduate, my primary interest had been traditional intellectual history, and I had written a senior thesis about the eighteenth-century English scientist, radical, and minister Joseph Priestley. As I began to read new kinds of historical work in graduate school, however, my ideas about important historical questions began to broaden. I found myself drawn to analyses of gender and race, and of the tensions between universalism and particularism in various world contexts, from the Jewish diaspora to postcolonial South Asia and the Caribbean.

Though I had not thought about it before in academic terms, this issue of universalism and particularism—of negotiations between one's inherited cultural traditions and those of a larger multicultural society, of a universal culture—had been one of the guiding themes of my life and that of many of my friends. Growing up in multiethnic New Jersey, most people I knew were hyphenated Americans (whether Italian-, Indian-, Jewish-, Irish-, African-, or Chinese-Americans); we sometimes struggled to find the right balance between our own cultural heritages and our desire to blend into American society. In graduate school, I discovered scholarly debates about universalism as a political ideology, and about whether it was flexible enough to include all or was defined in a way that inherently excluded some (a case that was made particularly with regard to women). I also became exposed to the range of responses groups had devised to deal with such challenges, from minority nationalisms to total assimilation to hybridity.

Fascinated by this new scholarship, I began to read more about gender, Jewish history, colonialism, and postcolonialism. These new interests competed, though, with the questions that had ignited my interest in history in the first place. These included issues such as why revolutions erupt, what role religious truth claims play in political and cultural life, and how ideas transform as they are diffused throughout society. My studies with Keith Michael Baker, a renowned scholar of eighteenth-century France, reaffirmed my desire to specialize in that field. I was pulled in multiple directions, however, by my new interests. As I considered possible dissertation subjects, one idea came from Aron Rodrigue, a specialist at Stanford in Ottoman and French Jewry: he suggested that the abbé Henri Grégoire was a perfect fit for my interests. I knew that biography seemed passé to many scholars, however, and I wasn't sure how a study of Grégoire, a famous white French priest, would offer new insight into the questions I wished to study.

What did I know of Grégoire at the time? For anyone studying the French Revolution or modern Jewish history, the abbé was inescapable. A priest from Lorraine, he had written a famous essay on Jews in 1788, urging that they be "regenerated" physically, morally, and politically, in order to be integrated fully into French society. The next year, he had come to Paris for the Estates-General and become involved in the Revolution, where he was the figure credited with effecting Jewish emancipation. I also knew that Grégoire had unsuccessfully insisted that the Revolution's Declaration of the Rights of Man and of the Citizen proclaim man's "duties toward God" along with his rights in society. It is possible that I also knew of his opposition to slavery. While I did not dispute that his activities had been important, I knew that they were hardly obscure; a quick glance in the library catalog showed a number of studies about him, some written quite recently.[2] What more, I wondered, could be said about him?

In search of an ideal topic, I investigated several alternatives, ranging from the Sephardic Jews of eighteenth-century Bordeaux to people of mixed race in colonial Saint-Domingue (now Haiti) to particular debates about the French Revolution. Each related either to the question of universalism and particularism or to my more traditional interests in French intellectual history. As I approached my final decision, however, I discovered an agonizing problem. I realized that I could not study everything—and yet, I still felt that many of my concerns were interconnected. One week, I decided I would give Grégoire a try, doing nothing other than reading about him. I expected that I would quickly tire of him, and the idea could be put to rest.

Once I began to trace the abbé's journeys across the eighteenth and into the nineteenth century, however, I found myself unwilling to stop. His life spanned a far longer period than I—or even my mentors—had realized (from 1750 to 1831); beyond the activities I already knew about were many other intriguing aspects of his life. Unlike most Old Regime clerics, he had not come from a background of privilege but had studied with the help of scholarships. Once he ascended to the position of parish priest, he did not seal himself within the clerical world, but instead tried to launch a parallel career in the world of the provincial Enlightenment. After being elected to the Estates-General, he helped spur the union of the three estates into a single National Assembly, thus launching the Revolution. He also appeared as a central figure in a host of other issues, including, but hardly limited to: Christianizing the Revolution, eradicating the dialects spoken around France and requiring standard French instead, extending full citizenship to all men regardless of wealth, smashing forces of "counter-Revolution," abolishing slavery, and maintaining government support for research.

Except for his ambition, Grégoire began to strike me as a real-life Forrest Gump, if a more intellectual version; like the title character in that famous 1994 film, the abbé was never far from the center of important political events. Depicted at the forefront of Jacques-Louis David's famous painting, *The Tennis Court Oath,* Grégoire also presided over the Assembly during the storming of the Bastille, led the efforts to justify the Revolution's nationalization of the Catholic Church, and authored many of the most famous reports on revolutionary cultural policy. One of the most radical members of the National Convention, he was the deputy who introduced the resolution abolishing the monarchy. And yet there he was again, after the fall of Robespierre, as one of the newly minted moderates who would now lead the Republic to stability. In the Napoleonic Senate, he led the opposition; in 1814, with the return of the Bourbons, he became a living symbol of the lost Revolution. Even when he died in 1831, during the first year of the July monarchy, his corpse remained a symbol, as conservative clerics and republicans fought over its disposition. Meanwhile, his international interests—from the Caribbean to India—were even more remarkable. I was further intrigued to discover that he had been seen as an inspiration for peoples around the world after his death (from American abolitionists to Ho Chi Minh), even as he also found bitter detractors.

As I learned more about Grégoire, I saw that he was in fact an ideal choice for exploring my interests. I remained uncomfortable with the idea of writing a "traditional" biography (described by one critic as "stories about the lives of prominent male subjects, . . . praising the subjects rather than questioning their characters").[3] I particularly wanted to avoid giving false coherence to Grégoire's life and falling prey to hero-worship. I had begun to realize, however, that there were other possibilities for the genre. Looking at historical developments through the prism of Grégoire's life, I had started to view the origins and nature of modern universalism in new ways, and to sense that certain truisms about the Old Regime and Revolution needed adjustment.

Unwittingly, I had been led to a field known as new biography or social biography. As I discovered, American social historians' recuperation of biography had been underway well before I started graduate school. In 1968, David Brion Davis had called for a new kind of biography that would focus on individuals in order to illuminate larger cultural developments. While biography ran the risk of "exaggerating the historical importance of individuals," he noted, it "may provide, nevertheless, a concreteness and sense of historical development that most studies of culture lack." A subsequent movement of social biography became popular in the 1980s and 1990s in American women's and social history; it focused on recovering the lives of marginalized individuals to reveal overlooked dimensions of the past.[4]

I discovered a parallel movement in progress in French history, as scholars from a variety of methodological perspectives were reclaiming the study of individuals as an effective way of dissecting complex issues. A pioneer in this movement turned out to be another one of my graduate mentors, Mary Louise Roberts, who was using postmodern notions of self-fashioning to do cutting-edge work in gender history. Some *Annales*-influenced historians also had been revising their perceptions of biographical studies. Bernard Guenée, for example, had argued that structural studies, while invaluable, often lent too great a sense of inevitability to historical change, and that biographical studies could restore attention to "chance, to events [and] to chronological sequence."[5]

Still, as scholars on the cutting edges of their fields turned to the individual, they were sometimes reluctant to call what they were doing "biography." In her 1996 *Only Paradoxes to Offer*, a study composed of essays on individual French feminists, Joan Scott rejected the idea of traditional biography. She nevertheless chose to focus on specific women as "sites" at which "crucial political and cultural contexts are enacted and can be examined in some detail." While Baker applauded my decision to study Grégoire, I later realized that he had exhibited similar reluctance about biography in his own first book. That study, of the Marquis de Condorcet, had begun with a disclaimer that it was not a biography—even though it was in many ways a model for new biography in focusing on Condorcet to explicate a larger issue, the creation of social science. Biography remained an unwanted stepchild in academic history, implying a study that presented every detail of an elite subject's life from cradle to grave, without shedding light on larger historical questions.[6]

Indeed, I was not sure I wanted to call my own study a biography, even a "new" one; at the time I wrote my dissertation, I often insisted it was not. In many ways, it did not fit available models in the genre. Many traditional studies of famous people took the importance of their subject for granted and focused on uncovering "what he or she was really like." Meanwhile, many "new" biographies chronicled the lives of unknown figures to illuminate social history. Neither of these models was suited for Grégoire, who was neither obscure nor universally famous. Other new approaches to well-known figures did not apply either. One theorist of new feminist biography argued for studying a subject's family interactions, but the celibate Grégoire was an only child, and evidence of his relationship with his parents was limited.[7] Meanwhile, I was interested in the everyday details of his life only insofar as they offered insight into larger questions. I also did not think that I should attempt a nonlinear narrative, an aspect of a number of innovative new biographies, since key sections of Grégoire's career—from his life before the Revolution to his international activities—remained largely uncharted. Moreover, I had unearthed several previously unknown manuscripts and letters that I wanted to place in chronological context.

In what follows, therefore, I offer a new prototype of biography, one that blends elements of old and new and is particularly suitable for a subject like Grégoire. While this study has a traditional narrative form, it analyzes Grégoire in three modes—as window, as agent, and as symbol. First, as with other writers of new or social biography, I suggest that my subject's life offers an extraordinary vantage point from which to view large issues in European and world history in the late eighteenth and early nineteenth centuries. Grégoire represents an especially revealing window because of the unparalleled length of his career, spanning four monarchs, one emperor, and no less than five different revolutionary governments.

Grégoire's life is not interesting only as a window, however, since he was not an unknown during his time but someone whose actions helped spark and define the Revolution, and in particular its approach to creating a unified nation out of a religiously, racially, and linguistically diverse populace. I therefore also analyze him as an agent of change, and chart the ways he subtly shifted his self-presentation over time. Finally, adopting elements of postmodern theory, I examine his currency as a symbol of both the Revolution and its universalism, for his contemporaries and for countless others after his death; during key moments in French history, from 1880 to 1931 and 1989, the memory of Grégoire has been resuscitated to defend or attack the revolutionary legacy. Invocations of Grégoire (positive or negative) have not been confined to France, but have been produced by actors as diverse as Ho Chi Minh, Harlem Renaissance intellectuals, American and French Jews, and the Nazis.

One thread of this study will thus chart Grégoire's life, introducing him to new readers and intervening into scholarly debates about him. Much of existing scholarship has offered a series of nonintersecting Grégoires: the egalitarian friend of Jews and blacks, the ruthlessly homogenizing Jacobin, the austere Christian republican. In contrast, I hope to explore how various parts of his oeuvre were linked, even while demonstrating that his ideas did evolve over time (something at odds with the claim made by Grégoire and other scholars that he never changed his ideas) and were sometimes contradictory. To the extent possible given Grégoire's enormous output (over four hundred published essays, discourses, and books, plus a voluminous correspondence) and the limitations inherent in reconstructing any life, this study thus aims at comprehensiveness. While every biographer inevitably brings his or her worldview to the study of his or her subject, I also have tried to avoid the twin poles of heroic or villainous portrayals of Grégoire, which have so often characterized studies of him.

Since a regenerated vision of biography involves moving beyond the individual life to larger historiographic issues, my discussion of each stage of his life will simultaneously tackle several macro questions. While I hope that this narrative can offer a variety of insights into late-eighteenth- and early-nineteenth-century life, I concentrate on three large sets of issues, which are presented in more detail in each of the three part introductions. The first set (which lies at the core of part 1) concerns the intellectual origins of the French Revolution and the relationship of Enlightenment to Christianity in prerevolutionary France. Grégoire's earliest decades call into question the notion that France (in contrast to other European countries) lacked a tradition of enlightened religion. They also suggest that the French Revolution had a more diverse intellectual lineage than is often imagined, and that Revolution and religion were not necessarily destined to be enemies in France.

The second set of issues, explored especially in part 2, concerns the Revolution's idea of universalism. I focus on Grégoire's idea of "regeneration" (remaking people anew, chiefly through political action) and its centrality to revolutionary ideology. I argue that revolutionary universalism was made possible only through the mechanism of regeneration, which was used to manage a society full of religious, racial, linguistic, gender and other differences and turn it into a unifed French nation. Regeneration allowed for including in the nation groups that had previously been mistreated, but at the same time it necessitated that they relinquish their particularities in order to be seen as full members. Because gender difference was viewed as fixed, women were not seen as capable of regeneration to the same degree as even long-hated groups like Jews or people of color. Part 2 also explores the relationship between Revolution and religion, and the reasons for the radicalization and failure of the Revolution.

The final set of issues, introduced in Chapter 6 and examined more fully in part 3, involves the Revolution's legacy from the nineteenth century until today. With its ideals of liberty, equality, and national self-determination, the French Revolution is often viewed as having inspired movements of liberation around the globe. Grégoire's life confirms this aspect of the Revolution's legacy; especially after the failure of republicanism in France, the abbé worked to export these ideals to other parts of the world, notably the Americas. His life also reveals, however, that French revolutionary ideals could justify colonialism and conquest just as easily as liberation. The legacy of the Revolution is thus contradictory. The recurring difficulty in France—and many modern nation-states—with resolving issues of religious, racial, and sexual difference stems from the tensions inherent in the idea of regeneration. Even when this word is absent, it also colors the way Europeans and Americans talk about their interactions with "non-Western" nations. Studying the abbé Grégoire, a central figure in his own time, can thus help illuminate ours.

Grégoire's Early Years

*Enlightenment and Religion
in France, 1750–1789*

Introduction to Part One

What were the intellectual origins of the French Revolution and its influential idea of universalism, which suggested—even more radically than in the American case—that all men were equal? From where did future revolutionaries like Grégoire draw their ideas for reform? What was the relationship in Old Regime France between the Enlightenment and other intellectual movements, including Christian ones? Much of late-eighteenth-century intellectual history has been overshadowed by the presence of the Revolution at century's end, as historians have read its factions and conflicts backwards in a search for origins. Tracing the Revolution back to Enlightenment philosophes like Voltaire, Montesquieu, and Rousseau has thus been a venerable tradition in eighteenth-century studies. This genealogy has competed in recent years, however, with studies highlighting the religious (particularly Jansenist) origins of revolutionary discourse, and those showing the importance of lesser-known Enlightenment popularizers. Meanwhile, whereas scholarship long depicted the Revolution as preplanned, new work emphasizes the way deputies to the Estates-General changed and radicalized their views once they arrived in Paris in 1789. Roger Chartier has argued that the Enlightenment did not create the Revolution but the opposite—that "it was the Revolution that invented the Enlightenment by attempting to root its legitimacy in a corpus of texts and founding authors reconciled and united, beyond their extreme differences, by their preparation of a rupture with the old world." Indeed, the mid-century philosophes, freethinkers in some domains but not others, would likely have been shocked at many of the actions later carried out in their name.[1]

Another important question in Enlightenment studies has been the relationship between Enlightenment and Christianity. Though historians have recognized the existence of "enlightened religion" in other countries in the eighteenth century, they often have been hesitant to do so for France, which is frequently portrayed as having had wholly separate Enlightenment and Christian camps. This unrelenting enmity is sometimes used to explain why France erupted into revolution instead of experiencing gradual reform like some European neighbors, and why its revolution was more violent than in the American case. Philosophes and conservative clerics did in fact clash regularly in France in the decades preceding the Revolution, and their conflicts would help inspire much of revolutionary policy. At the same time, the stark opposition often drawn between these schools of thought may be too simple. Was there no common ground at all between enlightened and religious ideas in France? Was it truly impossible for Frenchmen to find inspiration from both the Gospels and the *Encylopédie?*

Grégoire's story helps shed new light on these important issues, while also giving a more human-sized view of what it was like to be an aspiring cleric and intellectual in the last decades of the Old Regime. His early years, though little discussed in many studies, are vital to understanding his intellectual development and reconstructing late-eighteenth-century life.[2] First, Grégoire shows us that Enlightenment and religion could be less antagonistic than has frequently been thought. Historians such as Dale Van Kley and David A. Bell have nuanced our understanding of the relationship between religion and the Enlightenment by showing how ideas drawn from Jansenist Catholicism were subtly incorporated into Old Regime political debates. Grégoire's trajectory reveals other aspects of the intermingling of enlightened and religious thinking in late-eighteenth-century France. As we follow his travels through the seminary, to the Enlightenment world of the Nancy and Metz Academies, and into the quasi-Masonic Société des Philantropes of Strasbourg, we will see young Henri moving in circles that aimed consciously to mix philosophical and religious ideas. His seminal idea of regeneration would emerge not from the Enlightenment or Christianity alone, but also from eighteenth-century currents of enlightened religion. His activities therefore suggest that the Revolution and Christianity were not irrevocably destined for bloody conflict.

Second, we will see that Grégoire drew on a multiplicity of sources, suggesting a much greater diversity of ideas in France than has often been acknowledged, particularly in the border regions of the east, which were home to Protestants and Jews as well as Catholics. Rather than being the product of any one ideological tradition, his intellectual affinities linked him to churchmen and unbelievers, Jansenists and Jesuits, Jews and Gentiles, Protestants and Catholics, Freemasons and profanes, Frenchmen and foreigners. The roots of his thought—like those of Revolutionary ideology itself—were thus profoundly heterogeneous, with ancestry in Enlightenment, religion, and enlightened religion.

Finally, though Grégoire's ideas would evolve and change over the course of the Revolution, we will see that many of his revolutionary interests were already present in the 1770s and 1780s. Protestant friends would help shape his social views, and the programs he began in his own parish in the 1780s parallel ideas he would later propose on a national scale. By the eve of the Revolution, Grégoire would be in a position to win an essay contest sponsored by the Academy of Metz on ways to make Jews "more useful and more happy." This contest would give Grégoire a platform for articulating the idea of regeneration, that would become so central to the Revolution and to his own career.

CHAPTER I

From Tailor's Son to Enlightened Abbé

A Provincial Journey

We begin our journey in Lorraine, four decades before the Revolution, where a child named Baptiste Henry was born to modest artisans named Bastien Grégoire and Marguerite Thiébaut.[1] Aided by scholarships and endowed with unusual intelligence, young Henri (as he came to be known) would exhaust every opportunity he received for schooling and would soon ask his teachers to place him in a religious seminary. We might imagine an eighteenth-century seminary student as someone who had opted to close himself off from secular influences. Henri, however, was not only an aspiring cleric but also an ambitious provincial intellectual—like many young men of the time, he desired to make an impact on his society, to know important figures and to become known to them. Even while training in the church, Grégoire would vie for notoriety in the provincial academies and societies that were so important to late-eighteenth-century intellectual life; an extrovert, his search for good conversation would also lead him to make myriad friends.[2] As we seek to trace Grégoire's earliest years, we therefore need to look not in one place but in many: in the multiplicity of worlds the young Henri entered, in country and city, in seminary and court, among true believers and heretics. Though previous biographies have overlooked this, he would be particularly influenced by a quasi-Masonic group called the Société des Philantropes of Strasbourg.

BECOMING A PRIEST: THE EARLY YEARS
OF THE PRODIGY FROM VÉHO

The Lorraine in which Grégoire was born on December 4, 1750, was a countryside of rolling hills. Vého, Henri's natal village, was a tiny hamlet a short walk from Emberménil, the parish seat. The two towns were within twenty kilometers of the court at Lunéville (seat of the independent duchy of Lorraine) and the renowned crystal manufacturing town of Baccarat. They were also approximately fifty kilometers from Nancy and one hundred kilometers from Metz, Lorraine's largest cultural and commercial centers. Lorraine had had a complicated history, and the area was a tangled nexus of political jurisdictions. Much of Lorraine was part of the duchy rather than fully part of France, though Vého itself was within the French kingdom. Stanislas, the duke of Lorraine and former king of Poland, was also Louis XV's father-in-law.

Who were Henri's earliest influences in this region? He himself claimed that his greatest inspirations were his parents, who taught him that being virtuous was more important than being rich. An only child, Grégoire was extremely attached to them: "I thank the heavens for having given me parents who, having virtually no riches but piety and virtue, took pains to transmit this heritage to me." In the decades after their deaths, he would often say that he could not wait until they would all be reunited in heaven: "How many times have I anticipated this happiness in my thoughts!"[3]

Grégoire began his formal education by studying with the local priest, who may have been a Jansenist. Jansenism was a seventeenth-century Catholic theology which emphasized man's depravity in the wake of original sin and the role of divine grace in saving an elect few; it also advocated rigorous piety. Jansenists were particularly critical of Jesuits, whom they saw as overly lenient and too closely allied with papal absolutism. While popular among many segments of the French clergy and public, Jansenists' emphasis on predestination and their attacks on the Jesuits had led to their condemnation by the pope and the French monarchy; in 1710, Louis XIV destroyed the abbey of Port-Royal, the hub of French Jansenism. The suppression of the Jansenists created even more sympathy and enhanced popularity for them, though their tenets remained controversial. Vého, Grégoire's birthplace, was served by the regular canons (monks) of Saint-Augustin de la Congrégation de Notre-Sauveur, who are said to have "professed Jansenism openly."[4]

By the age of eight, Grégoire knew how to read and write. The nine-teenth-century Lorraine scholar Louis Maggiolo, who interviewed people who knew Grégoire as a child, wrote that the future cleric "would tell stories from the Bible with emotion, and the schoolmaster had nothing more to teach him. Grégoire would give the lesson to his younger classmates, who used to listen to him with respect." Since Vého held so little educational opportunity for the precocious Henri, he was sent to study in Emberménil with the parish priest, the abbé Cherrier. The other children who studied with Cherrier were the offspring of the great local families. While Bastien Grégoire's earnings as a tailor would not normally have allowed his son to continue his studies, young Henri was fortunate to become a scholarship student, aided by the clergy's funds for the poor.[5]

The books Cherrier assigned his pupils would have a profound impact upon the young Grégoire. According to Maggiolo, Cherrier had them read Racine, Virgil, the *Port-Royal Grammar,* and the *Histoire de l'ancien et du nouveau testament des juifs* by Dom Augustin Calmet. Calmet's work, which argued that "one can never have a truly distinct notion of Christianity unless one understands the history of the Jewish religion," seems to have had a particularly strong influence on the future abbé. Later, he would try to write a new history of the Jews; he would also visit Calmet's old order at the Abbaye de Senones. Grégoire also may have been influenced by the Christian universalism of the work's interpretation of Genesis; Calmet insisted that all nations, from China to Egypt to the Americas, had a common origin and that the history of Noah was also their history.[6]

Through these books and through Cherrier, the young Grégoire would also have an introduction to the school of Port-Royal (which centered around the abbey of Port-Royal). Though maintaining that Grégoire would never be a true Jansenist in doctrine, Bernard Plongeron has written that Cherrier taught his students about these controversies and may have thus sparked in Grégoire a general sympathy for Port-Royal.[7] Grégoire also may have gained a sympathy for the persecuted Port-Royalists through hearing about the author of his grammar textbook, Antoine Arnauld, a leading Jansenist and former resident of the abbey.

Grégoire's learning during this period was not limited to the classroom. According to Maggiolo, his loathing of class pretension stemmed from his experiences with his classmates. The family of one of these classmates (Euskerkem de Borroger) often invited all of the boys to spend vacations at their château in nearby Marimont-la-Basse. Rather than being enjoyable, Maggiolo asserted, the experience fostered resentment in Grégoire and gave rise to a lifelong hatred of aristocracy: "The contrast between the privations of his father's home and the splendors of château life exercised, if I can believe the stories I have heard [from conversations with Grégoire's childhood friend and lifelong confidant, the abbé Jennat], an unfortunate influence on the spirit of the young peasant from Vého." Citing an unspecified letter from 1789, Maggiolo argued that Grégoire had a "sort of poorly disguised animosity toward the nobility, who 'regard the people as their slaves, the king as their rival, and the clergy as their prey.' "[8]

Grégoire would soon outgrow what he could learn in Emberménil and its environs, however. At the age of twelve, he felt a religious calling, and Cherrier looked for a suitable school in which to place him. The choice of where to send him was complicated by continuing battles in France between Jesuits and Jansenists. In 1764, the Jansenists and their supporters succeeding in having the Jesuits banned from Metz and elsewhere in France, as they had been five years earlier from Portugal. In Nancy, however, which was part of the duchy, they were protected by Stanislas. Some details of Grégoire's schooling during this period—such as who taught him in Nancy and whether that city was Cherrier's first choice for him—remain unclear. We do know, however, that he studied there from 1763 to 1768 at a secondary school *(collège)* run by the Jesuits.[9]

Though Grégoire had had a number of teachers inclined toward Jansenism, he seems not to have become a partisan in these disputes. On the contrary, he embraced his Jesuit teachers as much as his earlier instructors. As he recalled in 1808 (at a time when his Jansenist sympathies were more fully developed): "I studied with the Jesuits in Nancy and received nothing but good examples and useful instruction." Even if he "did not like at all the spirit of the defunct society," he pledged that he would "maintain a respectful attachment toward my teachers until I am in the grave." He was also proud to discover during travels to England—forty years after his studies had ended—that his Jesuit teachers still remembered him and "loved me tenderly."[10]

Grégoire's days as a student of the Jesuits, however, were numbered. With Stanislas's death in 1766, the Jesuits lost their protector, and Lorraine passed into French hands. In 1768, the French government expelled the Jesuits from their last stronghold and disbanded the *collège* where Grégoire had been studying. The experience of seeing his Jesuit teachers expelled seems to have angered Grégoire and made him suspicious of political authorities; rather than being a Jansenist partisan who supported the expulsion, Grégoire saw this action as an abuse of power. Indeed, looking back on this episode in 1790, he would call the expulsion one of the "hundred thousand vexations of the old government, which burdened France so heavily."[11]

Grégoire next studied under a series of teachers from different orders. With the Jesuits expelled, he resumed his study in Nancy with the *collège*'s new faculty, who were apparently Jansenists from Notre-Sauveur, the order that had served Vého. After that he headed to Metz (probably in 1769–71), where he studied under the Lazarist Adrien Lamourette, who would later be his colleague in the National Assembly as well as the constitutional bishop of Lyon.[12] One scholar has claimed that Grégoire was not merely Lamourette's student, but more properly his disciple; this writer insists that Grégoire's first essay on the Jews (1778) was written so soon after he studied with Lamourette that the teacher must have had a great influence on it. Since Grégoire's studies with Lamourette seem to have occurred seven to nine years before his composition of this essay, we should be careful before assuming that Grégoire derived all of his ideas from this teacher. Lamourette's later writings do reveal him to be highly sympathetic to the idea of the *retour des juifs* (the "return" of the Jews to the church preceding the Second Coming) and he may have been one of the people who introduced this idea to Grégoire. The evidence suggests, though, that in Grégoire's elaboration of what to do about Jews, the student was probably leading the teacher.[13] Regardless of who inspired whom, however, Grégoire would retain for Lamourette a feeling of deep gratitude and esteem.

After his studies in Metz, Grégoire moved on to Pont-à-Mousson, where he encountered yet another set of ideas. There, Grégoire seems to have studied with Cherrier's friend, the abbé Sanguiné, and been introduced to Richerism. Sanguiné was an important advocate of this clerical movement, which was built around the ideas of Edmond Richer, an early-seventeenth-century cleric. Richer had aimed to raise the status of curés (parish priests) within the church structure, and his ideas became particularly popular in eighteenth-century Lorraine. Grégoire would be deeply influenced by Sanguiné, and would praise his teaching many years later, while defending the Civil Constitution of the Clergy.[14]

Even as an unordained student at Pont-à-Mousson, Grégoire's brilliance earned him a position as professor. According to contemporary evidence, Grégoire taught there for three years and directed study in the humanities. His selection for the important position of professor was closely watched and discussed by others. Summarizing Grégoire's early years in an otherwise critical assessment, the abbé Chatrian (another Lorraine priest and future Assembly deputy, who would become a critic and rival of Grégoire) noted: "After a few years at the seminary of Metz, while still only a subdeacon, he was judged suitable for directing the humanities at the *collège* of Pont-à-Mousson, and this choice was applauded. During the three years that he was form-master for the *troisième*, he lived up to the favorable impression that people had formed of his abilities." After his years studying and teaching, Grégoire was finally ready for the priesthood. According to the account of Antoine Sutter, he returned to Metz in 1774 for his ordination, which occurred on April 1, 1775.[15]

If Grégoire's years in the seminary had detached him at all from the harsh realities of peasant life, his first job would be an instant reminder. For seven months, Grégoire served as *vicaire* of the rural district of Chateau-Salins, an experience that may have crystallized his feelings about the oppression of peasants under the Old Regime and about the ability of the clergy to alleviate their suffering. Among all of the tax burdens in prerevolutionary France, peasants in Lorraine felt particularly squeezed by the *gabelle,* a salt tax that required them to buy their salt at high rates. While Grégoire served in Chateau-Salins, a poor man of eighty-four was imprisoned for having dared to dry some salt himself in order to make a thin soup; the man never saw freedom again, dying behind bars. Grégoire, who administered last rites to him, remained haunted by this incident fifty years later; he noted in 1824 that "the confessor who gave him the sacraments has climbed different ranks of the hierarchy. But of all the functions he has performed, none left more moving and *honorable* memories than that which we have just described." Once elected to the National Assembly, Grégoire would again remember this experience and campaign passionately against the *gabelle.*[16]

While we know little else about Grégoire's activities and ideas in Chateau-Salins, there is more evidence about his next position. In 1776, he became the *vicaire résident* of Marimont, a post he retained for six years. Two accounts exist of Grégoire's experience there, each of which sheds light, in its own way, on the state of his thinking at that stage in his life. According to the abbé Chatrian's recollections in 1794, Grégoire cared little about his duties, was anxious to depart from established practice, and was scorned by the pious. An ambitious cad who cared little about propriety or decency, Chatrian's Grégoire did nothing but cause trouble:

Le sieur Grégoire showed himself there to be very occupied with his clerical finery, leading a life of dissipation and amusement. He hardly cared
about honoring the priesthood with which he had been invested, to the
point of making others doubt whether he recited the breviary and of scan-
dalizing some pious persons through the philosophico-heretical tolerance
of which he made a show. . . .

It was also at this time that he caused a truly deplorable scene in the
Church of Bassing [the parish seat]. He was there at the time of the patron
saint's day; even though there was a Capuchin father who had been invited
in advance to preach the Panegyric of the Holy Patron, our young cad . . .
insisted on ascending the altar and declaiming a completely Protestant sermon, in which he attacked nearly all Catholic practices of saint-worship
as abuses. . . . M. Chapelier, the excellent curé of this parish, vigorously
repented having allowed him to preach in his church on that day, and
never again thought of the incident without pain.

Maggiolo offered a different view of Grégoire's years in Marimont. After
interviewing residents there in the 1830s, he judged Grégoire to have
been extremely popular—someone remembered fondly for his hard
work, aid to the sick, and attention to the local school.[17]

Certainly, there are reasons to view Chatrian's account as colored by
his intense dislike of Grégoire, especially after the latter's rise to fame
during the Revolution. Based on Maggiolo's having met at least some
people who remembered Grégoire fondly, we should not see Grégoire as
a careless dilettante. Nevertheless, it is doubtful that Chatrian fabricated
the idea that Grégoire was controversial; moreover, Chatrian did occasionally praise Grégoire when he felt that the young priest had done
something worthy of acclaim.[18] It seems likely that Grégoire was beginning to press for some kind of change in the Church, foreshadowing his
later activities in Emberménil. He also had begun, as we will see in a
moment, to pass much of his time with laymen in the court at Nancy. As
Grégoire moved from one world to the other, it is not surprising that he
offended conservative Catholics who were hostile to currents of Enlightenment and reform.

Meanwhile, we should remember that even if Grégoire was acting
worldly, he still earned a paltry salary, two hundred livres. In Sutter's
words, "The lot of a *vicaire résident* was not enviable. . . . This was the
proletariat of the Church, and some of them remained their entire life in
this miserable condition."[19] Grégoire would have better luck than many
of his fellows: in 1782, he was named curé of Emberménil, Cherrier having designated him as his preferred successor. From this post, he would
ultimately be elected to the Estates-General.

But we must not get ahead of ourselves. We are still trying to determine what would distinguish this young cleric from others around him, what would spur his development into the famous abbé Grégoire. So far, we have focused on Grégoire's life within the seminary and the ministry. Part of the answer to questions about his intellectual development lies within the Church; however, to fully comprehend Grégoire's development, we must look beyond this world.

INSTRUCTING ONESELF: INTELLECTUAL LIFE
IN ENLIGHTENMENT NANCY

Even while a seminarian, Grégoire was manifesting ambitions outside the church. He was also coming into contact with local luminaries and others from vastly different backgrounds. Grégoire tells us in his *Mémoires* that he sought mature intellectual mentors: "In my youth I always sought (and I love to say this) friends older than me; this, I believe, gives one a share in the experience of others." He suggested that his two greatest mentors were Pierre Joseph de la Pimpie Solignac, former secretary to Stanislas, and a cleric named Joseph Gautier. Solignac had written a history of Poland, along with other works that Grégoire claimed "hardly merited being cited"; Gautier had a varied literary career, publishing work on geometry and the English language, along with an apology for Christianity and a response to Rousseau's discourse on the arts and sciences. Gautier, who corresponded with the Academies of Paris and London and had assembled an impressive collection of natural history specimens, may also have been the source for Grégoire's lifelong fascination with natural history. Grégoire's relations with these men probably lasted from the late 1760s to the early 1770s. During these years, Grégoire also began to do work for the Nancy Academy.[20]

Grégoire also was displaying an independence of mind in his choice of reading material, choosing books far beyond what his teachers assigned. The world of books would be one of his first connections to intellectual life, and he would maintain an intense love affair with reading throughout his life. During his teenage years, he was an unusually voracious reader, a regular at the Bibliothèque municipale of Nancy. Indeed, Grégoire's *Mémoires* contain a revealing anecdote about his first visit there. He wrote, "I was a child when, for the first time, I entered the public library of Nancy. The abbé Marquet, then assistant librarian . . . , said to me, 'What would you like?' 'Books for *amusing myself.*' 'My friend, you have come to the wrong place; here we only give books for *instructing oneself.*' " Grégoire reported that he had replied, "I thank you; I will never forget this reprimand for as long as I live." As the young Henri matured, he would remain a passionate bibliophile.[21]

Of particular relevance in our search for Grégoire's early intellectual influences are two books he would later call his school-age favorites: Jean Boucher's *De justa Henrici tertii abdicatione*, and the *Vindiciae contra tyrannos*, which he attributed to Hubert Languet. The two books came from opposite ends of the sixteenth-century religious spectrum; Boucher was a Catholic who had supported the suppression of Protestants, while the author of the *Vindiciae* was a radical Protestant pamphleteer.[22] Still, as Plongeron has noted, the *Vindiciae* was as influential among Catholics as among Protestants. In positing the idea of a political contract between the ancient Israelites and their God, the work argued that the rights of subjects preceded those of their temporal rulers. As for Boucher, Dale Van Kley has commented that in vesting sovereignty in the entire Catholic community and asserting that kings should be elected by and accountable to the Estates-General, Boucher and other Catholic polemicists made similar arguments to—and even "shamelessly plagiarized"—their Protestant adversaries.[23]

In terms of Grégoire's intellectual development, what is essential is that both books defended the right of subjects to resist and even kill an unjust ruler. As Grégoire would later write, these books, along with others he liked at the time, shared a common theme: they were "in favor of liberty." Certainly, Grégoire's having retroactively called these books his childhood favorites does not mean that they were; it might simply reflect a desire to cast his childhood in a certain light. Still, Grégoire did seem to think that he was being courageous in revealing it: "How much my enemies will profit from this information, . . . in imputing to me a seditious character that I never had!" He also applauded his own "precocity" for having liked these works at such a young age.[24]

Beyond reading, Grégoire sought to make a name for himself in the intellectual world. In 1773, the Academy of Nancy held an essay contest on the importance of poetry, and Grégoire decided to enter. His entry showed both religious and secular influences. On the one hand, it revealed the pen of a writer with a religious bent; it hinted at his life-long desire to carry a religious perspective into the secular sphere. Instead of beginning with the pagan Greeks, he informed the reader that the first poetry was that of the Hebrews: "[It was] the most sublime poetry, the most majestic, & all the riches of the secular Muses will never equal it. I open David, and what energy! What nobility! What images! Sometimes I see a merciful God who opens his hand, and the earth swims in abundance. Sometimes it is a terrible God who arms himself with wrath and makes the universe tremble from the sound of his lightning." Grégoire exulted in the religious content of David's poetry, a theme he would later reprise.[25]

At the same time, the essay reads much differently than Grégoire's later works, many of which have a much more explicit Christian content. In many places, Grégoire sounded like any classically trained young man using romantic metaphors: "Born with a clear penchant for Poetry, I want to proclaim its praises; faithful lover, I will celebrate my beloved." He sang the praises of Virgil and Homer, Corneille and Jean-Louis Guez de Balzac. His references sound little like the antimonarchical, piously Christian firebrand Grégoire would later become. He flattered Stanislas by calling him "a tender Prince, beneficent and sensitive to the misfortunes of humanity"; he imagined the ruler standing among Greek gods and great French poets: "O Stanislas, I can see you in that illustrious assembly [of Muses and Greek gods]. Placed between Tituses and Theodores, an immortal crown is on your head, & the wishes of Lorraine are at your feet. The rare geniuses who have enlightened the universe are there. The Barclays, the Calmets, the Hugos, the Grafignis, & all those who have brought fame to my homeland [patrie], are also there." Grégoire also celebrated secular muses, like the Lesbie and la belle Laure. So different was the essay from many of his later works that Grégoire would later be embarrassed by its content; as the abbé Jennat told Maggiolo, the elderly Grégoire "seemed to regret that the tone of his Eloge de la poésie was hardly suitable to the dignity of his ecclesiastical functions."[26]

At the time, however, Grégoire was quite proud of his effort—and unashamed to show the Academy members how much he wanted to win. "A single desire remains in my heart," he concluded. "That would be, Messieurs, to please you. . . . This desire has directed my brush, and I have tried to paint an elegy for Poetry. I hope I have made one for myself." Grégoire's desire proved successful, and he won the contest. Rather than closing himself inside his parish, Grégoire was now firmly ensconced in the institutions of the provincial Enlightenment. He now had a basis from which to interact with the intellectual elite of Nancy.[27]

This heady experience posed unanticipated challenges, however. Grégoire reported in his Mémoires that in the face of his interactions with the Nancy elite (a "society of people of letters who, having lived in the court of the good Stanislas, were far from having religious sentiments") and being introduced to popular secular works, he became unsure of his faith. He noted that he was "devoured with doubt after reading so-called philosophical works."[28]

If Enlightenment works would pose the greatest challenge to Grégoire's religious beliefs, they also would provide the means with which he could extricate himself from this quandary. Several modern commentators, relying principally on Grégoire's later statements, have asserted that his only relationship to the Enlightenment was one of hostility.[29] Yet, as Grégoire later reported, after "examining everything," he used the intellectual tools of the philosophes to decide that "I am Catholic, not because my fathers were, but because reason, aided by divine grace, has led me to revelation." The philosophes were clearly having an impact on him in other ways; his footnotes reveal that he was reading Enlightenment works and taking their ideas seriously. In a description of his trip through the Vosges in the mid 1780s, for example, Grégoire let slip that he had read through Voltaire's collected works.[30]

Enlightenment works thus played a critical role in Grégoire's early intellectual development, even if his ultimate evaluation of them was negative. Grégoire's confession makes clear that he was initially convinced by the philosophes' antireligious arguments; it was only after soul-searching in response to their criticisms that Grégoire felt firm in his faith. As we will see, encounters with secular philosophes would continue to exercise a formative influence on his worldview.

Meanwhile, Grégoire continued to experiment with poetry, giving it to Gautier and de Solignac for their feedback, though he later burned all his early attempts. He again entered the Academy's contest in 1774, it seems, but with much less success; reports suggest that his entry drew only ridicule. Fortunately, however, his entry remained anonymous, and Grégoire continued to be involved in Academy life.[31]

ENCOUNTERING THE RELIGIOUS ENLIGHTENMENT:
THE SOCIÉTÉ DES PHILANTROPES OF STRASBOURG

After his literary successes at home, Grégoire was soon looking beyond Nancy for intellectual companionship. He began to travel in Lorraine and in Alsace, particularly to the city of Strasbourg. Late-eighteenth-century Strasbourg was a remarkable place, fusing French and German culture and attracting intellectuals from throughout Europe. Though the situation there, as in most places in France, was different for Jews, it also had an unusually diverse religious culture. Because of the Treaty of

Westphalia, Protestant groups were allowed to practice openly in Alsace, something denied them elsewhere in France. By the 1780s, Franklin Ford has argued, confessional differences produced little overt conflict, and "Catholics and Protestants had arrived at a social relationship going beyond mere coexistence."[32]

Strasbourg was thus a particularly fertile place for the development of currents of enlightened religion, and Grégoire would soon come under the influence of a circle of Lutherans there who were particularly active in mixing piety with Enlightenment ideas. Around 1770, these men and other friends in Strasbourg's cultural elite formed a quasi-Masonic society called the Société des Philantropes of Strasbourg (henceforth SPS). They imagined an international brotherhood like the Masons, which would have its headquarters in Strasbourg.

Though it has figured little in previous studies of Grégoire, the SPS played a crucial role in Grégoire's intellectual development.[33] Grégoire not only interacted with the founders of the SPS, but also helped to found a satellite branch of the Société in Nancy. Moreover, he participated in the society's contest on "the Jewish question" in 1778, four years before Christian Wilhelm Dohm's famous work on the Jews and seven years before his own entry in the Metz Academy contest of 1785–88. According to Grégoire's own later insistence—in evidence undiscovered by previous scholars—it was the SPS contest that in fact spurred his interest in Jews. He also claimed that his Metz entry was merely an excerpt from his SPS essay and that he would have won the SPS contest if the organizers had not run out of money and thus failed to award a prize.[34]

Furthermore, Grégoire remained friendly with the society's founders well into the nineteenth century, identifying them as some of his closest intellectual confidantes. By 1788, he was referring to SPS leaders Jean de Turckheim, Jean Laurent Blessig, and Frédéric-Rodolphe Saltzmann as old friends and asking to be recalled to "our friends in Strasbourg"; he would work with Turckheim on abolition campaigns even into the 1820s. His letters to these men, to Blessig's student Jean-Chrétien Ehrmann, and to the brothers Oberlin show his great affinity with them and the way their ideas shaped his understanding of the "problem" of the Jews and many other issues.[35]

What exactly do we know about this society? At the outset, it is crucial to mention its Masonic connections. While it has been asserted periodically that Grégoire himself was a Mason, the evidence for this is vague and mostly unconvincing.[36] Nevertheless, many of the founders of the SPS in Strasbourg and in Nancy were Masons, including the club's president, Jean de Turckheim, who held a high office in Strasbourg Masonry.[37] Moreover, sources suggest that the SPS was in fact a humanitarian offshoot of the heavily aristocratic lodge *La Candeur* in Strasbourg. Margaret Jacob has called the SPS a lodge with "masonic foundations and ambience. Such societies, of which there were many founded by lodges throughout Continental Europe, are often described in retrospect as quasi- or para-masonic. In them the idealists of the lodges could recruit non-masons and engage in specific projects for social reform and utility. . . . In eastern France the Strasbourg Society of Philanthropy and the Harmonious Society of Reunited Friends, both with strong associations with *La Candeur,* were the local version of the Enlightenment applied." Bertrand Diringer, the author of a thesis on Strasbourg Masonry, has added that there was a "very clear penetration of the Masonic milieu" in the SPS, and that it was "an antichamber for Masonry, and possibly a way of being associated with it without being initiated." Diringer also speculated that membership in the SPS instead of a lodge "presented the advantage of being risk-free for a priest."[38]

Of course, there were important differences between a quasi-Masonic society like the SPS and an actual lodge. For one thing, Diringer noted, the SPS did not draw from a cross-section of Strasbourg Masonry, but "only from the strata with the highest social status" and from the most intellectual Masons. More importantly, the lodges were committed to secrecy, while the societies tried to publicize their activities to the general public. It is clear, nevertheless, that the SPS was "pregnant with Masonic influence."[39]

Outside of Strasbourg Masonry, the society had another important influence, that of the philosophic or literary Enlightenment. As David A. Bell has noted in a study of Strasbourg intellectual elites on the eve of the Revolution, several SPS members were heavily influenced by French and German philosophes. Bell points out that the bookstore founded by Saltzmann (an SPS member, Freemason, and close friend of Grégoire) was the chief means by which "Alsace encountered the Enlightenment," while Blessig (another SPS Mason and dear friend of Grégoire) "frequently praised Voltaire and Rousseau" and "sought out d'Alembert" in Paris. Other sources show us that Turckheim—an aristocrat who belonged to Strasbourg's leading family—was a devotee of Voltaire, with whom he had an extended correspondence. These men were also deeply influenced by the German Enlightenment *(Aufklärung)*: several of them were intimate friends of Goethe and Herder.[40]

We should therefore not be surprised to see ideals drawn from the philosophes and from freemasonry (or, as Margaret Jacob has called them, the "Enlightenment of the philosophe and the popular Enlightenment") pervading SPS publications.[41] Indeed, the SPS began an announcement of its formation with a Lockian account of the origins of human society: men, it declared, "even among the most savage," naturally form societies. They used universal language to talk of the commonality of men throughout the world, and spoke of the need for widespread enlightenment. They also showed a belief in human perfectibility, something at odds with Christian notions of original sin: "An active beneficence is the basis of Philanthropy, & its principal goal is the physical and moral perfection of man, from which results the greatest happiness he can enjoy in civil society. All human knowledge that can help console, relieve, or enlighten man is the source of Philanthropy." Moreover, they aimed to foster equality and fraternity among the members; they would unite "rich men, sensitive to the culture of letters and to the pleasure of doing good, who want to make use of their fortunes respectably, and educated and hardworking people, ready to consecrate their leisure to the general utility and the moral, economic, and political perfection of society."[42]

Enlightenment principles also pervaded the concrete plans announced by the SPS. First and foremost, they wanted to support morality among the common people in the countryside; they would recognize local do-gooders by writing about their good qualities and honoring them publicly, and sponsor festivals "to conserve the purity of morals in the countryside." They would also support technical education for the poor, giving them "instruction suited to their status," and provide food for bastard children. Finally, they aimed to "enlighten men about their true interests."[43]

The SPS's two sections (economic and literary) also bore traces of Enlightenment thinking. In keeping with Enlightenment ethnology, the economic section would have a universal outlook: "The philanthropist-citizen observes man at all ages and in all climates. No nation, happy or unhappy, savage or civilized, will escape his penetration." In political economy, the section would focus on "legislation, morals in general, and especially education, the basis of public happiness, whose perfection has interested all the philosophes of our century," while its rural economy emphasis would be on helping "the simple inhabitant of the countryside to participate in the Enlightenment and in the beneficent philosophy of his century." The members vowed to emphasize practical and useful applications, to help farmers with techniques, and "to propose prizes for the invention of new and useful instruments." Like other Enlightenment writers, the society suggested that the common people were not fully aware of their own best interests and that their efforts might not be appreciated by the farmers themselves, who were "slave[s] to routine." The philanthrope, armed with science, would thus have to work hard to "destroy deeply rooted prejudice."[44]

Like the economic section, the literary section aimed at enlightening other men. Philanthropes could write poetry consecrated "to religion, to the great moral truths." They would also write histories and biographies whose goal was to educate others by highlighting "true sages, who, having made themselves useful to men through their knowledge [lumières] and their virtues, should serve as models for Philanthropes." Finally, they pledged to write accounts of their travels to provide ethnographic instruction: "The Philanthrope, who makes a vow to love men, must hasten to know them."[45]

In addition to the Enlightenment influence evident in the SPS's ideas, the society had another feature that it shared with lodges and salons: it made sociable behavior a condition of its functioning. Despite its universalist values, the society made clear that not all could participate. They pledged to exclude "those whom a negligent education, a dangerous ignorance, a reason without culture, render unworthy of bearing the beautiful name of Philanthropes." Members would also need "certain literary dispositions" and to "have made progress in the sciences." They could only be selected with unanimous approval, in order to ensure "the sweet intimacy that must reign between Philanthropes."[46]

Much of this should not sound surprising, as many eighteenth-century humanitarian societies were imbued with Enlightenment ideals. We should also not be surprised that there was skepticism about the Société's lofty goals. The always critical abbé Chatrian in fact viewed the Nancy branch as pretentious false humanitarians. The members of this "Société furieuse," he charged, were more interested in self-aggrandizement than in helping others; their "mania is to have themselves paraded and extolled in all the newspapers for even the smallest acts of charity." He accused Grégoire in particular of social-climbing, alleging that "charity has never been his great passion."[47]

What might surprise us, though, is the next aspect of the Société's outlook, which departs from an understanding of Enlightenment thinking that opposes it to Christianity. Homage to Voltaire notwithstanding, members made clear that Christianity would be an object of respect in their gatherings: "Any revealed religion that sincerely aims at the happiness of men merits the homage of Philanthropes. Christianity is the object of veneration in this regard." The SPS made it clear that they would not welcome irreligious people or atheists as members; Christianity was as much a part of their society as enlightened ideals. Yet though the society would be Christian, it also would be nondenominational to avoid battles between Protestant and Catholic members. The society noted that "aside from [Christianity's] sublime morality, the Philanthrope is forbidden to discuss the dogmas that have so often divided men." Indeed, society members were a diverse—but clearly Christian—lot, including several Protestant ministers and Catholic priests.[48]

Christian theology and Enlightenment ideals also mingled in the SPS's 1778 contest on what to do about Jews. Why would Jewish status have been fodder for an essay contest? Though Jews had been alternately welcomed and banished in France for centuries, by the eighteenth century there were approximately 40,000 Jews in France, divided into three main populations: around 30,000 Ashkenazi (Yiddish-speaking) Jews in Alsace and Lorraine; 4,500–5,000 Sephardi (Ladino-speaking) Jews in the southwestern cities of Bordeaux and Saint-Esprit-lès-Bayonne; and a clandestine community in Paris of 500–800 Jews of mixed lineage (there were also isolated communities in the south and approximately 2,000 Jews in the papal states of Avignon and the Comtat Venaissin, which did not become part of France until 1791). The Sephardim of the southwest, who originally had entered France in 1550 as *conversos* from Spain, had become well integrated, prosperous, and proficient in French; by the eighteenth century, their status was no different from that of similarly situated Christians. Some Sephardim even held civic offices.[49]

The plight of the eastern Ashkenazim was far worse. Though their status was more secure than that of the Jews of Paris, who had no legal right to reside in that city and were under constant police surveillance, they suffered from humiliating laws restricting their residences and occupations, and faced widespread popular anti-Semitism. Many worked in money-lending, peddling, or the grain and cattle trades—the only jobs permitted them—and were viewed as usurers by the surrounding population. Despite Strasbourg's reputation for tolerance among Christians, that city—SPS headquarters—banned Jewish residents completely (Jews could enter only by day, and upon payment of a tax). Meanwhile, in other parts of the east, most Jews lived in misery and in fear of the sporadic outbreaks of popular violence that were encouraged by local nobles and clerics.[50]

In the eighteenth century, some philosophes had begun to question the idea that the state should practice religious discrimination; though this line of inquiry was more often sparked by the fate of Protestants, it also extended to Jews. Nevertheless, advocacy of religious tolerance did not always imply sympathy for Jews themselves. While some writers, like Rousseau, portrayed Jews positively, other philosophes, most notably Voltaire, depicted them as contemptible and sneaky.[51]

When the SPS asked men of letters to consider whether Jewish status should be changed, it is thus unsurprising that its own position seemed ambivalent. In the program for the contest, the lofty principles of the SPS charter mixed with harsh anti-Jewish prejudices—probably drawn less from Voltaire than from popular and Lutheran traditions.[52] The contest seems to have been inspired not only by debates among philosophes but also by the violence associated with the forged receipts affair of 1777–79, in which a local official named François-Antoine-Joseph Hell (later a deputy to the National Assembly) coordinated the mass forging of receipts suggesting that Alsatian peasants had paid off their debts to Jews. During this same period, mass riots erupted against the Jews, and the government sided with the peasants and decreed the reduction of all debts owed to Jews. Hell later declared publicly that he had forged the receipts because Jews were Christ-killers who also murdered children, and in 1780 the government arrested him, mostly because the violence he was inciting was causing instability and because Jews who were owed money by peasants often needed it to pay the heavy taxes they were assessed.[53]

For the most part, the SPS contest program adopted the point of view of anti-Jewish peasants; it framed the problem as one of helping them escape the scourge of Jewish usury rather than of rescuing Jews from prejudice. It suggested that Jews, through their religious pride and cruel business practices, bore the responsibility for their outcast status: "For more than two thousand years, the Jewish nation, separated from all others by peculiar ceremonies and an exclusive form of worship to which it clings with enthusiasm, has been dispersed around the globe." In trying to eke out a living in their admittedly precarious situation, Jews had made themselves "onerous to the common people." The program cited (without contesting) arguments that "their industry has been ruinous and calculated on fraud; that in the cities they have received stolen goods and consume life savings with usury . . . ; that in the countryside they have devoured the assets of farmers with easy advances [and] extorted reimbursements at the wrong moment." Jewish usury, the society's program hinted, posed terrible dangers for the social, economic, and moral order of the French countryside.[54]

Still, despite these many sins, the SPS held out the possibility that the Jewish condition should be improved. One of the reasons Jews were so onerous to others, the members suggested, was because "the ordinary functions of citizens . . . and nearly any honest means of gaining subsistence" had been forbidden them. The program recognized that Jews were humans and had greatly suffered from prejudice: "The imprescriptible rights of humanity have often been denied to them by fanaticism. In the dark centuries of the Middle Ages, all of the physical ills that have desolated the earth were imputed to them." Yet though the last sentence suggested an explicitly Enlightenment view of history (i.e., that the Middle Ages were dark rather than a religious golden age), the program suggested that the Gospels, rather than secular political goals, should be the true determinant of Jews' fate: "The interest of the moment, rather than the spirit of the Gospels, has alternatively tolerated and oppressed them." The question posed by the society was thus how to reconcile these opposing considerations—humanity and the corruption of the Jews—to best protect peasants.[55]

The program's reference to the Gospels rather than "the interest of the moment" shows that members wanted their actions to be seen as rooted in Christianity. Nevertheless, the SPS's Christianity was decidedly reformist, paralleling—and incorporating—Enlightenment critiques of Christianity. Before it became defunct, the society published one volume of *Mémoires,* which, in good Enlightenment form, bore a foreign imprint, that of Berne. Alongside several signed articles was one anonymous article attacking ecclesiastical greed ("Considérations sur les abus de la Sécularisation des biens ecclésiastiques"). Though it has gone unnoticed by previous scholars of Grégoire, it seems highly probable that this polemic was written by Grégoire himself, thus providing us with rare evidence of his prerevolutionary thinking.[56]

Moreover, even alongside the declarations of Christian loyalty, the Société's description of its goals (its "Précis") yields a strikingly agnostic view of religion, perhaps reflecting a committee-drafted document. Echoing the deism of Rousseau's *Creed of a Priest of Savoy,* the document declared that, rather than look for an ultimate religious truth, the Philanthrope should simply believe in the universal aspects of religion ("love for his neighbor, for good deeds, and for purity of the heart") and follow the rites of his parents.[57]

How can we account for the coexistence of strong Christian and Enlightenment sentiments within the same society? While certain Enlightenment writers (such as Voltaire and Diderot) were notoriously anti-Christian, the French Enlightenment was not in fact hostile as a bloc to Christianity. Indeed, though the SPS's veneration of Christianity may have been inconsistent with atheistic forms of the Enlightenment, other philosophes praised the Gospels and Christian morality. Rousseau's *Creed* commanded a philosophe to practice a religion so as best to pay homage to the Supreme Being, and his other writings expressed veneration for Christianity. Moreover, even the group that put together the *Encyclopédie* had heterodox views on religion.[58] While it is true that the Church contained, as Darrin McMahon has recently noted, a vocal group of anti-philosophes who saw the Enlightenment as signaling the "onset of darkness," theirs was not the only position in the Church. Other clerics quietly embraced parts of Enlightenment thought that were not overtly hostile to religion, while still others sought to reform certain aspects of Christianity in acknowledgement of Enlightenment critiques. As R. R. Palmer noted in 1939, Enlightenment and religion could be more commingled than we have allowed.[59] The enlightened Christianity of the society therefore presents less a paradox than it might seem.

The society's Masonic connections are also illuminating in this regard. While Masonry may have a reputation for irreligion (particularly because Pope Clement XII condemned it in 1738 and the Catholic Church continues to frown upon it), much of eighteenth-century Masonry scorned atheism. Indeed, the SPS's deeming of non-Christians to be unworthy of membership closely parallels a founding document of speculative Freemasonry that similarly restricted membership to believers: it declared that if a Freemason "rightly understands the Art, he will never be a stupid Atheist, nor an irreligious Libertine." While banning interdenominational squabbles, this document required that Freemasons subscribe "to that Religion in which all men agree, leaving their particular opinions to themselves." In French Freemasonry, according to Margaret Jacob, the grade of *chevalier élu* required an oath to "adore God and to be faithful to my king and charitable toward my brothers and to defend the Christian religion with the last drop of my blood." Therefore, she notes, the "search to be enlightened need not have entailed the irreligious."[60]

What can we conclude from our foray into Grégoire's early years and into the writings of the SPS? First, the SPS had a crucial impact on the development of Grégoire's social ideals. As he later noted, "It was their contest that gave me the idea of being interested in the question" of the Jews; he would also share SPS leaders' ambivalence on this question, seeing Christians as responsible for persecuting Jews but also holding Jews culpable for maintaining wrong-headed ways. SPS ideals also bear a striking resemblance to many of Grégoire's other later activities and ideas. These included educating peasants, improving agricultural technologies, writing histories of great men to serve as models of virtue, and using cultural events to instill moral values. Certainly, Grégoire's concern for peasants was not something he suddenly gained in this society; no one needed to teach the prodigy from Vého that an individual's moral and intellectual worth bore little relation to his social status. Grégoire's inclination to help the forgotten members of society and his love for Jesus Christ also predated his involvement with this group. Here in the crucible of this quasi-Masonic provincial society, however, Grégoire found secular (and even Protestant) confirmation for his views, developed them among a cohort of kindred spirits and discovered practical ways to implement them. The SPS—which Grégoire would later call "a society now dissolved, to my great regret"—thus had a decisive role in his development as a thinker and as an activist.[61]

Grégoire's involvement with the SPS also suggests that the role of the Enlightenment in his intellectual development is more complicated than scholars have assumed. Grégoire's desire to affiliate with such a society (and his longtime friendship with its members) makes clear that Grégoire was quite receptive to many Enlightenment ideas. While Catholicism played an important role in his intellectual development, his social origins and his interactions with those steeped in Enlightenment and Protestant ideals helped him crystallize his views in the 1770s. Grégoire's early years thus reveal active currents of enlightened religion in France, even though this very notion was later seen as oxymoronic.[62] As developed by Grégoire and others, enlightened religion was not merely an internal church movement (the "Aufklärung catholique")[63] that aimed to counteract the secular Enlightenment, but a conscious mixture of philosophic and religious ideals.

Ultimately, however, the influences on an individual's thinking are less important than how he or she cobbles together these diverse ideas. How would Grégoire weave these diverse intellectual inspirations into his own vision of universalism? Without venturing far from Vého, the former prodigy would soon find himself with an important position from which to spread his ideas.

CHAPTER 2

The "Bon Curé" of Emberménil

In the last chapter, we saw the dramatic rise of the prodigy from Vého. Born to a modest tailor and his wife, Grégoire was welcomed not only into the aristocratically dominated world of the Church, but also into the highest intellectual circles of eastern France, equally comfortable with veterans of Stanislas's court and with the wealthy merchants and nobles in the SPS. Despite this ascent, however, Grégoire's future remained uncertain. The salary of a *vicaire résident* was paltry, and many priests never emerged from these positions. Moreover, as the abbé Chatrian made clear, Grégoire's unorthodox preaching style and worldly friendships were raising eyebrows among conservative clerics.

In 1782, however, Grégoire was named *curé* (parish priest) of Emberménil, as successor to his old mentor—something truly momentous for someone in his circumstances. No longer fated to be a struggling rural artisan or a poorly paid *vicaire*, Grégoire was now assured a modest but comfortable income. Though he could have remained an important man in Emberménil until his death, Grégoire was to set his sights higher. What happened in the 1780s to spark his universalism and to prepare him for his later political career? What would drive him to enter the Metz Academy's essay contest on Jews in 1785–88 and to run for election to the Estates-General?

A complete picture of Grégoire's years as curé of Emberménil remains elusive because sources for this period, as for his childhood, are few.[1] Nevertheless, we can still learn about his activities and ideas during these years from a number of sources, including some not before located by other scholars. These sources suggest that Grégoire had four main areas of activity in the 1780s: educating his parishioners and other country dwellers in moral and practical knowledge, traveling to meet famous intellectuals in Switzerland and Alsace, preaching and pushing for church reform, and writing about Jews (the last of which is discussed in the next chapter).

Though Grégoire's activities in the 1780s are far less famous than his later actions, tracing them is important for several reasons. First, examining his practical attempts to improve his parish helps us to better understand the roots of his ideas of regeneration and universalism, and how they were simultaneously inclusive and paternalistic. We will see in particular his early interest in spreading enlightenment to groups he felt had been denied knowledge (in this case, his poor parishioners); in having enlightened *bons curés* (virtuous priests) be the vanguard of social change in France; in eradicating patois; in forming friendships with members of other religions (even while hoping he might convert them); in traveling as a means for learning about different cultures; and in using Johann Caspar Lavater's ideas on physiognomy to understand moral behavior. We also will see the origins of his controversial stances on the Church during the Revolution, as he shaped Richerist and Enlightenment critiques into his own vision of an ideal, purified church.

Looking at these activities will also reinforce what we have seen so far about the heterogeneity of Grégoire's intellectual lineage. Though some scholars have claimed that his formative influence during this period was Jansenism, we will see that his chief influences during this period continued to include Catholics, Protestants, and deistic philosophes. Since some of the ideas he developed in this period were enshrined into law during the Revolution, this material reminds us that the origins of revolutionary ideology were as multiple as Grégoire's.

ENLIGHTENING THE PEASANTS: AN EDUCATOR-CURÉ

When Grégoire arrived in Emberménil in 1782, with his own benefice, he was keen to effect reform in his parish—something he had plenty of time to think about, given the parish's small size.[2] While there, he developed a model of the ideal *bon curé* that he would later see as key to social change during the Revolution.

Grégoire was hardly the first curé in France to rethink his role and seek to expand it. Indeed, curés had been working to increase their

status within their parishes—and to "improve" their parishioners—
since at least the Counter-Reformation. As scholars of Catholic renewal
have noted, parish priests in the sixteenth and seventeenth centuries saw
popular culture as vulgar, licentious, and chaotic. By introducing new
rituals and codes of conduct, they sought to wipe it out and replace it
with more Christian behavior. Following reforms made at the Council
of Trent (the Tridentine reforms), priests were particularly worried
about the populace's potential to direct violence against the authorities
and upend the social order. Clerical campaigns against popular festivals
and confraternities thus went hand in hand with government efforts to
control the masses.[3]

The eighteenth-century *bon curé* movement, of which Grégoire was
a part, sought to preserve some aspects of this post-Tridentine model
while altering its political valence. As Timothy Tackett has noted, a new
ideal developed in the eighteenth century among enlightened portions of
the clergy—that of the curé as "key agent of the king, tutor of society,
servant of Enlightenment in the countryside." This model preserved the
idea that the lower classes needed direction from above, but offered a
more enlightened model of the curé's basis for authority. While the priest
would still endeavor to change his parishioners, a *bon curé* saw his
authority as deriving from the knowledge he could bring to the parish
rather than from his hierarchical position. This model was not, however,
unanimously accepted in France, and choosing to be a *bon curé* was a
decidedly reformist stance.[4]

Within this larger movement, Grégoire's particular vision of the *bon
curé* began with moral probity. He thought it essential that curés be close
to their parishioners but also police their own conduct to avoid temptation. Without specifying what kind of temptation he meant, Grégoire
made clear that the Catholic priesthood offered easy opportunities for
immoral activities. As he later wrote in his *Mémoires:* "Confession
establishes in the Catholic religion more immediate relationships
between pastors and their faithful than in societies where this part of the
sacrament of penitence has been suppressed [e.g. Protestant ones]. Well,
such was the confidence of my parishioners that if I had not placed
mandatory limits on their spontaneous revelations, they would often
have exceeded them. From this I concluded how necessary it is for priests
to have a [standard of] conduct at least as severe for themselves, because
the ministry sometimes offers personal dangers." In addition to modeling Christian morality, Grégoire focused his attention on educating his
parishioners. Now that he had a benefice, he could at last implement

some of the ideas he had discussed with the SPS. Grégoire thus began his lifelong campaign to improve the inhabitants of the countryside and allow them to participate in the advances of the century.

In thinking about what, if anything, to teach the poor, Grégoire joined a lively Enlightenment debate. Many philosophes had suggested that the masses were simply incapable of being enlightened. Voltaire famously wrote friends that "I have no concern with the *canaille* [masses]; it will always remain *canaille*," and "We have never pretended to enlighten shoemakers and servants; that is the job of the apostles." Other philosophes, from Diderot to Locke, Kant to Rousseau, made similarly disparaging comments. Nevertheless, all of these men occasionally showed optimism about peasants' potential for learning; as Voltaire wrote in 1767, "All is not lost when one gives the people the chance to see that it has intelligence. On the contrary, all is lost when one treats it like a herd of cattle." While the philosophes mistrusted the masses and feared the possible effects of educating them too broadly, most believed that the poor should be given basic physical, occupational, and moral instruction.[5]

Where did Grégoire stand in these debates? From what we can tell, the curé of Emberménil went farther than many Enlightenment thinkers in his sincere commitment to educate the people among whom he lived. At the same time, he sought to tailor their education to their station. Though he himself epitomized social mobility, he did not want to encourage his parishioners to think about alternate careers. Instead, he aimed to enlighten them in moral and practical matters, while keeping them interested in farming. As he later noted, "I formed the project to carry, as far as possible, enlightened piety, the purity of morals, and the culture of intelligence among the country people: not only without distancing them from agricultural work, but fortifying their attachment to this type of work."[6] The curé wanted to bring new ideas to his parishioners, but he also idealized the agrarian character of the society in which he had been reared, imagining that rural societies were the most conducive to good morals.

One major element of Grégoire's campaign to educate his parishioners was the establishment of a parish library. Here too, he chose materials he deemed suitable for his parishioners' social station, filling the library with "well-chosen ascetic books and works relative to agriculture, hygiene, the mechanical arts, etc." Later in life, he continued to idealize carefully selected parish libraries as a means for improving the poor. In 1796, he recalled: "When I was a curé, I had a library for the use of my parishioners. Its object was all that was useful and possible to teach country-dwellers: books about rural economy, veterinary arts, knowledge of plants, care for the sick, and especially well-chosen pious books. They themselves [the parishioners] asked me . . . to lend them the books, to indicate the chapters most suited to their needs."[7] Grégoire's position on this matter differed markedly from many priests, who believed that reading the Bible was forbidden to parishioners, while reading nonreligious books was a waste of their time.[8]

Beyond Grégoire's later recollections about his efforts to improve his parishioners, little evidence exists about *what* he wished to teach them. We have some clues, however, from another source. On the eve of the Revolution, having won the Academy of Metz's essay contest on the Jews, Grégoire told a correspondent that he wanted to write four new works. One of them would be a manual on how best to educate country dwellers; it would pick up where an author named Philipon de la Madelaine had left off in his 1783 *Vues patriotiques sur l'éducation du peuple, tant des villes que de la campagne.*[9]

Because Grégoire never completed his work, we cannot know definitively what it would have said. We can gain some insight into what he was planning, though, by examining this letter and Philipon's work. Heavily influenced by Rousseau and Locke, Philipon aimed to apply Enlightenment ideals to education; his sources included the *Encyclopédie,* d'Alembert, Buffon, and Helvétius. He also valorized the detheologized *bon curé* who could bring secular education and morality to the common people. Philipon's work was hardly egalitarian; for him, "the true goal of educating the common people is to make them love their [social] station."[10]

While Grégoire presumably wanted curés' teachings to include more religious content, his letter (in which he called Philipon's work "praiseworthy") and later actions suggest that he aimed to extend Philipon's arguments, not counter them. For him as for Philipon, a project aimed at "educating the common people" implied that they needed an education different from those above them and that parish priests could best provide it.[11]

It is important to point out here that Grégoire differed in a key way from many other eighteenth-century reformers who sought to improve peasants. One important study depicts Grégoire as being like Parisian outsiders who had "stereotypes of a savage France" and saw the peasant as "a creature comparable to a farm animal."[12] The abbé was undoubtedly influenced by his urban education and by the elites of

Nancy and Strasbourg, and he had internalized the idea that country dwellers were inferior to city ones. As a product of the countryside, however, he never came to view the peasants as completely Other. Grégoire would remain suspended between the urban and rural worlds throughout his life, never belonging fully to either. He viewed himself as an outsider to the city and criticized its values but may have been embarrassed by origins he had learned to view as backward. Grégoire's efforts during these years to educate his parishioners, like his later efforts on patois, thus show a sincere commitment to helping improve his parishioners, even if this commitment can be viewed as condescending for assuming that the rural poor needed to become more like urban elites.

How did Grégoire's parishioners view his efforts? If we are to believe Maggiolo, the people of Emberménil seem to have appreciated them rather than regarding them as high-minded. Even though he himself disapproved of Grégoire's revolutionary-era activities, Maggiolo reported in 1873 that "I have met many of the children [of Grégoire's tenure in the parish] who have reached their old age. Not a single one had forgotten the instructions, the examples, or the virtues of the good curé." When Grégoire left his position to become the bishop of Loir-et-Cher during the Revolution, the local inhabitants wrote a letter filled with genuine regret; in turn, Grégoire felt so close to them that he called his decision to leave them the most difficult one of his life. He later described his days in Emberménil as his happiest, and in his will left a substantial amount of money for the poor of Vého and Emberménil.[13]

THE OBERLINS, LAVATER, AND SOCIAL CHANGE: A TRAVELING CURÉ

In the spirit of the SPS's discussions of travel, Grégoire was continuing to educate himself about his region and to seek ideas that could help him improve the lot of his parishioners. Though the SPS was now defunct, Grégoire still maintained intellectual connections with SPS members and their associates. Among them, the Swiss pastor and writer Johann Caspar Lavater and the Protestant educators Jérémie-Jacques and Jean-Frédéric Oberlin particularly influenced Grégoire's vision of social change. These men would spark Grégoire's interest in physiognomy and in eradicating patois, as well as offer him ideas for improving the peasants more generally.

During 1784–87, Grégoire traveled through the Vosges, to Alsace, and to Switzerland. Thanks to Strasbourg connections, he was lucky

enough during his 1784 Switzerland trip to receive an audience with
Lavater, then one of the most famous men in Europe; he also sought
out other noted intellectuals. The Vosges and Alsace trips, in 1784,
1786, and 1787, were also significant for him. He was thrilled to
return to Strasbourg (as he once commented, "I have always left this
city with regret and always return with pleasure") and see his SPS
friends; as Sutter notes, they were particularly interested in what was
happening "in the *patrie* of Jean-Jacques Rousseau." Grégoire also
journeyed to Senones, where he saw an original manuscript by
Edmond Richer, and paid homage to the late Dom Calmet, whose
work he had enjoyed as a schoolboy.[14]

More importantly, Grégoire cemented his long-term friendship with
the Oberlin brothers, who would exercise a crucial influence on him.
The brothers had grown up in Strasbourg, sons of a professor at the
Protestant gymnasium. Despite confessional differences, Grégoire
shared with them an abiding faith in God and a fascination with country dwellers and patois. Jérémie-Jacques, the older brother, was a professor at the university in Strasbourg, and it is likely he met Grégoire
through the Société des Philantropes. Though Oberlin does not appear
on its 1777 list, he was closely associated with several of its leaders,
having edited the short-lived Strasbourg newspaper *Der Bürgerfreund*
(which has been referred to as an SPS organ) with Blessig, Saltzmann,
and Turckheim.[15]

Grégoire's relationship with the older Oberlin was to play a key role
in his interest in language as a means for transforming the countryside.
Oberlin had been known in eastern France and Germany for his pioneer-
ing studies of local dialects, and had published some of this research in
1776 as *Essai sur le patois lorrain des environs du comté du Ban de la
Roche*. This work depicted patois as the "coarse language of their [rural
dwellers'] ancestors" dating from the fourteenth and fifteenth centuries;
Oberlin contrasted it to the refined language spoken by modern men of
letters and "le beau monde." For him, patois represented a corruption
of standard French, the result of "ignorance and laziness"; it had no purpose and needed to be modernized.[16] Grégoire admired Oberlin deeply
and owned a copy of the work. Though we do not know when he purchased it, it seems to have had an impact on him long before the Revolution; in 1798, he reported to Oberlin that his own language
investigation of 1790 (often cited as the beginning of the eradication of
patois in France) was spurred by having read Oberlin's *Essai*: "It was
you who once gave me the idea by your writings."[17]

Grégoire's relationship with Jérémie-Jacques transcended the study of language. Grégoire would ultimately help him obtain a scholarly grant from the National Convention, and the two would become colleagues in the Institut national. During their long correspondence, Grégoire often sent copies of his work to Oberlin for comments. After he returned from England in 1802, he told Jérémie-Jacques, "How many times I wished to have you there with me."[18]

Perhaps even more important in developing Grégoire's social vision was his relationship with the younger Oberlin, Jean-Frédéric (also called Johann Friedrich or Fritz). Jean-Frédéric, another friend of SPS members, assumed the pastorship of the Protestant Vosgien town of Waldersbach (Waldbach) in Ban-de-la-Roche in 1767 and remained there until his death in 1826. Extremely popular among Alsatian intellectuals even now, he is renowned for bringing education, roads, farming techniques, and commerce to this rugged wilderness. His efforts reached such celebrity in the eighteenth century that a congregation of Austrian Protestant émigrés to the United States asked him in 1774 to be their pastor. Oberlin wanted to go, especially in order to spread the Gospel to Amerindians and to build schools for "young Negroes." Though he never succeeded in emigrating, the founders of a small college in Ohio decided to name it for him posthumously (Oberlin College); they hoped to be as successful in bringing knowledge to their stretch of backcountry as Oberlin had been in his.[19]

Grégoire and Jean-Frédéric were destined to be close friends, for Oberlin represented exactly the kind of minister Grégoire aimed to be. Despite their different confessions, Oberlin and Grégoire were kindred spirits in nearly everything. Both were men of God who were conversant with a wide variety of eighteenth-century ideas. Both had a taste for austerity. Grégoire once noted that "the conduct of the minister of Walderspach [sic] is a lesson and a reproach to many Catholic priests." In turn, Grégoire was one of the only people with whom Jean-Frédéric felt comfortable enough to use the familiar *tu*.[20] Grégoire's comments (at the time and in the nineteenth century) on Oberlin's efforts in the countryside reveal what he thought of his own activities during this period.

Jean-Frédéric Oberlin first visited Grégoire in Emberménil in 1785 because he had heard about Grégoire's visit to Lavater (another close friend of certain SPS members) in 1784. Among his many interests, Oberlin was an enthusiast of Lavater's physiognomic theories. Building on an ancient "science" which held that people's external traits existed only to reveal their interior, Lavater provided extensive commentary on

what various facial features meant. Although strange to modern mind-
sets, Lavater's ideas enjoyed enormous popularity throughout Europe
in the eighteenth century, making him an important figure in popular
culture and turning physiognomy into a favorite parlor game. One
scholar has asserted that Lavater, with whom Jean-Frédéric had an
extended correspondence, was one of the key characters in the younger
Oberlin's life.[21]

Grégoire shared Jean-Frédéric's fascination with Lavater, calling his
work on physiognomy "great." He wrote that "Lavater, who has written on physiognomies, himself has a happy one. There are faces more
beautiful than his, but there is not one that announces more the great
thinker."[22] In a quest for self-understanding, Grégoire was anxious to
know what his own physiognomy signaled about his character, and
turned to Oberlin for help. Oberlin used a homemade device to make a
silhouette of Grégoire (probably the most exact likeness of him that
exists) and later responded to his request to analyze it using Lavaterian
theories (see fig. 1). Grégoire's profile suggested to Oberlin a man with
a promising future. His forehead and nose were "very happy, very productive, ingenious"; his chin implied someone "bold, active, enterpris-
ing, without being too thoughtless." All in all, Oberlin noted, Grégoire's
profile revealed a "restless man who can do much for the good of society by his activities and abilities."[23] Grégoire would display further
enthusiasm for Lavater's physiognomy in his *Essai* on the Jews, and
would gain a key part of his idea of regeneration from him.

Grégoire and Oberlin had much more in common than an interest in
Lavater. Grégoire particularly admired his Protestant friend's commitment to rural ministry and his success in educating his parishioners. In
his travel journal, the curé praised Oberlin's educational efforts, which
mirrored his own aims in Emberménil: "He has advanced education in
the countryside very far. It is surprising in this wild terrain of Ban-de-la-
Roche to find among the peasants such developed common sense, a del-
icacy of emotions, an amiable politeness and pure morals, of which one
finds few examples in some cities." He praised Oberlin for being "very
laborious, active, and educated," for facilitating students' apprentice-
ships of trades, and for teaching peasants relevant principles of botany.
He also felt that Oberlin was "very close to Catholicism on many matters," even if he was also prone to the "reveries of [the Swedish mystic
Emmanuel] Swedenborg" and other visionary sect leaders.[24]

Grégoire's descriptions of his visit to Waldbach reveal a growing critique of urban morality and preference for that of the countryside. "In

FIGURE 1. Silhouette of Grégoire prepared by his friend Jean-Frédéric Oberlin, using a homemade device, in 1785. Courtesy of the Archives municipales de Strasbourg.

Ban-de-la-Roche," he wrote, "nature has not lavished its favors, but the industry of its inhabitants and their patience combat the harshness of the climate. In their poverty, a near golden age exists for them. What a difference between these places and our cities, where one sees foolishness and vices of all kinds."[25] Though this idealization of the countryside was certainly not unique in the eighteenth century, we should remember that Grégoire was himself a country boy; his critique of the city was that of a newcomer rather than of a native urbanite idealizing a rural utopia. Even as Grégoire would be attracted by the cosmopolitanism and intellectual opportunities of French and foreign cities for the rest of his life, he would continue to see rural morality as superior to its urban counterpart.

Grégoire was also influenced by Oberlin's efforts to substitute French for the patois of Ban-de-la-Roche. Like his older brother, Jean-Frédéric viewed patois as a major obstacle to learning and was personally frustrated when he could not understand his parishioners. He thus tried to eliminate the "difficult" patois of Ban-de-la-Roche. According to one scholar, "He succeeded, if not in eradicating it, at least in relegating it to the interior of the family and substituting French as the public and official language." Grégoire never forgot Jean-Frédéric's efforts to eliminate patois, citing his friend as a model during the Revolution's educational debates.[26]

Despite their close friendship, however, Grégoire seems to have always hoped that he could convert Jean-Frédéric. According to John F. Kurtz, Oberlin, who had grown up in a family influenced by German pietism, had a religion more of the heart than of commitment to the dogma of a particular denomination. Because of Jean-Frédéric's heterodox ideas (such as offering communion to Protestant and Catholic alike and signing his letters "ministre catholique-évangelique"), Grégoire hoped he would "return" to Catholicism. Even though he never stopped proselytizing his friend, however, the two men retained respect for each other's beliefs.[27]

Grégoire's relationship with the Oberlins and his interest in Lavater remind us yet again of the importance of non-Catholics, particularly Protestants linked to the SPS, in shaping his worldview. The abbé seems to have idealized his friendships with these men and looked back to his carefree days of clerical leisure with some nostalgia. During the Directory, when he was working feverishly with several groups of men who seemed close to him, Grégoire suggested that his only true friends were in Strasbourg. As he wrote to Jérémie-Jacques in 1795: "When will I be able to be . . . my own master and to delight in the pleasure of seeing my friends, of conversing with them!" Until his death, Grégoire would regard Jean-Frédéric as one of his dearest friends and retain a connection with his family. Grégoire recalled in 1818 when recommending him for a prize: "Differing in our manner of thinking on religion, we were on everything else nearly in unison: the same taste and activity for sparking among the habitants of the countryside the progress of good morals and Enlightenment [lumières], improving the educational system [and] enlightening [éclairer] rural industry and economy." Despite their confessional differences, Grégoire saw Jean-Frédéric as his spiritual twin.[28]

RESTRUCTURING THE CHURCH: A CRUSADING CURÉ

Although he focused his reform efforts on his own parish, the abbé Grégoire was beginning to gain a certain renown in the larger clerical world of Lorraine. In addition to preaching in Emberménil, he sometimes was asked to lead services or give guest sermons in other churches. In September 1786, for example, he was asked to speak at a parish church in Lunéville on the opening of a synagogue in that city. He also gave an oration for the crowning of the village maiden *(Rosière)* at the festivals in 1782 and 1783 (and possibly 1779) in Réchicourt-le-Château. In keeping with his interest in spreading morality among the peasants, Grégoire treasured the opportunity to speak at this festival; he greatly admired the efforts of the local curé to eliminate libertinage in his parish and spread virtue through moralistic pageantry.[29]

Grégoire also was making himself infamous in some eyes. According to the abbé Chatrian, Grégoire was a highly unorthodox orator who shocked those who came to listen to him. Of a service Grégoire led one day in Lunéville, Chatrian wrote in his diary: "M. Grégoire will not allow in his Church paintings or statues. . . . He preaches without a square cap, does not bend to his knees in the pulpit before beginning, does not use a Bible, does not even pretend to preach but rather converses with his listeners. . . . But besides having no brilliant figures [of speech] and no oratorical movements, this 'English orator' finishes suddenly, without recapitulating, without which one has no idea what the point was of his worldly conversation from the pulpit." Chatrian also asserted that Grégoire scandalized his parishioners from the moment he arrived because of his hatred for iconography and his Protestant soul: "The new curé, Protestant in his soul—or rather nothing *[rieniste]*—did not waste any time in Emberménil in showing himself to be an iconoclast. He scandalously pillaged the *tableaux,* statues, and saints' portraits that were in his church, to the point where his parishioners, justifiably unable to contain their indignation, complained about it throughout the region as a vexation worthy of a Lutheran or Calvinist minister." Given Chatrian's taste for hyperbolic critiques of those he disliked, one should not accept this description at face value. Certainly, by the time of the Revolution, Grégoire would become renowned for his fiery oratory. Moreover, by the end of the 1780s, he would become a leader of other curés through what Réné Taveneaux has called his "imposing presence, his inflamed words, his art of handling the masses and dominating them." Chatrian did, however, reveal two key aspects of Grégoire's developing clerical style: his taste for simplicity and his unabashed willingness to turn convention on its head. Grégoire was ready to crusade for reform, regardless of what others thought of him.[30]

One of the changes Grégoire most desired, in accordance with Richerist principles, was in Church organization. As we have seen, Richerism, inspired by the seventeenth-century cleric Edmond Richer, aimed to improve the position of curés within the church structure. Richer posited authority in the entire church, not just among the bishops and higher officials; Richerism was therefore primarily a movement of parish priests. In the spirit of a Richerist tradition that was particularly strong in Lorraine, Grégoire saw curés as the basic and most important element of the church. Like other lower clergy members, he believed that bishops had monopolized power for too long, that curés were the descendants of the disciples, and that the Church should be an egalitarian society. Furthermore, like other Richerist curés, Grégoire felt that an egalitarian church could be achieved through the institution of national councils instead of clerical assemblies, and if priests were free to defend their rights when the bishops opposed them.[31]

Grégoire's first formal effort on church reform was the anonymous essay he published in 1778 in the SPS's *Mémoires*. Though this essay has hitherto been completely unknown to Grégoire scholars, it is extremely valuable for learning about the young Grégoire's ideas, especially because, with the exception of his essays on poetry and the Jews, it is his only extant pre-1788 work. While it drew upon ideas central to Richerism, such as the value of the lower clergy, the essay also reflected critiques made from outside the Church, by lay philosophes and Protestants, who viewed it as corrupt. Grégoire's effort shows that he was both influenced by and sympathetic to Enlightenment critiques of his church. Nevertheless, he still sought to justify its continued existence, in a purified form.[32]

Rather than denouncing Enlightenment and Protestant writers who called for the enormous wealth of the clergy to be confiscated and nationalized, Grégoire admitted that these critics had a point. Historically speaking, he insisted, the clergy's growth in stature had a logical basis: beginning in Roman times, priests had spread "the sweet light of Christianity," and had been met with gratitude by the people. "It was entirely natural," Grégoire wrote, "that the people would shower those whom they regarded as their benefactors with honors and riches." Voluntary donations from people grateful for the clergy's good deeds thus formed the original basis of the clergy's wealth. Nevertheless, Grégoire noted, this state of affairs had changed as the clergy began to include "imbeciles" more concerned with greed than with spirituality. The clergy, he continued, invented pretexts to bleed people, while convents became "splendid palaces, and bishops became the rivals [in material goods] of kings."[33]

Echoing Enlightenment critiques of the Church, Grégoire argued that reform had come only after it had been proposed by laymen. The clergy had been ignorant, Grégoire charged, while lay people had become more and more enlightened. They challenged the clergy about abuses, which Grégoire saw as a blessing in disguise, for it made the clergy understand "the necessity of reform." Grégoire also agreed with critics outside the Church that a poor clergy could spread religion just as easily as a rich one. "Religion," he wrote, "could subsist very well if bishops were not like princes, if cloisters were open [to allow monks the option of leaving], and if no priest earned more than 1000 ecus."[34]

Nevertheless, he claimed, revealing his growing distaste for the extravagances of court life, it would do no good if convents were shut down and the money saved was simply given to the king to mount more operas. Moreover, even if the status quo was untenable, so was any reform that would abolish monastic life completely. Grégoire therefore offered a modest proposal of his own—one that was nevertheless still certain to scandalize conservatives. First, cloisters should be opened so that monks could choose whether to remain or begin new lives elsewhere as useful citizens. Next, monks should be made to do useful labor in exchange for their subsistence. "Idle monks," he charged in incendiary language, "are no less useless than courtesans or dancing women." Nuns also could be useful, Grégoire argued, if they would set up "schools for youth and safe refuges for orphans and widows," and houses of rehabilitation for the "moral correction" of law-breakers who were "not yet corrupt enough to be thrown into prisons." Other convents or monasteries could be assigned "the touching work of consoling the sick" or "the advancement of rural economy, given that the first monks were industrious and cleared the land for cultivation."[35]

Grégoire predicted that his plan, which accepted certain critiques of the philosophes while still seeking to preserve the Church as a useful institution, would be controversial, satisfying neither the Church's opponents nor its fervent defenders. "Such a reform," he wrote, "would undoubtedly be one of the most prominent good deeds that rulers could do for the human race. But I readily admit that it would meet infinitely more obstacles than the complete suppression of the monasteries." Nevertheless,

Grégoire insisted, it was essential to try to fix the broken Church: "However insurmountable may be the obstacles, renouncing any attempt at reform, which would have such happy influences on the fate of the human family, would only reveal a reprehensible cowardice." He hoped that, even if his contemporaries were not yet ready for them, these reforms could be accepted in the nineteenth or twentieth centuries.[36]

Grégoire was right to assume his project would be controversial: the abbé Chatrian, who asserted that Grégoire's authorship of the pamphlet was an open secret, was undoubtedly not alone when he called the essay "truly stupefying [bien frappé]."[37] This did not discourage Grégoire's efforts to push for change in the Church over the next decade, however. In addition to his planned pamphlet on educating country people, one of the other tracts Grégoire hoped to write in late 1788 concerned the education of future clerics. Grégoire lamented that, in the eighteenth-century fever for rethinking education, no one had thought to write about this topic. Aside from Léon Berthe, the modern historian of the Academy of Arras who discovered Grégoire's letter about these projects, scholars of Grégoire have not referred to this work, and there is no definitive record of its completion. Berthe did locate a 1790 pamphlet about the education of clerics but could not determine if it was written by Grégoire or another cleric.[38]

It seems extremely likely that the author was indeed Grégoire, for several reasons. First, the pamphlet had the same Metz publisher as Grégoire's only other wide-circulation work during the Old Regime, his *Essai* on the Jews. Second, the language and word choice sound very much like his. Third, in addition to putting forward a *bon curé* model strikingly like Grégoire's, the pamphlet (which seems to have been drafted before the Revolution, of which there is barely a hint) closely resembles proposals Grégoire later made as bishop of Loir-et-Cher. If Grégoire was correct in asserting that no other authors were interested in this topic, that would be an additional reason to presume that the work was his.[39]

Assuming the pamphlet Berthe found was indeed the work of Grégoire, we can add more information to our knowledge of his prerevolutionary vision of the Church and its clergy. For him, theological training required careful thought. Curés could not be expected to help parishioners through metaphysical doubts if they entertained the same ones themselves. The author denounced the training of priests in the scholastic system of objections, arguing (perhaps in reference to his own case) that it frequently created dangerous crises of faith. Requiring students to debate propositions before they were convinced of them made them "regard the most certain principles as problematic"; it also led seminarians to be quarrelsome and to dislike each other instead of being genuinely interested in intellectual exchange. Grégoire therefore recommended the replacement of the scholastic system with one that taught the principles of faith in a "simpler and more natural order."[40] According to him, a future curé should also study natural law and moral theology, and learn to appreciate the simple style of the Holy Scriptures and the early church. Moreover, schools should be dominated not by monks ("regular" clergy) from one order only, nor for that matter by monks alone, but by the most highly qualified clerics, whether regular or "secular" (priests living among the world, i.e., non-monks). The pamphlet's author himself showed the influence of multiple teachers: he cited everyone from Locke to Arnauld, Bossuet to Montesquieu, even while denouncing Voltaire and the dangers of discussing impious ideas when seminarians were just learning about their faith.[41]

For Grégoire, theological exactness was only part of a curé's duties, however. The budding curé also needed training in instilling basic morality and a love of duty among his parishioners. He encouraged curés to draw pleasure from educating their flock rather than from clerical wealth.

> A pastor, in his village, is the only person from whom one can expect help in moral and religious instruction. If his education was flawed, if he neglects his duties, if he is ignorant, and if he attaches more worth to simple practices than to the accomplishment of essential duties, his people will remain ignorant of their principal obligations or will become superstitious and fanatic.
>
> Nations! Devote care to the studies of your priests. . . . Do not corrupt them with riches and with distinctions that flatter their pride. Talents and virtues should be the costuming of a minister of religion, not crosses and ribbons, which are the frivolous diversions of a childish vanity.

Grégoire also suggested that a priest should be capable of instructing his parishioners not only in religious matters, but also in political and social duties. Using a well-chosen library, a curé needed to educate himself about "sacred and profane history, natural history, physics, and medicine," and to be prepared to act as a sort of paramedic. As far as the peasants were concerned, the great medical discoveries of the eighteenth century were nonexistent; therefore, a priest (the most learned man in a rural parish) needed to find out as much as he could about medicinal remedies in order to prevent peasants ("the most useful portion of society") from dying needlessly. To those who might see such activity as too far afield from the ministry, Grégoire noted that Jesus Christ himself had worked to cure the sick.[42]

Taken together, these two essays give us a good sense of Grégoire's growing interest in church reform during this period. Though he published these essays anonymously, the ambitious curé of Embermésnil would become an increasingly important figure in Lorraine Richerism; Taveneaux has in fact called him the "soul of this presbyterian movement" in Lorraine of the late 1780s. During the writing of the *cahiers de doléance* (grievance lists) on the eve of the Revolution, Grégoire would play an active role in drafting at least two *cahiers,* that of the Embermésnil commoners and that of the Lunéville clergy, each of which was imbued with Richerist ideals. His enthusiasm for Richerism also influenced the way other local *cahiers* were written.[43] As we will see, Grégoire remained interested in redesigning the Church according to Richerist principles even after the Terror.

Despite Grégoire's growing prominence in Lorraine clerical circles over the course of the 1780s, his hopes to reform the Church and clerical education might have remained unfulfilled, two more among the vast heap of Enlightenment-era projects that never came to fruition. Changes were happening in France, however, that would catapult Grégoire to prominence and give him the opportunity to try to realize his vision of an ideal church. After drafting the Richerist-inflected *cahiers* for Embermésnil and the Lunéville clergy, Grégoire began campaigning for election to the Estates-General as a clerical deputy. In late January 1789, he joined with two other curés to demand that the lower clergy be represented in Paris. "First of all, we are citizens," they wrote. And "as curés, we [also] have rights. In 1200 years, there has perhaps never been as favorable an occasion to assert them."[44]

Grégoire won the *bailliage* (bailiwick) election from Lunéville, and was then sent to the regional voting assembly in Nancy. He gave a passionate speech there in which he declared the "incontestable right" of the curés to representation and declared that it would be "revolting" if they were deprived of this right. After all, as the king convened the nation to discuss ways to reform the kingdom, who understood the people better than their parish priests? "We [the curés] admire monks; but we know better than anyone about life in the provinces, about the needs of the common people, and the best ways to relieve them. . . . Are we not in some way the fathers and heads of the communal family? On what topic can we not contribute?"[45] Grégoire's oratory, along with support from Bishop La Fare of Nancy, helped push him ahead of all the other *bailliage* representatives, and he would be elected as one of only two clerical deputies from the entire region of Nancy (the other being the bishop himself).[46]

UNDERSTANDING GRÉGOIRE: A JANSENIST CURÉ?

We have seen in the last section that Grégoire aimed to reform the Church, and that one (though not the only one) of his intellectual stim-uli in doing so was Richerism. Does his Richerism mean, as has often been suggested, that Grégoire was also a Jansenist during these years? This question has sparked particular debate because Jansenism remains controversial in the Church. Grégoire's possible links to Jansenism have also drawn attention because of the argument made in a number of recent studies, most notably those by Dale Van Kley, that the French Revolution's intellectual origins lie perhaps more in Jansenism than in the Enlightenment.[47]

The case for Grégoire's early (and enduring) Jansenism has been made most emphatically by Rita Hermon-Belot and Paul Grunebaum-Ballin. Where Hermon-Belot detected in the abbé's thinking an "enduring familiarity with Jansenism that would need only to be expounded in adversity, and which is explained by the very strong presence of Jansenism in the Lorraine of his birth," Grunebaum-Ballin summed up Grégoire's view of the world in "three words: *Grégoire était janséniste.*" Jean-Michel Leniaud and Augustin Gazier have made similar argu-ments, at least in part.[48]

Though the evidence of Grégoire's identifying with Jansenism and Port-Royal after the Revolution is clear, the argument for Jansenism as Grégoire's capital influence before the Revolution is less convincing, especially given the many other kinds of intellectual inspirations we have seen. The evidence offered by Hermon-Belot dates primarily from after the Revolution, or is nonspecific, such as the idea that Grégoire must have gained Jansenist sympathies from his Jansenist teachers; as we have seen, however, he also admired his Jesuit teachers. As for that given by Leniaud, he mistakenly cites Maggiolo as stating that Grégoire's mother was a Jansenist (when Maggiolo simply contested someone else who had made this assertion). Hermon-Belot, Leniaud, and Grunebaum-Ballin also rely on the fact that the abbé Chatrian called Grégoire a Jansenist. As we have seen, however, Chatrian may not have been the most reli-able source when it came to Grégoire; moreover, he used *Jansenist* and

Protestant as epithets, often calling the same person a "Jansenist, Freemason, gambler, drunk, [and] libertine."[49]

Arguments about Grégoire's hopes for a *retour des juifs* to the Church—central to many Jansenists—are also inconclusive. Grunebaum-Ballin and Hermon-Belot have demonstrated that a longing for the conversion of the Jews was present in Grégoire's writings as early as 1788.[50] It is far less evident, however, that this belief came to him through Jansenism. The idea that the conversion of the Jews was necessary for the redemption of the church had deep roots among non-Jansenists in eastern France and in Germany—for instance, among Grégoire's Protestant friends. Jean-Frédéric Oberlin, for example, was interested in the "final conversion of the Jews" as early as 1767. As Christopher Clark has shown, the idea of the conversion of the Jews occupied a central place in German pietism, which influenced Oberlin and many Protestants in Alsace in the eighteenth century. Grégoire's interest in Jews was therefore not a certain sign of Jansenism; indeed, as we have seen, Grégoire himself would assert that it was the SPS that had raised his interest in Jews.[51]

Because of the paucity of direct evidence, several other students of Grégoire have asserted that he was never really a Jansenist. Ruth Necheles has made the strongest case for this position: "His use of predestinarian terminology and his sympathy with millenarian attitudes led his enemies to call him a Jansenist. And indeed he did exhibit the two traits of piety and puritanism which characterized all those who at one time or another have been called Jansenists. Grégoire's Jansenism went no further." Similarly, Plongeron has dismissed the possibility of any Jansenist influences. He argues that what Grégoire would later find attractive about Port-Royal was not its theology but its symbolic value as a Catholic movement to renovate Christianity which was persecuted by the French state.[52]

As Van Kley himself has suggested, denying any Jansenist aspect to Grégoire's worldview may go too far. That Grégoire was to identify after the Revolution with Port-Royal and with Jansenism is undeniable. Still, even Leniaud admitted that Grégoire's interest in Jansenism was sparked more during the Directory than before the Revolution and was never really theological. Meanwhile, Van Kley examined Grégoire's prerevolutionary and early revolutionary writings, and found many of the abbé's statements to be "simply incompatible" with Jansenist theology. Scholars like Catherine Maire have made a more persuasive case for Grégoire's identification with Port-Royal after the Revolution than before it.[53]

In what, then, if at all, did Grégoire's Jansenism in this period con-
sist? Though this could also have come from Enlightenment or Protestant sources, it is possible, as Hermon-Belot has argued, that Grégoire's
interest in getting his parishioners to read was inspired by Jansenists'
encouraging literacy among the faithful so that they could understand
the Bible. Moreover, even if we have no firm evidence of the abbé's holding doctrinally Jansenist beliefs before the Revolution, Chatrian's
description of Grégoire's services makes them sound Jansenist in their
austerity. This fits with René Taveneaux's account of the extent of Grégoire's Jansenism during these years; for him, Grégoire had "a sympathy of a moral kind more than a doctrinal adhesion" to Jansenism,
marked by "his piety, his taste for austerity, his lack of ornamentation
and his wanting to conform to primitive simplicity."[54]

Grégoire's Richerism might also seem on its face to hint at a doctrinal Jansenism. Richer was himself linked with Jansenism, and Richerism
would be adopted wholeheartedly by the Jansenist movement. Yet, as
many scholars have noted, Jansenism and Richerism were hardly coterminous by the late eighteenth century. Grégoire may have been an heir
to many Jansenist ideas that had become diffused in eighteenth-century
political language, but as Van Kley has convincingly shown in numerous studies, so had many others in the eighteenth century. Grégoire's
Gallicanism and Richerism alone do not therefore suffice to make him
a Jansenist.[55] Jansenism was thus only one of the many influences upon
Grégoire in this period rather than the major one.

In this chapter and the last, we have seen that Grégoire drew his ideas
in the prerevolutionary years not from a single school of thought but
from several. Some of his strongest inspirations continued to be drawn
from enlightened Protestantism, particularly via the SPS and its associates. We have also seen the earliest stirrings of his relentless efforts
toward reform. Along with many curés of his generation, Grégoire
aimed to purify and cleanse the church and to make it less hierarchical.
He also sought to improve his parishioners through religious, moral,
and practical teaching. While he departed from many contemporaries in
deeming these modest farmers *capable* of improvement, his attitude also
had a paternalistic air; it was predicated on the Counter-Reformation
idea that popular culture needed to be wiped out and replaced with
books and festivals of the clergy's choosing. Indeed, like the Oberlins,
Grégoire believed that the peasants should be made to switch the very
language they spoke if it prevented their pastor from understanding

them and thus being able to influence them. With his careful filtering of reading material, he also wanted to ensure that literacy would not alter the social aspirations of peasants.

We can thus see here the earliest version of Grégoire's idea of universalism. He looked at every person in France, even a humble peasant, as having essential worthiness and being an important member of the human family. He also believed, however, that the participation of peasants in that family should be directed from the top down by enlightened parish fathers. We can also see that Grégoire's plans for including all in the social body were deeply rooted in Counter-Reformation Catholicism and its vision of morality; indeed, even as Grégoire made friends across confessional lines, he never gave up hope of bringing them into the "true" church.

At this point, the future "friend of men of all colors" had not even begun to think about the problem of African slaves and whether they too deserved to be considered part of the human family. But in the wake of his SPS activities, he had already begun to think about the place of Jews in society. In 1785, the Academy of Metz would announce a new contest on the subject, and Grégoire would have a chance to gain national stature while articulating a nascent vision of social regeneration.

CHAPTER 3

A Physical, Moral, and Political Regeneration of the Jews

Even as Grégoire's star rose in the Lorraine clerical world of the 1780s, he continued to aspire to a reputation as a man of letters in the secular world. In 1787, building on the interests he had first developed in the SPS, the abbé entered a contest sponsored by the Société royale des sciences et des arts de Metz (the Metz Academy) on the topic "Are there ways of making the Jews more useful and happier in France?" *(Est-il des moyens de rendre les Juifs plus utiles et plus heureux en France?)*. Though the academy initially deemed all of the entries insufficient, Grégoire re-entered with a revised version and ultimately shared the top prize. The paradigm he chose for dealing with this question—that of *regeneration*—had a complicated history and a momentous future.

In focusing on the way Grégoire used the term *regeneration* on the eve of the Revolution, we can glimpse some of the contradictions in this paradigm as he would use it throughout his life. For Grégoire, whose usage of the word was seminal, regeneration was not merely a political action, but also a physical and moral one. Building on meanings of the word in Christian theology as well as in the Enlightenment, the new usage suggested that groups like the Jews who were seen as degenerated needed special help in all of these areas before they could be fully included in the social body. Understanding Grégoire's reshaping of the word is especially important since regeneration would become the dominant paradigm for the treatment of difference in modern France and its empire.[1]

Grégoire's Metz essay also needs to be understood not only as a defense of the Jews but also as a set of statements on the other issues he had been working on since the 1770s, such as spreading Christianity and protecting country dwellers. Like another famous eighteenth-century author on the Jews, Christian Wilhelm Dohm, Grégoire had a motive for entering the contest quite apart from the issue of the Jews themselves: winning a prestigious academy essay contest was an opportunity to gain standing on the national intellectual scene, thereby facilitating the winner's ability to publicize his ideas on other matters.[2]

We will begin by looking at the linguistic history of *regeneration,* then examine the debates on Jews to which Grégoire was responding, and finally turn to his way of answering the question. We will examine both the published version of his second entry and the manuscript of his first entry, which has long been presumed to have been lost, like his earlier SPS contest entry. Rather than being on the cutting edge of contemporary discourse about Jews, Grégoire charted a middle path between writers who had insisted that Jews were no different in any regard from (or, in some regards, were perhaps even better than) other Europeans, and others who saw Jews as incorrigible usurers and Christ-killers who could never be included in civil society. His middle position—an inclusion managed by regeneration—would be that adopted by the Revolution.

REGENERATION: A LINGUISTIC HISTORY

As Mona Ozouf and Antoine de Baecque have shown, regeneration would be a key slogan of the French Revolution.[3] Yet the definitions the word took on during the Revolution—that of a general improvement, a freeing from corruption, or a societal renewal—were departures from what regeneration had meant a century earlier. During the course of the eighteenth century, regeneration would shift from a rare word to a popular one while changing in definition. Starting as an almost theological term, it would gain secular and then physical connotations in the middle of the century in the hands of the philosophes.[4]

As late as the middle of the eighteenth century, *régénération* was a relatively rare word with only three meanings: two theological ones (baptism and resurrection) and an infrequently used medical one (repair of injured body parts or the flesh). While the ARTFL database of French-language texts suggests that baptism was by far the most common connotation of the word at that time, regeneration as the "new life of resuscitated bodies" (less common but used in the French Bible) would be especially important for the word's future life. Indeed, regeneration as resurrection implied not merely cleansing or purifying a living creature, but raising the dead, infusing new life into a corpse in order to revive it. It is also important to note that the active verb *régénérer* was almost never used, for regeneration could come only from God's action. Humans did not themselves have the power to regenerate; they could only *be* regenerated *(régénérés)* through divine volition.[5]

How then did the noun *régénération* change from its early-eighteenth-century meaning of baptism into the definition it would have in the Revolution? While an overused answer to questions about eighteenth-century ideological changes is "the Enlightenment," the cliché may be true here in its strictest sense: regeneration may have begun its transformation in the *Encyclopédie*, the project led by Diderot and d'Alembert that was central to the Enlightenment movement in mid-eighteenth-century France. How did the *Encyclopédie* use this concept? On the one hand, the entry for *régénération* defined it only as baptism. In the preliminary discourse, however, d'Alembert used the word in a new way, begging the reader's indulgence for his linguistic transgression. As he spoke of his hopes that the *Encyclopédie* would spark a new flowering of knowledge, d'Alembert noted: "In exiting from a long interval of ignorance, which was preceded by centuries of light, the regeneration of ideas, if one can speak that way, needed to be different from their primitive generation." In d'Alembert, we see a secularization of the word *regeneration,* a modest but crucial transformation of the word *generation* into its *re-* form, generation again. Regeneration could now signify the new dawn of something, its rebirth, in a way that was separate both from Jesus Christ and from medicine. Regeneration was becoming a displacement of the Gospels, with humans rather than God doing the reviving. By 1778, we see reflexive usages such as that of a writer who gushed that, upon Voltaire's arrival in Paris, "humanity is regenerating itself *[l'humanité se régénère]*."[6]

The physiocrat Marquis de Mirabeau's *Ami des hommes* would add a new dimension to regeneration by repeatedly using both the noun *régénération* and the active verb *régénérer*. His work aimed to increase population in France, and his use of *regeneration* represented a metaphorical application of the medical definition to politics. Because his goal was to enlarge the size of the state, he spoke of actively regenerating parts of the body politic.[7] This new usage reflected the Enlightenment belief in humans' ability to change the cosmic order through concerted action.

Regeneration and *regenerate* also found new life in mid-century natural history, particularly in the writings of the Swiss Protestant scientist Charles Bonnet. A close friend of Lavater, Bonnet aimed to prove the truth of Christianity by examining living beings. In an analogy with human resurrection, Bonnet noted that just as humans could reach a state of perfection through divine regeneration, so could plants: "This organ . . . will be the instrument of this *future regeneration,* which will elevate the polyp to a degree of perfection that is not included in the present state of things." *Regeneration* could now refer to the secularized, biological perfectibility of living species. The concept was also popularized in the influential writings of the naturalist Georges Louis Leclerc de Buffon, which Grégoire would cite in his *Essai* the first time he used a *re-* or *de-* form of *generation.* Though the active verb *régénérer* did not appear in Buffon's works, the noun *dégénération* and the verb *dégénérer* played a key role in them, as Buffon attempted to trace how particular animal and human species (the latter implying racial differences) degenerated.[8]

In the years just before the Estates-General, uses of the word exploded. Writers searched for ways in which the state could be regenerated and acclaimed Louis XVI as the great regenerator of France for having called the Estates-General and thus begun a process of reform. Louis XVI in fact declared that he had convoked the Estates-General "to work with me on the regeneration of the kingdom."[9] Regenerating was no longer only the province of God, but rather an operation that could be directed by humans. Moreover, regeneration could now be effected upon the body politic itself rather than simply upon the bodies of individual Christians.

THE CONTEXT OF THE *ESSAI:* GRÉGOIRE'S PREDECESSORS

So far we have looked at the history of the word *regeneration.* Let us next examine how Grégoire came to be in a position of entering another contest about Jews. While it is hardly true that Jews were Grégoire's main preoccupation before the Revolution,[10] the curé did continue to discuss them with his Protestant friends from the Société des Philantropes. In addition, in November 1785 he accepted an invitation to give a sermon about them at the parish church in Lunéville, which, if his later recollection is reliable, sparked a "remarkable sensation."[11] In 1785, when the Metz Academy announced its essay contest for the year

1787 on whether Jews could be made "more useful and happier," Grégoire was therefore delighted to have an opportunity to recycle parts of
his uncrowned SPS essay. Indeed, as we have seen, he later indicated that
he would not have thought of entering the Metz contest if not for the
influence of the SPS's earlier contest (fig. 2).

The impetus for the new contest came from the death of the esteemed
Metz rabbi Lion Asser and from the same sorts of debates on Jews that
had been raging in Alsace. Led in this matter by the future deputy Pierre-
Louis Roederer, the academy was also responding to the forged receipts
affair in Alsace and the violence it had unleashed on Jews. Works written in Alsace and Western Germany amidst this controversy had
included the anti-Jewish writings of Hell and Johann David Michaelis,
and two defenses of Jews written by the German civil servant Christian
Wilhelm Dohm at the request of (and in exchange for payment from) the
Alsatian Jewish leader Cerf Berr. Dohm's principal pamphlet, which
would become extremely well known, and other efforts by Cerf Berr had
also brought about two royal decrees (Letters-Patent) in 1784 that
effected changes in the status of the Jews of the east. How Jews should
be treated was thus a major question of the day in eastern France.[12]

The terms of the Metz contest seem to have come directly from the
French translation of Dohm's pamphlet, which referred to "means of
making them useful and happy."[13] *Über die bürgerliche Verbesserung
der Juden* (On the Civic Improvement of the Jews) appeared in German
in 1781 and was translated into French in 1782 as *De la réforme politique des Juifs* (On the Political Reform of the Jews). Because it did not
receive a formal approbation from the government censors, however,
nearly all copies were destroyed.[14] Despite its renown and its availabil-
ity in German, the pamphlet's ideas were therefore not as widely diffused
as Dohm's French admirers would have liked. Indeed, in his instructions,
Roederer specifically praised Dohm's work.

When the entries came in, however, Roederer and the academy were
unhappy with nearly all of them; they explained that the essays contained "some well-written morsels" but were generally incomplete and
poorly reasoned. Still, academy members were satisfied enough with
two of them—those by Grégoire and a Protestant lawyer named Claude-
Antoine Thiéry—to ask the authors to revise them, in accordance with
specific feedback. Another re-entrant was Zalkind Hourwitz, a Polish-
born Parisian Jew who had entered the contest and reversed the
academy's terms (explaining how the Jews could be made happier and
thus more useful). Hourwitz, although disappointed by his essay's not

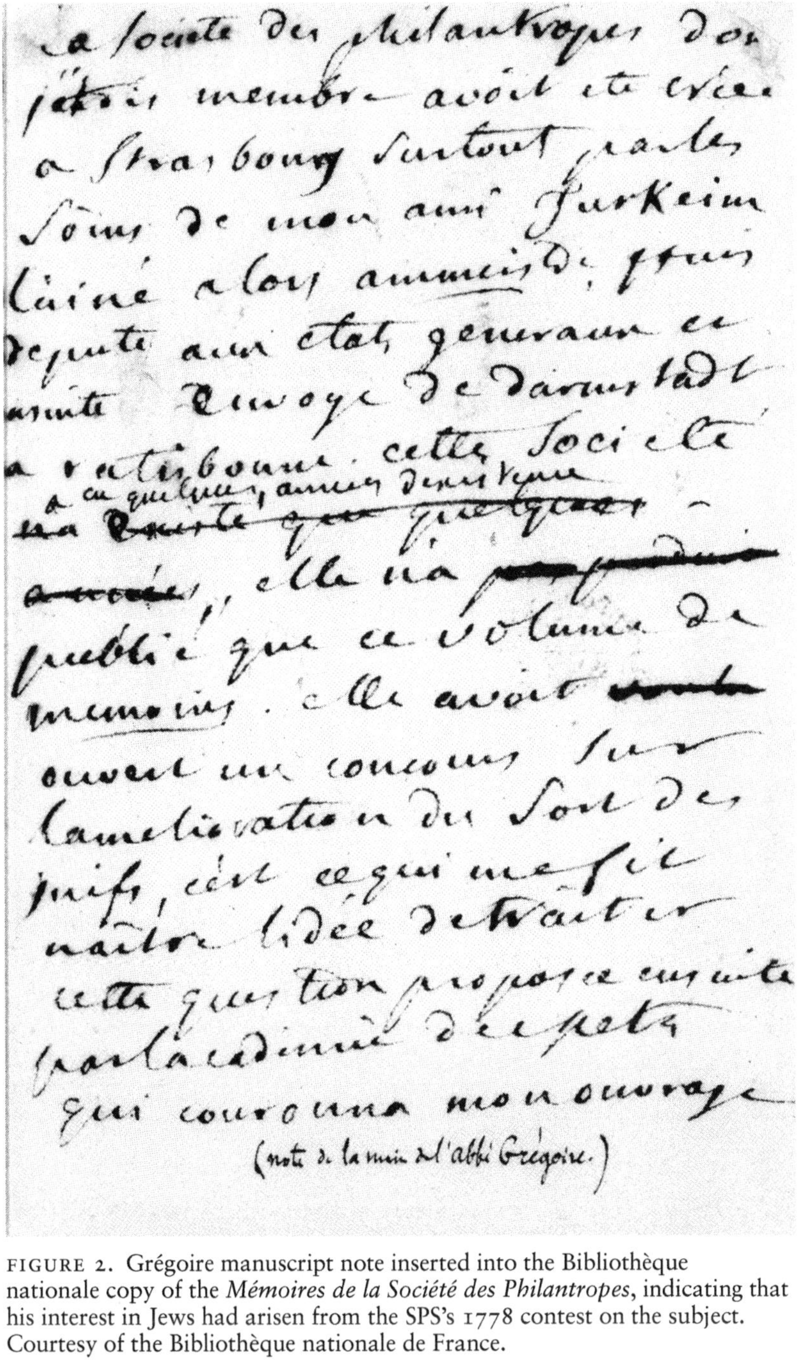
La société des philantropes dont j'étois membre avoit été créée a Strasbourg surtout par les soins de mon ami Turkeim l'ainé alors ammeister, puis député aux états generaux ensuite envoyé de Darmstadt a Ratisbonne. cette société a eu quelques années d'existence ~~n'a existé que quelques années~~, elle n'a ~~point~~ publié que ce volume de memoires. elle avoit ~~aussi~~ ouvert un concours sur l'amelioration du sort des juifs, c'est ce qui me fit naitre l'idée de traiter cette question proposée ensuite par l'academie de Metz qui couronna mon ouvrage

(note de la main de l'abbé Grégoire.)

FIGURE 2. Grégoire manuscript note inserted into the Bibliothèque nationale copy of the *Mémoires de la Société des Philantropes*, indicating that his interest in Jews had arisen from the SPS's 1778 contest on the subject. Courtesy of the Bibliothèque nationale de France.

being grouped among the best, submitted a revised version anyway. While the academy was still not fully satisfied with anyone's revisions, Roederer's committee decided in 1788 that the new entries of Grégoire, Thiéry, and Hourwitz had enough merit to share the prize.[15]

How did Grégoire understand the debate that he was entering? His footnotes reveal a man who read broadly; his sources on the Jews ranged from SPS friends and Enlightenment texts to papal decrees, travel narratives, and medical treatises. Referring frequently to the works of John Toland, Jacques Basnage, Pierre-Louis Lacretelle, Dohm, and Michaelis, Grégoire aimed to settle some of their debates.[16]

The three schools of thought among these authors presage the three positions on Jewish citizenship during the Revolution.[17] First were those who argued that Jews should be incorporated into society with no conditions other than those demanded of other citizens (a position we will call the unconditionalist discourse, typified before the Revolution in certain writings by Toland, Lacretelle, and Israël Valabrègue, and later by Hourwitz and certain radical deputies). The next position, which we will call the impossibilist position, suggested that Jews were inherently corrupt, could not be reformed, and would wreak havoc on society if incorporated into it; this position was espoused by Michaelis and Hell, and later by deputies such as the abbé Maury. Finally, the conditionalist discourse, that of Dohm and later of Grégoire himself, suggested that persecution should end and Jewish political status should be improved, but with conditions that would aim to strip Jews of their particularity in the long run. Grégoire's footnotes make clear that he was familiar with each of these positions.

John Toland's *Reasons for Naturalizing the Jews in Great Britain and Ireland,* published in 1714, was a pioneer in creating the unconditionalist discourse, which urged equality for Jews within European civil society without conditions. Among the texts Grégoire would read, it was also the most accepting of Jews' right to be different. Toland, a freethinker who saw his defense of Jews as one way of deflating the pretensions of Christianity, used a mercantilist and secular line of argumentation: he insisted that it was in Britain's economic interest to tolerate Jews. At least in this text, he stated that he saw no need to reform the Jewish character in any way, for he considered Jewish morals to be perhaps better than those of the average British subject. He noted: "My Purpose at present then, is to prove, that the *Jews* are so farr from being an Excrescence or Spunge (as some wou'd have it) and a useless member in the Commonwealth, or being ill subjects, and a dangerous people on any account, that they are as obedient, peaceable, useful, and advantageous as any; and even more so than many others." Toland added that the Jews had "infinitely more charity than the bulk of *Christians.*" From Toland, Grégoire would take the idea that Jews could become like other members of the country in which they lived if they were treated equally. He would reject outright, however, Toland's idea that the Jews were as moral as anyone else and did not need any change.[18]

The work of Pierre-Louis Lacretelle, a young lawyer who helped bring a famous 1775 test case claiming the rights of Jews to work in all trades, was similar in orientation to Toland's essay. Rather than emphasizing that Jews were degenerate and needed improvement, Lacretelle argued simply that the laws which oppressed them were unjust. For him, "the most important question in this case is to know whether Jews are men." Since they were, Lacretelle reasoned, and since the law in question did not allow for excluding people based on their religion, Jews could not be banned from the trades. In keeping with contemporary prejudices, Lacretelle admitted that the Jews were "a nation apart, a degenerate nation"; he also called them "base" and said they had developed a "habit for deceit and usury." At the same time, he did not dwell on these purported defects, and insisted that any nation persecuted like the Jews would end up in similar circumstances. Using a language of justice and right, he focused on the commercial benefits of evaluating people on merit alone and the illegality of excluding any single religious group. For Lacretelle, no special measures were needed to correct Jews; only their legal status needed reform.[19]

Another text that presented an unconditionalist perspective on Jews was the 1767 *Lettre, ou Réflexions d'un milord à son correspondant à Paris,* a well-known pamphlet to which both Grégoire and Roederer referred. Though its ostensible author was a Christian Englishman writing to a friend in France, it was actually the work of Israël Bernard Valabrègue, an Avignonnais Jew who lived in Paris. Valabrègue's text used logic similar to Toland's and Lacretelle's to assert that Jews were moral and useful, and that the state would benefit from their being able to enter any occupation for which they were suited. Citing a long history of Gentiles praising Jews for their achievements in learning and science, Valabrègue also asserted that prejudice rather than reason formed the only source of attacks against them. He contested the oft-repeated idea that Jews hated Christianity: "It is not the Christian religion that Jews hate: it is slander and the slanderer, persecution and the persecutor, the false Christian."[20]

While Grégoire himself read Lacretelle and Valabrègue, his knowledge of Toland seems to have come mostly from Basnage's *Histoire des Juifs*. Basnage's motivations for writing such a history were firmly rooted in Christian apologetics; he insisted that his only reason for doing so was "to prove the Truth of Christianity against the Jews." Having no great love for Jews and especially for rabbis, whom he ridiculed in the bitterest of terms, Basnage (a French Protestant in exile in Holland) also wanted to convince the Jewish masses of alternative explanations for their history. His final chapter focused on successful methods for inducing them to convert, especially by reducing their reliance on the Talmud. Nevertheless, Basnage felt that only God should punish the Jews, and he used his work to attack Catholic clergy for persecuting them (a charge that subtly evoked Catholic persecution of Protestants). While Grégoire would vigorously object to Basnage's critique of Catholicism, he would nonetheless rely heavily on Basnage's book for information about the Jews. He would also adopt Basnage's view of the Talmud and envision his work as a Christian (though Catholic) apologetic.[21]

Another author whose name appears repeatedly in the *Essai* is Michaelis, a prominent German Orientalist who styled himself an expert on the Jews but hated them profoundly. Grégoire would try to refute some of Michaelis's more vituperative comments on Jews (such as the statistic that twenty-four out of twenty-five criminals were Jewish), and he combated Michaelis's idea that "the Jews are incapable of being regenerated, because they are absolutely perverse." At the same time, Grégoire adopted a tone of respectful disagreement with the German writer and often relied on him for other kinds of information about Jews. Though Michaelis and like-minded skeptics were Grégoire's main target audience, it was a dispute "within the family," for many of Michaelis's French friends were SPS members and therefore also friends of Grégoire.[22]

A final work to which Grégoire saw himself as responding was Dohm's famous essay on the Jews. Like the unconditionalists Toland and Lacretelle, Dohm agreed that tolerating Jews would help the prosperity of the state; he also portrayed Jews as potentially honest. Unlike Toland, however, Dohm depicted most Jews as utterly corrupt, even while noting that their corruption resulted from Christian persecution and that some Jews, like Moses Mendelssohn, were exceptions. To reform the Jews and the conditions that had corrupted them, he suggested granting them political rights (while banning them from high offices), annulling the laws that had restricted them to money-lending, and allowing them to enter the trades. He also recommended that Jews be permitted to buy land but only if they worked it themselves, that they be educated by the state instead of by their communities, and that they be made to mix with Christians so that prejudices on both sides would end. Dohm also recommended that Jews be allowed to keep their communal autonomy. Although Jews were hardly perfect, he maintained, they were certainly perfectible; moreover, Christians should see them as brothers. With certain conditions and restrictions in place, they could be safely integrated into the state.[23] Dohm's work was cited numerous times by Grégoire, and readers of the two texts will notice key similarities.

The similarities between Grégoire's work and Dohm's have led some scholars—and newspapers at the time—to suggest that the former was derived from the latter.[24] According to Grégoire, however, Dohm's essay was written after Grégoire had already made his ideas public in the SPS, to which both belonged. So sensitive was Grégoire about this imputation that he began his essay with a disclaimer.

> The work that I have the honor of presenting to the Metz Academy is merely an excerpt from a longer work I wrote eight years ago, which has been hidden away among my papers since then. It is not at all modeled after the Edict of Joseph nor on the work by M. Dohm for a simple reason: it existed before both the issuing of that edict and the publication of that work. This is a fact that I can prove by the testimony of more than twenty men of letters; my work was read along with several others on the same subject in a literary gathering [the SPS], which had proposed the same topic, and which had desired to crown my work until unforeseen events wiped out the funds destined for the prize. I mention these facts because they are of course unknown by all of the members of the Metz Academy.... One will find some items that I later appended to my work in which I cite M. Dohm, but they are a very small number. I did not have the translation of the first part of his work, the second is not yet translated, and I have only begun to be able to understand the German language.[25]

One might say that Grégoire was either protesting too much or simply unlucky—for while his unpublished SPS entry sat among his papers, another man garnered continental fame for publishing something that bore many of the same arguments. It also is plausible that Dohm heard about Grégoire's 1778 essay from friends in Strasbourg. Nevertheless, even though both men used a conditionalist discourse and made some of the same arguments, there were important differences between their works, as we will see below, stemming from their very different religious agendas.

What exactly did Grégoire say when he intervened in this debate in his first Metz contest entry? This entry, like his earlier SPS entry, has long been presumed lost, since it was not in the Metz Academy archives with the other original entries. Scholars' only way of knowing its contents (a source of much interest) was therefore Roederer's critique of it in his call for a second contest. In that announcement, Roederer praised Grégoire's entry for covering a great deal of material and for recognizing almost all of the difficulties involved in incorporating the Jews into the body politic. At the same time, he opined, it suffered from massive disorganization, and was "embarrassing[ly]" filled with "incidental and sometimes trivial observations." On the whole, Roederer asserted, it was not forceful enough to induce social change. A little-known article by Maggiolo, who claimed to have come upon a manuscript of a previous version of Grégoire's *Essai,* offered some further hints about its contents. He included what he said were excerpts from this essay, including Grégoire's contention that the text was simply a shortened version of his SPS entry. Maggiolo's account was impossible to verify, however, since the manuscript's location was unknown.[26]

Grégoire's first Metz contest essay was not lost, however, but only in private hands and later in the storerooms of the Musée lorrain. The Musée lorrain called attention to its holding a manuscript of Grégoire's *Essai* by including it in the Blois-Nancy exhibition of 1989 on Grégoire; one local scholar seems to have heard about it as early as the 1970s. The Musée thought, however, that what it held was simply the "original manuscript of the second entry of 1788"; scholars who heard about the manuscript shared this assumption.[27] The manuscript has thus lain unexamined until now.

A careful examination of the Musée lorrain manuscript reveals that it is in fact the first rather than the second entry and contains information crucial for understanding the eventual published *Essai.* While the manuscript does not indicate whether it is the original version of the 1785–87 or 1788 entries, its being the earlier is indicated in several ways. First, Grégoire refers in it to his SPS essay as having been written "eight years ago" (thus dating the essay to eight years after 1778). Second, the manuscript fits Roederer's description of Grégoire's first entry, particularly in its poor organization. Third, it has only sixteen chapters, as opposed to the twenty-seven in the published *Essai.* Most importantly, Grégoire would receive government permission to publish the second entry only in the exact form crowned by the academy, so the manuscript of the second entry should have been identical to the published *Essai,* aside from typographical errors.[28]

With the first entry recovered, what can we add to our knowledge of the essay? This entry (which does contain the passages cited by Maggiolo, though he altered a few words) suggests that Grégoire did not submit, strictly speaking, a shortened version of his 1778 SPS essay, since the Musée lorrain manuscript includes citations to works published in the 1780s (especially Dohm's 1781 essay and Michaelis's 1783 critique of it). Grégoire also did not completely rewrite his essay between the first version and the second; most of the passages in the former reappear in the latter, though often in a different order and sometimes reworded. Because of the similarities, and because the second entry, as published, was the one that would become known to the public, we will focus on that version as we examine Grégoire's intervention in the contest.

Nevertheless, it is worth calling attention to several key changes that reveal an evolution in his thinking between 1785–87 and 1788. One difference is that the word *regeneration* is used far more extensively in the second entry. Where in the first entry Grégoire refers to correcting *[corriger]* and civilizing *[civiliser]* the Jews, each of these verbs mutates to *regenerating [régénérer]* in the published *Essai.* The first entry also did not yet have the title *Essai sur la régénération. . . .*[29] Nevertheless, though some scholars have claimed that Mirabeau was the first to use the term *regeneration* in connection with improving the Jews (in a 1787 essay that used the term only once), Grégoire's first entry used the term three times, in a way that seems to differ from previous usage in combining the multiple meanings of the word. This new usage was thus present in his work even before 1788.[30]

Comparing the first essay with the second yields another crucial insight. Many scholars of Jewish history, noticing Grégoire's acknowledgments in his footnotes to certain Jewish intellectuals, have claimed that they co-authored it with him or at least that one of them (Isaïah Berr Bing, a leader of the Jewish community in Metz) had been his friend since the mid 1770s.[31] This has led to suggestions that Grégoire entered the contest in order to help pre-existing Jewish friends. However, all of the notes and the material to which they refer (which constitute a tiny portion of the *Essai*) are absent from the first version, as is any hint of the Jewish perspective on their status. This suggests that Grégoire befriended these men (Bing, plus Simon von Geldern and Moses Ensheim) only during the revisions for his second entry, as he sought to respond to Roederer's comments and thus win the contest. The material Grégoire added on their account, including comments about Bing in particular, also suggest impassioned conversations with his new Jewish friends over passages critical of Jews and Judaism.[32]

By the time Grégoire made the revisions requested by the academy and prompted by his new Jewish acquaintances, what did the second entry actually say? While Grégoire's essay echoed many of the arguments made by his predecessors, he also departed from them in important ways. Most important is the way he synthesized various arguments and transformed the debate into one about regeneration, something that appears to be Grégoire's innovation. Grégoire's early version of regeneration already expressed some of the paradoxical aspects it would display in the Revolution: in this case, it allowed him to both defend and criticize Jews.

In recent years, the *Essai* has drawn heated debate, with analysts dividing into defenders and critics of Grégoire.[33] The work, however—a particular version of the conditionalist discourse—defies facile characterization as friendly toward Jews or as hypocritical in its enmity. The *Essai* remained considerably influenced by the way the SPS had framed the question in its earlier contest program; it was at once filled with pleas for tolerance and highly unfavorable depictions of Jewish character and physique. Unlike Michaelis and Hell, the abbé held that Jews were not essentially depraved, and that it was human society that made them different from Christians. Yet Grégoire also backed away from the more tolerant positions of Toland and Lacretelle—and even that of Dohm—in extensively detailing the *current* state of Jewish degeneracy. For him, Jews would need to undergo a long process of correction before they could become fully regenerated.

The idea that Grégoire would criticize Jews in such a work might seem paradoxical if we look at it as chiefly a defense of them. On one level, it was: though the Jews were the "greatest enemies of my religion," he noted, they also were human beings. By the time of the second entry, Grégoire had befriended Bing, von Geldern, and Ensheim, and also admired Mendelssohn. For him, Jews were brothers, if errant ones; rather than demonize them, he stressed that they were part of the same family as Christians. Jewish degeneracy, he suggested, resulted from their circumstances: "Any people placed in the same circumstances as the Hebrews . . . would become just like them." Recounting the long history of Jews' sufferings in Europe, the abbé was also ashamed that the persecutors purported to be Christians. This universalistic aspect of the essay paralleled Toland, Lacretelle, and Dohm, while rejecting the views of impossibilists who suggested that the Jews "are incapable of being regenerated because they are absolutely perverse." These statements were striking coming from a priest; where Enlightenment and Protestant intellectuals like those in the SPS had begun to reexamine persecution of the Jews, an abbé making these declarations was highly unusual.[34]

Grégoire was also motivated, however, by concerns that were external to Jewish suffering: an additional purpose of the *Essai* was to prove the truth of Christianity to readers. Grégoire would write a series of texts in the nineteenth century on oppressed peoples around the world that aimed to showcase Christianity's generosity in alleviating their burdens and its superiority over other faiths. The roots of this agenda were already present in the *Essai*, as Grégoire highlighted the benevolence of the Catholic clergy toward Jews over the centuries even while insisting that their unhappy fate confirmed Christian prophecies. He particularly wanted to show that anti-Christian philosophes were wrong when they called the church intolerant. He advanced a universalist understanding of Christianity: "Charity is the cry of the Gospels, and when I see Christians being persecutors, I am tempted to believe that they have not read them."[35]

Grégoire was not just interested in proving the truth of Christianity in general, however; his essay also was rooted in Protestant-Catholic polemics. Though he had been heavily influenced by Basnage, Grégoire objected to the Protestant writer's emphasis on Catholic persecution of Jews. Even Basnage, the abbé argued, had been forced to admit that the popes had shown constant humanity toward Jews—even as Jews frequently "repaid them with ingratitude." One day, Grégoire promised, he would combat Basnage in greater detail.[36]

Finally, Grégoire's interest in Jews grew out of his desire to help country dwellers. Echoing the SPS, Grégoire seemed concerned that many peasants were being "ruined by the Jews," both economically and morally.[37] Though Grégoire did not believe that the Jews were essentially defective, he did believe that they had *become* degenerate; without reform, they would continue to oppress peasants. Indeed, chapter titles included "Dangers of tolerating the Jews as they are, because of their aversion for other peoples and their lapsed morality" and "Danger of tolerating the Jews as they are, because of their commerce and usury."

Grégoire's simultaneous interest in defending Jews, in extolling Catholicism, and in helping peasants can be seen in the *Essai*'s method of approaching the contest question. Alongside his universalist defenses of Jews (which paralleled Valabrègue and Toland), he suggested that

Jews shared the blame for their condition. For him, Jews had been made inferior to other men not only because of Christian persecution and arbitrary laws, but also because of the "ridiculous" teachings of rabbis and the Talmud. He maligned Jews' "exclusive religion," their "obstinate adhesion to their dogmas," and their "hatred for the nations"; he further declared that God's fury had dispersed them. This line of argumentation followed the SPS's program as well as Basnage.[38]

Grégoire was also more critical of Jews than Dohm was; writing from a more theological perspective, the abbé charged that Dohm (a deist) had been naive to suggest that Jewish beliefs were not as different from Christian ones as many contemporaries imagined. He specifically rebuked Dohm for claiming that Jews venerated the same religious books as Christians (the Old Testament); except for the small sect of Karaites, the abbé alleged, the vast majority of Jews had replaced the morality of the Bible with "Talmudic reveries." In fact, he argued, Jews were even tougher to regenerate than heathens, because they had knowingly rejected the Gospels: "If the Jews were only savages, it would be easier to regenerate them. It would only be necessary to plant seeds in a virgin field in order to reap an abundant harvest. But they have an acquired ignorance that has depraved their intellectual faculties."[39]

Grégoire also exceeded Dohm in criticizing other aspects of Jewish life. His second essay did show a softening of position in some ways as a result of his conversations with his new Jewish friends. Nevertheless, the second essay included some new, even crueler comments about Jews. In addition, Grégoire criticized outright Valabrègue's and Lacretelle's assertions that Jews had made important contributions to European culture.[40]

Another negative aspect of the essay was the chapter Grégoire devoted to the danger of Jews' growing population. While he conceded that, in general, a large population might make a society more prosperous, he felt that the Jews were an exception. He used biological discourse to warn his readers of the "alarming" speed at which Jews were "multiplying," and to invoke a time when "the Jews, having become too numerous, will inundate and infest our country." He even included a detailed appendix at the back of the *Essai* (omitted from Hermon-Belot's and Badinter's editions), suggesting that Jews were reproducing too rapidly.[41]

In addition to their multiplication, Grégoire highlighted their usury, saying it had driven peasants to immorality. Some commentators have tried to downplay Grégoire's complaints on this topic, musing that he included them for the benefit of his audience. The abbé went beyond merely acknowledging that critics of the Jews might have a point, however; he went out of his way in the *Essai* to defend the notorious Hell. By 1788, when Grégoire wrote the second entry, it was well known that Hell had organized the forged receipts affair and that he viewed Jews as child-killers. Grégoire nevertheless inserted the following defense of Hell into his footnotes: "People have contested [Hell's] allegations, and I do not want, as he does, to blame today's Jews for the death of the Savior. *However, has it really been proven that everything he said was false?*" (emphasis added). It is noteworthy that this comment was absent from the first entry and came directly after a new footnote apologizing to Bing for any offense his criticism of Jews might cause. Once again, Grégoire made clear that defending Jews was less the target of his concern than protecting peasants from them.[42]

Still, though Jews were sinners for rejecting the Gospels, Grégoire believed that justice should only be exacted by God. Moreover, he thought that some of the more extreme charges against Jews (such as well poisoning) were ridiculous, and he did not believe in collective punishment. Persecuting Jews, he suggested, was not only contrary to the Gospels, but also counterproductive: it would not prevent them from being forced to prey on hapless peasants for a living, nor make them less hostile to Christianity.[43]

The curé of Emberménil was therefore candid about toleration's ultimate aim: the voluntary conversion of the Jews. Noting that "persecuting a religion is a sure means of making it even dearer to its adherents," he continued that "complete religious liberty accorded to them is a great contribution to reforming them, and I dare say, to converting them." "If we encourage the Jews," he added, "they will insensibly adopt our way of thinking and acting, our laws, our customs, and our morals." Though Grégoire sincerely denounced forced conversions, he had no objection to requiring Jews to attend mandatory lectures on Christianity: "Obliging the Jews to instruct themselves is not forcing them to convert." This voluntary conversion was especially important because the return of the Jews to Israel and their conversion were necessary precursors to Jesus' second coming.[44]

One essential means of persuading Jews to convert, Grégoire asserted, would be humor and sarcasm. He commented that the Talmud was "not funny enough to excuse its stupidity," and that only "irony" could get Jews to see this. Success in loosening the grip of Judaism would come, he predicted, when "works are produced that examine the mystical puerilities of 'Rabbinism,' expose them to ridicule, and substitute the fruits of a luminous reason for the ecstasies of delirium."[45]

For Grégoire, however, a moral regeneration of the Jews—and even
a theological conversion, as they recognized the absurdity of "Rabbinism"—would not be enough to correct their acquired faults and thereby
protect the state from danger. Nor would political measures suffice; as
Grégoire declared in the first entry, "Let us not believe that naturalizing
them will be enough to make them useful." To Grégoire, even the well-
integrated Sephardim were "still not French, and the work of their transformation has only begun." Grégoire also disagreed with Joseph II of
Austria's 1782 Tolerance Edict (which lifted some burdens on Jews but
preserved others), because he felt that correcting the degraded condition
of the Jews could only be done at a gradual pace, and required both
political and extrapolitical measures.[46]

If moral, theological, and political regeneration were not enough,
what else did Jews need? As we can see in the eventual title of the essay
(which placed physical regeneration first), Grégoire also saw Jews as
needing physical correction. Synthesizing ideas from Lavater and natural history, he depicted them as degenerate sexually and physically. He
criticized their precocity with regard to puberty, argued that "solitary
libertinage is extremely common among them," and intimated that
"Jewish women would be strongly subject to nymphomania" if they did
not marry early. Grégoire saw this discussion as central to the book,
telling a female correspondent that she should keep her children from
reading his *Essai* because of these details. Moreover, far from disagreeing with Michaelis on the negative physiognomy of the Jews, Grégoire
noted with pride that he had spoken himself to Lavater (whom he called
"a virtual legislator in pronouncing on physiognomy") and learned that
"in general, they have a pallid face, hooked nose, sunk-in *[enfoncé]* eyes,
prominent chin, and strongly pronounced muscles constricting the
mouth." Showing his agreement with Lavater's idea that Jews' physical
problems affected their moral character, Grégoire added, "I congratu-
late myself on seeing the moral consequences that he deduced from this
coinciding with what I argued in the last chapter."[47]

Grégoire thus felt that physical measures were necessary for Jews' full
regeneration. First, he argued, Jews needed to eliminate religious rules
like the kosher laws, which required them to remove all blood from meat
and therefore be deprived of its nutrients. Second, drawing upon natural history and the idea of crossbreeding species to improve them, Grégoire proposed an idea that had not appeared in other well-known
polemics on Jews and which would reappear in his discussions of blacks:
the "crossing of the races" through intermarriage. Jews had become

weak by inbreeding too much; race-crossing would be essential for regenerating them physically. Intermarriage would also establish intimate links between Jews and Christians and thus facilitate conversions. Physical and moral regeneration thus went hand in hand. The wise reformer would not only help Jews "elevate their souls" but also "give them energy."[48]

Building on his multiple intellectual influences, Grégoire thus united for the first time all of the eighteenth-century connotations of the word *regeneration*.[49] From his Catholic training, regeneration retained its theological meaning of conversion; in accordance with natural history, regeneration would also aim to correct the physical deterioration of the Jewish "species." Finally, à la d'Alembert, regeneration would come from the efforts of humanity, not by waiting for divine action.

All of these ideas did not coexist as well as Grégoire would have liked, however; a key tension can be seen in his idea of regeneration. Were individuals perfectible through education, or would generations of intermarriage be required to correct a people's faults? Could regeneration be achieved quickly through moral means or would it require long-term biological changes? On the one hand, Grégoire believed individuals to be capable of spiritual and moral rebirth through education and faith. On the other hand, he shared Lavater's belief in national physiognomy, which implied that people's characters were fixed by their physical attributes. This tension would lie at the heart of Grégoire's idea of regeneration into the 1820s, and would also remain in French colonial ideology, which in its most optimistic forms of assimilation theory saw intermarriage as a necessary component of regeneration.[50]

We thus can see that Grégoire's *Essai* was neither a straightforward defense nor an attack on Jews. His discussion of regenerating them was liberating and inclusive, for it implied that all people—Jews included—belonged to a single family and that no one group was inherently defective. This was a radical notion at the time for a priest, for it implied that Jews were not forever tainted by the death of Jesus. At the same time, *regeneration* suggested that a group already was degenerate and would endanger the state if not reformed. Grégoire's discussion implied defects so great that no single human could overcome them, as much as education or legal changes might begin to reverse these failings in the short term. To be truly regenerated, Jews (like the other groups Grégoire would seek to regenerate in the future) would need to change their customs, character, and even their bodies. Grégoire had rejected the unconditionalist paradigm.

The negative elements of the *Essai*'s stance toward Jews were commented upon by at least some contemporaries. A London newspaper, reviewing the translation of the *Essai* into English in 1791, called Grégoire's attitude hypocritical: "How easy it is, to point out follies and fancies, of a ridiculous nature, in the customs of others, while we neglect those which are equally so in our own. A Roman Catholic priest must have been witness to, or engaged in, several practices, which can hardly be exceeded, for folly and absurdity, by any that prevail among Jews, or even Heathens."[51]

Leading Jews of the time also seem to have viewed certain aspects of the text critically, even if it was difficult for them to complain about this outright because of their lowly position in society. Bing, Ensheim, and Hourwitz were among the most reform-oriented Jews in France and shared Grégoire's assessment on many levels of the sorry state to which Jews had been reduced because of Christian persecution. Nevertheless, they had more positive views of Judaism than he did and differed with him on a number of issues. For example, Grégoire's footnotes, even as they thanked Bing for his input, reveal heated exchanges between the two men as Bing politely but unsuccessfully tried to convince Grégoire to delete some of the *Essai*'s most negative comments about Jews. Moreover, in their own writings, Hourwitz and Bing challenged the Metz Academy's very question as insulting, suggesting that it would be better to ask how to regenerate the Christians persecuting Jews or how the Jews had survived in spite of this treatment. Hourwitz also denied that Jews were multiplying more rapidly than any other group or that it would be dangerous for the state if they were. While admiring the abbé for being interested in Jews' fate and cherishing their relationship with him for a variety of reasons, those Jews who knew Grégoire's text most intimately thus had concerns about the way Jews and Judaism were portrayed in it. Whatever plans they had for regenerating Jews from within the community, they nevertheless were far more unconditionalist than the abbé.[52]

PUBLISHING THE *ESSAI*

With his crowning by the Metz Academy in August 1788, Grégoire seemed poised to become an intellectual of some standing, and on a more national scale than when he had won the Nancy contest on poetry. News of the contest and its winners began to spread that fall, and within a year there would be reports on it in newspapers from England to Italy.[53] Grégoire was getting closer to his goal of having a platform for his ideas.

Grégoire had a small problem, however: he did not have a publisher for his essay. Thiéry (the Protestant lawyer who had shared the prize with Grégoire and Hourwitz) did not have the same difficulty; Berr-Isaac-Berr, the most prominent Jew in Nancy, was so taken with Thiéry's entry that he arranged to get it printed. Like Grégoire, Thiéry had talked of Jews needing correction and said their degradation had been caused by Christians; he also suggested that their penchant was for making money. Nevertheless, his essay spoke of Jewish faults far less than Grégoire's; indeed, Roederer had criticized Thiéry in the first contest precisely for being too optimistic. Thiéry also presented a much more positive account of Jewish religious beliefs than Grégoire and insisted that they be named citizens immediately while still preserving their communal autonomy (something the Jews of the east would themselves demand at the start of the Revolution). Berr did not offer to publish Grégoire's essay, indicating that he found Thiéry's ideas more in line with Jews' own aspirations for change.[54]

Still without a publisher in September, Grégoire sought help from the royal minister Malesherbes, who had spent 1788, at the king's directive, reexamining the status of the Jews. In an example of Grégoire's tendency to sometimes exaggerate his accomplishments, he told Malesherbes that his essay had been honored the most by the academy: "The newspapers have announced that the King asked you to prepare a report on how best to put to use the Jews. . . . I did research on this subject ten years ago, Monsieur, and the Academy of Metz has just crowned three works on this subject, with mine at the head." Omitting Roederer's critical comments about his first entry, as well as the academy's criticism of all three winners in its report on the second contest, Grégoire told Malesherbes that the academy had considered his text to "deal with nearly all the questions [originally proposed] and to resolve nearly all the difficulties" involved in integrating the Jews. Several months later, Grégoire was still trying to become an indispensable intermediary between the government and the Jews, promising to introduce the minister to several "likable and learned" Jewish friends.[55]

Most importantly, Grégoire asked Malesherbes for assistance in getting the essay published. As Gregory S. Brown has pointed out, becoming an author was a career to which many bright men of humble backgrounds aspired in the eighteenth century, yet they needed elite patrons for their words to appear in print. To gain this patronage,

Brown writes, "aspiring men of letters had to appear disinterested in their own gain to demonstrate their honorability, while at the same time gaining enough acclaim to come to the attention of potential protectors in the first place." After telling Malesherbes about the praise his entry had attracted, Grégoire thus assured the minister of the purity of his motives and his lack of interest in self-promotion. He insisted that his ambition of becoming an author was "subordinate to the desire for public good, to the hope of seeing the Jewish nation escape from its abjection in order to raise itself to virtue and to happiness." As Grégoire ominously warned Malesherbes, national stability depended on doing *something* about the Jews, since "we are retaining in France a degraded and unhappy horde that it is essential to regenerate."[56]

Grégoire seems not to have realized, however, that by the fall of 1788, as the king turned to the national fiscal crisis, Malesherbes had lost Louis's ear and was no longer preoccupied with Jewish matters. Grégoire might also not have realized that Malesherbes had already met Jews from across the country and received advice from figures like Lacretelle and Roederer. Malesherbes therefore declined to assist Grégoire in publishing his essay, though he wished him well. At this time of need, Grégoire again turned to his friends in Strasbourg. He wrote to Saltzmann to see if he might publish the *Essai,* but lamented to Ehrmann in October that he had not yet received an answer.[57]

Meanwhile, November came, Thiéry's pamphlet appeared, and Grégoire still had no publisher. He then turned to his backup plan: having the essay published under the auspices of the academy itself. Though all three laureates were entitled to be published in this way, Grégoire was the only one who chose to do so. One reason why this option was unattractive may have been that receiving government permission to print a prize-winning essay precluded modifications; only if the printed work was identical to what the academy had deemed meritorious could its judgment be substituted for that of the censors. We know that Grégoire had hoped to expand his essay, since he wrote to von Geldern with questions for the revisions. With no one willing to fund his plans, however, the essay finally appeared in print on February 14, 1789 with the academy's *imprimatur,* just as the curé was in the midst of his election campaign for the Estates-General (having already won the district election in Lunéville and before winning the diocese-wide election from Nancy).[58]

By the time the essay appeared, Grégoire also had begun working on other projects, which we learn about in a long letter he wrote in December 1788. While Jews had not been his primary interest throughout the prerevolutionary years, writing a new history of them became a major preoccupation of his in the wake of the contest. He particularly aimed to defend the Catholic Church against Basnage's accusations and thereby ensure its reputation for tolerance. Other works he was planning included those already discussed on the education of clerics and of country people, and a project on Gypsies, which he abandoned when he discovered that another scholar was further along on a similar study.[59]

Grégoire also tried to drum up favorable reviews for his *Essai* in the newspapers. A week after its publication, he contacted Bing and encouraged him to write to newspapers with his own ideas about how the Estates-General could help Jews. While he genuinely wanted to encourage his friend, Grégoire also had an additional motive for wanting Bing's words to appear in public: "This would also be for you an occasion to announce my work in the newspaper, and this would be a favor you could do for me. What do you think of my idea?" Grégoire seems to have believed that having a Jew praise his work would give him further publicity and credibility.[60]

Just as Grégoire was beginning to attain the fame he had long sought in the world of letters, however, his life took another turn; his works-in-progress (excepting the one on clerics) would remain incomplete. Grégoire was not fated to remain obscure, however. With his election to the Estates-General, the curé of Emberménil turned clerical deputy from Nancy would gain a national—if controversial—reputation, with a chance to enshrine his ideas into law. So far, we have traced Grégoire's early years and the development of his idea of regeneration from Enlightenment and religious roots. Let us now cross the Vosges and move to Paris, where the curé of Emberménil was about to become a celebrity.

Grégoire in Paris

Revolution and Regeneration, 1789–1801

Introduction to Part Two

What role would Grégoire play in the French Revolution? What would he do with the ideas he had developed in Lorraine and Alsace, and how would his views change? Furthermore, what can we learn about the Revolution (not just the period from 1789 until 1794, but also its less-studied stages, from 1794 until Napoleon's rise) from observing his activities? The French Revolution has been one of the most written-about eras in all of human history, and countless studies have sought to explain its development and consequences. The experiences of the curé of Emberménil can nevertheless add much to our understanding of the Revolution.

Grégoire arrived in Versailles in the midst of a crisis more profound than anyone had imagined when the Estates-General was called. Louis XVI's financial problems (the result of huge war debts from the Seven Years' War and the American Revolution) had been rumored throughout the 1780s; in 1787, he called an Assembly of Notables, hoping to persuade the clergy and nobility to consider structural changes that would allow him to pay down his debts. These two groups, however, were unwilling to pay new taxes and relinquish cherished privileges without a clearer picture of the king's finances, which the monarchy was unwilling to provide. Meanwhile, a catastrophic hailstorm and severe drought in 1788 destroyed much of the grain crop and led to higher prices. Though an Estates-General (a formal gathering of clergy, nobles, and commoners) had not been convened since 1614, the king soon realized that calling for one might be his only option if he wished to keep the monarchy from bankruptcy. He also asked every district to send a *cahier de doléances,* a list of complaints, hoping that his subjects would be willing to pay higher taxes in return for reforms. Deputies to the Estates-General, elected from across the empire, gathered in Versailles in May 1789.[1]

In May, the deputies could hardly have imagined that, within only a few months, a full-scale popular revolution would break out, with the Bastille destroyed and the monarchy forced to accept "the will of the people." Even if the deputies understood the financial crisis, they could not fathom the extent of the monarchy's inability to maintain order. After a series of mistakes on the monarchy's part (such as locking a room where the Third Estate was to meet) led to increasingly radical demands, however, the deputies of the Third Estate soon realized that the monarchy was powerless to control them and that they could set their own agenda. Soon, they would declare themselves a "National Assembly" and, with the support of the Parisian populace, dictate their desires to an increasingly frustrated Louis.

In the midst of this tumultuous change, the curé of little Emberménil might have gotten lost amid the sea of luminaries who had arrived from every corner of the French empire. Rather than disappear into the background, however, he caused a sensation from the moment he arrived. His forceful oratory made him a leader among the deputies; based on Edna Lemay's description of the physical difficulties of speaking in the Estates-General, he must have had a strong set of lungs. He persuaded the lower clergy to join the Third Estate, a key act in the Revolution, and was one of the first to take the Tennis Court Oath. In Jacques-Louis David's famous painting of that event, Grégoire occupies the central position; standing at the center, he brings together Dom Gerle (a Carthusian monk elected from central France) and the Protestant deputy Rabaut Saint-Etienne in a moment of patriotic unity (fig. 3). Colleagues marveled over his youthfulness—younger-looking even than his thirty-nine years—and his being different from most priests, the legacy of his sustained involvements outside the clerical world. One described him in July 1789 as bursting with "patriotism" and "energy"; another called him a true lover of humanity and a man of "rare talents." Poems, epistles, and songs toasted the youthful curé. To his reputation as defender of the Jews, he would add that of "friend of men of all colors"; in this new age, which vaunted universalism and tolerance, the atypical priest was capturing the imagination of the public (fig. 4).[2]

This new fame thrilled Grégoire's Strasbourg friends. As Blessig would write him in 1791, "How many times have I been deeply moved in seeing your name in the newspapers, always at the head of these grand discussions."[3] The ambitious young man from Vého had become a figure of national importance. The SPS alumni were extremely proud of him.

Even as Grégoire made a name for himself, however, some observers took an instant dislike to the unconventional priest with the razor-sharp tongue; the curé of Emberménil would prove to be a polarizing figure throughout his career. Where some saw energy and rhetorical flair, others detected an aggressiveness in his speech, a way of making those he disagreed with seem unpatriotic. Some who had known him in Lorraine felt he had become pretentious; they were stunned by the way the small-town

FIGURE 3. "Tennis Court Oath" by Jacques-Louis David (1791). Grégoire
stands in the center, bringing together Dom Gerle and Rabaut Saint-Etienne
in a moment of patriotic harmony. Courtesy of RMN/Art Resources.

curé had transformed himself, first through the publicity he generated
from the Metz contest and then by joining with the Third Estate. Fellow
Lorraine deputy Adrien Duquesnoy complained that Grégoire's notoriety only worsened his inflated ego; he found his colleague's writings
"incendiary," "scandalous" for a priest, and full of libels. Similarly, the
abbé Chatrian, also a clerical deputy to Paris, was distressed by his controversial neighbor's popularity. In July 1789, he lamented: "Ever since
M. Grégoire . . . spread in public this letter [his nominally anonymous
Nouvelle lettre d'un curé] with which honest men . . . are not happy, he
has an enormous reputation in Paris, where he is principally referred to
as the 'abbé *Ardent*.' Everyone wants to see the abbé *Ardent*; one con-
gratulates oneself on having seen the abbé *Ardent*, on having spoken to
him, on having eaten with him. . . . Voilà, it seems to me, a sad case of
celebrity. It is not ardor and vehemence . . . that the king requested for
the deputies to the Estates-General." Chatrian would write several
poems in his diary lampooning Grégoire's conceit; one claimed that the
curé-deputé "wants the world to think about him seven days a week"
and that no one would bother if he did not gesture so wildly and act like
a nuisance. Still, as La Fare, the bishop of Nancy, with whom Grégoire
had already clashed over the rights of curés—and would again over the

HENRI GRÉGOIRE,
Ancien Evêque de Blois.

FIGURE 4. Engraving of Grégoire, former bishop of Blois. One of the myriad engravings made of the popular priest, this portrait dates to the postrevolutionary period but uses the same youthful image common among many revolutionary likenesses of him. Courtesy of the Bibliothèque nationale de France.

direction of the Revolution—had to admit, the abbé had enjoyed a stunning rise to fame: "Grégoire is no longer an unknown. His imposing presence and his appearance, simple but well-groomed, are striking."[4]

Grégoire's newfound prominence and radical positions also shocked his constituents. During the elections, Grégoire had coordinated his campaign efforts with a group of Richerist priests, particularly the veteran Nancy curé Charles-Louis Guilbert. Grégoire had been very grateful for Guilbert's "priceless" help and told him that the entire Lorraine clergy would be forever in his debt for ensuring the victory of a Richerist. Guilbert and other Lorraine lower clergy soon felt betrayed by their delegate, however; he had promised to send reports from the capital but left several inquiries unanswered. As Guilbert complained to him in June: "The torrent that drags you along must be truly raging, my dear colleague, and the patriotic fever that burns you truly devouring for you to not have been able to write a single word to your order [the Lorraine clergy] for nearly two months. . . . You pledged that you would do this, and you owe it to us." Grégoire's colleagues were also upset to hear reports that he had been feuding with La Fare; even the most fervently Richerist clergy considered themselves part of a hierarchy, and many Lorraine clergy liked the bishop of Nancy. These reports were especially troubling, Guilbert noted, since it was La Fare who had helped propel Grégoire to victory. Moreover, even though they also wanted to root out the abuses of the upper clergy, many Lorraine Richerists saw Grégoire's *Nouvelle lettre d'un curé* (which attacked the nobility, praised the Third Estate, and encouraged curés to revolt against the upper clergy) as appallingly extremist.[5]

In July, shortly before the storming of the Bastille, Grégoire finally responded to Guilbert; he insisted that he was not neglecting his duties but rather had no time to write because the fate of the *patrie* rested on his efforts. He touted his accomplishments in Paris ("I will forever take pride in having been the most active and most ardent promoter of the union of the clergy with the towns [the Third Estate]"); he also told them that his *Nouvelle lettre*, while perhaps seeming too ardent to some readers, was necessary in "present circumstances." Guilbert was not convinced, however. By the next year, he and other former friends of Grégoire in Lorraine were complaining about their deputy's "vanity," "demagoguery" and "self-love." In 1791, Guilbert would lament that he would "carry to my grave a profound sadness for having contributed" to Grégoire's election in the first place.[6]

Among most Parisian revolutionaries, however, Grégoire's popularity continued to grow. As the Estates-General turned into the Constituent Assembly (the body that was to draft the new constitution), Grégoire became a key member of the Assembly's leadership structure. His colleagues elected him secretary on July 3 and 18, 1789 (he presided during the storming of the Bastille), and president on January 18, 1791. He was also placed on several committees, including the Credential-Verification and Report Committees (the latter of which he chaired, keeping him especially busy). Unlike some members, he took his responsibilities extremely seriously and thus shouldered a disproportionate workload.[7]

Because of his popularity, Grégoire was able to move in a wide variety of circles in the years 1789–91. It must have been a heady time for the Vého prodigy. Alongside the dazzling array of organized social activities (during the Estates-General, deputies could choose from dining out, classes, lectures, parties, theatrical performances, and concerts), Grégoire became a particularly sought-after guest for unofficial gatherings. He was admired now by the same people whose works he had read in the provinces; he also became close to the future Girondins, helping Brissot edit *Le patriote françois* and attending the salons of Mme Roland, Helen Maria Williams, and Mlle Helvétius (the latter in Auteuil). Grégoire was also invited as the only honorary member to join the patrician members of the Société des Amis des Noirs (Society of the Friends of Blacks), even though he could not afford the high membership fee.[8] He became an active member of the Breton Club and its successor the Jacobin Club; with Robespierre, he would become one of the leaders of the Jacobin Club's radical democratic faction, with broad support from the revolutionary populace. The curé of Emberménil, who loved intellectual discussions and socializing as much as he had in his twenties and thirties, was now hobnobbing with the giants of Parisian intellectual life and straddling many of the Revolution's fault lines. His prominence also brought him special treatment on the rare occasions when he left the capital.[9]

Under the National Assembly's religious policy (the Civil Constitution of the Clergy), which mandated popular election of bishops instead of their appointment by the pope, Grégoire would even be offered the choice of two different bishoprics, something beyond the wildest dreams of someone of his origins. In early 1791, he accepted that of Loir-et-Cher, centered in historic Blois; he moved there full-time at the end of the Constituent Assembly in September. Grégoire loved Blois and was enchanted by the countryside around it; he told his childhood friend the abbé Jennat that it was "one of the most beautiful *pays* [regions] under the heavens."[10] The Revolution—and Grégoire's days of being a legislator in Paris—might have seemed over.

With the outbreak of war, however, Grégoire would once again return to Paris, arriving in fall 1792. He became a key member of the new National Convention and a fervent believer in republicanism. He would soon realize, however, that his countrymen did not uniformly share his zeal. He found that opposition to the Revolution was highest among religious people who were suspicious of the revolutionaries' designs regarding Christianity.

A close look at Grégoire's activities—and his idea of regeneration—during the revolutionary years (defined here as stretching from 1789 until Napoleon's rise to power) can shed new light on major debates in scholarship on the French Revolution and the making of the modern nation-state.[11] In modern Europe, republicanism and religion have long been at odds, sparked by what is seen as the French Revolution's crusade against Catholicism. Grégoire's career, however, reinforces the findings of a number of recent studies about the way Revolution and religion seemed to many in the Revolution's early years to be perfectibly compatible. For faithful like Grégoire, " liberté, égalité, fraternité" was an inherently Christian motto; only as the Revolution progressed would the idea of Christian republicanism unravel.

These years also help clarify debates about revolutionary universalism. Many scholars—and the French public in general—highlight the ideals of universal rights that emerged from the French Revolution as one of its major achievements and legacies in modern world history. Some recent scholarship has pointed out, however, that revolutionary universalism was applied unevenly, that women in particular were never accorded equal citizenship. Meanwhile, some critics have argued that the category of universalism itself is flawed, that it was inherently exclusionary and therefore is not a political ideal that should be retained.

Looking at Grégoire makes us realize that universalism was never adopted on its own, however, but was made possible only through the homogenizing mechanism of regeneration. This term, used to refer generally to recreating society after the corruption of the Old Regime, was also used to target groups seen as needing "special" regeneration. Just as the abbé had suggested before the Revolution that Jews needed to transform themselves to become fully integrated into society, he now envisioned a similar process for other groups, such as dialect speakers and nonwhites. Regeneration would allow for including groups who had previously been persecuted or marginalized, but it depended on the erasure of their difference. One key mechanism for this would be intermarriage. Since sexual difference was not as easily expunged as racial, religious, linguistic, or other differences, however, the framework of regeneration would ultimately reinforce the exclusion of women, even as it facilitated the inclusion of other groups.

A final lesson offered by these years concerns the relationship between the Revolution's early years, full of harmony and promise, and its later turn to fratricidal violence. Many scholars, understandably sympathetic to the Revolution's goals of liberty and equality, have argued that the two main phases of the Revolution can be separated and that the Terror came about only when the Revolution's internal and external enemies refused to give up power. Grégoire's activities, though, help support the view that the seeds of the Terror were implicit in choices made earlier by the revolutionaries themselves, even if this was wholly unintended. One of these choices—which would also help distinguish the French Revolution from its American counterpart—was the slogan of regeneration. Grégoire's belief in the Revolution and regeneration were so great that he could not understand opposition to them, and he was one of the revolutionaries who most demonized those unconvinced by revolutionary rhetoric. The logic of regeneration soon led other revolutionaries to seek to destroy not only the Revolution's enemies but also those who seemed to lack enough zeal for it; as factions opposed to Christianity gained power, the Revolution began to create adversaries out of those who had initially supported it. Despite remaining a staunch republican, Grégoire himself would come to regret some of his early choices, and he would especially renounce the idea that regeneration necessitated complete destruction of the past. After Robespierre's fall, he and other newly styled moderates would search for ways to save republicanism, along with a reformed church and empire.

CHAPTER 4

Creating a French Nation

When Louis XVI first called the Estates-General to deal with his financial crisis, little did he imagine that he was launching a chain of events which would spur everything from the abolition of aristocratic and clerical privileges to his own execution. The early years of the Revolution, when the clergy and nobility unexpectedly joined with the Third Estate to form the National Assembly, launched dreams of a utopian future. As François Furet has noted, an "illusion of politics" was created, where anything seemed possible if only humans willed it.[1]

Grégoire himself was swept up in this fever; in the fall of 1789, in the wake of dramatic events like the storming of the Bastille, he believed in the instantaneous power of these events—and of the new constitution being drafted—to spark a radical regeneration of the entire kingdom. In a November 1789 sermon, the abbé invoked the utopia he thought the Revolution would effect: "In the near future, I see all the channels of agriculture and commerce opening to allow abundant goods to circulate . . .; all of the Arts, liberated from their fetters, deploying their energy; . . . Christianity recovering its splendor; regenerated education repairing the outrages done to the majesty of the altar; and the nineteenth century opening under the auspices of happiness."[2] Through political action, Grégoire and others imagined, France's problems could disappear.

THE DECLARATION OF THE RIGHTS OF MAN,
REGENERATION, AND UNIVERSAL CITIZENSHIP

The drafting of the Declaration of the Rights of Man and of the Citizen
in the summer of 1789 was a major impetus for these dreams. Whereas
the old system had been characterized by differential layers of privilege,
in which a person's legal status varied depending on his or her lineage, religion, occupation, place of residence, and gender, the Declaration used a
universalistic language to talk of the rights of "all men." Why did the revolutionaries use this new universal language? Where an older scholarship
saw the Revolution as a preplanned effort to put a coherent set of Enlightenment ideals into practice, much of the best recent work on the Revolution has shown that these ideals were often embraced retrospectively by
the revolutionaries, as the unexpected political crisis spurred them to create improvised responses to unforeseen situations. As Antoine de Baecque,
Keith Michael Baker, and Timothy Tackett have argued, the political
choices of 1789 were contingent, made in the heat of political contestation, rather than the result of longstanding ideological convictions.[3]

The choice of the Declaration's universalistic language was one of
these practical solutions. Though it might seem that the deputies were
consciously thinking of issues like the unequal status of the Jews, they
used this language, as Marcel Gauchet and other scholars have argued,
for reasons both more pragmatic and more circumscribed. First, the
deputies were aiming to destroy the system of privilege that had given
the Third Estate far fewer privileges than aristocratic and clerical elites.
By choosing a language which posited that "all men" should be given
the same "rights," they were in fact trying to ensure their own legal
equality. Second, as Gauchet has noted, the revolutionaries' decision to
speak of all men was rooted in a desire to substitute popular for monarchical sovereignty. Drawing on an idea most closely associated with
Rousseau, and hoping to legitimate their wresting control from the king,
they wanted to suggest the existence of a unified nation with a sovereign
and unitary will, so that it could appear that the nation was speaking as
one to reclaim its legitimate rights.[4]

The revolutionaries did not fully understand the consequences of their
choice, however, and were surprised to discover that they did not control
the meanings of their utterances. They soon faced an onslaught of unanticipated petitions from groups across the empire—from peasants and
Jews to people of color and actors—using the Assembly's new language
to declare that they too were "men" and deserved the same rights as "all

other Frenchmen." The revolutionaries thus faced an unexpected challenge: how to apply the universalism of their Declaration to the realities of French society.[5] How could they create a unified nation out of a country seemingly bursting with diversity—in religion, language, wealth, gender, geography, and race? How could difference be reconciled with equality, in order to cement the notion of a common French identity? These questions coincided with anxieties over the French nation; as David A. Bell has pointed out, at the very moment when it needed to emerge, people worried that it did not really exist.[6] Even minor differences thus seemed to represent a danger to French national character.

Into the void stepped a solution we have seen before: regeneration. As de Baecque has noted, it was Grégoire who had "defined most precisely the new uses" of this term on the eve of the Revolution, giving it the meaning of "correcting man physically, morally and politically."[7] Regeneration would become a central slogan of the French Revolution, describing a process in which every feature of French society would be purged of the corrupting germs of the Old Regime (fig. 5). While the entire nation was seen as needing regeneration, portions of it loomed as too different to be united with the rest. In its formulation by Grégoire, well before other revolutionaries were willing to fulfill the Declaration's promise of universality, regeneration thus promised to solve the problem of difference; it offered to create a unitary people where one did not yet exist. At the same time, it was not flexible enough to incorporate equally all portions of society, particularly women.

On the one hand, Grégoire's conception of regeneration was radically inclusive; it demanded that all potential members of the French nation be gathered into a single family. Grégoire had not forgotten the Jews and still believed that their integration was essential to social harmony. Working with Jewish leaders like Berr-Isaac-Berr, Grégoire pressed the issue of their citizenship early in the Constituent Assembly. Prevented from speaking on this issue in the Assembly itself when other members saw his views as too radical, he published a *Motion en faveur des juifs* in October 1789 restating the arguments of his Metz *Essai*. Denouncing the laws that prevented Jews' integration into French society, the abbé invoked the Gospels to argue that "it is as unjust as impolitic to leave the Jews vegetating in their current degradation." An unregenerated group within society, he suggested, could endanger everyone else.[8]

Similarly, Grégoire argued for rights for people of African descent in the French colonies. While his interest in Jews continued his prerevolutionary concerns, the cause of nonwhites was new for him. In his *Essai*

FIGURE 5. "Droits de l'homme" [or "L'homme enfin satisfait"] by
Jacques-Louis Pérée. A classic image depicting the regenerated man of the
French Revolution who has destroyed the remnants of the Old Regime
through masculine vigor and the political ideals of the Rights of Man.
Courtesy of the Bibliothèque nationale de France.

on the Jews and again in fall 1789, Grégoire had condemned philanthropists more concerned with blacks "two thousand leagues distant"
than with Jews at home. During his time in Paris, however, Grégoire
began to meet British and French abolitionists, as well as mixed-race
property-holders from Saint-Domingue (modern-day Haiti). He discovered that the French colonial system in the West Indies, which produced
a large portion of the world's sugar and coffee and fueled the French
economy, had a brutal human cost. He heard about the inhuman conditions and high death rate of the Middle Passage, and about the nearly
half a million slaves who labored in Saint-Domingue alone, facing savage repression if they dared revolt against their white masters. He also
learned of the legal and social discrimination faced even by those blacks
and people of mixed race who had purchased their freedom.[9]

Learning about conditions in the West Indies had a profound impact
on the abbé, and he soon changed his mind about the importance of the
colonial question. By late fall 1789, Grégoire decided that the colonies
needed regeneration as urgently as the metropole, and he pressed his colleagues to apply the Declaration's universal language to all areas of the
empire. Instituting racial equality, he suggested, would be one of the key
components in revitalizing the colonies. When mixed-race property-
holders (who were called *mulâtres* by their opponents but who preferred
the term *gens de couleur*) petitioned the Assembly in 1789 about their
disenfranchisement, Grégoire denounced what he called the "aristocracy of color." Later, when revolt broke out in Saint-Domingue over the
Assembly's failure to grant them rights, Grégoire insisted that France
could recognize only two classes of men: either the people of mixed race
were citizens or they were a foreign people rebelling against their despots.
Paralleling his concern with arbitrary laws that exiled Jews from the
social and economic mainstream, Grégoire called it outrageous that people of mixed race were not only prohibited from voting but were legally
prevented even from eating with whites in certain areas (a claim disputed
by his critics). Grégoire's demands for including people of color proved
too radical for the majority of the Assembly, and he found himself
attacked as a trouble-maker by the colonists and their allies. He nevertheless remained a leader in efforts to eradicate legal and social racism,
and influenced others to take up the cause.[10]

Grégoire also was a principal spokesman in the Assembly for
another group he saw as deserving of equal rights: the common people
in the French countryside. As one of the few deputies from a humble
background, he was a leading advocate of the idea that the common

people deserved full political rights and inclusion in the nation; for him, having different sets of rights contingent upon wealth simply perpetuated the injustices of the Old Regime. In 1789, he and Robespierre were among the only revolutionaries to object to the concept of passive citizenship, by which those who could not afford a tax would have fewer civic rights than those who could; the abbé argued that citizenship should be based on patriotism, not wealth. By 1791, other deputies began to share this sentiment, and Grégoire continued his efforts to eliminate the active/passive citizenship distinction. He blasted efforts to prevent the common people, "precisely those who have grievances to present," from petitioning the Assembly. "The declaration of rights," he noted, "is common to all men."[11]

"IT IS THEIR FAULT": REGENERATION AND CULTURAL HOMOGENIZATION

We would misunderstand Grégoire's idea of regeneration, however, if we thought it only meant crusading for kindness toward previously excluded groups and giving them citizenship. His frustrations—and silence—with regard to Jews are revealing. Despite his early interest in the Jewish issue, he turned his attentions elsewhere after 1789; when Jews ultimately received citizenship in 1790 (Sephardim only) and 1791 (all other Jews in France), other revolutionaries were more involved than he. Necheles found evidence suggesting that the abbé was prevented from speaking during the debates on citizenship for non-Catholics in December 1789 but that, afterwards, he voluntarily remained silent on the Jews to avoid jeopardizing his other projects.[12] This would suggest that Grégoire's interest in Jews was only one part of his larger plan for social reform, as it had been before the Revolution; while he relished being seen as their indefatigable defender, other issues had a greater claim on him, and he was hardly willing to let their citizenship campaign derail his political career, particularly when he had his own reservations about Jews' suitability for it.

Indeed, new evidence gives a candid view of Grégoire's frustrations and hesitations with regard to the Jews. In July 1791, seventeen months after the Sephardim had been deemed citizens, Grégoire explained to a Swiss friend why the Ashkenazim had not yet succeeded. Far from blaming the Jews' opponents, he wrote: "The Portuguese and Avignonese Jews enjoy the rights of citizens, those of Alsace and Lorraine not yet— *and it is their fault.* They would like to keep their communities and a torrent of customs that conflict with our current government [emphasis added]." He noted that he wished them well, but that it was necessary to "dissolve them into the national mass" instead of allowing them to remain a culturally definable group.[13] To him, the Ashkenazim's notion of citizenship—that they could be patriotic Frenchmen while maintaining distinct Jewish practices—was absurd.

Grégoire's comments remind us that his vision of regeneration entailed not only the immediate granting of citizenship to oppressed groups and thus their formal inclusion in the nation, but also special measures to change them. Just as Grégoire had made clear before the Revolution that Jews needed to change physically, morally, and politically to become fully French, Grégoire now applied similar ideas to non-whites and country dwellers. The nation required a unitary character.[14]

As with the Jews, Grégoire suggested that a key means for the full regeneration of nonwhites would be through interracial marriage. Interracial liaisons had been rendered degenerate under the Old Regime; depraved *colons* had forced themselves on their slaves and destroyed families of color, along with overall morality on the islands. Compounding matters, he alleged, many women of color had lost all "conjugal purity" and sought sexual relations with whites in hopes of improving their status. Any good that might have come of these relations, however, was impeded by law: the legal system penalized white men for marrying women of color but not for extramarital affairs with them. Furious about this system, Grégoire invoked a regenerated vision of interracial relationships; if they were sanctified by church, state, and society, the colonies could display "regenerated education and purified morals."[15]

Interracial marriage would improve not only the morals of nonwhites, but also their physiques; nonwhites, Grégoire contended, would benefit from exchanging blood with Europeans. As David Geggus has pointed out, Grégoire differed from other advocates of rights for freedmen by speaking of rights for "mixed bloods," "mulattos," or "people of color," and almost never for "free blacks." Though the abbé did in fact support rights for all freedmen in the colonies, this suggested that he saw the *gens de couleur* as having a greater claim to citizenship on account of their "white blood." Indeed, Grégoire saw the blending of the races as a key step toward national harmony; as offspring became lighter over time, prejudice would disappear because there would be no marker of racial difference. Grégoire did not view "black blood" as being without value; foreshadowing ideas he would expound in the 1820s, he argued that interracial marriage would produce a better population than whites or blacks alone. In particular, he praised the robustness of men of "crossed race" and their military bravery. We can see, however, that even as he denounced racial prejudice, he still suggested that each race had developed natural traits.[16]

The fact that regeneration did not only entail inclusion can also be seen in Grégoire's attitude toward slaves during these years. Despite his desire to obtain citizenship for the *gens de couleur* (as long as it was accompanied in the long term by other regeneratory measures, such as mixed marriage), Grégoire did not want it extended to slaves. While invoking the universalism of the Declaration of Rights in favor of mulattos, he stated that black slaves did not yet merit rights. Their cause "has nothing in common with that of the [free] mulattos. . . . One must not rush into anything . . . and give complete political rights to men who do not know all their duties. This would be putting a sword in the hands of the furious." Indeed, one of his arguments in favor of the *gens de couleur* was that they could help whites "contain the slaves."[17] Grégoire did admit that the revolutionaries would eventually need to address slavery in order to be true to their principles (an idea that was too radical for many of his colleagues). He nevertheless believed that slaves needed a long period of moral regeneration before membership in the nation could be considered. In the meantime, he appealed to the *gens de couleur* to spread Christianity to their "Negro brothers" and to recognize that they would have to free their own slaves one day.[18]

A parallel attitude about the need for cultural change to accompany political rights can be seen in Grégoire's view of country dwellers. Even as one of the most loyal champions of their equality, the abbé argued that changes in their cultural practices were essential for regenerating the nation. He was particularly anxious to wipe out local patois (by which he meant not only dialects of French, but also non-French regional languages); he also wanted to infuse peasants with learning from the cities, even while he was critical of urban immorality. Grégoire had argued in 1788 that the "annihilation of the patois is important to the expansion of enlightenment, the purified knowledge of religion, the easy execution of laws, national happiness, and political tranquility." In 1790, sparked by riots in the southwest that he attributed to language confusion, he sent questionnaires all over France asking how the patois could be eradicated. He was especially concerned about their influence on the morality, religiosity, and prejudices of the people; he also asked about schools and whether the curés monitored curricula. Foreshadowing his attempts to wipe out patois altogether, Grégoire suggested that linguistic diversity posed a great problem for national unity.[19]

As Bell has argued, Grégoire's analysis of this problem was not a self-evident one; he saw "massive and paralyzing heterogeneity" where others saw "only relatively minor differences" of accent or regionalisms. "It is simply not correct to say," Bell continues, "that the French revolutionaries confronted an obvious, inevitable 'language problem.' " Grégoire's analysis became extremely popular, however, and linguistic diversity began to loom for many revolutionaries as a serious challenge.[20] Once again, Grégoire's efforts suggested that universalism involved not only political inclusion but also cultural melting.

For Grégoire, difference thus appeared as a problem that needed to be solved through homogenization. The abbé was a great believer in the universal language of the Declaration; unlike many of his colleagues, he advocated immediate political rights for nearly all men. At the same time, he saw rights as only a first step. The nation needed a unified character, and groups who were different would need to alter their customs and values. The new ideal was not an entirely pre-existing one, since all of France needed to be regenerated. Some groups, however, had farther to go to get there. Country dwellers who spoke patois would need to speak only French; Jews would eventually need to convert; people of color would have to intermarry and adopt regenerated French values. Fully regenerated citizens would be French-speaking, Christian, enlightened, and light-skinned.

THE GENDER POLITICS OF REGENERATION

If nonwhites, Jews, and patois-speakers had the potential to change themselves into full members of the nation, there was one group that, in Grégoire's eyes, did not: women. Even as Grégoire campaigned against all kinds of generalizations about human difference and sought to eliminate artificial barriers differentiating people, he did not hesitate to make sweeping claims about natural differences between males and females; for him, gender, unlike race, was a fixed and comprehensive characteristic. Like many of his colleagues, Grégoire believed that women were so far from being able to fulfill the rights and duties of citizenship that the universal category of *men* should be restricted only to males.[21] Especially as the Revolution encountered increased opposition, the abbé began to scapegoat women for the Revolution's troubles and to urge that they refrain from expressing any political or religious ideas.

Grégoire's feelings about women over the course of his life were extremely complex and ambivalent, and he did make exceptions for individual women. The most important of these was for Mme Dubois (née Marie-Anne Brenier), his closest friend, "adopted mother" (despite being only a few years older), and confidante until his death. Grégoire first met Mme Dubois and her husband during the first year of the Revolution; his own mother had accompanied him to Paris to take care of him during the Estates-General, but she decided to return to Lorraine as the Revolution continued and found him a place in the Dubois's home.[22] While M. Dubois was frequently ill, Mme Dubois moved with Grégoire to Blois, hosted dinners for him in Paris, and shared his circle of friends and his most intimate thoughts. For a half-century, she would also take care of Grégoire's financial affairs, leaving him free to focus on political and spiritual matters. Early on in their friendship, he already called her "one of the most virtuous people that I have ever known."[23]

Though Grégoire's enemies occasionally whispered that the two were having an affair, their friendship was by all appearances extremely chaste. Grégoire was too pious and austere to have permitted himself to violate his vows of celibacy, and he would later prove to be merciless toward priests who had done so under duress during the dechristianizing fervor of the Terror. Mme Dubois nevertheless seems to have fulfilled all the social, practical, emotional, and intellectual functions of a "helpmate" for Grégoire, even during the years while her infirm husband was still alive. Over the next four decades, letters to Grégoire would frequently ask for regards to be sent to her; his own letters would often carry messages from her and convey "our wishes" on topics ranging from health to world politics.[24] She may have served occasionally as his secretary; some contemporaries speculated that she was his muse; and when Grégoire died, she would be his sole heir. Their bond was no doubt strengthened by the fact that Grégoire had no siblings and does not seem to have been close with his extended family.[25]

Apart from Mme Dubois and other individual women he befriended, however, Grégoire saw most women as frivolous and malevolent creatures whose immorality threatened the next generation. His antifemale diatribes went beyond those of many of his contemporaries. He did not insist, as many of them did, that women had superior moral qualities but lacked intellectual ones and thus needed to avoid politics. This kind of separate-spheres argument served to exclude women from public life but also suggested that women possessed admirable qualities that men lacked. While occasionally using the trope of feminine virtuousness in reference to pious peasant women, Grégoire more commonly denounced the majority of French women as immoral and vain. Bordering on misogyny, Grégoire's views in this regard can perhaps be seen as one of the legacies of his engagement with Rousseau.[26]

The first sign of Grégoire's hostility toward women came in 1790, in his *Lettre aux philantropes*. His attack was hidden in a footnote and its target was ambiguous; it was unclear whether he meant to criticize all French women or only female *colons*. The abbé was angry that the *colons* had questioned his motivation for defending the *gens de couleur* and were claiming he did so only because he had a mulatto sister-in-law. Grégoire retorted that the charge was preposterous, since he was an only child! But rather than stopping there, Grégoire lashed back at the *colons*, attacking "their" women in the harshest of terms: "If I did have a virtuous mulatto woman as my sister-in-law, I would prefer her to the near totality of your women, whose amiability is extolled, but who do not even know how to mask, under the facade of a dubious modesty, the ugliness of vice, which unites the shamelessness of gaze, the brazenness of remarks, [and] the cynicism of actions."[27] In contrasting a virtuous *mulâtresse* to the "near totality of your women," was Grégoire damning white women in general or only the female *colons*? Blaming the harshness of colonialism on white women was a common trope in European literature, one Grégoire himself would use later in life.[28]

Though the insult was hidden in a footnote, Grégoire's statement shocked his hardly feminist contemporaries; far from backing away from it once people noticed it, he repeated and expanded it. Adopting Rousseau's view of independent women as symbols of societal corruption, the abbé confirmed in a letter to Jacques-Pierre Brissot that he had indeed meant to attack the vast majority of women in French cities. Whether there or in the colonies, white women were largely immoral and shameless.

> You astonish me in announcing to me that the white *colons* are stung by what I said in my *lettre aux philantropes* against the libertinage of women. I will begin by saying to you that I only meant to talk about the women in our cities, starting with the capital. I repeat: nearly all of them unite the shamelessness of gaze, the brazenness of remarks, and the cynicism of actions. But since someone may demand an explanation on my part, I do not believe that our islands abound in vestal virgins and Lucretiuses. Incontestably, there is a great dissolution in morality there. I ask as much to creole women as to French ones: Are you virtuous? [If so, then] what I am saying does not concern you. I admit that there are exceptions; you do not have the right to take offense. Have you feigned virtue? The guilty ones must suffer and be quiet.[29]

This proved not to be an isolated statement uttered in frustration; Grégoire made similar comments in later years. In a discourse in honor of the Festival of the Federation in 1792, he blamed women for the moral degradation of children: "Who would not become indignant in seeing, near a very small number of women whom virtue decorates, a vile multitude who do not even deign to mask the ugliness of vice under the facade of a feigned reserve, which flaunts the shamelessness of gaze, the brazenness of remarks, the cynicism of attitudes? And who would not shudder in seeing their unbridled license, compared to many individuals of our sex?"[30] Because women's faults threatened to affect the next generation, Grégoire spent a great deal of energy appealing to women to improve themselves. Like other revolutionary leaders, Grégoire was obsessed with the next generation, for it would be the first born into the new regime. If it was to remain untainted, women needed to rediscover their natural mothering instincts and work to instill revolutionary values in their children.

While Grégoire did not seem to believe that women could ever be regenerated to the point that Jewish men or men of color could, he thus saw it as essential that women undergo drastic moral and behavioral change. He begged women to "prefer the love of your duties to those frivolous tastes that are always an indicator of hearts in war with virtue. May those to whom you have given birth learn to cherish religion and the *patrie* on your breast and in your arms." Grégoire's low opinion of women—and his belief that complete regeneration necessitated physical eradication of difference, something women could not undergo—thus led him to oppose political rights for them. Nevertheless, his concern about their behavior led him to a progressive position on one issue: because of mothers' crucial role in forming the next generation, he was a proponent of education for girls, calling in the Jacobin Club for "children of both sexes to be taught their rights and duties."[31]

Even as Grégoire appealed to women to be better mothers, however, he assailed them for allowing their maternal instincts to get in the way of patriotism. He cited classical examples of mothers who courageously valued their country more than their own children, and told them that, if they begged their husbands and sons to stay home out of selfish interest, the *patrie* would be deprived of soldiers and the Revolution would fail. Grégoire thus created a difficult situation for women: they needed to place their natural mothering duties above all else for the good of the nation, while repressing those instincts for the good of the nation.[32]

What accounts for Grégoire's bitterness toward women? It is unclear what specific experiences led him to his wholesale condemnations of female virtue, though one can imagine the seminarian from Vého having been scandalized both by the behavior of elite women in aristocratic Nancy and by the confidence and impiety of Parisian working women. The post-Tridentine church's efforts to prevent clergy from taking mistresses may also have shaped his apprehensions. His ill-ease with women was likely further strengthened by the political situation in Blois. When he first visited there in spring 1791, following his election as bishop, the local administration was warning of disorder and blaming it on women's seditious behavior. "The diversity of opinions on the Civil Constitution of the Clergy," they complained, "produces disastrous effects each day. In seducing an infinity of women by the false motives of religion and conscience, ill-intentioned people have succeeded in destroying the peace of households. Many women, Messieurs, have left the home of their husbands." In the minds of Blois revolutionaries, gullible women were the tools used by Thémines (Grégoire's episcopal predecessor, replaced because of his opposition to the Civil Constitution of the Clergy) and his associates to rebel against the Revolution. Nuns were a source of even greater suspicion for him. Though the Ursulines welcomed him, other nuns made clear their loyalty to Thémines and distaste for the new bishop from the moment he arrived in the diocese. The elite Dames de Calvaire, for example, refused to ring their bells when Grégoire visited their convent.[33]

Under the Republic, Grégoire's anti-woman rhetoric increased. As opposition to the revolution he loved so much became more and more evident, Grégoire increasingly placed the blame on women for persuading the rest of the people to follow counterrevolutionaries. Like the other Convention members who would vote to shut down women's political clubs, Grégoire contended that the polity could only be built if women were prevented from trying to influence the national will.

Scholars of gender have debated in recent years whether the universalism of the Revolution was inherently exclusionary with regard to women. Where some writers have suggested that the exclusion of women from membership in the nation was an integral part of revolutionary values and that the Revolution set back women's equality, others have maintained that women's exclusion was merely contingent, the result of lingering prejudices, while the idea of rights in general was advanced tremendously during the Revolution.[34]

Looking at Grégoire suggests an answer between the two. On the one hand, the later embrace of Grégoire by advocates of national liberation and *négritude* (a twentieth-century movement that celebrates African rather than European ideals) reminds us that the Revolution's universalism did help feminism, antiracism, and other forms of social protest to become more thinkable. At the same time, however, Grégoire's campaigns reveal the restrictive conditions that made universalism operational. Universalism did not stand on its own; on the contrary, its implementation depended on the homogenizing action of regeneration. Women could not transform themselves into fully regenerated citizens in the same way as patois-speaking, Jewish, Protestant, mixed-race or black males; women's difference was a fixed one that could not be erased by converting, adopting a new language, or intermarrying. While women thus required regeneration of some sort, they would never be fully regenerated, and universal citizenship could not apply to them. Women's exclusion began to seem even more natural to Grégoire and others as women became more firmly identified with religiosity and counterrevolution, as we will see in the next chapter.

THE CHOICE OF REGENERATION

So far, we have discussed the revolutionaries' choice of a universalistic Declaration, their anxieties about the "nation," and the way the paradigm of regeneration aimed to solve the problem of difference through widespread inclusion combined with cultural homogenization. We have also seen that, for Grégoire and others, women's difference was impossible to overcome, in contrast to that of Jews and nonwhites; though the latter groups were farther from the social mainstream as far as most Frenchmen were concerned, their biological differences were seen as erasable through intermarriage and other means of physical regeneration. If regeneration represented a choice, though, what other options did the Assembly have for dealing with marginalized groups?

On the one hand, there was an active impossibilist contingent in the Assembly, including some of the same people with whom Grégoire had debated in his *Essai* on the Jews. These deputies, such as the abbé Maury, La Fare (the bishop of Nancy), and the infamous Hell (the forged receipts mastermind), were willing to extend citizenship to Protestants, who, like Jews, also had a tenuous status under the Old Regime outside of Alsace. They rejected, however, the idea that the Declaration's universal principles should be applied to Jews and nonwhites. Paralleling

Michaelis, they claimed that Jews were both naturally corrupt and too different from the rest of the nation to be included in it.

Indeed, as Maury contended in December 1789, the Jews were not French but a separate nation of usurers. Similarly, La Fare chose a discourse of order over the Declaration's universalistic language of justice. Referring to the anti-Jewish riots that had occurred in Alsace, he claimed that "a decree which would grant Jews the rights of citizens could set off a great fire." Hell, meanwhile, adopted the strategy of pretending to apply the Declaration while completely distorting it; he proposed a motion that would have granted Jews the title of citizen, yet subjected them to so many humiliating restrictions (e.g., they would need permission of local authorities to marry, and could never comprise more than one-sixth of a local population) that it would have stripped the title of any real meaning. A similar proposal came from the prince de Broglie, an Alsatian aristocrat, who suggested that Jews demonstrate to their Gentile neighbors' satisfaction that they had regenerated themselves before receiving citizenship.[35]

Outside the Assembly, opponents of the Jews were even less generous. One pamphleteer invoked banishment of the Jews as a plausible alternative to giving them citizenship. He ridiculed the very idea that the Jews could be regenerated: "To achieve this metamorphosis on the Jews of our day, would require a true miracle, and the heavens have long tired of doing anything for this people." The municipality of Colmar followed a similar logic, arguing that the Jews' "distaste for any form of manual labor" and their hatred for Christians ensured that they could not be absorbed into the nation.[36]

Grégoire's belief in the possibility of regenerating people of color encountered similar opposition. The white *colons* and their metropolitan allies viewed nonwhites as wholly unworthy of citizenship, and worked to prevent the Assembly from even discussing a change in their status. They argued (successfully, during the earliest years of the Revolution) that the stability of the nation depended on the colonial status quo, and that colonial assemblies rather than the National Assembly should determine the status of nonwhites. Outside the Assembly, pro-colonial pamphleteers denounced Grégoire, maintaining that God had created blacks and whites to have different destinies, and that only rarely did nonwhites attain whites' level of intelligence. As one writer insisted, nonwhites were "men without education [and] without enlightenment"; it was therefore absurd to say "that all men are born and remain equal."[37]

Similarly, Médéric-Louis-Elie Moreau de Saint-Méry, a prominent slaveholding lawyer, was so upset about Grégoire's 1789 *Mémoire en faveur des gens de couleur* that he wrote a sixty-eight-page response, in which he charged that Grégoire was ignorant about the true situation in the colonies, that he blindly copied the most outrageous libels, and that his language was inappropriate for a priest and legislator. Moreau insisted that the Declaration was not made for the colonies, and that the true object of the Revolution was the "peace of the Kingdom and the happiness of its inhabitants." He contended that colonial commerce put bread in the mouths of millions, and that Grégoire played with their lives when he endangered the colonies' future. Moreover, he charged, Grégoire's attempts to gain immediate citizenship for the *gens de couleur* violated the principles that the abbé himself had announced in his *Essai* on the Jews. In that renowned work, Moreau noted, Grégoire had argued that it was necessary to work slowly in a situation fraught with prejudices and to carefully prepare both Christians and Jews before the latter's integration could be granted. Even while appealing to Grégoire's idea of regeneration, Moreau suggested that Grégoire was moving too quickly and trying to legislate equality before, instead of after, regeneration had taken place.[38]

Many Frenchmen, in the colonies and the metropole, agreed with the *colons*' position; as Geggus has noted, anyone who wanted to change the status quo risked being labeled unpatriotic. In November 1789, Grégoire was shouted down and prevented from speaking in the Assembly when he tried to present a report favorable to the *gens de couleur*. Moreover, when revolution broke out in Saint-Domingue in 1790–91, he was blamed for having incited it, and whites there burned him in effigy.[39]

At the same time, however, more liberal alternatives existed, which did not stipulate that these groups needed to change. These alternatives came primarily, though not exclusively, from members of these groups themselves. Those who held such views did not deny that patriotism and commitment to the polity's laws were requirements for citizenship. Nevertheless, they resisted efforts to put further restrictions on citizenship; they were thus heirs to what we have called unconditionalism.

When free people of color like Julien Raimond petitioned the Assembly, for instance, they argued simply that they deserved the same "sacred rights of humanity" that the Declaration had promised to others. Even as Raimond worked closely with Grégoire on the campaign to achieve rights for nonwhites and admired him greatly, he argued that free people of color did not need any special measures for improvement. Indeed, as Dominique Rogers has noted, middle-class freedmen had already enjoyed an "embryonic form of true citizenship" before the Revolution. Implicitly referencing the title of Grégoire's essay on the regeneration of the Jews, Raimond thus insisted that "we are [already] free, physically, morally, and politically. . . . [C]onsequently we must constitute one and the same class, one single category with all the free men of this colony." A slaveowner himself, Raimond nevertheless shared with Grégoire the conviction that slaves were not yet ready for rights.[40]

Just as Raimond challenged Grégoire's concept of targeting the *gens de couleur* for special regeneration, so too did the Jews of Bordeaux, in an open letter they addressed to him in August 1789. Grégoire often referred to the flowery opening of this letter as evidence of contemporary Jews' unconditional acclaim for him, an idea that has been repeated more recently by Hermon-Belot. Grégoire did not mention, however, the letter's crucial middle section, which implored him to change his position on Jews. In this section, which was deleted from Grégoire's *Mémoires* (where the rest of the letter was reproduced as if whole), the Jews of Bordeaux urged the abbé to stop speaking of laws about "Jews." For these Jews, who already enjoyed de facto equality with Gentiles before the Revolution, Jewish regeneration should be no different from the regeneration of the "entire Kingdom." Simply by being granted religious and civil liberty with others, they argued, "the Jews will find the means of becoming useful." Furthermore, they insisted, targeting Jews for anything other than the general regeneration of France would be "an injustice as gratuitous as it would be cruel."[41]

This plea was shared by non-Jewish revolutionaries like Brissot and the leaders of the Paris municipality, such as Jean-Claude-Antoine de Bourge. These revolutionaries rejected the idea that extralegal measures would be necessary to regenerate Jews; as de Bourge wrote, "Jews, like Christians, must be regenerated by the Constitution [alone]." Unlike Grégoire, many of these men (who later became allied with the Girondins) were not fervent Christians and therefore wanted to create a polity in which a person's religious beliefs were irrelevant. They therefore criticized the idea that there should be separate regulations about Jews, since "all men living in an Empire must participate in the same title and in the same rights." Their views were shared by other deputies, such as Adrien Duport, whose championing of the Jews' right to citizenship was predicated on the argument that the Declaration applied equally to all.[42]

Patois-speakers also contested Grégoire's idea that they needed to change their language to belong to the nation. When Grégoire sent out his language inquiry, for example, an anonymous respondent from Toulouse answered him as follows:

> *[Grégoire's Q. 29]:* What would be the religious and political impor-
> tance of entirely destroying the patois?
> *[Respondent's A]:* The religious and political importance of destroying
> the patois is nil.
> *[Q. 30]:* What would be the means of doing so?
> *[A]:* To destroy it, it would be necessary to destroy the
> sun, the coolness of night, the whole category of
> food, the qualities of water—and man altogether.[43]

Similarly, a respondent from Alsace told Grégoire that, rather than requiring French citizens to speak only French, bilingualism should be extended. This writer insisted that requiring people to speak the language of their rulers was oppressive and contrary to revolutionary principles. On the contrary, government employees should have to learn local languages: "No one is afraid today to claim that kings are made for peoples, and not vice versa. Yet one can still dare argue that the people must know the language of their judges, while the judge is allowed to be ignorant of the language of the people he is supposed to judge." This writer lauded German as a beautiful and rich language whose suppression would be a great loss for France.[44]

Finally, radical women such as Etta Palm d'Aelders and Olympe de Gouges contested the idea that they were unworthy of citizenship. In 1791, Palm d'Aelders challenged the Assembly to extend the Declaration's universalism to the female residents of France. "Yes, Gentlemen, you have broken the iron sceptre in order to replace it with the olive branch; you have sworn to protect the weak. . . . You have restored to man the dignity of his being in recognizing his rights; you will no longer allow woman to groan beneath an arbitrary authority; that would be to overturn the fundamental principles on which rests the stately edifice you are raising by your untiring labors for the happiness of Frenchmen." Similarly, in her famous Declaration of the Rights of Woman, de Gouges rephrased the Declaration of the Rights of Man to make an unambiguous proclamation of women's equality. Rephrasing Article I of the Assembly's Declaration ("Men are born and remain free and equal in rights"), she wrote: "Woman is born and lives equal to man in her rights." Transforming Article III ("The principle of all sovereignty resides essentially in the nation"), she wrote, "The principle of all sovereignty resides essentially in the nation, which is nothing but the union of woman and man." De Gouges hardly thought that women did not need moral regeneration; just as all of society needed to be liberated from the corruption of the past, so too did women. Nevertheless, she rejected the idea that women were somehow less deserving of rights than men, and she argued that the regeneration of women would best be accomplished by "including them in all the activities of men."[45] Women like de Gouges and Palm d'Aelders were supported in their claims for citizenship by a handful of men, most notably the Marquis de Condorcet.

In the end, though, the Assembly adopted a strategy that very much paralleled Grégoire's; if anything, it erred on the side of wanting to know that groups were capable of being regenerated before it was willing to grant them rights and include them in the nation. On December 24, 1789, the Assembly gave citizenship rights to Protestants and to actors, but it took until September 1791 before it finally accorded citizenship to all Jews (having granted it in January 1790 to Sephardim only, on the grounds that they were already assimilated into French culture). The deputies extended the limits of citizenship in May 1791 to a small portion of the *gens de couleur* (those born of two free parents), but to all mulattos and free blacks only in April 1792; they did not decree the end of slavery until 1794, and then mainly in an effort to quell the insurrection raging in Saint-Domingue. As for the rural and urban poor, the Assembly maintained the active/passive distinction that deprived them of equal rights throughout the Constituent Assembly; not until August 1792, when the revolutionaries began to destroy the monarchy, would this distinction be abolished.[46] Many in France were extremely enthusiastic about Grégoire's proposals to wipe out patois, however, and shared his belief that this action was essential for national unity; indeed, Grégoire's ideas are commonly viewed as the basis for language policy in nineteenth-century France and its empire. Nineteenth-century French Jews and Haitians would also find themselves using the concept of regeneration, in order to combat impossibilists and to suggest that they were in fact becoming worthy of equal treatment.[47]

Just as Grégoire had hoped, however, the revolutionaries ultimately deemed women too unregenerable to be part of the national community. Even as they granted citizenship rights to long-excluded groups of men, they refused to grant women the same legal status; during the National Convention, the government would even ban women's participation in political clubs.[48] As Joan Scott has noted, when radical women demanded that the Assembly's universalism be applied to them, they were placed in the delicate position of having to petition as women, thus "undermining the attempt to declare [their gender] irrelevant for political purposes."[49]

Regeneration seemed poised to facilitate, however, the creation of a unitary nation of "French" men. As Camille Desmoulins had noted in 1789: "Saint Paul . . . once wrote: 'Those of you who have been regenerated by baptism, you are no longer Jews, no longer Samaritans, no longer Romans, no longer Greeks: you are all Christians.' It is in the same way that we have just been regenerated by the National Assembly; we are no longer from Chartres or from Monthléri, no longer Picards or Bretons, no longer from Aix or Arras: we are all Frenchmen, all brothers."[50] In choosing *regeneration,* the revolutionaries had chosen a path between the impossibilists and unconditionalists—a path that promised to build unity by effacing difference.

CHAPTER 5

A Religious Revolution?

Regeneration Transformed

In the last chapter, we looked at a few of the paradoxical effects of regeneration: it facilitated the inclusion of oppressed groups while mandating that they change, and allowed for inclusion of some groups even while legitimizing the exclusion of women. These were not the only paradoxical aspects of regeneration, however: this concept would also serve to support a Christian Revolution and to work against the Church. Though regeneration began the eighteenth century as a theological term, it would soon be adopted as a revolutionary slogan by many people who considered themselves irreligious. What in fact was the relationship of religion to the Revolution? Were terms like *regeneration* completely stripped of their Christian content, their sacrality transferred to the nation in order to legitimate the new regime?[1] Would Grégoire be able to maintain his enlightened Catholicism as a coherent program throughout the Revolution? What choices would enable him to survive when colleagues were purged, and how would he feel about his decisions later?

In modern-day France, the involvement of Catholics like Grégoire in the Revolution has appeared puzzling at best, traitorous at worst. Because of the violent dechristianization of the later Revolution, which saw churches vandalized and royalist priests deported or executed, religion and Revolution have often been seen as sworn enemies. Many secular revolutionaries would not have objected to this depiction; for them, the Church was as much of an obstacle to progress as the monarchy. Moreover, when they used *regeneration,* they saw it not as a Christian

term but as an anti-Christian one. Many revolutionaries did not think
at all about the word's Christian origins; as Van Kley has noted, they
were "reluctan[t] to acknowledge intellectual ancestry in what they
denounced as superstition."[2] Nevertheless, we would fundamentally
misunderstand the Revolution if we saw it as uniformly anti-Christian
from the outset. Rather than defining church and Revolution as oppo-
sites, Grégoire and many other Catholics saw the Revolution as a fulfillment of the Gospels and a way to extend regeneration (political, social,
and theological) to all of France.

When Grégoire discovered that others did not share his passion for
the Revolution, however, his attacks on them became more fierce. While
never one of the most bloodthirsty revolutionaries, he would play an
integral role in the National Convention—something he would later try
to downplay. He would also lead denunciations of the Revolution's real
and perceived enemies, from nobles to women to conservative clerics.
Nevertheless, his idea of Christian republicanism became increasingly
idiosyncratic, and he would make choices he later found unpalatable;
indeed, his later claims that he had never varied in his opinions tend to
obscure the slipperiness of some of his revolutionary positions. Unwilling to join those supporters of the Revolution who turned against it as
it radicalized, the abbé endeavored to remain central in political life by
emphasizing the enlightened portion of enlightened religion. He also
continued to work toward the regeneration of France through his work
on the Committee of Public Institution (CPI), even when others began
to interpret this idea to mean dechristianization.

A RELIGIOUS REVOLUTION: THE EARLY YEARS

In the early years of the Revolution, Grégoire sought to use his new
authority to infuse Christianity throughout French society, expanding
the efforts he had begun in his parish. During the debates on the Declaration of Rights, for example, he aimed to ensure that God would be
present in the new regime's founding documents: "Man was not thrown
by accident onto the corner of the earth that he occupies. If he has rights,
we must speak of Him from whom he possesses them. If he has duties,
we must remind him of He who stipulates them. What name more
august and more grand can be placed at the head of the Declaration than
that of the divinity?" The abbé also emphasized the Christian aspects of
regeneration, particularly in regard to the Jews; though the "wind of
divine anger" had dispersed them around the globe, he argued, God

"reserves for us the glory of preparing the revolutions that must regenerate this People." He also noted in a 1789 sermon that his politics were guided by the Gospels. Furthermore, building on his prerevolutionary Richerism, Grégoire argued that the clergy should play a leading role in regenerating France. In his view, citizen-pastors would be the vanguard of the Parisian authorities in the provinces, reinforcing in their parishioners "the duties of citizen and Christian."[3]

To help regenerate France, however, Grégoire argued that the priesthood itself needed regeneration. First, priests would need to redirect their energies so that they could lead agricultural innovations and spread knowledge in addition to ministering spiritually. When the Assembly tried to close all religious orders in 1790, Grégoire insisted (building on his 1778 SPS essay) that "religion, the sciences, and agriculture require that some of them be conserved." In addition, Grégoire advocated land grants *(dotation en bien-fonds)* for the clergy, which could return them to the honest labor of the early Christians, while ensuring sufficient income for them to spread new scientific ideas. The curé of Emberménil also offered various proposals to ensure that clergy be patriotic.[4]

In addition to his own proposals, Grégoire supported the reforms initiated in the Church through the Assembly's 1790 Civil Constitution of the Clergy. He was at first reluctant to support this set of reforms, which nationalized the clergy by requiring priests to swear an oath of allegiance to the Assembly and to be elected by the people; like many priests, he feared its seeming rejection of the pope would produce a schism. Once his fellow deputies passed the Civil Constitution, however, Grégoire made himself a symbol of Catholic patriotism by being the first to pronounce the oath. Unaware of the chasm that the oath would open in French society, Grégoire declared: "We see nothing in the constitution that could harm the holy truths we believe and teach. It would injure and slander the National Assembly to suppose that it wishes to lay a hand on the thurible [incense vessel]." He appealed to priests to "defend the constitution, whose principles of equality and justice are based on the Gospels."[5]

Grégoire's efforts to ensure that the Revolution would be a Christian one only increased once the constitution was completed and the Constituent Assembly disbanded in September 1791. Though he had been elected bishop of Loir-et-Cher in February 1791, he had been too busy with his legislative duties to occupy the position full-time; now, he moved to his diocese and began reorganizing it. It is clear that he relished his new status; *évêque de Blois* (with *ancien* added after the Concordat) was the title on which he insisted until his death.[6] The Richerist firebrand was now a bishop himself—something unthinkable for someone of his birth before the Revolution; in addition, he now presided over the departmental Conseil général. Even from Blois, his national stature rose so much that he became the virtual figurehead of the Constitutional Church.

From this august platform, Grégoire had the opportunity to lay out his vision of a regenerated church, extending the reforms he had proposed in Emberménil and the SPS. What would this new church look like? Like the existing church, it would be hierarchical. Nevertheless, the hierarchy would more explicitly reflect democratic choice. Indeed, Grégoire himself claimed that he would have been perfectly happy to retire to Lorraine after the Constituent Assembly, but that when "several departments" elected him bishop, he decided that "THE VOICE OF THE PEOPLE IS THE VOICE OF GOD" (emphasis in original). While he was their father as bishop, he insisted that they all belonged to the same family.[7]

Another element of this purified church would be priests' increased attention to social and national issues, something he tried to instill through reforming the local seminary curriculum. Drawing on his pre-revolutionary interest in seminary reform, Grégoire declared that the education of clerics, which had been "vicious" and "a great plague to the Church," would henceforth be overhauled. Where religious teachers had previously "harmed love of their neighbor in quarreling over love of God," the new ecclesiastical training would emphasize the majestic aspects of faith and the social duties of the ministry. Pastor-citizens would "present to the French the Gospels in one hand and the Constitution in the other"; they could help "private and public morals regenerate themselves, and thus bring about more quickly the reign of Jesus Christ."[8]

In general, Grégoire held up the early church as a model for what the French church could become; regeneration could involve returning to an ancient ideal rather than a complete break with the past. Indeed, Grégoire modeled his own role after that of Jesus and the apostles, proclaiming his desire to live simply so that his diocesans would not have to spend their wages on his expenses. He promised that the most important portion of his job was helping individuals to see the light when they had questions; he further pledged that he would visit every corner of his diocese, spreading the Gospels as Jesus had throughout Judea—something, he noted, that his predecessor Thémines had not done for thirteen years. In early 1792, he set out on an eighteen-day tour during which he preached fifty-two times.[9]

Even as he venerated the ideals of the ancient church, Grégoire also used eighteenth-century ideals as he tried to win converts. Rather than telling nonbelievers they would be damned if they did not practice Christianity, he appealed to their reason: "Christianity is as necessary to your existence as air and light." He cited Plutarch on the value of a civil religion, adding, "It is under the guarantee of religion that public happiness rests; without it, a people will never be more than a despicable horde."[10]

Grégoire was hardly alone in seeing religion and Revolution as compatible. On the contrary, his Assembly colleagues included a host of other patriotic clerics, such as Claude Fauchet, Adrien Lamourette, Jean-Baptiste Royer, and Jean-Pierre Saurine. Patriotic priests such as François Mulot and Antoine Bertolio also held leadership positions in the Paris municipal government. For these priests, enlightened religion was not a contradiction, and Revolution and religion were inextricably linked.[11]

This idea was not unique to the priests who participated in the Revolution; it also had support among the populace. As Mona Ozouf writes, "The first revolutionary religion was quite simply the Christian religion. . . . In these early years of the Revolution, a thousand speeches, sermons, pamphlets, and patriotic prayers bear witness to an effort to popularize the notion that the message of Christianity was consonant with that of patriotism." Indeed, one of the things that spurred Grégoire's meteoric popularity was his willingness to place religion in service of the Revolution. One revolutionary in Rouen, for example, wrote a song for Grégoire; even as he said that he would rather drink brackish water than toast the pope, he praised the abbé as a "Pasteur Philosophe": "Beloved curé, you can safely say / Every Frenchman is my parishioner." Moreover, Suzanne Desan describes villagers who saw no contradiction between Revolution and religion, and who used revolutionary language to justify traditional religiosity.[12]

A religious Revolution was thus not anathema—at least, as Tackett and others have argued, until passage of the Civil Constitution of the Clergy. The Civil Constitution and its required oath of loyalty polarized many moderate clerics and lay people, forcing them to take a definitive position for or against the Revolution; in the oath's wake, as Tackett has noted, "French society would never again be quite the same." Notwithstanding many Catholics' bitter opposition to anything that smacked of Enlightenment, the ultimate break between the Revolution and the Church was therefore hardly inevitable in 1789.[13]

THE RELIGIOUS REVOLUTION ENCOUNTERS OPPOSITION

Even as Grégoire sought to be a "bon évêque," he soon found that Loir-et-Cher was not as receptive to change as Embermenil had been; the Civil Constitution—and Grégoire's arrival—had polarized the region. Though he was welcomed enthusiastically by many, and though he denied that constitutional Christianity represented any departure from true Christian principles, he faced a deluge of anonymous attacks even before he arrived. The ousted bishop, Thémines, refused to leave town; he and his supporters (such as the hostile nuns we encountered earlier) opposed Grégoire at every turn. An anonymous writer, for example, circulated a pamphlet contending that Grégoire was only interested in money and that his election was illegitimate. To compound matters, Grégoire's selection of *vicaires* (his clerical deputies) turned out, by his own admission, to be ill-advised; they included two men who later denounced Christianity and another who was a thief.[14] Meanwhile, outside the country, France's enemies threatened war.

Grégoire may once have thought, with his Girondin friends, that the Revolution was over once the constitution was completed. In the face of this opposition, however, he soon realized that the real work of regeneration was just beginning. Like other Jacobin Club members, he began to view regeneration as something not so quickly attained, but requiring constant vigilance.[15] In the service of religion and Revolution, regeneration necessitated war against enemies of the state.

When he found himself unable to win over his flock, Grégoire's attacks on his critics became increasingly virulent. He attacked the refractory priests (clergy who opposed the Civil Constitution) as "enemies of the *patrie*" and assured his flock that the Assembly wanted to found public happiness on the eternal truths of Jesus Christ. Since the Assembly had hardly rewritten the Gospels but had made only minor changes to church structure, he insisted, the dissidents' objections were not grounded in religion, but were merely a cover for counterrevolutionary sentiment: "Religion is the sacred veil that the wicked abuse to mask their plots. The only heresy they find in the constitution is *equality*." The Assembly and the constitutional clergy, he proclaimed, were "inviolably attached to the Catholic, Apostolic and Roman Church."[16]

Labeling opposition to the Revolution and to constitutional Christianity treasonous, Grégoire appealed to his flock to display their patriotism. Though the French church had believed in supporting the regime in power while it was a monarchy, many faithful were not prepared to support a revolutionary regime. Grégoire worked to convince his diocesans that loyalty to the government was not only a civic good but also a religious commandment; since despotism and feudalism violated Christian principles, Christians should be ready to die to prevent their return. "It is a crime," he declared, "to be indifferent to the fate of the *patrie*." He urged the residents of Loir-et-Cher to see church and state as twin pillars of regeneration: "Religion and constitution: that is our motto. We will be the apostles of it; we will be, if necessary, its martyrs, and our last breath will be for God, for law, and for liberty."[17]

Grégoire felt increasingly unconvinced, however, about the patriotism of his flock and of the people more generally. In 1791, he complained that "the most dangerous enemy of the people is the people themselves. It is the fluidity of its character, the mobility of its ideas and affections. It is this propensity for infatuation that makes a single fault efface fifty years of virtue in its eyes, and the wrongs of an entire century disappear in the face of a single promise to fix them." He declared publicly in 1792 that people in the region were overly royalist and "inclined toward idolatry," and later wrote in his *Mémoires* that they had less backbone than anywhere else in the country.[18]

As he became more suspicious of the local populace, Grégoire increasingly defined patriotism in negative terms. "Remember that the enemies of the Revolution are not all on the other side of the Rhine," he cautioned his flock. "A great number of them have infected our land, and even some public officials are traitors, salaried by a generous nation that they betray."[19] With all of Europe threatening war against France, Grégoire declared ominously, "we need to exterminate despotism, to annihilate this stupid arrogance, to purge the earth, to crush these monsters . . . , to reveal to all peoples their imprescriptible rights, and to emancipate the human species."[20]

He also urged his diocesans to display military zeal. In the wake of France's preemptive declaration of war on its neighbors in April 1792, Grégoire compared the people of Blois unfavorably to the inhabitants of Nancy, who, he told them, were volunteering in record numbers. With other members of the local administration, he challenged the citizens of Loir-et-Cher not to "close themselves in a cowardly manner in their houses" in the interior of the country, but to leave for the frontiers and defend France with their lives: "You have pledged to *live free or die*. The moment has arrived to fulfill your oaths."[21]

Militaristic patriotism, however, was not as obvious a corollary of the Gospels as Grégoire wanted it to seem; maintaining his Christian-revolutionary synthesis required some intellectual gymnastics. How could one reconcile the pacifistic universalism of the Gospels with the militaristic patriotism of the Revolution? How could one appease those portions of the populace whose enthusiasm for the Revolution inclined them to violent dechristianization? How could one retain the support of churchgoers, especially women (as Grégoire and others declared) who saw religion and Revolution as opposed? The revolutionary Christianity of Grégoire and his fellow priest-*conventionnels* was an increasingly unstable mixture, drawing national opposition. Yet, even as Grégoire and his clerical allies found themselves isolated from conservative Catholics, their differences with secular Jacobins became evident as well. While his revolutionary colleagues, as Lynn Hunt has noted, viewed the king as increasingly irrelevant and began to imagine themselves as a nation of brothers, Grégoire still clung to the idea that there was a father: God.[22] Grégoire's former teacher, Lamourette, tried to repair the divisions developing among revolutionaries with his famous kiss of reconciliation. By the next year, however, he would choose to join his Lyon flock in their revolt against the Revolution's increasingly radical course; the following year, he would be executed.

SMASH THE MONARCHY, SPREAD THE REVOLUTION

Even before leaving Paris for Blois, Grégoire had shown discomfort with the constitutional monarchy adopted by his colleagues. He was especially disgusted that the deputies had allowed the king to stay in power instead of imprisoning him after his ill-fated flight to Varennes in June 1791. Along with Robespierre and other radical Jacobins, Grégoire demanded that the king be held accountable. Similarly, as the Constituent Assembly wrapped up its business in September 1791 and prepared the transition to its permanent successor, the Legislative Assembly, the bishop of Loir-et-Cher advised the incoming deputies that the king could not be trusted. In an address to the Jacobin Club that proved so popular that the Jacobins ordered it sent around the country, Grégoire referred to kings as bloodthirsty and lecherous but complained that it was difficult to voice this idea in public. He asked the king's defenders sarcastically, "If it is a crime to imagine that another form of government might be preferable to monarchy . . . , shall we tear up the Declaration of Rights? It is insulting to proclaim freedom of opinion, even while you try to dominate mine. Despite you and all tyrants, I will continue to exercise my ability [to think for myself]. Based on what right, and with what force, can you make me happy with monarchy, if it is repugnant to my worldview? This task would require super-human force."[23] Even as he made these radical suggestions, however, Grégoire knew that the constitution, which he himself had sworn to uphold, preserved the king as an important political actor. He therefore could not yet give full voice to his intense hatred for the monarchy.

Within less than a year, however, Grégoire would no longer have to keep his ideas to himself. While in Blois, he was thrilled to receive news of the popular revolution of August 10; demonstrations had spurred the Legislative Assembly to suspend the king and call for a new constitution, to be drafted by a National Convention. After convening the other departmental administrators, composing a response, and staying up all night supervising the typesetting, Grégoire "had the department inundated" the next day with printed copies; he reported that the announcement "electrified" even the sedentary inhabitants of Loir-et-Cher. Elected unanimously as that region's deputy to the Convention at a meeting over which he himself presided and with support from the national Jacobin Club, Grégoire readied himself to leave for Paris.[24]

Grégoire now unleashed the brunt of his anger toward Louis. During a sermon he gave before he left Blois, he likened kings to monsters ("Someone said long ago that princes are commonly in morality what monsters are in the physical order") and added that "the most immoral class of men was always that of kings." He proclaimed that the history of kings was also that of the "martyrology of nations." While he was willing to admit that not all French kings had been bad, he could identify only two out of seventy that he respected. At this time of crisis, Grégoire declared that moderation was unacceptable. Chiding his flock for infrequently making principled stands, he lambasted those who "hide themselves behind the names *impartials, monarchists, feuillans,* and *moderates*" (emphasis in original). He also appealed to his countrymen to not let the Revolution die.[25]

So far, the events of summer 1789 had failed to spur the complete regeneration of France, as had the Constitution of 1791. Meanwhile, the Catholic faithful were resisting Grégoire's model of a religious Revolution, and their opposition was only hardening the anticlerical resolve of secular deputies. In this context, the abolition of the monarchy began to seem to Grégoire a panacea for France's problems. On the second day of the Convention, September 21, 1792, it was the bishop of Loir-et-Cher who proposed the abolition of the monarchy—a motion that was adopted unanimously. Repeating his dictum that the history of kings was the martyrology of the nations, he portrayed kings as bloodsuckers: "All the dynasties have been nothing but devouring races who lived only on the blood of peoples. . . . We must destroy this word *roi*." Though he had the previous year spoken with such force to the Jacobins about the right to freedom of opinion on the subject of the king, he did not look kindly on those who wished to exercise theirs in the king's defense. Intolerant of any opposition, Grégoire tried to put an end to debate: "Eh! what need do we have to discuss this when everyone is in agreement? Kings are in the moral order what monsters are in the physical order."[26]

Just how much hope Grégoire pinned on destroying the monarchy can be seen in a letter he sent the following day to the departmental administrators of Loir-et-Cher. The success of his motion was a dream come true, and he was filled with rapture. "On this September 21, we have annihilated the throne of this crowned monster. Since yesterday, I have been suffocated by joy to the point of being unable to eat or sleep. The royalty abolished in France is the first step toward the federation of peoples."[27]

The establishment of the Republic represented the fulfillment of Grégoire's long-held beliefs. Though it is impossible to be certain about the source of his hatred, he himself suggested that his position came from the Bible. Other influences came from seventeenth-century examples, such as the books by "Languet" and Boucher that Grégoire had read in his youth. Grégoire would cite the former on a list of republican forerunners who deserved to have French streets named after them, along with men like William Tell, Hampden, Pym, Milton, Locke, and Franklin.[28]

Even as Grégoire drew inspiration from the Bible, he also seems to have been influenced by Enlightenment critiques of monarchy, and especially by the republicanism of Thomas Paine, a deist. While still in Blois, Grégoire had given credit for the overthrow of the Old Regime to the Enlightenment: "*La philosophie* made feudalism wilt." On the very day he proposed the abolition of the monarchy, he welcomed Paine to Paris, and introduced him to the Convention; the next day, he was elated about being able to join the republican activist for dinner.[29]

Whatever the origins of Grégoire's political philosophy, the fire-tongued republican who sneered at his adversaries became a natural leader in the Convention. He was named immediately to some of the Convention's most important committees (Colonial, Diplomatic, and General Security); he would also serve as secretary and then as president of the entire body. Like-minded colleagues continued to praise him in their diaries.[30]

Grégoire used his new positions to call for annihilating monarchies throughout the world and federating their peoples. Even before arriving in Paris, he had prophesied that "Enlightenment is spreading like a torrent from the Bosphorus of Thrace to the strait of the Sund, and from the banks of the Tagus to those of the Neva. . . . Peoples, wake up! Return to your heritage. You only need to will it and the clay giants will return to nothingness." In the Convention, he predicted: "The volcano is going to explode and effect the political resurrection of the globe." Though he was less enthusiastic about the prospects for republicanism among "the Barbary pirates, the thieves of Arabia, and the cannibals of the South Sea," he hoped that republican ideas would spread "into the heart of Asia."[31]

Grégoire also became a specialist in advocating global revolution. Especially during the time he served as president of the Convention, he was often charged with responding to visiting republican delegations; he used their presence to urge other nations to imitate France. In addition to Paine, Grégoire allied himself with foreign republicans like the American poet and diplomat Joel Barlow. He even suggested that France should use force to help other nations achieve republicanism; in a report advocating the annexation of Savoy, Grégoire proclaimed that other countries must be delivered from monarchy so that they could choose their form of government.[32]

But how could cosmopolitan republicanism be reconciled with the needs of a country at war? What if a neighboring country opted against republicanism? If France's neighbors chose monarchy, Grégoire argued, France had a natural right to crush them. "Returned to liberty, the nations will never see us harm their sovereignty [or] disrupt the exercise of their rights. Free to organize themselves on their own, they will always find support and fraternity from us, *as long as they do not want to replace tyrants with tyrants.* If my neighbor feeds snakes, I have the right to suffocate them, by fear of becoming a victim [emphasis added]."[33] Despite Grégoire's professions of universalism, sovereignty of other nations could be allowed only if it coincided with France's military needs.

FRUSTRATION *EN MISSION*

Grégoire's dreams that abolishing the monarchy would lead France's neighbors to revolt against their tyrants did not materialize, and the war continued. Indeed, smashing the monarchy had not even brought all peoples within France to the side of the Revolution. Grégoire would learn this lesson even more sharply when he headed out of Paris in December 1792 as one of four deputies selected to go to the newly annexed region of Savoy—and then one of two sent to Nice and Monaco—to organize new departments there. Though speeches in the Convention had given the impression that the people of Savoy yearned to join their French neighbors in revolution, the actual situation was far different.

In a confidential letter from Chambéry to their colleague Danton in Paris, the deputies (called "représentants en mission") gave a true account of what they faced. From the moment they arrived in Savoy, they had encountered endless protests fomented by "privilegiés recalci-trants" (nobles unwilling to give up their privileges) and "fanatic and desperate priests." The provisional administration members were full of "egoism and intrigue"; the municipal administrators would not help the *représentants* unless they were paid; and even the local Jacobin Club was "full of suspicious men, spies, [and] aristocrats." On the whole, they complained, Chambéry was a greedy city, teeming with spies "from the mayor down to the beggars," where those hostile to the Revolution aimed to "discredit us, to neutralize us, to convoke popular assemblies against our work, to keep us in the dark about everything."[34] In Nice, as Henri Moris has noted, the situation was similar; the men who had voted for annexation had no popular mandate but had been installed by French military officials. Both new departments, Mont-Blanc (Savoy) and Alpes-Maritimes (the Nice/Monaco region), had a particularly high population of émigrés who had fled there before the regions were made part of France, and many inhabitants viewed the *représentants en mission* as occupiers. In Savoy, Grégoire would later charge, "a moral putridness emanates from the majority of cities." In Monaco, a congregation refused to allow Grégoire to say mass.[35]

How could Grégoire continue to portray the Revolution as one of, by, and for the people, when the population did not seem to want it? As he had in Blois, Grégoire blamed the Revolution's troubles on the people's character flaws, on émigré aristocrats and refractory priests, and on women's attempts to participate in politics. Grégoire found himself fighting the same battles he had waged in Blois in 1791. As in Loir-et-Cher, the bishop charged that the refractory clergy were obsessed with earthly goods and opposed the Revolution only because it had stripped them of riches. As for the aristocrats, he noted, the people should not be duped by them; though they had lost their titles, they remained danger-ous because "aristocracy is an incurable disease." Both groups, Grégoire declared repeatedly, tried to lead the public astray by misrepresenting the Revolution's religious policy.[36]

At first, Grégoire tried to make the will of local citizens seem like a perversion of true popular will based on misinformation. "Everywhere, *le peuple* is good," he declared in March 1793. In addition to being misled by aristocrats, however, they often allowed their judgment to be clouded by their passions; referring to them as diamonds in the rough who needed shaping from above, he suggested that they were turning to the wrong "stonecutter's chisel."[37]

As time went on, Grégoire moved beyond gentle admonitions; he used the law to repress popular behavior that conflicted with his own views. When local popular societies made motions objectionable to Grégoire and his colleague Jagot, he declared that the only "will of the people" was that expressed by the National Convention. As Grégoire told the defiant leaders of Menton, what they called popular demands represented nothing more than local, sectarian interests: "There is not a 'people' of Menton, nor of any other city in France. There are citizens of Menton, of Nice, of Paris, but there is only one 'people,' that of the entire Republic. . . . You tell us that the Council obeyed the people. . . . The people! We tell you yet again that there is only one people, consisting of the entire nation." Grégoire and Jagot nullified elections (and dissolved local legislatures) when they did not like the results and turned increasingly authoritarian in enforcing the "national" will on rebellious local administrators.[38]

The will of the people was also being distorted, Grégoire suggested, by the political activities of women—crowds of whom had torn up his and Jagot's proclamations and tried to chop down liberty trees, a symbol of the Revolution.[39] In the early years of the Revolution, as we have seen, Grégoire had attacked urban women and female *colons* but left open the possibility that rural women could be virtuous. In Blois, he had begun to fear women's religiosity and to see it as a civic danger. In this latest incarnation of his antifemale discourse, he portrayed women not only as religious fanatics but as stupid people best left to their housework. Unlike men, who could be trusted to sort out good and evil in forming the general will, women did not have sufficient intellectual tools; they could be too easily led astray.

On the one hand, these new attacks on women seem less severe than the ones Grégoire had made earlier in the Revolution. Nearly two hundred leagues from Paris and its "shameless" women, he conceded that women could have pious intentions, and he did not damn them as a class for their immorality. Women's biggest problem, he now suggested, was their gullibility. Women who were "timid and virtuous but without instruction" had been deliberately manipulated by the Revolution's enemies, who tried to convince them that "an insurrection against tyranny is an attack on religion."[40]

On the other hand, even while leaving women blameless for what cunning men made them do, Grégoire's words had a much more pernicious implication than in the past. If women were so gullible that they could not be trusted to make good decisions, then the total exclusion of women from political and religious debates was essential. Grégoire used examples from the Bible and the Jansenist-Jesuit quarrels to suggest that evildoers with silver tongues had long benefited from the misplaced eagerness of the weaker sex. For him, it was outrageous—even laughable—for women to imagine that they could think rationally. They were nothing but mothers who needed to attend to their homes: "When one sees mothers who, instead of enlightening their neighbor or taking care of their households, take it into their heads to make themselves into *théologiennes,* to reason—or rather to talk nonsense *[déraisonner]* about things they don't understand—to be honest, there is cause to laugh in pity."[41] The same Grégoire who had long argued against seeing entire classes of people as ignorant and incapable of governing their own affairs did not see himself as inconsistent when he dismissed all women. Rather than seeing gender prejudices as equally pernicious as religious or racial ones, he identified women with counterrevolution and hoped that their political exclusion might be the key to achieving harmony in the nation at last.

Grégoire therefore declared that the new regime must prevent women from exercising political influence in any way. Anticipating the Convention's decision in October 1793 to shut down women's political clubs, the bishop used women's influence as a sign of the shift between old and new; whereas the Old Regime had allowed porous gender boundaries, the new regime would not. In decrying the refractory clergy's opposition to episcopal elections, Grégoire noted that, under the monarchy, local nuns had sometimes helped to choose curés. "Which is the man who would dare to tell you," he taunted, "that these elections of women were worth more than those of an entire people?" He also complained that royal mistresses ("une Pompadour, une Dubarry") had succeeded in getting "schemers and court valets" named to important bishoprics. In Grégoire's eyes, the political power and scandalous behavior of female aristocrats typified the ills of the Old Regime. Women who were "gangrened with debauchery" had been permitted to control the destiny of the nation, and had been referred to as "women of quality"! Grégoire's anxiety on this point mirrored that of many colleagues; as Bell has pointed out, many revolutionaries worried that Old Regime Frenchness had been too closely associated with feminine characteristics. They thus imagined not only purging women from public life but also shedding all feminine traits. A regenerated France would be a masculinized one, with meddling women unable to distort the general will.[42]

"I WOULD HAVE ALLOWED MYSELF TO BE MASSACRED . . ."

While *en mission,* Grégoire worked passionately to spread the Revolution's message and defeat France's enemies. Fifteen years later, he recalled a time while visiting the French armies in Italy on an outing from Nice, when "I raced on a horse in my violet [bishop's] habit around the various battalions and harangued them all, under fire from Piedmontese cannons."[43] Humorous as this recollection may have appeared to an elder Grégoire retired from revolutionary life, the image aptly captures the way the curé of Emberménil had turned himself into a bishop-commander, urging his troops to fight to the death in service of the Revolution.

Soon, however, Grégoire's mission in the provinces was over, and it was time to rejoin the Convention. In his 1808 *Mémoires,* Grégoire reported that he felt himself an outsider as soon as he moved back to Paris; the Convention he found there in late May 1793 was completely different from the one he had joined eight months earlier. Portraying himself as a powerless outsider in these tumultuous days, he claimed to look back with regret, for example, at the exclusion of the Girondins. On May 31, he insisted, he had been forced to decline acting as president because of chest pains and laryngitis. If he had been able to serve, he noted wistfully, "perhaps I would have had Henriot [the leader of the popular forces pressing for the Girondins' removal] seized, or I would have allowed myself to be massacred rather than allow the Convention to be thus outraged."[44]

We would be misled about Grégoire's revolutionary activities, however, if we took his later account as an accurate depiction of these years; his discussion of this period is perhaps the least reliable part of his *Mémoires,* reflecting Napoleonic-era misgivings about his earlier actions and his desire to shape the way they would be viewed by posterity. Indeed, Grégoire was hardly the outsider he later claimed to have been, even when the emergence of factions and growing anticlerical sentiment made it more difficult to preserve his influence. To remain an important figure, the bishop made several choices that he later regretted or wished to conceal. It was not that he retained complete confidence in the Revolution's direction; doubts emerged for him as the idea of Christian republicanism looked increasingly tenuous and the Revolution did not turn out as he had hoped. It was also true that his idea of a Christian Revolution had never been universally accepted; the Assembly had declined his proposal to refer to God in the Declaration of Rights and refused in 1790 to declare Christianity the national religion. Grégoire's crisis of faith in the Revolution would become particularly acute in November 1793, when he nearly lost his life over his refusal to denounce Christianity. The bishop remained a leading member of the Convention, however, even when many other priests and moderates began to flee rather than make unpalatable choices.

Two incidents illustrate choices made in the heat of the Revolution that the abbé later wished to forget: the expulsion of the Girondins and his comments on the death of the king (particularly after he returned to Paris). Regarding the Girondin affair, Grégoire's *Mémoires* were accurate on two counts: he did not serve as president of the Convention during the day of June 1; and on June 2, he made statements similar to what he claimed he had wanted to say on June 1. Like many other deputies on that day, he denounced the popular armies surrounding the Convention for not having allowed the body to make its own decisions.[45]

Though Grégoire's *Mémoires* were true on these two factual issues, his description was nonetheless disingenuous; Grégoire's position in the Girondin affair was quite central. In making it seem as if he wanted to help but was unable, Grégoire omitted the likely reason for his "hoarseness" on June 1: he had served as president on May 31, during the revocation of the Girondin-dominated Commission of Twelve. On that day, President Grégoire vigorously congratulated a popular Parisian delegation that had condemned the commission as "enemies of the *patrie*"; he enthusiastically responded that "the moment approaches when the people *en masse* will crush our exterior and interior enemies!" Applauding the bravery of these Parisian patriots, Grégoire vowed that "in vain do aristocrats, royalists, and federalists try to divide us!"[46]

What happened on June 1 reveals another inconsistency in Grégoire's account. Despite his claim that chest pain and laryngitis kept him from serving as president on that day, he served in this capacity during an exceptional session that *evening*, conveniently convoked when no Girondins were present. Though he spoke little on that occasion, he graciously welcomed several Parisian delegations demanding the Girondins' removal. On June 2, Grégoire no longer presided but still managed to speak. On that day, he finally seemed to resist the pressure from Parisian radicals and suggested that the Convention should be free to make its own decisions. Still, without any protest from Grégoire, the Girondins were removed that day from the Convention and arrested. Though he insisted two days later that the *procès-verbal* show that the Convention had made its decision to remove the Girondins under armed pressure from the public, his words meant only that the Convention should have been able to consider the Girondins' fate itself. Grégoire's later claims about his helplessness in this affair were thus misleading. Though at least one recent scholar has tried to defend him on this front, Grégoire did in fact preside over the deliberations on purging longtime friends like Brissot and the Rolands. Indeed, Mme Roland denounced him for his cowardice before she was killed in November 1793.[47]

Grégoire's choice was not the only one to be made: other patriotic clerics spoke out publicly against the purge. Fauchet, who narrowly escaped being imprisoned at the time (only to be executed later with the other purged Girondins), left Grégoire off a list of courageous bishops who had protested the action. Royer and Saurine, despite being members of the Jacobin Club, went to prison and into hiding, respectively, for their protest of the Girondins' treatment.[48]

Another issue where Grégoire later sought to camouflage his past was his position on the king. In his *Mémoires* and throughout his later life, Grégoire decried the idea that he had been a regicide; in addition to saying that "I never voted for the death of anyone" (since he was *en mission* during the vote), he also contended that he had explicitly opposed the king's death. He customarily relied upon two arguments. First, even before the trial began, the bishop had called for imprisoning Louis instead of putting him to death, in spite of his hatred for this "monster." Grégoire had proclaimed in November 1792 that, as a man of the church, "I condemn the death penalty and hope that this remnant of barbarism will disappear from our laws. . . . If you abolish the death penalty, Louis Capet will share the benefits of the law and can be assimilated in everything to other criminals. You will thus condemn him to existence, so that the horror of his enormous crimes will constantly plague him."[49] A second argument Grégoire made concerned the collective letter that the *représentants en mission* to Mont-Blanc had sent to the Convention during the king's trial. He insisted that, whereas his colleagues had written that Louis should be subject to "condamnation à mort," he refused to sign it until they crossed out the words *à mort,* leaving only the ambiguous approval of "condemnation." After the Revolution, Grégoire was often called a regicide by monarchists, and he frequently repeated this defense.

The debate on whether Grégoire was in fact a regicide reignited in France in the mid 1990s. A young researcher, Jean-Daniel Piquet, found a letter printed in the newspaper *Le Créole patriote* that purported to have been written by Grégoire and his Mont-Blanc colleagues. In introducing the letter, the newspaper's editor wrote that he was publishing it to clarify the ambiguities of their collective letter. In this second letter, the *représentants* declared their clear preference for the death sentence:

> Your opinion [that of Jeanbon Saint-André, who forwarded the letter to the *Créole patriote*] in favor of the death of the monster is well known; you have made it with the courage and constancy of a true republican. Does not everyone agree with you? We have tried to imitate you, and we are writing our formal wishes on the deliberation of tomorrow to the Convention. *It is for the death of Louis without appeal to the people [Créole patriote*'s emphasis]. Please do us the service of ensuring that this letter will be read [by others].
>
> Hérault, Grégoire, Simond, Jagot
Chambéry, January 13, 1793

Because the purported original letter with cross-outs could no longer be located in the National Archives, where Grégoire claimed it was in the nineteenth century, Piquet concluded that Grégoire and his colleagues had always intended to be regicides. He suggested that the letter in the *Créole patriote* proved that Grégoire in fact supported the death penalty for Louis and only later concocted the story about the cross-out. Piquet also noted that it would not have been unusual for Grégoire to have changed his mind from November 1792 to January 1793; several deputies reversed their opposition to the death penalty after evidence mounted of the king's alignment with counterrevolutionaries.[50]

The eminent Catholic historian Bernard Plongeron, a longtime admirer of Grégoire, vigorously contested Piquet's claims. Noting that one article in a single newspaper hardly constituted definitive evidence, Plongeron denounced Piquet personally, charging even that French universities were failing to teach students how to read documents. Though differing with Plongeron on a number of issues related to Grégoire, Hermon-Belot joined Plongeron in opposing Piquet's argument. Given that the French government had just pantheonized Grégoire precisely because he was a nonregicidal revolutionary, passions ran high.[51]

Was Grégoire in fact a regicide, or was Piquet unfairly maligning his honor? It is conceivable that the bishop of Loir-et-Cher did cross out "à mort," and that the letter printed in the *Créole patriote* was either forged or had his name affixed without his approval. Evidence also suggests that the abbé was attacked in the Jacobin Club in 1793 for his failure to vote explicitly for death and that the Convention decided to count the signers of the ambiguous letter as "no" votes.[52] Even if Grégoire's later claims were true on these counts, however, he nevertheless left a series of damning statements applauding the regicide. In reporting on his mission after returning to Paris, he chided the Convention for its overly lengthy deliberation on the king's fate. The Convention had harmed the cause of the Revolution, the bishop contended, by not sending the king to the scaffold immediately: "Among the causes that have frozen or cooled patriotism in this region, one must include the conduct of the National Convention. Legislators, after having royalized Europe by the length of your discussions on the *fate of a tyrant whom you should have hastened to send to the scaffold*, you have encouraged the enemies of the Republic [emphasis added]." By the time Grégoire wrote his *Mémoires,* he had hardly forgotten this passage but was, on the contrary, quite embarrassed by it. Glossing over his mission report quickly, he noted only that it was so full of interesting touristic details that it should have been called *Voyage dans les Alpes maritimes*—and that "there is one sentence in the printed pamphlet that I disavow."[53]

Grégoire's *Essai historique et patriotique sur les arbres de liberté,* which later became a collector's classic, was filled with similarly violent denunciations of the monarchy. Here too, Grégoire later disavowed the incendiary statements, claiming that the printers had inserted them without his knowledge. The statements were not so very different, though, from things he had said previously. "All that is royal," he declared, "can figure only in the archives of crime. The destruction of a ferocious beast, the termination of a plague, the death of a king, [all these] are reasons for humanity to rejoice." The bishop of Loir-et-Cher shunned peace until the last enemy was dead: "We declare war on anyone who dares speak of peace before all our enemies have bitten the dust." He also argued that free people should not stop fighting "until they exterminate the last offspring of the bloodthirsty race of kings." Indeed, as early as 1792, Grégoire had made comments like, "We vow to annihilate all those who would want to annihilate liberty."[54]

Statements like these have led Norman Ravitch to suggest that Grégoire's anti–death penalty defense was merely retroactive and that

Grégoire "was a regicide in spirit, if not in fact." Even without making that claim categorically, it is safe to say that Grégoire tried to have it both ways. He opposed the death penalty in 1792 to assuage his religious conscience but was ambiguous about his feelings during the sentencing—and supportive of the execution afterward—to ensure that the king was punished and to retain political influence. The ambiguity of the supposed letter (he had, after all, not proposed writing the more explicit "condamné à vie"), in the context of his violently antimonarchical statements, allowed him to remain in good standing among the patriots of the Revolution, while not feeling he was violating his Christian beliefs. Grégoire's later assertions that he had never changed his views thus gloss over the strategic choices he made at particular moments.[55]

ENLIGHTENMENT, RELIGION, OR ENLIGHTENED RELIGION?

Another choice Grégoire made during the Convention years was muting the religious content of his speeches and writings and praising the philosophes in glowing terms. Without having paid attention to his early career, one might argue that he did so only in order to survive, or that invoking Voltaire and Rousseau was a sly attempt to gain support from secular colleagues. Grégoire's repeated references to various philosophes, however, were not insincere ploys invented during this period but continuations of his prerevolutionary interest in enlightened religion. Though Grégoire would later come to regret his enthusiasm for Enlightenment ideas as his perspective on the revolutionary experiment changed, he never claimed that his praise had been false at the time.

During these years, Rousseau remained a particular inspiration to Grégoire, as to many other cleric-legislators. While *en mission* in Savoy, Grégoire invoked the "immortal author of the *Social Contract,* the King who had the courage to tell Governments and men so many truths." Upon his return from Chambéry, the bishop of Loir-et-Cher cited Rousseau as a revolutionary precursor and exulted at having been in "the city where Rousseau contemplated ways to regenerate the body politic." He cited Rousseau in many other instances and declared that it was scandalous that the *Social Contract,* the bible of the state, had been attacked in some academies. Even after Thermidor, he would invoke "Jean-Jacques" as an inspiration for projects with which he was involved.[56]

When Grégoire commented on the Convention's educational projects, he also drew heavily from Rousseau. Inserting himself into

Enlightenment debates on human nature, Grégoire stated that he did not agree "with Diderot and some other writers, that nature creates malicious people [méchans]." Siding instead with Locke and Rousseau, Grégoire argued that man was perfectible; if he was bad, it was because of his society: "We cannot inculcate enough a truth that is proved by experience: man is in large part the product of his education, or as J. Jacques said, man is good, men are mean." Since, as Palmer has noted, a belief in perfectibility was something that separated hard-line Catholics from philosophes—and was certainly un-Jansenist—Grégoire's position was decidedly unconventional for a cleric. Grégoire himself admitted as much in the nineteenth century, when he retracted his belief that "man is good" and reaffirmed his belief in original sin.[57]

Sometimes, of course, Grégoire disagreed with the irreligious aspects of certain philosophes' arguments. In 1789, for example, he successfully blocked the National Assembly from sanctioning a new edition of Voltaire because, as he later wrote, "an honest man would blush to see this work in the hands of his wife and children." In 1791, during the discussions surrounding the Civil Constitution of the Clergy, the abbé attacked anti-Christian philosophes in no uncertain terms. As Ruth Graham has noted, Grégoire and the other revolutionary bishops drew freely on the ideas of Rousseau and other deists, even while rejecting the ideas of more anticlerical philosophes, such as Voltaire and Diderot.[58]

Grégoire did not agree even with Rousseau on every subject. Later in life, he—like other revolutionary bishops—would change his appraisal of the Genevan and emphasize the "scandalous" aspects of his writings. Grégoire would even start to use language that sometimes resembled that of the antiphilosophes chronicled by McMahon. Still, as Ravitch writes, "Grégoire clearly was a man of the Enlightenment, and if he often appeared one of its strongest critics, he much resembled Rousseau in being a critic from within the Enlightenment camp itself. Grégoire and Rousseau both did their utmost to disassociate themselves from currents of thought to which they owed a great deal."[59]

Despite his hesitations, however, Grégoire drew upon the ideas of a range of philosophes, including Voltaire and the materialists. His footnotes reveal that he had read several of Voltaire's works; he cited him as an authority on a number of issues, including the value of French over Latin. Moreover, during a discussion of reorganizing the scholarly academies, Grégoire borrowed the rhetoric of the Parisian sans-culottes, and argued that funding priority be given to the poor man of letters "in his basement room or on the sixth floor" rather than to powdered "intellectuals." To illustrate his point that the state-sanctioned academies had lost their way long before the Revolution, Grégoire cited a list of "great men" who had been excluded from eighteenth-century academies; they included not only the deists Rousseau and Mably, but also the materialists Helvétius and Diderot. As late as 1821, even as he tried to distance himself from Enlightenment thinking in the wake of the Revolution's failure, he still owned copies of works by Helvétius and Baron d'Holbach, as a previously unknown catalogue reveals.[60]

Grégoire's reports while on the Committee of Public Instruction also contained dechristianizing elements. A report he cowrote permitted communes to change their names if "their origin stemmed from religion, feudalism, or the royalty"; in a report he authored on street names, he lumped religious orders with aristocrats, saying that both had brought nothing but misery and did not merit having streets named after them.[61] In one report, he invoked not God but "the God of liberty"; in another, he invoked the "beneficent hand of providence." Both of these sounded more like a deist acclaiming the Supreme Being than a Christian believing in the Holy Trinity.[62] Though most of his nineteenth-century letters were signed with a cross († Grégoire évêque), Grégoire never used one during the Revolution, preferring instead the standard citoyen Grégoire.

REGENERATING HEARTS AND MINDS

Still, even while Grégoire worked to remain central in the Revolution and became still more notorious among its Christian opponents, his doubts about the Revolution were growing. In October 1793, the Convention turned its back on the Civil Constitution of the Clergy and began an official program of dechristianization, legitimizing popular efforts that had begun earlier in the provinces. Churches were closed, priests encouraged to marry, and a new calendar adopted to break the rhythms of the Christian year.[63] Meanwhile, several of Grégoire's fellow bishop-legislators were imprisoned or executed for not being sufficiently radical.

Even while largely muting his religious beliefs, Grégoire retained his strong faith and hoped the Revolution might right itself. He refused to obey a law banning clerical dress and soon became a striking sight in the Convention in his violet bishop's robe, the only deputy still wearing clerical garb. In October 1793, he wrote to another constitutional bishop about the urgency of continuing to build their ideal church: "Let us instruct, build, and continually make people realize by our words and deeds that Christianity is the friend of the Republic [and] the religion of liberty, equality and fraternity." Grégoire linked the continuing fight to democratize the Church to the Richerist struggles of the 1770s, and he blamed the "despotic" actions of many clerics, rather than the Convention, for having provoked the measures against the Church.[64]

On 17 brumaire an II (November 7, 1793), however, Grégoire realized just how much the Revolution had deviated from the path he had imagined it would take. After a turbulent session in which numerous priests renounced their oaths, Grégoire was brought in from a Committee of Public Instruction meeting and encouraged to do the same. His refusal to denounce Christianity was the first time he made—and was forced to make—an unequivocal stand in the conflicts between religion and *philosophie*. Years later, he remembered the chilling response he received: "Descending from the rostrum, I returned to my seat. Everyone moved away from me, as if I had the Plague. When I turned my head, I saw looks of fury directed at me. . . . Threats and insults rained down on me. . . . In saying [what I did], I believed that I was pronouncing my death sentence. For eighteen months, I was expected at the scaffold." Though some deputies respected Grégoire for his defiance, he faced great personal danger in the next few weeks: "For the next few days, my house was besieged by emissaries and bandits. . . . On 21 brumaire, a placard was posted on all the street corners in Paris, entitled: *A message for Bishop Grégoire*." Mme Dubois, whom Grégoire later called the "sole confidante of my troubles and sharer of my feelings" at the time, was frightened that he would soon be taken to the gallows. Grégoire endured a terrifying two weeks, until Robespierre attacked the dechristianizing faction and called atheism aristocratic.[65]

Even in the face of this scary episode, Grégoire maintained his commitment to the Revolution and to the goals of regeneration; he did not wish to join the ranks of former supporters of the Revolution who were now renouncing it. He decided, however, that his earlier efforts had been insufficient. Neither the storming of the Bastille nor the new constitution had changed human nature overnight, and the Jews had retained their religion. In four years, the French masses had not rallied in support of Revolutionary Christianity, and the killing of the king had only engendered further hostility toward the revolutionaries. Indeed, full-blown war had broken out in France's Vendée region in spring 1793, with peasants joining nobles and refractory priests against the forces of the Revolution.

Though Grégoire himself had helped pioneer the polarizing and violent language that accompanied calls for regeneration, he now began to seek an alternative to it. For regeneration to work, Grégoire decided, the revolutionaries would need to change the *mentalités* of future generations by methods so subtle they might not even realize what was happening. To create a comprehensive cultural policy in the midst of what later became known as the Terror, Grégoire threw his energies into the Committee of Public Instruction and into what Hermon-Belot has called a politics of voluntarism, a gentle alternative to Jacobin repression.[66] It may not be completely true that, as Grégoire remembered in his *Mémoires,* "When the Convention was delivered to *brigandage* . . . , the Committee of Public Instruction seemed to me to be the only one where a semblance of good sense took refuge." Nevertheless, it was in the CPI that Grégoire focused his energies during this period. He was feverishly busy, attending Convention meetings all day and CPI meetings every other night, and drafting "the majority of the important reports" into the morning. At one point, Grégoire told an acquaintance, he had barely slept in two weeks.[67]

While on the CPI, Grégoire aimed to create a new kind of French person, through formal and informal education; as he would write in 1794, building on Rousseau's ideas, "The two most useful and most neglected sciences are the cultivation of man and that of the earth." Revolutionary schooling would be a key component of creating a new mentality among the populace. In contrast to older generations (whose ideas might still be altered, but who retained the corrupting germs of the Old Regime), the youngest generation had been born free and was completely open to influence. Grégoire worked particularly on creating universal education for the poor, questioning how society could write off an entire class of men. He also focused on early childhood education, noting that if a young child was badly educated, it was like "throwing a ferocious animal" into society. In addition to basic moral and civic education, Grégoire worked to advance education in agricultural technology, a project that took on new urgency with the shortages of the war.[68]

Grégoire also took charge of the reorganization of knowledge in the CPI. Continuing another of his prerevolutionary interests, he promoted the spread and increased organization of libraries. "Carefully formed libraries and books," he declared, "are in some sense the workshops of the human spirit." Without books, scholars wasted time reinventing the wheel. He also worked to save the academy system, while ensuring that intellectuals would use their abilities to serve the Republic. Though many literary academies were exclusionary, petty, and "gangrened with an incurable aristocracy," and were therefore better suppressed and replaced by freely formed equivalents, Grégoire argued that the scientific academies should be preserved. They had adjusted to the new order and were producing socially useful knowledge.[69]

Knowledge could not be spread, however, if men did not speak the same language. Grégoire thus renewed his earlier efforts to wipe out patois. In his famous 1794 report on "annihilating patois," Grégoire depicted a tight link between language and citizenship. "Reading, writing, and speaking the national language are the indispensable skills that every citizen must know," he declared. "The unity of the Republic requires the unity of idiom." Grégoire was troubled that "at least six million French people, particularly in the countryside, do not know the national language." Language retained the divisiveness of the Old Regime: "With these thirty different patois, we are still, as far as language goes, at the Tower of Babel, even though, as far as liberty goes, we form the avant-garde of nations." For Grégoire, unity of language was essential as France tried to create a unified national identity: "Our language and our hearts must be in unison."[70]

Ignorance of French, Grégoire warned, would breed counterrevolution. In the departments, he charged, opponents of the Revolution "base the success of their counterrevolutionary machinations on the ignorance of our language." For people to obey the laws, it was necessary that they—and their local leaders—understand them. Linguistic diversity was especially dangerous on the frontiers, where citizens shared a common tongue with their foreign neighbors and could thus "establish dangerous relations with our enemies." "Language," he declared, "must be one, like the Republic."[71] Even as he saw French as necessary to help create a unified national identity within the borders of France, he also viewed it as the world's best language; he hoped it would eventually be adopted elsewhere as the language of liberty, fulfilling Leibnitz's hopes for a universal language.[72]

In addition to his efforts on language, Grégoire was concerned with imprinting the Revolution onto physical geography, hoping this would bring revolutionary education into people's daily lives. He advocated that monuments have simple inscriptions in French (rather than Latin) to inspire patriotism in understandable language. How thrilling for the average citizen, he noted, to arrive at the Bastille and see a simple plaque: "Ici on danse!" He spoke not only of creating new monuments but also of destroying outdated ones; though he would later make a specialty of denouncing vandalism, he advocated the destruction of royal monuments as a cathartic experience. He gleefully recounted an anecdote from his days in Blois, when local revolutionaries had vented their feelings toward a statue of Louis XII: "Even before the destruction of the royalty, the republicans of this city had done justice to his statue. They smashed it and threw it in the Loire, to the repeated cries of 'The king drinks! *[Le roi boit].*' " All ancient monuments (a term he did not define, but by which he seemed to mean artifacts from the classical past), he allowed, should be spared. But "as for modern monuments, the National Convention wisely ordered the destruction of anything that carries the imprint of royalism or feudalism." He argued that only modern monuments without royal or feudal inscriptions be conserved.[73]

Grégoire also pointed to other ways of creating an everyday landscape of patriotism. Building on efforts begun by others earlier in the Revolution, Grégoire authored the CPI report on changing French street and place names to honor classical and modern republicans along with republican virtues. He also advocated the widespread use of liberty trees and envisioned a patriotic emotional catharsis occurring around them: "There the citizens will feel their hearts palpitate in talking of love of the *patrie,* of the sovereignty of the people, of republican indivisibility."[74]

Though Grégoire envisioned his cultural policy as one that would please people, he also intended it to be directed by elites instead of by the people themselves. Even as Grégoire proclaimed that "the people are everything, and everything must be done for them," he argued that the people needed the "paternal solicitude of the government" to direct them and prevent local cultural initiatives from causing disorder. Indeed, as John Markoff has shown, Grégoire tried to change the meaning of liberty trees, effacing their plebeian origins and assigning them another history, as the "gift of a paternal priest." This had the effect, Markoff argues, of removing the populist message of the trees and reinterpreting them as symbols of support for the central authorities.[75]

While Grégoire's emphasis during this period was on cultural regeneration, he continued to believe in the need for a physical regeneration of the French. He argued along with other revolutionaries, following Rousseau, that breastfeeding by mothers (something unfashionable in the eighteenth century) needed to replace that done by wet nurses, or republican citizens would not be healthy. Indeed, several images produced at the time depicted a fountain of regeneration, in which milk spouting from a female statue's breasts would spark the nation's regeneration! (fig. 6). How mothers treated children before the age of seven largely determined their future conduct, Grégoire alleged, and a failure to breastfeed would have nefarious consequences. Grégoire also

FIGURE 6. "Fountain of Regeneration" at the 1793 Festival of Unity and Regeneration. Water from the statue's breasts, representing mother's milk, will regenerate the nation. Courtesy of the Bibliothèque nationale de France.

complained that immorality had led to a weakening of the French body, and he again singled out mothers as its cause. If the Revolution succeeded, however, it could reverse this physical degeneration, wipe out disease, and return humans "to a natural state" in which the species would be "reconstituted."[76]

During his turbulent half-decade in politics, Grégoire had fought for a Catholic Revolution, and then watched it disintegrate. He had called for the annihilation of those he considered enemies of the people and emphasized the enlightened parts of enlightened religion; at other times, he had worked to create a cultural policy that could effect societal regeneration gently. Nevertheless, the future of enlightened religion looked very different in 1794 than it had in 1778 or even 1789. During 1793 and 1794, anti-Christian revolutionaries created what Michel Vovelle has called a "regenerative liturgy," which worked to destroy the "corrupt" Church in the name of "Jesus the sans-culotte." The desire to regenerate everything, while demolishing anything that hinted of the Old Regime, had produced overzealous fanatics—while alienating portions of the populace who might have supported a less ambitious revolution. This is not to say that a revolution of any kind did not have ready enemies from the outset.[77] The mandate of regeneration and the force

of language like Grégoire's had polarized the French into camps of royalist Catholics and dechristianizing revolutionaries, however; after
promising unity, it had spurred the onset of purges.

The choices of 1789 had thus helped create the very situation in which
Grégoire found himself in the midst of the Terror—where the Revolution
no longer had a Christian complexion, and it faced hostility from a sizable portion of the faithful. The selection of regeneration as a central slogan of the French Revolution may have held utopian promise for Grégoire
and others at the Revolution's start. It also contained, however, the seeds
of unforeseen division.[78] When humans failed to change their nature
overnight and the "illusion of politics" began to shatter, revolutionaries
like Grégoire felt forced to narrow the circle of true patriots. Looking for
scapegoats, they used increasingly violent language to denounce those
who wavered even slightly in their support for the Revolution. By the time
Grégoire began to speak the more peaceful language of the Committee of
Public Instruction, battle lines had hardened. Grégoire thus provides a
vivid example of the connection between the utopian hopes of 1789 and
the repressive violence of 1793–94, even if the deputies in the Revolution's
early years neither imagined nor desired this violence.[79]

On 9 Thermidor (July 27, 1794), there was yet another choice to
make. When *conventionnels* who opposed Robespierre arrested him and
the Convention deliberated his fate, all deputies faced a decision: vote
to defend him and the Jacobin principles he stood for, or condemn him
and thus disassociate oneself from the Terror. Grégoire chose to abstain;
the next day his erstwhile ally was executed.[80] Even as republican Christianity appeared permanently endangered, however, Grégoire still held
out hope for its survival. His next task was to save republicanism itself.

CHAPTER 6

Overcoming the Terror, Rebuilding the Empire

In what century were men of talent persecuted more
atrociously than under the tyranny of Robespierre?
—Grégoire, September 1794

I do not think that the history of Christianity contains as
blatant a persecution as that which we have just suffered.
We saw sacrileges and cruelties heretofore unknown to
the human race. Thousands of pastors who were equally
attached to religion and the Republic perished in dungeons,
on the seas, and upon the scaffold. . . .
—Grégoire, May 1796

Sensible men will never confuse the Revolution with the
crimes and disasters that accompanied it.
—Grégoire, August 1801

Though he had been an active member of the Convention throughout
the Terror and a longtime ally of Robespierre, Grégoire became a vocal
critic of both after Robespierre's execution. He did not view the Revolution as a mistake; he remained firmly attached to republicanism and
still sought global change. Grégoire's doubts about the Revolution's
course were evident even before the Terror ended, however; in radical
dechristianization (and in what he would call "vandalism"), he saw the
consequences of unbridled discourses of innovation and regeneration. In
the rush to regenerate, he felt, men had targeted the good as well as the
bad. Like the other moderates who came to be known as Thermidorians, Grégoire felt that the Revolution, despite its excesses, could still be
saved.[1] Nevertheless, he felt it was time for dramatic change in how the
Revolution was conducted.

One of the things Grégoire most wanted to reverse was how his fellow revolutionaries had come to view the past. As we have seen, the
bishop of Loir-et-Cher had long had a reverence for history; before the
Estates-General changed his destiny, he had dreamed of becoming a

137

famous historian, using past events to illuminate contemporary issues. Later, during the Revolution, he employed his historical knowledge in service of his politics; he also used history as a source of cautionary lessons and to provide paternity for the Republic. In this respect, Grégoire's historical consciousness was not altogether different from other deputies; indeed, according to Joseph Zizek, many revolutionaries looked to history for cautionary lessons and to lend legitimacy to their arguments. Also like them, though he saw history as useful, he did not see its lessons as binding, since he felt that France had transcended the experience of nations past.[2]

Nevertheless, Grégoire differed with secular colleagues in a key way. For them, the past was more or less expendable; they might opt to look to it for examples or warnings, but it did not restrict their choices. For Bishop Grégoire, however, as much as history could prove instructive, it could never be *only* that; aspects of the Christian past retained an absolute authority for him. Though he could advocate breaking with political precedents, he viewed Jesus' teaching and church law as immutable constraints on the present. As much as he spoke of regeneration, therefore, he would never want to start completely afresh.

Another way Grégoire differed from his legislative colleagues concerned his longtime love for books. He drew upon a clerical veneration of texts as well as an Enlightenment tradition that regarded the past as a record of progress, something to be preserved and examined to ensure future advancement. Employing Orientalist tropes, Grégoire contended in 1794 that destroying historical records made the civilized French appear to be "worse barbarians than those Muslims who walk with disdain over the ruins of a majestic antiquity."[3]

Grégoire consequently recoiled when fellow revolutionaries began to destroy historic artifacts simply because they bore marks of the Old Regime. Though he had once called for selective destruction of artifacts, Grégoire could not accept radical forms of what he came to call "vandalism." After overzealous republicanism led to widespread destruction of statues, buildings, paintings, and books, Grégoire led a national campaign to preserve France's cultural patrimony—a crusade that garnered him as much national acclaim as any of his earlier activities and that did much to stem the tide of destruction. Though the Committee of Public Instruction initially opposed his efforts (which began even before the death of Robespierre), Grégoire's three reports on it became a veritable phenomenon, reprinted, distributed and applauded across the country.[4] Newspapers praised him, other Thermidorians took his words to heart, and letters poured in to him from around the nation. Fanny de Beauharnais dedicated a poem to him, while others commented that, had his first report been published even sooner, "it would have prevented a torrent of irreparable destructions."[5]

Since regeneration had come to mean a complete repudiation of the past to many revolutionaries, Grégoire found himself struggling to portray the national agenda differently: as a cleansing of corrupted traditions, a connecting of the best of the past with that of the present. Even when he, like many others, blamed the excesses of the Terror on Robespierre, he also reexamined his own principles to understand where the Revolution had gone wrong. Grégoire's new vision of regeneration was not a radical reconceptualization; after all, the root of the word was *regeneration,* creating something again. Nevertheless, vandalism revealed to Bishop Grégoire that many partisans of the Revolution had imagined regeneration differently.

Even as he lessened his parliamentary involvement during the Thermidorian Convention and the Directory (the regime that succeeded the Convention), Grégoire remained enormously busy—and influential—in other spheres. In his efforts to root innovation in a usable past and thus avoid the mistakes of the Terror (a term that was adopted retrospectively, even by those who had been its leaders),[6] he looked particularly in three directions: creating a science of society, reestablishing a republican Church, and reorienting—while preserving—the French colonial system. Even though some of his ideas were not universally shared, he remained an extremely popular figure, a man for the times. His efforts would help refound republicanism, while ensuring the future of French imperialism.

ENSURING MORALITY AND LIBERTY: EDUCATION AND
THE SOCIAL SCIENCES

As Grégoire and other contemporaries endeavored to stabilize the Revolution, one of their main goals was the creation of a science of society and of politics. The people had won democracy, the Thermidorians argued, but had squandered it by permitting a reign of despotism. Only an advanced social science could prevent them from repeating this mistake.

In trying to invent such a science, the Thermidorians were hardly doing something new. The holy grail of a science of society had been pursued well before the Revolution, most notably by Condorcet, who had hoped that this science could attain the same degree of certainty as physics or mathematics. A firm believer in human perfectibility, Condorcet had sought to discover the basic principles of the moral and political sciences, so that they could be taught to all citizens. If people were ignorant, democracy would be a dangerous business; the people would not know their true interests and would be "always subject to the corrupt will of some hypocritical tyrant." "The more men are enlightened," Condorcet believed, "the less those with authority will be able to abuse it."[7]

Though Condorcet died before realizing his goals, the Thermidorians took up his search with a vengeance. Social science promised a path toward a tension-free, scientific social consensus; Condorcet's *Esquisse d'un tableau historique* was, in Baker's words, "adopted as the philosophical manifesto of post-Thermidorian reconstruction." On the ruins of the prerevolutionary academies, the Thermidorians built an Institut national; one of its three sections was the Class of Moral and Political Sciences. Grégoire was one of those elected to this class, and he would be extremely active in it.[8]

With his interest in the social sciences, Grégoire built upon his longtime veneration of scientific knowledge more generally. While on the CPI, he had tried to preserve the academies, even as he rejected the snobbishness of some of them. During the Thermidorian Convention, he continued to reject the anti-intellectualism of many colleagues. Scholars, he argued in 1794, were the ones who had enabled France to become a republic: "Scholars and men of letters struck the first blows against despotism. . . . If the career of liberty is open before us, they were the pioneers." He campaigned for government funding of scholarly research of all kinds, no matter how dire the state's finances; today's research in chemistry or physics could yield untold benefits tomorrow. "Did the first person who studied gases," he asked, "ever think that one day they would elevate balloons, and that these balloons would be used to batter our enemies?" He deplored the lot of most men of genius, whose lives were often filled with poverty even though they received posthumous acclaim.[9]

Grégoire saw particular value in the political and moral sciences. Unlike others in the Class, Grégoire was not a great theoretician; he did not let himself be drawn into the turbulent debates over the best methodological approach. He drew instead on all of the available models of Enlightenment social science, from Montesquieu to Condillac to Condorcet and the physiocrats. He was also intrigued by the promise of statistics for understanding political economy.[10]

Even without a unique vision of the social sciences, Grégoire still had great hopes for what they could achieve. When he was tapped to give a public address on the opening day of the Institut in April 1796, Grégoire offered a passionate defense of republican values and of scholars' rights to pursue truth without being censored. He argued that political science should not focus only on inventing perfect laws, because the turbulent revolutionary experience had revealed that legislation alone could not guarantee a good society. Even the Thermidorians' best version of a constitution, he believed, had major flaws.[11]

In place of legislation, Grégoire (like other Thermidorians) seized on education as a panacea against despotism. Humanity could still be regenerated; humans could be cultivated, Grégoire declared, like an "extremely vast field open to the efforts of genius." Once people had been educated, freedom would be more durable, since the masses would not act irrationally. Grégoire also argued for the necessity of practical, civic, and moral education, though he laid out only the rudiments of a curriculum. First, he asserted, people needed to learn the basic skills that would enable them to be happy in their everyday lives. To this end, he worked toward founding the national Conservatoire des arts et métiers, which aimed to place the trades at the top of the national education system, at a level previously reserved for more abstract pursuits. He also worked to spread agricultural technology through the Société d'agriculture du département de la Seine. Second, Grégoire argued that citizens needed to learn the two most fundamental principles of political science: separation of powers and representative government. Finally, Grégoire stressed moral education, arguing that moral citizens were a better guarantee of a good society than even the wisest laws.[12]

At the height of the Convention, revolutionaries had also dreamed of education as a path toward regeneration. Now, a more practical Grégoire made clear that advances in education and social science could happen only if advances in physical sciences continued. Impoverished republics were doomed to suffer fighting between haves and have-nots, as the Terror years had shown; the stability of the Republic therefore rested upon material progress. Unlike clerics who opposed scientific experimentation and saw it as threatening religion, Grégoire praised physical and applied scientists. He felt that their work enabled people to live healthier, more peaceful lives through their discoveries, and he urged scholars in all disciplines to work together.[13]

To achieve new heights in scholarship and education, Grégoire also suggested that past advances needed to be better known. The institutions of the republic of letters had been destroyed during the Terror; everything from scholarly journals to international correspondence among researchers needed to be revived. "The periodicals that served as depositories of new inventions and that recounted the march of the human spirit are nearly all gone," he lamented. Grégoire also became an energetic advocate of public libraries in the Thermidorian Convention, pushing for their growth and rational organization, and for the creation of new reference works. "Carefully formed libraries and books," he declared, "are in some sense the workshops of the human spirit." Without books, scholars wasted time reinventing the wheel: "How many men, lacking books, have wasted precious time trying to find a solution to problems that have already been resolved."[14]

Finally, building on efforts he had begun with the SPS and the CPI, Grégoire advocated using visual symbols to deepen republican sentiment among the populace. During the Thermidorian Convention, he successfully proposed an elaborate system of colored uniforms for public officials, which would instill respect for leaders among the populace and reinforce a sense of dignity for their wearers: "We are all susceptible to receiving, by this means, profound impressions. Those who claim that a people can be governed by philosophical theories [alone] are hardly philosophers." Later, while serving on the Council of Five Hundred (the lower house in the Convention's successor legislature), Grégoire convinced his colleagues that the Republic, like the monarchy, needed an official seal. Visual images, he argued, could strike people's imaginations more than words alone: "A legislator who ignored the importance of symbolic language would be unworthy of his post; he cannot pass up a single opportunity to grab someone by his senses, in order to awaken republican ideas. Images constantly reproduced before people's eyes will soon penetrate their souls."[15]

With proper education and the extension of knowledge, the Republic might survive. Still, Grégoire was not naive about what lay ahead, and he warned against complacency. Invoking the cautionary lessons of the past, he told the public gathered at his 1796 speech that the historical record was full of "miserable people in chains," and that the distance between what people were and what people could be was enormous. Millions of men throughout the world languished in ignorance and misery, ruled by tyrants determined to keep them that way. Meanwhile, tremendous battles lay ahead for the Republic, as those who would defend knowledge and liberty would fight to the death against those who despised it. Ending on an optimistic note, however, he suggested that France might win the battle if it proceeded carefully: "The republic of letters will give birth to republics. A new century is about to begin . . .

[and] emancipated and regenerated nations . . . will make a solemn entry into the universe."[16]

Despite Grégoire's great hopes for social science, however, the Class proved unable to agree on how to construct such a science. As Martin Staum has shown, the Class splintered into three camps: Ideologues searching for a secular moral science, deists who wanted new civic rituals, and conservative Catholics who had opposed the Revolution and rejected the very idea of social science.[17] Though he had often socialized with the Ideologues, Grégoire—a committed republican *and* Christian— found himself without a natural camp. Alienated from the Christian opponents of the Revolution, he also saw a secular moral science as anathema and had begun to blame the excesses of the Revolution on its abandonment of the church.[18] How could society be stabilized, Grégoire wondered, if it was missing the institution most essential to the future of France: the Catholic Church? "Has not the experience of every century proven that political theories and human laws are insufficient for the maintenance of social order? . . . Only Religion encompasses all virtues in order to command them, all vices in order to forbid them. . . . Religion, as someone has said, is the cement of society. Necessary in all political states, it is even more necessary in a republican regime, in which the criminal code, wisely made less harsh, can find its indispensable supplement only in religion." The Republic had nearly destroyed the one institution it most needed and was now trying to replace it with the civic cult of Theophilanthropy.[19]

Grégoire was determined to rescue the one true religion. Within the Class, he tried to do so by promoting the ideas of Kant, which he hoped might persuade his secular colleagues to anchor the Republic in Christianity. Grégoire was one of the first points of entry in France for Kantian ideas; his old friends in Strasbourg introduced him to the German philosopher's work as early as 1794, and Grégoire reportedly joined with Sieyès to propose Kant for election to the Class in 1796.[20] As we will see in chapter 9, however, Grégoire would become disaffected with Kantism when he decided that it actually undermined the foundations of Christianity. Reviving Christianity within the context of the Class, Grégoire determined, would be impossible.

Grégoire also tried to revive the Church through his legislative activities. In the face of official sanction for the cult of Theophilanthropy, Grégoire gave a December 1794 speech advocating freedom of religion (particularly for Catholics). This discourse, which he delivered in his bishop's garb, had a striking impact on his colleagues at a time when the

Church had been virtually destroyed. After he spoke, churches were allowed to reopen, and Grégoire and several other bishops reclaimed the keys to Notre-Dame. According to Alphonse Aulard, Grégoire's speech sparked a revival of Catholicism across the country.[21]

Just as Grégoire could not revive the Church in the Institut, however, neither could he do so through parliamentary means. In the next few years, Grégoire became increasingly inactive as a legislator. Aside from his report on seals, Grégoire gave only one other major discourse in the Council of Five Hundred. This speech concerned a religious issue: a proposal to hold official festivals on the *décadi* (the tenth day of the week in the revolutionary calendar) so as to replace public loyalty to Sunday worship. His speech against this plan drew opposition even from sympathetic deputies, who deemed it inappropriate for Grégoire to be speaking as a priest instead of as a legislator. Some also depicted him as intolerant; despite his defense of oppressed groups, one pamphlet writer noted, it was clear that he considered non-Catholics to be in error and longed to convert them. Grégoire began to realize at this time that the attitudes of Directory leaders toward Catholicism ranged from hostile to indifferent.[22]

THE CEMENT OF SOCIETY: REBUILDING THE GALLICAN CHURCH

Grégoire now believed himself in a battle to save Christianity—the thing more important to him, as we saw in brumaire an II, than life itself. If he had learned anything from the Terror, it was that he could not count on secular colleagues to respect religion. If the church was to reclaim its place of glory in France, Grégoire could no longer sublimate his Christianity to other goals, nor suffer silently when others called for a dechristianizing regeneration. He was convinced that the new French polity needed to be based on a moderate republican Christianity. Without it, France would not be regenerated, but would sink back into anarchy.

Working outside the legislature, Grégoire became the national leader of a group of constitutional bishops who called themselves the United Bishops *(évêques réunis)*; they included Jean-Baptiste Royer, Jean-Pierre Saurine, Guillaume Mauviel, Antoine-Hubert Wandelaincourt, and Eléonore-Marie Desbois de Rochefort. As a spokesman for the group, Grégoire corresponded with patriotic priests in every corner of France, wrote pamphlets outlining what the church should look like, and helped coordinate the national episcopal councils of 1797 and 1801. Their efforts would be crucial in reviving religion in France after the Terror, predating the 1802 publication of François-Réné de Chateaubriand's famous *Genius of Christianity.*

Grégoire's efforts to revive Christianity in this period have been the subject of a number of specialized works, and it is unnecessary to recount all the details of these efforts.[23] At the same time, we cannot understand Grégoire's efforts to remake society without looking at the basic principles of the reorganized church. The United Bishops wanted not to readopt the philosophy of the prerevolutionary Church but rather to realize the Richerist ideals they had longed for as young curés. In calling themselves the Gallican Church, they placed themselves in the French church's conciliar and independent strain, rejecting the notion that Rome had absolute authority over all church decisions.[24]

What were the principles of this Gallican Church? The United Bishops did not want to create a schism, and they still saw the pope as the church's head. At the same time, they did not see him as infallible, and they decried Rome for trampling on the historic rights of the national churches. They therefore advocated religious government by council rather than by the pope and the "court of Rome." Though the councils would assemble only the church elite, they would nevertheless be representative, since the bishops would continue to be elected by the people. The bishops further declared that they had no intention of becoming a wealthy, powerful body competing with the state. Unlike Rome or the Old Regime church, the Gallican Church would focus instead on its spiritual mission.[25]

In keeping with Grégoire's hope of preserving the best aspects of the past, the United Bishops idealized the early church, a belief that had been fundamental to Richerism. As Grégoire said in 1795: "May religion be reborn among us . . . as pure as it left the hands of Jesus Christ, as it was in its first centuries. Those were its days of glory." Returning to the early church meant stripping away layers of corruption and reuniting with other national churches in fraternal unity.[26]

Another element that Grégoire wanted to preserve was church hierarchy and discipline. Though the church would be purified and cleansed, that did not mean it would be less institutional or strict. Grégoire and the other bishops hardly wanted the deinstitutionalized Christianity desired by some other admirers of the early church, like Joseph Priestley across the English Channel. On the contrary, Grégoire sought to root the church firmly in the authority of ancient discipline and hierarchy.

People could not choose when it was convenient to be Catholic; they needed to accept all rules. "One can't be half Christian," he declared. "You cannot have half of your soul saved."[27]

Grégoire saw the breakdown in clerical discipline—particularly the marriage of priests during the Terror—as a special problem. Married priests had accommodated too much to the Revolution; not even those who now denounced their marriages as unconsummated ruses, contracted for self-protection, could be forgiven. In 1795, Grégoire and three other constitutional bishops denounced married priests as "unworthy of their status and of the confidence of the faithful in matters of religion."[28] As Grégoire would later admit, the practice violated no divine law; any infraction was only against church regulations. Grégoire tenaciously opposed these marriages, however, because they violated the "general discipline" of the church. Even when he received a torrent of letters from formerly married priests begging to resume their lives as clerics, Grégoire insisted that church rules prevented being indulgent toward them. Lines needed to be drawn somewhere. If he and his friends had managed to survive the Terror without getting married, others could have done so too.[29]

The stridency of Grégoire's opposition to married priests' efforts to rejoin the church surprised those who wondered why he clung so much to rules of recent vintage. Given his denunciations of anti-Christian persecution during the Terror, could he not show more sympathy toward these unfortunate men? Sanadon, the bishop of Bas-Pyrénées, appealed to Grégoire to be more tolerant of married priests: "I am far from approving the marriage of ecclesiastics. But since the law that requires them to live in celibacy is nothing but discipline—and dating from modern times—does the violation of this law really rend them irremissibly [']unworthy of their status and of the confidence of the faithful in matters of religion[']?" Similarly, Grégoire's SPS friend Blessig wondered why he needed to make this such an important issue. All of their friends in Strasbourg were puzzled:

> Your severity toward the married priests and your indulgence for certain rituals that you yourself seemed to want to reform, like using Latin in liturgy, did not really astonish me. . . . Still, I was distressed to see that the good you want to do cannot be carried out for the marriage of priests. . . . You undoubtedly want to wipe out this scandal. . . . But I must ask you, was it absolutely necessary to express yourself on this issue in such universal terms? It was this austerity that astonished many of your friends, even when they support the same cause [the reconstruction of Christianity in France].

Grégoire was attacked on this issue equally by partisans of dechristian-ization and of the Old Regime church. One anti-Christian newspaper urged him to find himself a wife, while a supporter of the old church told him that he was being hypocritical, since it was his own principles that had landed the church in its current mess. "Why don't you end your career with a good marriage?" this anonymous author taunted Grégoire. Referring to Mme Dubois, he jeered, "We all know a *citoyenne* who will divorce her ancient constitution of a husband and throw herself in your arms as soon as you give the word."[30]

Why was Grégoire so inflexible on this issue? It was hardly that he opposed all forms of church reform; on the contrary, he and the other bishops still hoped to make significant changes. "Certain parts of disci-pline, unhappy remnants of the barbarism of the middle ages and of the subversion of principles introduced by false *Décrétales*, still carry the imprint of ignorance," they declared. Grégoire tried to cast the church's near-destruction as a blessing in disguise, an opportunity for rebuilding a regenerated church from scratch: "The persecution directed against the Gallican Church was undoubtedly part of God's plans, a salutary cri-sis for regenerating it. The tranquility that the church seemed to enjoy before the Revolution was less a state of peace than a state of stagna-tion."[31] In their national councils, the bishops debated many reforms, like changing the liturgical language from Latin to French.

As much as Grégoire and the other bishops wanted reform, however, they wanted to control it and direct it from above; otherwise, the church would break down in chaos. Earlier in the Revolution, Grégoire had venerated democracy in the church; after all, he owed his bishopric to the "voice of the people." Now, however, he opposed local initiatives. In many of the widowed parishes and dioceses (those whose leaders had fled or left the priesthood), the lay faithful had begun to recreate the faith themselves. Grassroots reform, the bishops contended, would destroy the church: "If each bishop and each diocese—particularly the 'widowed' dioceses—permitted themselves to make innovations in church discipline, . . . soon anarchy would be the disastrous result." As Grégoire and the other United Bishops made clear, change needed to come from above, not below.[32]

Another important reason for their inflexibility came from the circum-stances of the post-Terror world. In the Revolution's early years, the men who became the constitutional bishops had called for an enlightened restructuring of the church and blasted Catholics who opposed them as misguided and ill-intentioned. In the wake of Thermidor, however, conservative Catholics had reemerged, calling themselves prescient for having predicted that Enlightenment morality could lead only to violence. Whereas, in the past, Grégoire and his colleagues might have combated their enemies' interpretation of the Enlightenment, dechristianization had led them to share a good deal of it. With Grégoire referring to himself in 1795 as "the enemy of this so-called philosophy that would like to rip all religious principles . . . from the heart of man," they sought to distance themselves from their earlier radicalism and from deists they had previously praised.[33] Whereas republican religion remained as important to them as ever, the idea of enlightened religion now grew suspect. No matter how much Grégoire now criticized the "so-called philosophes," however, their influence upon him remained.

While Grégoire and his colleagues moved away from the philosophes, however, they began to link themselves to another persecuted Old Regime movement, this time from within the church: the Jansenists. Two institutions they created alongside the Gallican Church had particular affinities with Port-Royal. One was the *Annales de la Religion,* a weekly newspaper that helped the embattled constitutional clergy in the provinces feel tied to a larger church structure. The second, with more explicit ties to the Jansenist tradition, was the Société de philosophie chrétienne (SPC). Though the SPC publicly described itself as an "open literary society" to imply that it was nothing but a casual gathering of citizens, it actually had a central institutional role in the new Gallican Church. It acted as a de facto ecclesiastical council, tying together the constitutional bishops and Gallican sympathizers from other countries. Moreover, it served as a sort of theological appeal board for the Gallican Church, an alternative to writing to Rome. Finally, it functioned, in Grégoire's words, as a "kind of academy," a Christian version of the Institut.[34] The society, which included longtime Jansenists like Adrien Le Paige, Armand Gaston Camus, and Pierre-Jean Agier, made a concerted effort to identify with Port-Royal. Members made an annual pilgrimage to the ruins of the abbey, something that would inspire Grégoire to write his famous *Les Ruines de Port-Royal,* in which he called the scholars of Port-Royal the "precursors of the Revolution" and the source of "all that is good, grand, and generous" in France. Another possibly Jansenist aspect of the SPC can be seen in Necheles's finding that members "frequently discussed the Jews and the millennium," though Grégoire apparently never participated in these debates. Such a coupling was a hallmark of Jansenism, even if not exclusive to it.[35]

Some of this identification stemmed from the strong links between Gallicanism and Jansenism. Though Gallicanism and Jansenism were not coterminous, and one could be Gallican without being Jansenist, overlap between the two was often quite strong. A speech given to the SPC by a Sardinian Gallican sympathizer explicitly equated the society's Gallicanism with Jansenism. Grégoire's friendships with Italian Gallican sympathizers like Scipione de' Ricci and Eustachio Degola, both noted Jansenists, only strengthened this connection. Grégoire's history-writing also linked the Gallican Church to the Jansenists; through the *Annales,* he gathered materials for a history of the Revolution's persecution of the church. He imagined a direct line between the Constitutional Church and other mistreated religious groups in French history, especially Port-Royal.[36]

As suggested earlier, however, this identification with Jansenism seems to have been something new rather than having been carried forward from before the Revolution. Trying to revive a Gallican Church and being attacked for his beliefs led Grégoire to an intense empathy with the Jansenists, if not to a complete theological Jansenism. Catherine Maire argues convincingly that "Grégoire *became* a Jansenist and a figurist at a certain moment." For her, "Grégoire cannot be clearly labeled as a Jansenist in any of his initiatives within the Constituent Assembly and the Convention, nor even in his pastoral works in Blois." Only after dechristianization, she argues, did the bishop look back to Port-Royal to find the origins of a republican Christianity. Even then, she noted, he did not adopt "Jansenist beliefs" but instead refigured them: "The Port-Royal which Grégoire exalts . . . is a Port-Royal which owes very little to the reality of the Jansenist movement"; "His ingenuity in misappropriating the meaning of texts is unlimited."[37]

In his various church activities, then, Grégoire tried to reconnect the best of the new system (a reorganized Republic) with that of the old (a spiritual, circumscribed Gallican Church). Opposing an anti-Christian notion of regeneration and the idea of a secular moral science, he maintained that republican society needed Christianity to help create moral citizens. Without it, the Republic would be doomed to failure.

REGROUNDING EMPIRE: THE AMIS DES NOIRS ET
DES COLONIES

If the Republic needed religion, it also needed to keep its empire to maintain stability. Continually amazing contemporaries with his frenetic activity, Grégoire engaged in a whole other sphere of action during the period: rethinking the empire through the *Société des Amis des Noirs et des Colonies* (Society of the Friends of Blacks and of the Colonies; SANC).[38] In the society, which met frequently from 1796 to 1799, Grégoire joined other old-time Amis des Noirs, prominent legislators, and white and mixed-race *colons,* in making a case for colonialism to continue, although in reformulated terms.[39] At a moment when France could have given up its empire, Grégoire and the other members urged that regenerated colonies remain at the heart of the Republic. Abolishing colonialism was impractical and unwise, and would harm France's interests as well as those of the colonies.

What were the stated purposes of the new SANC? Like its predecessor, the Société des Amis des Noirs, the SANC's ostensible goal was the abolition of slavery. One of the society's four commissions aimed to write a history of the slave trade, and Grégoire himself often read antislavery works in progress. In 1799, in conjunction with the government, the society held a large public celebration of the fifth anniversary of France's abolition of slavery. Unlike the first society, however, abolition was not the SANC's primary concern, since it had already been decreed in France. Despite the emancipation of French slaves, the members of the SANC warned, "the task of the friends of humanity is not yet finished."[40] Far from resolving the problems of the colonies, the abruptness of abolition had created new ones.

Indeed, in the wake of abolition and the insurrection in Saint-Domingue, the future of the colonies—which many saw as the lifeblood of the French economy—was in doubt. Slave-owners had long warned that, without slavery, colonial production—and French commerce itself—would grind to a halt. Even men who conceded that the colonies would eventually become independent argued that the newly freed slaves were not in a condition to use the land to its "fullest advantage." Moreover, they worried that, once they had a choice, free blacks might not opt to consume the European manufactured goods on which the colonial trade had been based. Indeed, if left to his own designs, the consistently antislavery *Décade philosophique* fretted, the newly freed *nègre* would only want "a shirt and a pair of underpants to cover his nudity"; he would "view as insane anyone who wanted to engage him in work that would drain him of energy and continually drag him away from the side of his lover, in exchange for dishes that his unrefined palate could not appreciate or a European-style outfit."[41] Furthermore, in addition to the disorder created by abolition, French possessions in the Caribbean were threatened by the war with Britain.

In addressing this crisis, some intellectuals reprised physiocratic arguments that colonies were inefficient and therefore unnecessary. Horace Say, brother of the famous economist and *Décade philosophique* coeditor J.-B. Say, argued that colonialism was absurd. Having a government situated "two thousand leagues away from the governed," with a single system of laws, was ridiculous; independence for all colonies was inevitable. Nevertheless, he insisted, it was folly for France to "unilaterally detach itself from its colonies"; this would effectively abandon them to England. Meanwhile, he argued, "let us conserve our colonies, in anticipation of the era when, without danger for them or for us, they can be independent." In another article, the *Décade* urged that as long as England was trying to establish new colonies throughout the world, France should too.[42]

Like a number of republicans at the time, the SANC went even farther, arguing that the colonies not only could—but needed to be—preserved in a postslavery world. Though one of the society's four committees was dedicated to abolition, the other three aimed at spreading colonization. Moreover, alongside abolition, the society's three other purposes ("the moral and physical improvement *[perfectionnement]* of the inhabitants of the colonies; the progress of agriculture, industry, and commerce there; and the formation of new colonies") aimed to reorient the philosophy of colonialism. Through moral regeneration, freed slaves would learn to be industrious and ethical; through technical instruction, they could bring forth bounty from their land. New colonies would ensure that these values were spread throughout the world and that the benefits of this labor would accrue to France and not Britain.[43]

Though they wished to anchor old and new colonies more firmly in the French empire, the republican intellectuals who composed the SANC confronted a problem: how to incorporate colonial inhabitants into a secular republican system? This issue was far more acute for them than for earlier, nonrepublican critics of slavery, such as the abbé Raynal or Thomas Clarkson. Even antislavery authors who had been more disposed toward republicanism, such as Diderot, had been writing when emancipation was an abstract proposal rather than a legislative fait accompli. SANC members therefore had to think about issues of integration and equality in a more profound way than previous opponents of slavery, even though they were able to draw upon earlier antislavery texts.[44]

To resolve this dilemma, members harkened back to Grégoire's earlier arguments about regeneration; they insisted that political emancipation of people of color needed to be followed by efforts to improve and
instruct them. Their plans to regenerate nonwhites did not stop, however, with those seen as having been degraded by slavery; they also
argued that improvement was needed by free blacks in Africa. Africans
everywhere were in a profound state of ignorance, and Europeans had
a duty to improve them morally, physically, and practically: "In their
native land, the Africans are unaware of all the advantage they can draw
from their soil and their climate for their own use and that of others.
They are without instruction and without knowledge of useful arts. As
for their like in our colonies, who have become our fellow citizens and
brothers, are they not abandoned to a profound ignorance? Do they not
have an urgent need for moral and physical instruction?" With their
superior knowledge of science, the SANC suggested, Europeans knew
Africa far better than the Africans. The SANC made similar claims
about "peoples who live around the Mediterranean," whom it called
"too ignorant [and] too hostile to any kind of improvement, for us to
wait for it to happen from their own efforts."[45]

The emphasis on instructing people of color reflected the preoccupation with education that lay at the heart of the new social science. Since
the SANC included Class members like Cabanis and Grégoire, we
should not be surprised to see it emphasize education as a way of reshaping societies of color. Indeed, the SANC's Commission des colonies anciennes declared that, though Directory leaders were no doubt busy, they
should make time to promote the "regeneration of morals in our
colonies" and to research how to "educate Negroes in all the virtues that
are appropriate to free men, to Frenchmen."[46]

Education alone could not ensure a stable empire, however; in keeping with Thermidorian ideas on the importance of material prosperity,
the SANC devoted much of its time to investigating how the colonies
could continue to generate wealth for the metropole. With many in
France worried that a slavery-free empire would be a bankrupt one,
members sought to ensure that colonies based on free labor would
remain productive. Discussions of agricultural techniques and machines
dominated society meetings and reports.[47]

In addition to their efforts to increase production in existing colonies,
the members of the society worked to establish new ones, particularly in
Africa. Some members expressed reservations about colonialism; even
as they sought to benefit the metropole, they insisted that they did not

wish to exploit the colonies. "We must not forget that all commercial relations between France and the colonies must be based on a principle of reciprocal utility," one member noted. "To be exact, growing rich for the mother country, and increasing cultivation and commerce for the colonies." Similarly, a commission of Lasteyrie, Théremin, and J.-B. Say declared its opposition to colonial "domination," musing that "if the British [East] India Company were to be chased from the countries it oppresses; and if the gentle and industrious peoples there, delivered from the absurd and ferocious power of these bourgeois sovereigns, would raise themselves back to the level of [other] nations; it would not be in accordance with our principles to establish our domination in place of the one that we had destroyed." The commission denounced the very notion of having new colonies, in the sense that the idea of " 'colonies' implies a territorial sovereignty."[48]

Despite these members' semantic opposition to the term *colonies,* however, the SANC was very much in favor of establishing new spheres of influence around the world. As Yves Bénot has noted, being antislavery in this period did not mean being anticolonial; someone opposing colonies based on subjection could still support colonial "establishments" that would benefit the Republic economically. While members thus suggested that new establishments would be based on "affection and gratitude" instead of brute power, they still envisioned them as serving the mother country's economic needs. Indeed, Lasteyrie, Théremin, and J.-B. Say followed their hesitancy about colonies with a spirited recommendation to create foreign "establishments equally useful for us and our hosts." The SANC in fact aimed to build many more new colonial establishments throughout the world.[49]

Given Grégoire's active participation in the SANC, the enduring image of him as an anticolonial militant appears problematic. Necheles has portrayed Grégoire as out of step with the rest of the society, a lone moral idealist uncomfortable with the economic issues discussed by others.[50] Yet Grégoire was hardly a wild-eyed utopian; during the Convention, he had been a consummate strategist, a man very much concerned with international rivalries and with the exploitation of resources. Though he himself spoke mostly about the slave trade during SANC meetings, he explicitly endorsed the goals of increased agricultural production and new colonization. He arranged, for example, for another member's essay about sugar production to be printed in the *Décade* and underwritten by the SANC. There is no evidence to suggest that Grégoire (the guiding force behind the Conservatoire des Arts et Métiers, a proponent of agricultural innovation since his days as a curé, and a member of prestigious agricultural societies in France and abroad) was suddenly made uncomfortable by discussions of agricultural technology when it came to the colonies. Although his own arguments for new colonies focused on their moral advantages, Grégoire enthusiastically promoted the new "philanthropic colonization."[51]

Grégoire's enthusiasm for new colonization comes through clearly in his speech to the Class of Moral and Political Sciences about the British colony at Sierra Leone, in which he praised European colonization for its ability to spread civilization. While complaining about the slave trade, Grégoire did not argue for the regeneration of the Europeans who had conducted it, but for that of Africans; he agreed with other "philanthropists who believe that a way of eradicating this horrible trafficking would be to gradually bring civilization to Africa." Europeans were indispensable to Africa, Grégoire noted, to "console and encourage" freed blacks returning there and to "make them taste the first fruits of the social condition." Though he was aware that some inhabitants of Africa had their own religion (he referred to "Islamists" in the continent's interior), he insisted that Christianity was necessary for them. In addition to reducing their desire for vengeance, it had begun to make Sierra-Leonians into "friends of order and peace" and "taught them to cherish and fulfill their duties, to look after the education of their families." With European help, "a moral revolution operated rapidly among them."[52]

Even after the SANC dissolved in 1799, Grégoire remained committed to the idea that world progress would come through a European presence on other continents. Chosen by the Institut in 1799 to prepare a report relating to Napoleon's invasion of Egypt (itself planned by the Institut), Grégoire praised the expedition and declared French conquest to be necessary to the rebirth of the Orient. In the wake of Napoleon's arrival, Grégoire gushed, "Liberty and science will bloom again in a country where, in ancient times, they had displayed such brilliance. What a memorable epoch in the annals of humanity!" His ideas on this conquest were thus hardly out of step with those of Bonaparte, who depicted his ultimately unsuccessful expedition as liberating the Egyptians from their Mamluk and Ottoman tyrants. Grégoire clearly saw European conquest as a powerful motor of the drive to improve humanity, and encouraged Napoleon and others to pursue it.[53]

Though Grégoire's various activities during the Directory years may seem unrelated, his SANC activities fit perfectly with his other efforts of the period. Though the SANC itself was resolutely secular, Grégoire's interest in the colonies remained linked to his church and Institut activities; he hoped that creating a free empire would both ensure the stability of the Republic and help spread Christianity.[54] Even if his religious faith was not shared by most other intellectuals and abolitionists, his advocacy of a moderate republicanism—one that did not require destroying all aspects of the past—made him a man for the times. Though the Directory itself would be short-lived, destroyed by Napoleon's infamous coup of 18 brumaire (1799), many of Grégoire's efforts during the period would have an enduring legacy. His efforts toward cultural reconstruction in this period, for instance, are celebrated even now. His visage adorns the gates of the Conservatoire national des arts et métiers, while the Institut still pays homage to him as one of its founders.[55]

The arguments of Grégoire and his abolitionist comrades about how to proceed with the colonies would have perhaps even greater impact. Despite their abolitionism, Grégoire and his friends continued to view empire as a central part of the Republic. They would depart from the old system in abolishing slavery; moreover, treatment of colonial subjects would no longer be based on brute force. Regardless of Grégoire's private motivations, SANC members and other like-minded Directory intellectuals did not make gaining new souls for the church a basis for empire. They opted to preserve colonialism, however, at a time when it could have been abandoned, because they saw it as crucial to the material stability of France and to the success of its contests with Great Britain. The new colonial system would have a regenerated justification. Rather than the colonies simply serving the mother country, the claims of empire would now be based on the service of colonizers to the colonized: in helping freed slaves to regenerate themselves and in teaching them how best to exploit their resources. At some future time, Grégoire and his friends imagined, when non-Europeans had learned their lessons well, they might be ready for independence. But that time had not yet arrived. Meanwhile, the SANC had created a republican, secular civilizing mission, rescuing colonialism for republican government.[56]

Keeping the Faith

Grégoire, Regeneration, and the Revolution's Global Legacy, 1801–1831

Introduction to Part Three

How would Grégoire look back on the Revolution in the wake of its definitive failure? To what extent would his views change to reflect the realities of a France returned to monarchy? What would be the legacy of the Revolution's ideals—most notably that of regeneration? That the French Revolution had worldwide consequences is a truism of modern historiography, a staple of textbooks and more scholarly writing alike. Discussions of the Revolution's legacy often focus on abstractions, however; it is hard to follow individual revolutionaries into the nineteenth century, since few survived and remained true to republican principles. Grégoire, in contrast, would live through Napoleon's Empire, the Bourbon Restoration, and the first year of the July Monarchy—and retain his republicanism throughout.[1] Once again, his experiences in this period have much to teach us.

After Thermidor, Grégoire and his like-minded friends had tried to save French republicanism. To replace the Convention, the Thermidorians had adopted the Directory system, which featured a five-man Executive Directorate and an elite Council of Ancients alongside the lower Council of Five Hundred. The leaders of the Directory struggled to keep power away from both royalists and unreconstructed Jacobins, and to win the ongoing war against the European monarchies. Nevertheless, the system eventually fell prey to corruption, crushing the Thermidorians' idealism.

Meanwhile, Grégoire was experiencing personal difficulties. In the 1798 elections, he lost his seat in the Council of Five Hundred and his political career came to an abrupt end. Mme Dubois's economical management of his finances could not save him from poverty, and he was forced to sell books from his private collection to survive. Fortunately, François de Neufchâteau helped him get a post as assistant librarian at the Bibliothèque de l'Arsenal, and the bishop had a new source of income. He nearly lost this position, though, when the chief librarian, the former abbé Ameilhon, complained that his new deputy was not a professional librarian, no matter how great his interest in books and his policy expertise. Though well-connected friends helped him keep the post, another blow struck in 1799 when his beloved mother died in Emberménil. Meanwhile, Grégoire remained anxious about the future of France itself.[2]

Amidst the uncertainty of the time, the rise of Napoleon did not alarm Grégoire but rather gave him cause for optimism. Like other members of his circle and like a public exhausted by a decade of turbulence, the bishop of Loir-et-Cher was at first excited by the coup that brought the young war hero to power in 1799. He contrasted "the crimes of the National Convention and the Directory" to "the wise and measured conduct of General Bonaparte, who always respects religion and wants to use the moral force of religion to consolidate the Republic." Grégoire enjoyed cordial relations with Bonaparte, a fellow Institut member, and he often socialized with the general's friends and family, including his brother Joseph, a fellow habitué of the Auteuil group.[3] Even Napoleon's ongoing negotiations with Rome did not worry Grégoire, who hoped they would bring peace between the republican church and the pope. Indeed, Bonaparte consulted with Grégoire numerous times about the negotiations, which were impeded when Napoleon insisted that the Gallican clergy be accommodated in the settlement.[4]

In 1801, Grégoire was therefore more optimistic than he had been in years about the possibility for reconciliation between the Republic and religion. Napoleon seemed more sympathetic to the Gallican Church than the Directorate had been; moreover, the new pope had a reputation for flexibility, having praised the Civil Constitution of the Clergy when he was only a bishop. A settlement between Rome and a quasi-revolutionary France seemed so likely that rumors circulated that Grégoire would soon be named a cardinal. Hopes were high that the new pope would make peace with France and reward the United Bishops for their battle against irreligion.[5]

Fate took a turn in the other direction, however, and Grégoire soon realized that his optimism had been misplaced. Napoleon, whose own religious beliefs were famously instrumentalist (he once remarked that "in Egypt I was a Mohammedan; here I will be a Catholic"), quickly determined that Grégoire's church lacked widespread support and that reinstituting Rome's religious authority would better cement his power. The Concordat, the agreement he reached with the pope in 1801, ended France's experiment with a revolutionary Christianity; Grégoire was forced, like other constitutional clergy, to resign from his bishopric and realized that he would never receive a cardinal's cap. As he wrote to a friend later that year, "This supposed ornament is not destined for heads that are simultaneously religious and republican."[6]

Certainly, there were aspects of Napoleon's reign that Grégoire favored, from the continuation of certain revolutionary policies to the general's treatment of Jews. Rather than simply reviving the Old Regime, Bonaparte continued many of the Revolution's innovations, such as the merit system; he also emphasized currents of the Revolution that had been to Grégoire's liking, such as the political exclusion of women. Grégoire was additionally pleased by Napoleon's convening Jewish leaders in 1806–7 into an Assembly of Notables and a Sanhedrin, an ancient rabbinical institution. Through these bodies, Napoleon asked Jews to declare their loyalty to France, renounce usury, and profess their willingness to intermarry. This singling out of Jews by the state—and the implication that they were both usurious and less patriotic than others—reversed the universalistic posture taken by the late Constituent Assembly, which had repudiated laws aimed at Jews instead of at all citizens. Nevertheless, Grégoire, who had become increasingly skeptical about Jews' desire to regenerate themselves, applauded Napoleon's actions vigorously.[7]

On the whole, however, Napoleon's reign served to repudiate many values that Grégoire held dear. In 1802, the general reinstituted slavery in the French colonies and attempted to reconquer Saint-Domingue, where Toussaint Louverture, the leader of the slave insurrection, had proclaimed himself "governor-general." Though Napoleon's expedition was successful in capturing and imprisoning Toussaint, it failed to reassert control over the island, and an independent "Haiti" was proclaimed there on January 1, 1804. Nevertheless, Napoleon's actions preserved slavery in other French colonies. Equally galling to Grégoire was Bonaparte's crowning himself emperor in 1804, a true death notice for French republicanism.

Though he was elected to the Napoleonic Senate, thereby resuming a political career, Grégoire did not follow former colleagues like Sieyès and Roederer in transferring his loyalties to the new regime. His continued attachments to republicanism, abolitionism, and Gallicanism led him into occasional skirmishes with Napoleon, even as the general had a bemused respect for his frankness. Their exchanges are the stuff of legend. One popular anecdote involves Napoleon's convoking a group of senators who were expected to support his reestablishment of slavery. The sole person to disagree, Grégoire quipped: "If someone was blind, it would be enough to hear such speeches to be sure that they were made by white men. If all these gentlemen had their skin color altered right now, they would probably change their tune." Another legend involves Bonaparte's taunting Grégoire about associating with the atheist former *conventionnel* Dupuis. The former bishop supposedly retorted: "General,

Dupuis and I do not agree on everything. But at least we have one religion in common: that of the Republic!" Whatever truth resides in these
legends, we do know that Grégoire was the only member of the Senate
to denounce the 1808 law creating a new nobility, and that he condemned Napoleon's divorce from Josephine in 1809. When the former
law made Grégoire a count, along with all of the other senators, Grégoire refused to use the title. Even as his ability to influence France's destiny grew increasingly dim, however, he remained sufficiently well
connected to avoid official persecution. Moreover, he now had income
from his Senate post, which allowed him leisure to write.[8]

If Napoleon's reign had troubled Grégoire, the victory of the European
monarchies in 1814—and their promise to reinstall the Bourbons—was
worse. Emperor Alexander of Russia (speaking also for Britain, Austria,
and Prussia) charged the Napoleonic Senate with drawing up a monarchical constitution "suitable for the French people"; arguing that a civil
war might be sparked by a long power vacuum, he gave them three days
to comply. The senators responded with a brief statement in which they
declared that the French people were "freely calling to the throne Louis-
Stanislas-Xavier de France" (who, they added, happened to be the
brother of the last king); many of them hoped they might thereby
achieve a constitutional monarchy akin to that of 1791, with separation
of powers and consultative government. Grégoire was on the commission charged with examining the document, and the newspapers
reported that the document was approved unanimously.[9]

Whatever the record showed, however, Grégoire was not at all happy
with the Senate's declaration, nor with the conditions under which it had
been coerced. At the same time, he was also disturbed by the monarchists who began publishing pamphlets denouncing the Senate for pre-
suming to grant authority to the king. These men denied that the
Bourbons had any obligation to obey a constitution. Grégoire, seeing
himself as one of the last true republicans in France, waged a final battle for liberty in the court of public opinion. In one anonymous pamphlet (and possibly a second one), he defended the idea of a constitution,
even as he criticized the Senate's version as hasty and ill-conceived. As
one of the pamphlets declared, the royalist attacks on the Senate were
astounding: "What! That one could want a state like France not to have
a constitution? They dare, in the nineteenth century, after twenty-five
years of Revolution, and ten years of the reign of Buonaparte, to propose that thirty million Frenchmen deliver themselves with feet and fists
tied to a man, giving themselves without reserve? . . . I did not believe

there were Frenchmen capable of thinking such an idea, let alone publishing it." Grégoire found it incredible that, just as other nations had begun to move toward constitutional government, some of his fellow citizens would renounce it. He suggested that he could have accepted a constitutional monarchy as a compromise, if the senatorial constitution had been a well-considered one, which guaranteed stable liberty and represented popular choice. This constitution, however, was not worthy of its name, particularly because the people supposedly granting power to the new king had never been consulted.[10]

Grégoire's pamphlet *De la constitution de 1814* enjoyed enormous popularity and went through five editions. In the midst of a flurry of pamphleteering on all sides, one contemporary called Grégoire's "the best" and "most famous" of all the writings that then appeared. Other republicans championed him as an alternative leader for the country.[11] Nevertheless, his willingness to defend the republican legacy publicly—nearly alone among former revolutionaries—offended royalists, and he bore the brunt of their anger. He was attacked endlessly as a "vile hypocrite" and "one of the most hotheaded apostles of the Revolution." Readers, many of whom had not been born in 1789, were told that "the experience of the past has not cured Grégoire of his mania for utopias," and that his actions had caused the colonies to be "watered with the blood of the whites."[12]

If the Constitution of 1814 seemed problematic to Grégoire, Louis XVIII's ultimate decision about how to regard it was even more offensive. Rejecting the notion that a Bourbon could ever owe his crown to popular choice, the king replaced the Senate's document with his own charter; though it instituted parliamentary institutions, its justifications of royal power read almost as if the Old Regime had never fallen. During the Restoration, royalists and republicans sparred repeatedly about whether Grégoire had been a regicide, but the former bishop was never formally punished. Still, royalists did everything they could to make his life unpleasant. In addition to endless attacks in the press, he was stripped of his beloved position in the Institut, an act that drew sporadic but unsuccessful public protests for the next fifteen years.[13]

Grégoire was also beginning to feel old. Though he and Mme Dubois still enjoyed the many visitors who came to chat or enjoy her cooking, he frequently complained in letters that both of them were suffering from illness; on a number of occasions, they journeyed to the Lorraine countryside to try to restore their health. The former bishop was also increasingly pessimistic about human nature; he told a Danish scholar in 1817 that one needed to have spent two decades in politics "to under-stand the extent to which the majority of public figures and intellectu-als in France are weak, ungrateful and vile."[14]

Despite his official exclusion and these personal disappointments, Grégoire remained important in France as a living symbol of the repub-lican past. In 1819, at the age of sixty-nine, he was elected to the Cham-ber of Deputies from the Isère region as part of a republican protest, in a nationally watched contest. His feelings of powerlessness in public life only deepened, however, after his election was nullified by the Cham-ber's ultra-monarchists, and a flurry of pamphlets and newspaper arti-cles denounced him.[15] To Grégoire, this controversy proved that he could have no further impact on France. The Revolution to which he had devoted so much of his life, "gladly sacrific[ing] my fortune and my health," was defeated, and his diocese was now in other hands. Though he had claimed as a younger man that his days as a curé had been his happiest, he now tried to portray his forced retirement positively, telling the abbé Jennat that "I thank the heavens for having discharged me of the burdens of the ministry."[16]

In addition to Grégoire's ejection from political and ministerial life, his financial worries had returned. Upon their return to power, the Bour-bons had agreed to offer pensions of 24,000 francs to the former Napoleonic senators. The monarchy revoked this promise in 1816, though, and Grégoire was once again forced to sell books from his library to economize, a painful task for such an ardent bibliophile. Though he had used part of his Senate income in 1807 to purchase land in Mme Dubois' natal region (the Yonne, in Burgundy) as an investment, he also seems to have been having trouble collecting rents on it. In 1820, however, a new law restored the senatorial pensions; newly flush and with Mme Dubois continuing to manage his practical affairs, Grégoire could focus again on writing, spending time with friends, and donating money to the poor.[17] During the Empire and Restoration, he would write approximately two hundred essays, articles, and books on history and other topics.

Lest we think Grégoire had turned his back on political reform, how-ever, we should note that his histories continued to have political impli-cations. His 1808 *De la littérature des nègres* was not an innocuous literary chronicle but an abolitionist manifesto, a barely veiled challenge to Napoleon's reinstitution of slavery. His 1818 *Essai historique sur les libertés de l'Eglise gallicane*—and his publishing the newspaper *La chronique religieuse* with like-minded friends—defended the Civil

Constitution and the Gallican Church; his projected biographical history of Lorraine aimed to highlight men who embodied republican and Christian virtues.[18] Finally, his massive *Histoire des sectes religieuses,* which we will analyze more fully, contrasted the true Catholic faith with various modern sects. In returning to historiography at a time when the government sought to revive the Old Regime, Grégoire wanted to offer an alternate reading of the past in which republicanism and Gallicanism remained viable options for the future.

Grégoire could hardly remain confined to his study or to friends' receiving rooms, however. In the last thirty years of his life, he would redirect the major part of his energy overseas, to an untainted new world full of possibilities. Though these last years of his life have received little attention from scholars, who have mainly focused on his career at the height of the Revolution, they have much to teach us about the Revolution and its impact.[19]

First, they remind us that historians get a partial view of French history when they focus attention only on the hexagon. The story of French republicanism and its struggles to reassert itself in early-nineteenth-century France can be deepened by looking at transnational interactions. Grégoire's career shows how, in the immediate postrevolutionary period, vanquished French republicans tried to spread their ideals abroad (particularly to the Americas), in the hopes that republicanism could later be reimported into France. Their efforts, even when they proved frustrating, are an overlooked aspect of the Revolution's legacy.

Second, Grégoire's later years show vividly that enlightened religion in France, whatever its prerevolutionary existence, had become anathema by the nineteenth century. Grégoire increasingly blamed the Revolution's failure on its embrace of Enlightenment impiety, and he came to regret his enthusiasm for writers he now considered scandalous. Though the philosophes' influence upon him never disappeared completely, he began to denounce them as a group, and he increasingly highlighted Christianity as the answer to all of the world's problems. Although he retained his faith in republicanism, he began to distance himself from the notion of social regeneration, with its reliance upon political action and voluntary transformation. On the one hand, the term had become suspicious to contemporaries, who saw it as a dangerous reminder of revolutionary utopianism;[20] on the other, he increasingly felt that only divine intercession could change people. While he still hoped for global regeneration, he reaffirmed his belief in the taint of original sin, and increasingly argued that only theological regeneration could unite the universal human family. His writings in this period also show that his interest in oppressed groups should not be seen merely as humanitarian, but rather as part of the Christian apologetic tradition. Just as writing about Jews in 1788 had been a way for him to defend the Catholic Church against Basnage, Grégoire's discussions of oppressed groups or other religious denominations served to prove the truth of Catholicism.

Nevertheless, despite Grégoire's own disenchantment with the idea of political regeneration, the idea would take on a life of its own, particularly with regard to colonial and postcolonial situations. Regeneration became a useful concept for victorious leaders of revolutions in Haiti and elsewhere to argue to foreigners that they were fully capable of self-rule and to convince countrymen that they were the most qualified to direct it, in reversing the legacy of colonialism and creating a new society. Nevertheless, the term would retain the paradoxes and contradictions it had had when applied to "degenerate" groups within France. Just as regeneration could be used to promote national liberation, it could also be used in service of European paternalism and new waves of colonialism.

CHAPTER 7

The Joys and Frustrations of the Atlantic Republican Network

Grégoire and the Americas

Friendship traverses the seas and we are often in spirit in
Washington City. Oh, if you only knew how many times and
with what tender emotion we speak of you and Mr. Barlow!
Why are you so far away? Will the heavens allow us to see
you again?

—Grégoire, 1806

When Grégoire wrote these impassioned lines to his American friends
Ruth and Joel Barlow in 1806 on behalf of himself and Mme Dubois,
little did he guess that in a few short years, a poem would tear their
transatlantic friendship apart. In 1807, Barlow published his eight-
thousand-line opus *The Columbiad,* and Grégoire was stunned by its
contents. The poem's republicanism did not offend Grégoire, nor did its
abolitionist message; agreement on these issues had long united the two
men. Nor was Grégoire bothered in the least by the poem's vision of an
America on the rise, ready to overtake its European rivals. On the contrary, Grégoire was dismayed by the fate of republicanism in Europe,
and pinned many of his hopes for the future of humanity on the New
World. One passage in particular in the poem, however—in which the
deist Barlow attacked the superstition and corruption of the Catholic
Church—would spark a rift that would never heal.

As they had for many Europeans since the abbé Raynal, the Americas held a special fascination for Grégoire; in contrast to Europe, they
represented for him a world of uncorrupted possibilities. Grégoire particularly admired the United States, which had sparked the modern
republican trend; he also supported would-be republicans throughout

Latin America. He knew, nevertheless, that a new republic was a shaky proposition; many initially successful revolutions crumbled, turning back to monarchy or toward military dictators. For Grégoire, Americans' ability to avoid these pitfalls and sustain their republic would be crucial to the future of republicanism worldwide. As a veteran of the Terror, Grégoire felt he had valuable lessons to impart to republicans throughout the Atlantic world. As part of his hopes to create a worldwide network of republican intellectuals, he thus carried on a correspondence with a varied set of New World residents, from American statesmen to Mexican priests.[1]

Grégoire's pan-American engagements highlight the existence of an Atlantic republican network in the early nineteenth century, as republicans around the Atlantic eagerly sought relationships with each other. Despite their eagerness, however, this network was fragile and sometimes contentious. Views of republicanism were not always the same, and Grégoire would discover that American republicans were not always as interested in corresponding with him as he was with them. His disagreements with them often centered on two matters: slavery and religion—particularly as Catholicism became even more central to his political program. Grégoire's dealings with Thomas Jefferson—and the public disagreement that erupted between the French priest and Barlow over the *Columbiad*—would be emblematic of his simultaneous admiration for and frustration with American republicans.

THE LURE OF THE AMERICAS

Grégoire viewed republican initiatives throughout the western hemisphere with a great deal of interest. He had personal relationships with intellectuals in Mexico, Bogota, and Guatemala, and was excited about the progress of Latin American colonies toward independence. He supported the efforts of Simon Bolívar to break free of Spain and argued passionately that Spain's American colonies had an "imprescriptible right" to independence. He also kept an eye on the status of Catholicism in Latin America, monitoring Catholic writings in Mexico, for example, to see whether *ultramontanes* (fervid supporters of Rome) or Gallican sympathizers would predominate there. He was also worried about the "masses of obscene and impious books" being sent to Mexico by other Frenchmen, which "can only corrupt [people's] minds and hearts." Grégoire also tried to remain up-to-date on the status of indigenous peoples in the Spanish Americas.[2]

Most importantly, Grégoire tried to stay current on the abolitionist movement in Latin America and the Caribbean. Along with other European abolitionists, he tracked the efforts of the new republic of Colombia to abolish slavery, which he saw as a sage way of preventing violence. He hoped that this example would spread to others and that "the force of public opinion and coming events will force the United States, Brazil, Cuba, Jamaica, Martinique, and Guadeloupe to occupy themselves seriously with freeing the slaves." In the face of lax enforcement of the ban on the slave trade (agreed to by England, France, the United States, and others in the period 1807–1818), he also asked a friend to provide him with documentation about its illegal continuation so he could prod the authorities to take action.[3]

Grégoire's interest in Latin America was reciprocated, and he had a steady stream of Latin American visitors anxious to meet the famous French republican. For example, when Fray Servando Teresa de Mier, who has been called "the chief theorist of the Mexican insurgency," escaped Spanish imprisonment in 1801, he fled to France, where Grégoire welcomed him and became, in the words of one historian, his "French mentor." The two had perhaps the most in common of any of Grégoire's American friends. Catholic, republican, and abolitionist, both men shared an admiration for Bartolomé de Las Casas, the famous sixteenth-century defender of Amerindians, as well as for Gallicanism and Jansenism. Other founders of Mexico also invoked Grégoire's work as they sought to reconcile the competing claims of church and state.[4]

Grégoire's work could also prove controversial, though, among Latin American writers. His *Apologie de Barthélemy de Las-Casas* was one of his most divisive works in this respect. Like Servando de Mier, a number of Latin Americans shared Grégoire's admiration of Las Casas and were sympathetic to Grégoire's effort to rehabilitate him; Las Casas had been tarnished by writers who accused him of launching the African slave trade by urging that Amerindian labor be replaced with African labor. Grégoire vigorously contested this charge, insisting that the Spanish priest was a true universalist and one of the few Catholic heroes of the antislavery movement. Others, however, took offense at Grégoire's impugning of certain Spanish historians while trying to defend Las Casas; they insisted that Las Casas had indeed supported African slavery. Pamphlets appeared in a number of countries criticizing or defending Grégoire's *Apologie*.[5]

Grégoire's interest in the United States—the first republic in the hemisphere and republican France's inspiration in many ways—was even greater. He therefore corresponded eagerly with Americans to learn more about their system and to offer his advice. One of his most sustained relationships was with the American Philosophical Society (APS) in Philadelphia, the preeminent American intellectual institution. Even before the rise of Napoleon, Grégoire began to donate books to the APS in the hopes that intellectuals in the United States would read them.

Examining the selection of books Grégoire sent the APS expands our knowledge of his republican vision in the postrevolutionary years. To Grégoire, the best government needed a stable source of agricultural wealth, a vigilant commitment to republican ideals, a morality rooted in Christianity, an inclusive attitude toward people of all religions and races, and an unyielding dedication to abolitionism. One frequent theme of Grégoire's donations was thus agricultural technology.[6] He also wanted Americans to monitor retreats from republicanism in France, so they would recognize the dangers of insufficiently protecting their republic. To this end, he sent the APS a copy of his *De la constitution française de l'an 1814,* and another pamphlet endorsing meritocracy.[7] Building on his longtime commitment to regeneration, he also sent the APS copies of two of his writings on Jews and addressed a questionnaire to an American friend about the integration of different religious and racial groups in the American republic. He also sought information from Mordecai Noah, an important New York Jew whom he had met in Paris. In addition, he solicited material about the status of Protestant sects in the United States, which he used in his *Histoire des sectes religieuses.* He also wanted to know about the status of American Catholics—not only in the United States, but also in Louisiana and Canada.[8]

Although Grégoire hoped that the United States would be tolerant of people of all religions, he continued to see Catholicism as the one true religion, and he hoped for universal conversion. Grégoire's interest in Jews in the United States thus also related to whether they might be persuaded to become Christian. To this end, he corresponded with Hannah Adams and other American Christians who desired to convert the Jews. Grégoire and Adams appear to have discussed the progress of conversion in their respective countries; Adams reported her excitement at learning from Grégoire that some Jews in eastern France, in the wake of emancipation, were adopting Christianity. Grégoire also wanted to make sure Amerindians would be brought into the American polity and the church; he asked a correspondent several questions about them, and was particularly interested in what books were being given to them. Finally, Grégoire was interested in American Protestants and how different their beliefs were from Catholicism.[9]

Precisely because of his religious desires for the United States, Grégoire looked to American Catholics as a natural source of alliance. He was particularly interested in corresponding with John Carroll, the archbishop of Baltimore and leader of the Catholic Church in the United States. Grégoire hoped he would find a kindred spirit and eager correspondent in the American prelate; Carroll was after all a bishop living in a republic, and he had gained a reputation in the 1790s as an enlightened republican Catholic who wanted the American church to be independent of Rome. Like other Americans who became more conservative in the wake of the French Revolution, however, Carroll had by the late 1790s become a Federalist and a more traditional supporter of the pope. To the older Carroll, Grégoire's support for the French Revolution was suspect; though he wrote a few times to the infamous Jacobin over a six-year period, his letters expressed a polite if unyielding disapproval of the French priest's writings and positions. Grégoire thus found himself unable to build a solid relationship with the leading American Catholic.[10]

Grégoire's inability to connect with American Catholics compounded two other frustrations he encountered in dealing with the United States. First, he felt that American ideals held great promise but were not always implemented. On the one hand, Grégoire had long seen the United States as a model in its church-state policies. In late 1794, when urging his countrymen to adopt ideals of religious liberty and separation of church and state, he had called their attention to the American example. America owed its very "power and happiness," he told the Thermidorian Convention, to its welcoming of those whose faiths and practices had led to their persecution in Europe. Moreover, he deemed it laudable that Mordecai Noah had been named sheriff of New York despite being Jewish. Grégoire was nevertheless upset when he felt that the American government was inconsistent in implementing its ideals. He was disturbed to learn that, after serving as U.S. consul in Tunis, Noah had received a letter from President James Monroe revoking his position on account of his being a Jew.[11]

More importantly, Grégoire was disgusted by the American accommodation of slavery. He considered it a scandal that the young republic not only had not abolished but had in fact *enshrined* slavery in its constitution through the three-fifths compromise. Grégoire therefore endeavored to convince American leaders of the brutality of slavery and the necessity of abolishing it. One way he did so was through his correspondence with the APS, to which he sent several antislavery works.[12] He also corresponded with American abolitionist organizations, such as the Pennsylvania Society for the Abolition of Slavery, and abolitionists such as Gulian Verplanck, president of the New-York Historical Society.[13]

Grégoire's most important effort to influence American opinion on slavery was his 1808 *De la littérature des nègres*. Grégoire had been incensed by Thomas Jefferson's comments in *Notes on the State of Virginia* to the effect that blacks were naturally and irrevocably incapable of the same intellectual achievements as whites. Though Grégoire praised the Virginian in the preface for his work against the slave trade, he attacked the view of Jefferson and others that blacks were inferior intellectually. The abbé countered the idea of separate origins of the races with the argument that all human beings belonged to a single species: "Who would dare . . . deny that all humans are variations on a single type, and who would claim that some of them are incapable of attaining civilization?" Only historical events—particularly the brutality of slavery, he insisted—had degraded blacks. Any logical person, he thundered, must recognize that the injustice of whites, rather than any innate defect, had made blacks seem inferior: "What sentiments of dignity, of self-respect, can possibly exist in beings treated like beasts . . . ? What can become of individuals degraded below the level of brutes, overloaded with work, covered with rags, devoured with hunger, and torn by the bloody whip of their overseer for the slightest fault?" Anticipating the many counter-arguments against his position, Grégoire declared, "Those claiming the superiority of whites are none other than whites defending their own interests."[14]

Grégoire's criticism of Jefferson did not remain implicit; he rebuked the Virginian by name numerous times. Of whites' self-interested arguments about black inferiority, Grégoire noted, "It is maddening to find the same prejudice in a man whose name is ordinarily pronounced among us only with a deep esteem and a well-deserved respect: Jefferson, in his *Notes on the State of Virginia.*" After recounting the virtues and talents of people of African descent from the ancient world to the nineteenth century, Grégoire added in exasperation, "These details make it clear what one must think when . . . Jefferson tells us that they have never erected a civilized society." Grégoire was particularly upset that the drafter of the Declaration of Independence could not concede genius even to those blacks who had most distinguished themselves in the arts and letters. "The more imposing and respectable the authority of Jefferson," he declared, "the more essential it is to combat his judgment."[15]

Grégoire's abolitionist efforts attracted much positive attention in the United States. In 1818, Verplanck lauded Grégoire and compared him to Las Casas. Offering Grégoire honorary membership in the New-York Historical Society, he called the abbé "a man, who, like Las Casas himself, has devoted a long life to the defence of liberal principles, and to labours of humanity, who, like him, too, has been in turns a mark for the calumnies of the bigot and of the infidel; . . . at one time the champion of toleration against bigotry, at another of his religion against triumphant and persecuting atheism; the defender of learning and the arts . . . and always the friend of the oppressed." The American statesman Robert Livingston also praised Grégoire's defense of Las Casas.[16]

American intellectuals followed other aspects of Grégoire's work as well. The Library Company of Philadelphia, the leading subscription library in the country at the time, purchased a number of Grégoire's writings.[17] Furthermore, the abbé's American admirers endeavored to meet him when visiting France. For example, Noah first met Grégoire after seeking him out in Paris in 1814, inspiring him to later describe Grégoire as "my venerable and pious friend . . . to whom the Jews owe an incalculable debt of gratitude." Grégoire's notoriety in the United States continued well into the Restoration. The Bostonian Rev. William Ellery Channing, for example, a leading American Unitarian and abolitionist, and a key figure in the development of Transcendentalism, told a friend that he longed to meet the famous Grégoire. Similarly, the young lawyer and future Harvard professor George Ticknor was a regular in 1817 at the nightly gatherings at Grégoire's residence.[18] Furthermore, a number of Grégoire's works were translated in the United States.[19]

At the same time, other Americans viewed Grégoire with suspicion. Many Americans, like many Britons, had turned against the French Revolution during its more violent phases. With the passing of the 1798 Alien and Sedition Acts and the aftermath of the XYZ Affair, it was particularly dangerous for an immigrant to be identified with French radicals. Benjamin Vaughan, a republican born in England and living in Maine, was a close friend of Grégoire from having lived in France in the late 1790s. In 1798, however he narrowly escaped prosecution under the Alien and Sedition Acts when a confiscated letter was published referring to his close friendship with several prominent French revolutionaries, including Grégoire. It even proved dangerous to spend time with the abbé in Paris, as Ticknor discovered when the French police began to harass and follow him on account of his association with Grégoire, Lafayette, and other French republicans.[20]

Moreover, to Grégoire's consternation, the republican—and abolitionist—network he was attempting to build often seemed fragile, as some correspondents ceased writing to him. By 1805, Grégoire was regularly complaining to Barlow that the Pennsylvania Abolition Society was ignoring him and that he had not heard anything from them in two years. He was particularly upset that his essay on Las Casas seemed not to have been translated in the United States, as the society had promised him.[21]

Jefferson, meanwhile, seemed unpersuaded by Grégoire's arguments on the unity of the human species. In a well-known letter to Grégoire, Jefferson politely thanked the abbé for the copy of *De la littérature des nègres* and swore that he had been impressed by it. He also pledged that his mind was still open on the subject of blacks' natural intelligence: "No person living wishes more sincerely than I do, to see a complete refutation of the doubts I have myself entertained and expressed on the grade of understanding allowed to them [blacks] by nature." Moreover, he insisted, his doubts about their abilities had nothing to do with their rights. In a lesser-known letter to their mutual friend Barlow, however, written a few months later, Jefferson showed a different face. He depicted Grégoire as simple-minded and commented that he had given the Frenchman a "soft answer." Jefferson accused Grégoire of naïveté and implied that whatever achievements had been reached by those chronicled in *De la littérature,* it was only because they had some white blood.[22]

Grégoire himself worried that his efforts to convince Americans about the ills of slavery were having no effect. Indeed, to him, racial prejudice was perhaps worse in the United States of the 1820s than in any European colony of the time. In 1826, Grégoire would lament: "Skin-color prejudice exists in its most extreme degree in the French, Dutch and British colonies, and especially in the United States." He noted that George Washington had owned many slaves, and praised a letter to Washington published by an English author, Edward Rushton. Rushton, Grégoire reported, had found Americans to be "extremely reprehensible" with regard to slavery, and asked Washington how he could deny Negro slaves the same natural rights claimed by white Americans in regard to the British. The abbé was further exasperated by an 1825 speech given by President John Quincy Adams; though Adams supported abolishing the slave trade, Grégoire complained that he and others were doing nothing to force the abolition of slavery itself.[23]

THE *COLUMBIAD* CONTROVERSY

Slavery was not the only issue that separated Grégoire from New World republicans, however. His friendship with Barlow reveals another point of fissure in the Atlantic republican world: religion. Since the Revolution, Barlow and his wife, Ruth, had been two of Grégoire's closest friends. His relationship with the American writer began when the latter arrived in Paris with other foreign republicans and Grégoire pushed to have him named a French citizen. Their friendship deepened when Barlow accompanied Grégoire *en mission* to Savoy.[24] Grégoire prized their relationship, which continued for many years and blossomed after the Revolution, when the Barlows lived close to Grégoire and Mme Dubois on the Left Bank. Grégoire, Mme Dubois, and the Barlows had a common circle of friends, and spent vacations in the same spa town in the Vosges, Plombières.[25]

So close were they that when the Barlows returned to the United States, Grégoire and Mme Dubois were crushed. Though Grégoire often displayed his emotions in letters to friends, his epistles to the absent couple were striking. "Please believe, my good friends," he assured them in 1805, "that no matter what physical distance the seas place between you and us, whatever the locations where providence places us on the globe, our inviolable attachment for you will accompany you across the Atlantic." The next year, his affection had hardly dimmed. "Our friends, along with Mme Dubois and I, will never forget you. Our friendship would be as strong in fifty years as today if we remained on this earth. We cannot pass by your house on the Rue Vaugirard without feeling tender emotion and regrets at remembering that you are so far from us. . . . I defy you to write to someone who is more attached to you than we are." Grégoire's occasional letters to Ruth Barlow repeat the same sentiments. "Friendship crosses the seas, and we are often in Washington City [D.C.], in spirit. Oh, if you only knew how many times and with what tender emotion we speak of you and Mr. Barlow! Why are you so far away? Will the heavens allow us to see you again?" Mme Dubois, he told Joel Barlow, "loves Madame Barlow like a sister," and was pained by her absence. Grégoire and Mme Dubois even hired the Barlows' beloved former servant Parise as their own and continued to reminisce with him about the departed Americans. Parise was a special blessing for them, since Grégoire complained at other times about servants who gave them or their friends nothing but heartache.[26]

Grégoire's relationship with Barlow was built not only on an intense personal bond, but also on common political views: attachment to revolutionary republicanism, opposition to slavery, and an interest in the status of Jews. Grégoire was also a great admirer of Barlow's writings and had long awaited his *Columbiad,* hoping it could fuel antislavery sentiment in the United States.[27]

The friendship would ultimately shatter, nevertheless, over religious matters. For inasmuch as Grégoire shared republican principles with his American correspondents, he rarely saw eye-to-eye with them on theological issues. Religion had not been a force of division between the two men during the Revolutionary years, when Grégoire sometimes subordinated his religious agenda to his larger social goals and Barlow undoubtedly hid his skepticism from his devout friend. By the 1800s, however, the abbé was no longer willing to tolerate attacks on Catholicism. When Barlow's *Columbiad* finally appeared and arrived in France, Grégoire was shocked to discover sentiments he felt were deist and anti-Christian. He was particularly flabbergasted by an engraving that portrayed the stamping out of prejudice with an image of the crushed remnants of a cross and crown, and by the closing passage of the poem, which seemed a direct assault on all Grégoire held dear. It included the lines,

> Beneath the footstool all destructive things,
> The mask of priesthood and the mace of kings,
> Lie trampled in the dust; for here at last
> Fraud, folly, error all their emblems cast.
> Each envoy here unloads his wearied hand
> Of some old idol from his native land;
> One flings a pagod on the mingled heap,
> One lays a crescent, one a cross to sleep,
> Swords, sceptres, mitres, crowns and globes and stars
> Codes of false fame and stimulants to wars
> Sink in the settling mass; since guile began,
> These are the agents of the woes of man.[28]

In March 1809, Grégoire published an open letter to his friend, entitled *Observations critiques sur le poème de M. Joel Barlow*. He began these *Observations* gently, by noting that there were many aspects of the work which had pleased him: "This monument of genius and of typography will immortalize the author and bring glory to American printers."[29]

Grégoire quickly moved, however, to a bitter condemnation of the poem's religious content. He noted that he could not stay silent in the face of what he considered Barlow's anti-Christian sentiments: "In the letter that accompanies your book, you ask me for a critique. . . . Thus I exercise a duty . . . in fighting back against an insult to Christianity—an insult about which I would keep silent, if Barlow was a common writer and his poem was a mediocre work." Precisely because Barlow was such an important author and one of his dearest friends, Barlow's depiction of Christianity required a response. Grégoire focused his anger on certain verses and an engraving that bears the following inscription: *Final destruction of prejudices.* Prejudices!. . . [ellipses in original]. No one more than I, perhaps, wishes for their destruction. But to what are you referring with this ambiguous term? And what is that I see in the middle of the ruins that, in this engraving, serve as their emblems? The symbols of the Catholic ministry and especially the standard of Christianity, the cross of Jesus-Christ! What?! Is that what you call *prejudices?*

The abbé was even more disturbed by what he perceived as the excellent reception the poem received from other intellectuals.[30]

By the time Grégoire published these remarks, Barlow had already begun to hear about his friend's anger from mutual acquaintances; he tried to mend fences by sending Grégoire a personal letter, in which he argued that his friend had misinterpreted the poem. "I am pained to tears," he wrote, "and my heart bleeds, to learn from Mr. Warden that my poem wounded your religious principles, which I respect as much as you do yourself. Nothing was further from my heart. . . ."[31]

Once Grégoire's letter was translated into English and began to be reprinted widely in American newspapers, though, Barlow worried that the critique was damaging his public standing. Indeed, one scholar of Barlow has argued that, although Barlow was a deist, he feared that his political views would be ignored if his full opposition to Christianity was known. He therefore published a separate open response to Grégoire in September 1809. Regarding the famous engraving, he swore that it was inserted into his book without his ever having seen it. In fact, Barlow insisted, he had defended the true principles of morality and virtue in a more powerful manner than "all the writings of christian authors of the three last ages, whom you have cited as the glory of christendom." His poem was hardly deist, he claimed, but reflected "the genuine principles, practice, faith and hope of the christian system, as inculcated in the gospels and explained by the apostles. . . ." Using a language of natural religion, he insisted that any religious differences between him and his friend were only on the surface.[32]

Despite proclaiming their fundamental agreement, however, Barlow suggested several key differences between the two men. First, he underlined a major disparity in how he and his friend saw the world: Grégoire, he felt, was confusing the core values of Christianity and its outward symbols, viewing an attack on the physical emblems of the Catholic Church as an assault on the Gospels. Secondly, Barlow turned the tables on Grégoire's analysis of the French Revolution's failure. Where the abbé had blamed the violence of the Terror on anti-Christian excess, Barlow insisted that it was the Catholic Church's overemphasis during the Old Regime on ceremonies and symbols that had led to Frenchmen's ignorance of true religious principles. If the Catholic Church had not accustomed the French people to worshipping icons, Barlow contended, they would not have built the "golden calf" of their goddess of reason nor launched dechristianization.[33]

Barlow was particularly concerned about the damage the controversy was causing to his reputation, because Grégoire's letter was circulated much more widely than his own response. As one prominent friend of Barlow's wrote him from Vermont, "The Bishop's letter has been read and applauded thro[ughout] this part of the country. Yours has not been published in the papers." Friends elsewhere in the country promised Barlow that they were working to persuade local newspapers to insert it but had not yet been successful. Even a New York press that published Grégoire's *Observations* together with Barlow's response made sure to praise Grégoire's comments on Christianity: "To the enlightened liberal christian, the critical remarks of the bishop Grégoire on the Columbiad will not fail of being highly pleasing."[34]

Despite his frustration with Barlow, Grégoire was dismayed when he learned that newspapers were portraying his friend as an atheist, which he knew him not to be. In a personal letter responding to Barlow's open one, he continued to call the American "my dear friend," and acknowledged Barlow's regret about the notorious engraving: "I am more persuaded than ever that you did not intend the least offense to your Catholic brother." Moreover, he apologized for the way in which his *Observations* had been used to discredit Barlow's integrity and that of Republicans more generally. "I view with sadness," he wrote, "that, in America, you have enemies who are not personal ones but political ones, who abuse my letter to you to denigrate you, to divert attention away from their misdeeds." He cited his own experience being vilified for his beliefs and tried to console his friend.[35]

While accepting Barlow's lack of malice, however, the former bishop did not retreat from his attack on the poem's religious content. "I persist," he wrote, "in all that my *Observations* said on the subject of religion." He insisted that Barlow had been the one confusing the essence of religion with its outward appearance; he argued that corruption was not the essence of the Catholic Church but a "parasitic plant" attacking it. Moreover, Grégoire countered Barlow's critique of Catholicism with one of Protestantism. Grégoire saw Protestantism as dangerous precisely because it "authoriz[es] each individual to interpret the Bible as he pleases."[36]

Despite their best efforts to work through this disagreement, the friendship between the men was never again the same. As deeply as they shared a commitment to republicanism, tolerance, and antislavery, Grégoire and Barlow could not agree on theological matters. Grégoire saw the ideal republic as Catholic, while his American friend found Catholic iconography and "idol-worship" to be inimical to free thought.

Though Grégoire would prove to have an important influence on American abolitionism and on the rise of African-American historiography in the long term, the controversy had a chilling effect in the short term on his efforts to influence the United States. Though some Federalists praised his critique of Barlow, he had little in common with these men otherwise, since they tended towards staunch anti-Jacobinism. Though Republicans' views of the French Revolution were more positive, Grégoire's *Observations* ended up distancing him from many of them. Men like Jefferson found in his public attacks on Barlow a reason to remain distant from the French priest. Indeed, Jefferson commiserated with Barlow in 1809 over what he called Grégoire's "diatribe to you," and said the abbé "did not deserve" Barlow's apologetic response.[37] The controversy thus left the French priest isolated from most of those on whom he hoped to have an influence.

Religion and slavery were two other important issues that divided Grégoire from many Americans. Most American republicans did not see the abolition of slavery as essential; whereas their French counterparts had decreed the abolition of slavery only two years after proclaiming their republic, it would take more than seventy years—and a civil war—for the Americans to do the same. Most Americans also did not share Grégoire's religious beliefs. His attack on deism was hardly appealing to deists in the American intellectual and political elite; meanwhile, those closest to him in matters of faith, like the Catholic bishop John Carroll, viewed his Jacobinism and Gallicanism with suspicion.[38]

One might have expected Grégoire to have more in common with Latin American republicans, since the majority of them were Catholics and many of them were Gallican sympathizers. He would in fact find much support there, with many republicans anxious to realize his vision of a free New World. Nevertheless, though religion and politics united him with Latin American republicans, attitudes toward slavery often did not; abolition would take even longer in many Latin American countries than in the United States. Grégoire would continue to monitor issues important to him in North and South America, such as religion, slavery, and the status of republican government; he and Mme Dubois would receive visitors from both continents until his death. Grégoire found, however, that Atlantic networking could have frustrations as well as joys. While his republican ideas continued to find new adherents, his vision of Catholic republican abolitionism remained largely idiosyncratic.

The white republics of the United States and Latin America were not the only hopes for republicanism in the New World, however. In the next chapter, we will look at Grégoire's ties with Haiti, which began in earnest after the Barlow controversy and the return of the Bourbons. With the right decisions by leaders there, worldwide regeneration—and the spread of universalist Catholic republicanism—might still be possible.

CHAPTER 8

Exporting the Revolution

The Colonial Laboratory in Haiti

May the Heavens allow that . . . one day liberty will cross
the Atlantic and come to vaccinate politically this decrepit
Europe, where we have *dreamed* of liberty.

— Grégoire, 1825

Despite his turn to the Americas in the nineteenth century, Grégoire had
not completely lost faith in the Old World. From 1797 to 1805, he had
traveled extensively in Europe, investigating the status of republicanism,
religion, and scholarly pursuits. He made like-minded contacts from
England to Denmark, reconnected with old heroes like Lavater, and had
a chance to meet new ones, such as Goethe (with whom he delighted in
passing what he later recalled as some "delicious moments"). The abbé
also discovered that he had many foreign admirers, even if newspapers
abroad occasionally noted his visits with displeasure. After his travels
ended, correspondence with his new acquaintances sustained him. In the
wake of the Bourbon return in 1814, for example, he told a Swiss friend,
Paul Usteri, of his hopes that "the Heavens will allow your country to
serve always as the asylum of liberty." He also made plans for an international network of republican scholars and worked with other European abolitionists.[1] Nevertheless, Grégoire was greatly pessimistic
about the future of republicanism in Europe, at least for the period of
his own lifetime, since the majority of his former comrades had long
since abandoned their revolutionary hopes. By 1821, he therefore told a
Dutch acquaintance that correspondence with the New World "absorbs
all my time."[2]

Within the Americas, the Haitian republic seemed to Grégoire the
most promising site for preserving and perfecting the Revolution's
legacy. Unlike the United States, Haiti had abolished slavery, and its

leaders professed Catholicism. Unlike the Jews, Grégoire believed, the Haitians did not already have a civilization and deeply rooted preju- dices; they represented a tabula rasa. Finally, in contrast to Latin Amer- ica, Haiti's political leaders of African descent offered proof of his longtime contention that people of color could be intelligent human beings capable of self-government. If the republican experiment worked in Haiti, Grégoire reasoned, it might be reimplanted in Europe and exported worldwide. Starved for information about the state of affairs in the young West Indian nation, Grégoire began to correspond with the men and women who composed Haiti's intellectual and political elite.

Grégoire's involvement with Haiti during the Restoration has much to teach us about his vision of regeneration for the world during these years, since Haiti was the beacon *(phare)* that would spread light to all other nations, including France. "Free Haiti," Grégoire noted, "is a bea- con elevated from the Antilles toward which slaves and their masters, oppressed and oppressors, turn their gaze."[3] Grégoire's Haitian involve- ment also yields a fascinating glimpse into the complexities of abolition- ists' relationships with those they wanted to help. Grégoire was more progressive than his contemporaries in many ways. Even as his compa- triots attacked him for his "Negrophilia" and treated Haiti as an out- law nation, he applauded Haitian independence and thirsted for reports on the progress of civilization in Haiti. Although the abbé supported non-European peoples' efforts to resist colonialism, however, parts of his work helped provide ideological support for that colonialism and reinforced their international subservience. Grégoire's relationship with Haiti also sheds light on the legacy of the Revolution itself, by further demonstrating the links between revolutionary universalism and the nineteenth-century idea of the white man's burden.

Indeed, one of Grégoire's main aims in his Haitian involvement was to spread "civilization" to non-European peoples. He recognized, how- ever, that such an endeavor could be counterproductive. As he wrote a European friend in Africa in 1815, "Without a doubt, the most difficult problem to resolve would be how to appropriate all the advantages of European civilization, without including the vicious and hideous parts. European civilization has done much for the spirit, but often it has fal- sified judgment and perverted reason. The education of the heart has especially been neglected or deteriorated."[4] Though Grégoire felt that Haiti's troubles had been caused by the negative aspects of French civi- lization, he hoped these troubles could be reversed by exporting a bet- ter form of European civilization.

Although he proved very popular among Haitian leaders, however, here too he would sometimes find himself ignored. While Haiti's leaders professed Catholicism and admired Grégoire, they sometimes had different standards of personal behavior or different visions of the best course for Haiti's future. They would nevertheless see regeneration as an extremely powerful concept and adopt it as their own.

GRÉGOIRE, CLARKSON, AND THE NORTHERN MONARCHY

After the assassination of Emperor Dessalines in 1806, Haiti had split into two regimes: a black-led state in the north (run by Henry Christophe) and a military republic led by Alexandre Pétion and other people of mixed race *(métis)* in the south.[5] The north had become a monarchy in 1811 when Christophe declared himself King Henry I. Tension endured between the two states, with each vying for international recognition.

Christophe's foreign minister, the Comte de Limonade, asked Grégoire for help in 1814. Applauding the abbé's work on behalf of blacks, he reported that the king loved Grégoire's *De la littérature des nègres*. Christophe had "ordered from London *fifty* copies," and wanted "the most interesting passages to be inserted in the newspapers to introduce them to the Haitian people, particularly to the inhabitants of the countryside." De Limonade's letter was not merely adulatory; he hoped to persuade Grégoire to campaign for French recognition of his kingdom. He begged Grégoire to "raise his voice and publish" in support of the monarchy. Calling Grégoire Haiti's only European friend, he echoed the idea of regeneration:

> You, Monseigneur, have consecrated your whole life, your vigilance and your writings to effect the regeneration of the human species. . . . You are the only European who has had the courage to tell the truth without fear of attracting hate. . . . A new Las Casas, your name is pronounced among Haitians only with the eulogies that are due to the defender of the cause of liberty and unfortunate people. . . . The happiest day for my sovereign would be the day he could see you and press you to his heart.[6]

Was this sincere adulation or merely flattery aimed at winning Grégoire's support? It was probably a little of both. Grégoire was indeed one of the few Europeans to speak out for Haitians and people of color, and the northern kingdom desperately desired international recognition.

What is certain is that Grégoire refused to enter into correspondence with de Limonade and Christophe. Disgusted with the return of monarchy and hereditary aristocracy in France, Grégoire hardly wanted Haiti to follow the same path. Unlike modern historians who are inclined to sympathize with Christophe's kingdom rather than the southern republic (which has been viewed as an oligarchy of a few wealthy *métis* with no concern for the formerly enslaved poor), Grégoire could not see past Christophe's royalism.[7]

In an unpublished essay on the north's constitution, Grégoire sharply criticized its adoption of monarchy. He was appalled that, as much of the world was slowly adopting republican principles, the north of Haiti was abandoning them. He was especially incensed at the irony of blacks' creating a system based on arbitrary titles: "The nobility of parchment is just as absurd as the nobility of skin color, which the *colons* wanted to award only to the color white." He also condemned the monarchy's expensive public ceremonies for diverting money from the task of civilizing the former slaves. In addition, Grégoire blasted what he saw as the racist paternalism of the monarchy, whose apologists "say that a free government is more suitable for the situation of the southwest, where people of mixed race dominate, because in general civilization and enlightenment are more advanced among them than among the blacks, who are the great majority of the northern population." While agreeing that the *métis* had greater civilization than blacks, Grégoire countered that the latter's lack of education did not disqualify them from political rights. Distinguishing between civilization and common sense, Grégoire noted that even former slaves had enough sense to choose their own leaders.[8]

Whether this essay was ever sent to anyone in Haiti is unknown, though its archival location makes it probable.[9] But those in the north perceived Grégoire's hostility. As the north's chief propagandist, Baron de Vastey, complained in 1819, Grégoire, "praiseworthy as he is in many ways, has allowed himself to fall into grievous injustices toward us."[10]

Still, like de Limonade and other members of the northern elite, de Vastey had already adopted the idiom of regeneration. Though stung by Grégoire's hostility, they still saw themselves as spreading civilization to Africans and their work as regenerating the Haitian people. Nevertheless, de Vastey was ambivalent about this term even as he appropriated it. Though he felt that Haitians needed to spread the civilization they had learned from Europeans to Africans, de Vastey disputed the view that whites were superior to blacks. He used natural history against whites and identified *them* as degenerate: "When the race of an animal whitens, this is a proof of degeneration."[11]

The leaders of the north found themselves in a bind that would befall many postcolonial leaders. Foreigners like Grégoire had encouraged them to abandon their traditional ways and to emulate European customs. But which European customs should they emulate? Christophe and his aides had hedged their bets incorrectly and cast their lot with the wrong European model. Instead of being praised for acculturating so completely to European ideals, the leaders of the north found themselves subject to Grégoire's scorn.

Not all European abolitionists shared Grégoire's instinctive opposition to the Haitian monarchy, however. After being rejected by the man they called Haiti's only European friend, the leaders of the north approached Thomas Clarkson, the leading English abolitionist. Unlike Grégoire, Clarkson accepted the role of advisor with pleasure, offering Christophe counsel on everything from international strategy to domestic administration. As an English subject, he felt more comfortable with Christophe's monarchy than with the republicans in the south; for him, Christophe had chosen precisely the right model.[12]

Clarkson and Christophe soon came into conflict on a key issue, however: Haitian sovereignty in negotiations with France. While Christophe pleaded with Clarkson to persuade England to be the first European nation to recognize his kingdom, Clarkson insisted that England could only follow France. His advice (that Haiti pay an indemnity to France for nationalizing its property and treat the Bourbons as nominal sovereigns) met with insistent refusal from Christophe. But Clarkson, astonished at Christophe's unwillingness to compromise, would not relay the Haitian's messages to the French court, fearful that he would be ejected.[13]

After Christophe committed suicide during a revolt in 1820, the north was absorbed into a single Haitian republic under General Jean-Pierre Boyer, who had replaced Pétion in 1818. As Clarkson's correspondence with the king faced a sudden end, he tried to sustain his ability to help Haiti by contacting Boyer; he insisted that the only reason he had corresponded with the north instead of the south was that "you never asked me to do it." He urged that Christophe's widow and daughters be treated well.[14]

Yet Clarkson's overtures faced a chilly reception. Boyer declined further relations, noting that "a long series of misfortunes has taught us that only we can guarantee our rights." Haitians had to be selective in choosing their friends, even among abolitionists. When Boyer dispatched Christophe's widow and daughters to England to live with Clarkson, the abolitionist was caught by surprise; he revealed an ambivalence toward the people he was happy to defend from afar.

Though his initial apprehensions disappeared when he found them "delightful" and "enlightened," he reported that even longtime abolitionists like William Wilberforce evinced a "sort of shrink at admitting them into high society." Those who had advocated abolition were not always ready for its consequences: the romanticized icons whose enslavement they had denounced (like the kneeling, enchained African slave represented on a famous abolitionist medallion) now revealed themselves as men of flesh and blood, determined to chart their own course.[15]

GRÉGOIRE AND THE REPUBLIC OF THE SOUTH

Despite their rebuff of Clarkson, Boyer and his lieutenants were delighted to correspond with Grégoire, whose loyalty to their cause was unquestioned. Even before Christophe's fall, Grégoire had been a magnet for Haitians, whether through correspondence or through visits to Paris. The grand judge of Haiti instructed his sister in 1818 that she should try to meet the abbé while in Paris. Noël Colombel, chief secretary to President Boyer, wrote Grégoire in 1819 that he would never forget the warm reception Grégoire had given him in Paris many years before, when Colombel was an unknown. A firm believer in regeneration, he recalled his delight at hearing the abbé's opinion that "the Haitian nation is raising itself to the level of current civilization." General B. Inginac, another of Boyer's closest advisors, swore to Grégoire in 1820 that those in Haiti were hungry for news about him. "We console ourselves," he declared, "in the hope of soon seeing the image of the new Las Casas." Inginac reported that Boyer had purchased a copy of Grégoire's portrait and that a public collection was being taken for a second copy to be placed in the Salle du Gouvernement. Boyer's admiration for Grégoire extended even deeper; in 1818, he invited Grégoire to be the bishop of Haiti, an invitation Grégoire declined on account of his advanced age.[16]

What did these Haitians hope to receive from Grégoire? Certainly not the kind of international legitimacy Christophe had sought from Clarkson. As his Haitian correspondents did not fail to recognize, Grégoire was now an outcast in France, the subject of endless attacks. He occasionally helped them by ordering provisions for them from sympathetic merchants in France, and he sometimes helped in recommending priests and scientists when they requested his aid. Moreover, in 1818, he sent them two hundred French religious books to form a small library. They more than reciprocated, however, sending expensive gifts like coffee, inviting him to be the official biographer of Toussaint Louverture, and exuding enthusiasm at his every response.[17]

Why were they so enthusiastic? On one level, they were genuinely grateful for his writings on their behalf, particularly in contrast with other Europeans who portrayed Haitians as brutal savages. On another, while the idea of regeneration began to seem suspicious in monarchical France, Haitian elites found it to be a politically potent tool; it gave them a framework with which to legitimate their rule. If progress was to be made by spreading Western civilization, then only the wealthy, well-educated, and mostly mixed-race elite of the south could be leaders. The former slaves, though more numerous, could only hope to imitate and learn from them. Claiming Grégoire as the father figure of the south, as Pierre Buteau has noted, also helped preserve the myth that Boyer's government was republican, despite its oligarchic reality.[18]

Pictures of Grégoire thus hung in many government buildings, and calls for regeneration abounded in southern writings. To cite only a few, the pro-Boyer newspaper *La Concorde,* which lauded Grégoire's works like other Haitian newspapers, included an assurance from a Haitian deputy to his constituents that the government "has taken to heart the work of Haitian regeneration" and that all officials were "working arduously to attain this goal." Another paper, *Le Phare* (which took its name from Grégoire's quote about Haiti's future), frequently called for a "complete regeneration" of Haitian society and boasted about "the successive progress of civilization [making] itself felt in all the classes of Haitian society." In a line that Grégoire would cite approvingly, the Haitian author Desrivières-Chanlatte predicted that "Haiti, long ago called the *Queen of the Antilles,* will become the center of civilization, enlightenment and liberty in this regenerated archipelago." Government leaders from Boyer on down spoke urgently of regeneration and the need to spread civilization in Haiti.[19]

What did Grégoire want in turn from the Haitian leaders? His letter of June 22, 1821 to Boyer displays many of the complexities of his relationship with Haiti. Unlike Clarkson, who instructed Christophe on all manner of topics, Grégoire professed awkwardness about interfering in internal Haitian matters. "Certainly," he noted in this letter, "I have no right to insinuate myself into your government." He refrained from offering advice about politics, administration, or diplomacy. Also unlike Clarkson, Grégoire emphasized his admiration for Haitians' hard-won independence and his profound identification with them. The very existence of the Haitian republic, he declared, was a "victorious response to

all the fallacies spread in Europe against the children of Africa." Unable
to live in the world he had dreamed of creating in France, Grégoire imagined himself a citizen of this new republic. Like them, he had felt the
sting of persecution, and he promised to help them until his dying day.[20]

Still, at the risk of angering Boyer, Grégoire could not restrain himself from offering advice on moral and religious matters. He clearly envisioned himself in the role he would lay out in his *Histoire des confesseurs
des empereurs, des rois, et d'autres princes*; in this work, which he sent
to Boyer, he applauded priests who had courageously told rulers
unpalatable truths instead of toadying to them, thus adding a moral
influence to political affairs. Portraying himself as an older and wiser
man, he appealed to Boyer not to divorce morality from politics. He
insisted that "religion, the object most dear to my heart . . . , is the fundamental rock of all society." Moral matters were the heart of Haitian
civil strife, as he saw it.[21]

In subsequent writings, Grégoire called Boyer's attention to issues he
thought were preventing harmony on the island. When he heard that
Methodist missionaries had been pelted with rocks, Grégoire dashed off
an essay in favor of religious tolerance. Instead of seeing the issue as one
of Haitians repelling foreign provocateurs (a key problem in Haiti), the
former bishop reminded Boyer that the French revolutionaries had
granted citizenship to "Jews, Protestants and Anabaptists." In fact, during the French Revolution, the abbé had called for fiercely wiping out
any hint of counterrevolution and for banning foreigners from clerical
positions. Now, however, he instructed Boyer that foreigners should
have free run to spread their ideas in Haiti. "Persecuting men for their
religious opinions is not only an injustice and a crime," he maintained,
but also stupid and weak. He saw the situation wholly in terms of European religious quarrels, not recognizing Haitians' attempts to retain
their own religious practices and to prevent being reconquered. Grégoire
also pleaded with Boyer to respect the intelligence of the common man
by adopting a jury system, something he saw as essential to republican
government but which had been "defaced" in France.[22]

More importantly, Grégoire directed Boyer's attention to the same
issue he had long condemned among whites: skin-color prejudice, or
what he would elsewhere call the *noblesse de peau*. Saddened by reports
of discrimination by people of mixed race against blacks and whites,
Grégoire urged Boyer to take measures to prevent the "eruption of hate
between the colors." No divisions should be allowed to arise among
Haitians, "whatever the nuances of their skin." Grégoire's concern with

skin-color prejudice stemmed directly from his religious beliefs. Though he had for years followed Enlightenment debates about natural history and race, he was frustrated with both sides on the question of human origins. On the one hand, he denounced the idea propounded by Voltaire and other writers that distinct races existed. On the other hand, he was irritated by the other side in these debates; years of scholarly inquiry had yielded nothing more advanced than Buffon's argument that all men belonged to a common species, something Grégoire believed to be evident from Genesis.[23]

Grégoire thus used a family metaphor in several writings he composed for a Haitian readership. In his *Manuel de piété,* aimed at creating a Haitian liturgy, Grégoire spoke of "men of all colors emanating from a single stem, created by the same God, equally redeemed by the blood of Jesus Christ, equally called to the Eucharistic table." In his *Considérations sur le mariage et le divorce adressés aux citoyens d'Haïti,* he proclaimed that "men of all colors" should recognize that they were "all brothers before a common father."[24]

Centuries of colonial adventurism by whites had destroyed this family, however, and no one remembered its existence. The former bishop of Loir-et-Cher did not place the blame for the colonial morass on missionaries; in fact, he felt that Christianity had an undeservedly bad reputation for its racial track record. He continued to feel, however, as he had during the Revolution, that irreligious *colons* and the French legal system had wreaked havoc in the Antilles: "European libertinage, spread throughout the Antilles, left hideous traces and habits of disorder."[25]

To rectify these negative aspects of the European legacy, Grégoire proposed many remedies, including one long favored by him: education. Even as he had become more pessimistic about human perfectibility in the post-Terror years, he still believed that educating citizens was a fundamental republican value, essential for ending social divisions. He was fascinated by the new Lycée national in Haiti, corresponded with educators, and sent books for Haitian students.[26]

Just as Grégoire had decided during the Directory that education alone could not rebuild a society, however, he also advocated the widespread adoption of Christianity. With its message of universal love and redemption, Grégoire believed, Christianity could console the unfortunate and make men stop hating each other. He was particularly interested in the development of an indigenous clergy. Never acknowledging voodoo, which combined West African religious elements and Christian rituals, he insisted that Haitians were simply not sufficiently converted. He cited as common knowledge that "men of mixed race and blacks love the pomp of Catholic solemnities and religious ceremonies." He instructed the Haitians that ceremony was only the exterior form of Christianity and that they needed to observe its other precepts.[27]

Education and true religiosity would take time and could not be achieved by government action alone, however. Looking beyond government action, Grégoire focused on the family, which represented the most important site for regeneration. Holy matrimony was the all-important bedrock of society, the best safeguard of Christian values and a stable polity, while divorce was as unthinkable as promiscuity.[28] Boyer himself, living in concubinage, was hardly an ideal audience for Grégoire's plea to wipe out all extramarital relationships. Grégoire persisted nonetheless in his battle to eradicate all but church-sanctified monogamy.

Grégoire was not concerned only with couples' marrying and remaining together, however. He had specific instructions to offer on the content of spousal roles. Women, he insisted, needed to act as civilizing forces on their husbands and sons. Though many Haitian mixed-race women had long become accustomed to independence in business and personal affairs, Grégoire directed them to assume their natural civilizing roles. If they did not enforce morality and spread civilization, no one would.[29]

As we have seen, Grégoire had in the past displayed a mostly negative attitude toward women's participation in public life. During the Revolution, he scapegoated pious peasant women for the problems the Revolution was encountering and depicted city women as immoral and dangerous. He also argued for the exclusion of women from political debates, even while insisting on the inclusion of Jews, patois-speakers, and people of color. During the Directory, he blamed "villainous and seditious women" for blocking his Constitutional Church.[30]

At the same time, Grégoire's general pronouncements on women had been moderated by a number of factors, and he differed from Jacobins who believed categorically that women should be limited to roles as mothers. For one thing, though he certainly resented the nuns of Loir-et-Cher who had supported Thémines, he admired the charitable efforts of other nuns, whose lives were by definition built around functions other than marriage and motherhood. Especially in the years after the Revolution when his Jansenist sympathies became most evident, he held a special fondness for the sisters of Port-Royal. Grégoire's love for learning had also offset his overall feelings about women's immorality and lack of intelligence. Despite his denunciations of women in general, he had come to make exceptions for a number of individual women who made contributions to scholarship; he developed good relationships with them and even recommended some for government scholarly pensions. His longtime friendship with Mme Dubois may also have tempered his views on women's inferiority, at least to some extent, as is hinted in his letters to her while traveling abroad.[31]

Grégoire even talked occasionally of a world in which gender inequality would be erased, in which what we might call a *noblesse de sexe* would be eliminated along with the *noblesse de peau*. In an essay on Christian doctrine, for example, the abbé collapsed several favorite biblical passages into one, portraying a future egalitarian world with all arbitrary distinctions erased: there would be "neither Greek nor Gentile, neither Scythian nor Barbarian, neither circumcised persons nor uncircumcised persons, *neither men nor women,* neither serfs nor freemen" (emphasis added). He continued, "You are all one in Jesus Christ; you are all brothers." As far back as 1788, Grégoire had argued that the way women were treated was "the measure of the progress of a nation in civic life."[32] In these instances, Grégoire's universalism seemed to imply that gender prejudice should be abolished along with all other kinds of prejudice. Such thinking would hardly have been impossible for a man of his time, particularly one who during the Revolution had gravitated to the same circles as Mary Wollstonecraft and who had read her *Vindication of the Rights of Woman*.[33]

Grégoire's admiration for certain individual women and his abstract proclamations of human equality, however, were dwarfed by his more common mode of discussing women: attacking them for interfering in— and thus creating havoc in—public life. In the nineteenth century and particularly in his *Histoire des sectes religieuses,* he continued to complain about the risks that women posed to society. Despite his biblical references to a genderless world with "neither men nor women," women's equal participation in French public life still seemed to him too dangerous.[34]

Despite his belief in most women's inaptitude for participation in European public life, Grégoire spoke differently about the situation in Haiti. While still not advocating political equality or seeing women as capable of complete regeneration, he nevertheless felt that Haitian women had certain duties essential to the country's future. Because of Haiti's perilously low level of civilization and its generations of men accustomed to violence, he decided, women needed to act as peacemakers and civilizers. If they neglected to exercise these roles, Grégoire suggested, Haiti could never recover from the debilitating effects of colonialism. Haitian women were hardly angels, he felt, but they had not become as corrupted as their white sisters; if most women were currently

immoral, that was a perversion of their true nature. Altering his pronouncements about women's basic inferiority, Grégoire began to speak
instead of gender complementarity. Women "have more aptitude than
men" for charity, he told Haitian women. Moreover, "as the gentler and
more sensitive half of humankind, it is up to you most of all to purify
morals, to make them loved and respected by your examples." He
appealed to Haitian women to be the enforcers of chastity, since uncon-
trolled sexuality had sparked so much immorality in Saint-Domingue.[35]

Grégoire also appealed to Haitian women to help educate their children, and argued in turn for the improvement of women's education. As
he had argued in the Jacobin Club during the Revolution, Grégoire
insisted that to teach her children, woman herself needed an education
"corresponding to the goal of the Creator and to her destination in society." In the 1820s, Grégoire denounced contemporaries who did not recognize that ignorant women would transmit vice; critiquing Rousseau
and others, he complained that in "what is abusively called *education*"
for women, "the useful is sacrificed to the agreeable." At the same time,
when Grégoire wrote to women in Haiti, he did not forward the same
books on political and social issues that he sent their male countrymen;
he only recommended religious books appropriate for their sex.[36]

A final domain in which women needed to reclaim their natural roles
was in religion. Despite his earlier complaints about fanatically religious
women (complaints that would reappear in the *Histoire des sectes
religieuses*), Grégoire very much wanted women to help spread Christianity in Haiti—provided they carefully obeyed the clergy. Women
would be the first point of entry for true Christianity in Haiti, he hoped;
since it protected them more than their "savage" systems had, they
would be deeply grateful to Christians for having rescued them. Grégoire's letters to Haitian women—but not to men—are marked by
requests that they pray. Grégoire would make clear his displeasure when
he felt they had not fulfilled this duty, and he denounced the way elite
Haitian women were resisting a European missionary in Port-au-Prince.
While he encouraged their establishment of a charitable society, he was
also upset by reports that several members avoided going to church.[37]

Even as Grégoire moved to distance himself from the Enlightenment,
he still drew on its ideas, even without always knowing it. Here, he
seems to have been reprising an Enlightenment discourse that viewed
woman, in Dena Goodman's words, as "a civilizing force . . . : the benign
force that brings out what is noble in men and suppresses not only their
brutality, but their hostility toward each other, thus making them both

civil and civilized."[38] This attitude could have a positive cast. By speaking of women as better at certain roles, Grégoire gave them crucial (if restricted) standing in society-building. To bring men of all races together, stop them from fighting, and help them progress, Grégoire's suggestions implied, women's efforts were essential.

Alongside the empowering possibilities of this portrayal, however, Grégoire hardly ceased representing women as potentially dangerous. He argued that white women in the colonies often "deny the natural goodness of their sex [and] are more cruel toward Negroes than men." He also portrayed women as potential adulteresses who would go astray from their husbands and break up the family. Moreover, he called any women who would not breastfeed their children or fulfill the other duties he assigned them "cruel."[39]

These comments seemed to suggest that, if women were left out of the business of society-building, white and black men could band together and unite. Women had an important role to play, but only by abandoning their independent roles and returning to their natural civilizing ones. Paralleling what Joan Scott has observed about the function of gender during the National Convention, Grégoire thus used gender differentiation to facilitate the abolition of racial differentiation.[40]

But even women's influence within their families would not be enough to sustain a stable, harmonious society. Another ingredient was necessary: interracial marriage. As in the 1780s, Grégoire argued that interracial marriages could restore harmony among men—not simply returning Haiti to an idealized precolonial world, but also moving the world forward. Echoing Buffon, Grégoire argued that the new race would be better than either blacks or whites separately had been. "All the physiologists attest," he asserted, "that the crossed races are together more robust." He dreamed that the new mixed race could farm the land and learn advanced agricultural technologies far better than either race had done separately. Interracial marriage would remain at the heart of Grégoire's conception of global regeneration. In addition to improving Jews and Africans, he hoped it could solve tensions between Greeks and Turks, unite French Protestants and Catholics, and bring civilization to India by joining European men with Hindu women.[41]

"HAÏTIENS, ADIEU!"

Grégoire would soon discover that his pupils had minds of their own. When Boyer began to receive overtures from previously hostile European

governments in the mid 1820s, some Haitian leaders were quick to distance themselves from Grégoire, referring to him as a lemon whose juice
had been squeezed. When representatives of Charles X came to Port-au-
Prince, Boyer quickly removed the portrait of Grégoire that hung in the
presidential palace. Moreover, a toast to Grégoire at the state dinner welcoming the French was suppressed from the government newspaper.[42]

Despondent at being abandoned by those for whom he had suffered
ostracism at home, Grégoire wrote a bitter *Epître aux Haïtiens,* which the
Haitian government was charitable enough to print and distribute in
1827. He claimed that, at the risk of persecution at home, he had always
tried to help Haitians enjoy the rule of law and the benefits of civilization.
He noted that his right to intervene in their affairs derived solely from their
confidence in him and that he had offered his opinions only after being
invited to do so. He had tried to guide them on the right moral path; liken-
ing himself to the prophet Samuel, he noted that he might not always have
told them what they wanted to hear. And he harped again on the marriage
theme, implicitly criticizing Boyer. Even as he removed himself from direct
involvement in Haitian affairs, however, he promised he would always
remember them in his prayers. "I have ardent wishes for your spiritual
happiness and your temporal prosperity," he noted. "But I regret not
being able to raise my hopes to the level of my desires, on either count.
Haïtiens, adieu!" On his deathbed, his final words reportedly included the
exclamation, "*Pauvres haïtiens!* [Poor Haitians]."[43]

Nevertheless, since his death Grégoire has been remembered with
fondness by many members of the elite in Haiti, even those oriented
toward ideas of *négritude.* The anonymous editor of Grégoire's *Epître*
claimed that Grégoire must have been misinformed about the lemon
comment because of "the sentiments of recognition and veneration"
that the vast majority of Haitians felt towards him. Haitians erected a
statue to the abbé in the nineteenth century, and an elite academy was
named the Collège Grégoire. According to Jean Price-Mars, the statesman and "dean of Haitian intellectuals," who has been called the father
of *négritude,* Haitians "always devoted a fervent cult to his memory."
Even now, the main shopping street in Pétionville (a wealthy suburb of
Port-au-Prince) is called Rue Grégoire.[44]

THE LIMITS OF GRÉGOIRE'S UNIVERSALISM

Was Grégoire in fact a prophet of *négritude* and an anticolonial militant? David Brion Davis and others have complicated the notion of

abolitionists as disinterested moral paragons by showing how many abolitionists benefited from their opposition to slavery and continued to have hierarchical worldviews.[45] As we have seen, Grégoire was more progressive than many other abolitionists in several ways, including his support for Haitian sovereignty, his respectful attitude toward its leaders, and his intolerance for skin-color prejudice.

It would not, however, be accurate to see him as an unqualified opponent of colonialism or an advocate of "Haitian culture." Certainly, Grégoire had problems with European civilization; following Raynal and others, he questioned whether European immorality really was an improvement over savage mores. Moreover, he hardly wanted Haitians and other non-Europeans to parrot the depravity of fashionable European society.[46] Although he had doubts about certain aspects of European civilization, however, Grégoire thought it was non-Western peoples' only hope for salvation. Indeed, his idea of regeneration and calls for civilization reinforced the prejudicial ideas he detested about nonwhites, for they implied that Haitians were presently degenerate and savage. Where Vastey had argued that the whites who had enslaved his people were the degenerate ones, Grégoire continued to insist that Haitians needed to follow Europeans.

Moreover, even as he tried to empower Haitians, Grégoire depicted them as almost entirely passive. Any problems existing in Haitian society had come from the *colons*; once these corruptions had been expunged, the empty-vessel Haitians could be refilled with new and better ideas from Europe. Only then could these "children of Africa" start down the path toward a happy future. Creole and voodoo, both efforts to retain elements of traditional culture, thus appeared to him only as corruptions of French and Christianity that needed to be wiped out.[47]

Another irony of Grégoire's Haitian involvement was that his well-intentioned efforts to help the weakest members of Haitian society may have done the opposite. Grégoire's republicanism precluded him from sympathizing with Christophe, yet many modern historians argue that his monarchy was actually more progressive than the south's republican oligarchy. Vaval claimed that Boyer lied to Grégoire, kept his books from the public, and falsified reports of increasing education.[48] At a time when the *anciens libres* (primarily mixed-race and upper-class Haitians who had been free before the Revolution) were vastly outnumbered by *nouveaux libres* (primarily black), Grégoire's idea of regeneration and his support for Boyer may have served to deepen the political and cultural disenfranchisement of the latter group.

An additional discrepancy concerns what Grégoire really thought about race. Though he often denounced racial generalizations, he sometimes resorted to biological racial theorizing. When he spoke of interracial marriage, for example, he resorted to a physiognomic discourse that treated it as an advantageous mixture of two species. Grégoire seems to have believed that Haitians could be improved only by losing their racial particularity.

We should also remember that Grégoire was not as unequivocally anticolonialist as legend would have it. Though he supported Haitian independence after it happened, he had earlier participated in efforts to keep the colonies firmly in the French orbit. He supported colonialism while the metropole was run by republicans like himself, moving closer to an anti-imperial stance only after Napoleon broke with revolutionary principles (and again when the Bourbons returned to power).[49]

Recognizing these aspects of Grégoire's thinking does not necessitate condemning him on colonial issues or seeing him as a manipulative and false friend. At the risk of social ostracism, which followed him to his deathbed, Grégoire courageously gave aid to Haitians when few others would. It is important to note, however, the complexities of his universalism and his relationship with non-Europeans. While Grégoire wanted racial differences to be wiped out, a key way to abolish them was by reinforcing gender differences and the exclusion of women from political life. While he fervently desired to help Haitians enjoy their sovereignty, his idea of regeneration put them in a state of long-term tutelage.[50] The universal human family that Grégoire sought to build would ultimately place Europeans and other peoples in brotherhood. These other peoples would have to abandon their cultures and adopt the republican Christian values of Europeans like Grégoire, however, before they could belong. Until then, they remained younger brothers in the family, subject to perpetual advice from their older siblings.

Compounding the ambiguities of Grégoire's positions during his own time, his words took on a double life after his death. Regeneration and the idea of philanthropic colonization helped supply later colonialists with some of the ideological tools necessary to justify their actions, allowing them to claim that they were not exploiting the colonies but spreading the benefits of Western civilization.[51] Grégoire's vision of wiping out dialects and his elevation of French as the only language of unity and culture would provide a key element of French imperialist cultural policy, from Africa to Indochina. Regeneration also forced colonized peoples forever to play catch-up, to measure their own progress by their conformity to European standards.

FIGURE 7. "The Benefits of the Printing Press in Africa" by David d'Angers (c. 1840). Depicts Clarkson, Condorcet, and Grégoire bringing a printing press to the shores of Africa, to grateful enchained Africans. Photograph courtesy of Betje B. Klier.

Indeed, although anticolonialists championed Grégoire, he would also be seen as a forefather by proponents of colonialism. A sample of how Grégoire could be used in a colonial context comes from a 1931 speech at a school run by the Franco-Jewish Alliance Israélite Universelle in Rabat, Morocco. Teacher Y. D. Sémach invoked Grégoire to suggest that Moroccan Jews had a duty to be faithful to France; he traced the founding of the paracolonial Alliance—and the introduction of French in Morocco—to Grégoire's ideas:

> French Jews, free and happy, heirs of his [Grégoire's] thought, would work in the future for uplifting their coreligionists in other countries. Thus the Alliance Israélite was founded in Paris in 1860, to emancipate the Jews. Through its schools, it would spur the spread of the *idée française* by popularizing the French language which Grégoire sought to universalize.
>
> In Morocco, the Alliance was the first to teach French. Like the Jews of France once, like the Jews of Algeria yesterday, Moroccan Jews today have only one desire: to elevate themselves to the dignity of citizens and to serve the country which liberated them.[52]

Sculptor Pierre David d'Angers's bas-relief, *Les bienfaits de l'imprimerie en Afrique* (The Benefits of the Printing Press in Africa, c. 1840; fig. 7), similarly displays the ambiguities latent in Grégoire's idea of regeneration, even as it celebrates his involvement with Haiti. Rather than praise the abbé for recognizing Haiti's independence, d'Angers made him the model for a philanthropic colonial adventurism that would carry civilization to infantilized peoples. The contradictions of Grégoire's involvement with Haiti thus encapsulate the two sides of the Revolution's international legacy. Like the Revolution, he provided inspiration for liberation movements around the world but also helped create renewed justification for colonial expansion.

CHAPTER 9

Christian Apologetics and the Universal Human Family

Despite occasional frustrations, Grégoire remained an activist in world politics until his death. In addition to New World republicanism, he used his money and pen to support the rights of Catholics in Ireland, republicans in Europe, and enslaved Africans throughout the world; he worked on these issues with like-minded young intellectuals and artists (like David d'Angers) and older friends (like Lafayette). One 1828 visitor noted that Grégoire—then seventy-eight—was "as active as a twenty-year-old," while another marveled that he must have found a way to "have more than twenty-four hours" in a day.[1] Despite growing skeptical about the possibility of social regeneration, he continued to hope that, with God's help, mankind could be regenerated into a united Catholic family.

In addition to his international campaigns, Grégoire continued his scholarly pursuits. His histories continued to have political and religious goals, in that he hoped to influence his contemporaries and leave a record of his ideas for future generations. Two of his longest and most neglected works from this period, the *Histoire des sectes religieuses* and the *De l'influence du christianisme* corpus, are excellent examples of Grégoire's attempts to use scholarship in this way; they also remind us of the universal extent of Grégoire's interest in the human family. The abbé tried to apply the universal ideals of the French Revolution—and of Christianity—to a broader group of men than perhaps anyone else in his generation. Oppressed groups continued to be a particular target of his attentions.

Nevertheless, rather than defining his interest in oppressed groups as simply humanitarian, we need to situate it within his ongoing defense of Catholicism against attacks by philosophes, Protestants, and other non-believers. While Grégoire's Christianity was certainly a motivating factor in his defense of the oppressed, the equation was also reversed: his discussions of the oppressed served precisely to demonstrate Christianity's superiority. Before the Revolution, Grégoire had been clear that defending Catholicism against Basnage was one of his main goals in writing about Jews. Although he had avoided such language during the Revolution, it now returned and expanded, as marginal groups of all kinds became vehicles for him to laud Catholicism. Grégoire would even talk in these years about improving the lot of women. Here too, however, his writing was more Christian apologetics than egalitarian manifesto; he continued to assert that women were inherently inferior and to attack those women who transgressed conventional gender roles.

THE *HISTOIRE DES SECTES RELIGIEUSES*

Grégoire's greatest opus during the postrevolutionary period was his *Histoire des sectes religieuses,* printed in a two-volume edition in 1810 (banned until 1814) and expanded into a six-volume edition beginning in 1828 (with the final volume published posthumously in 1845). Though Grégoire spent a tremendous amount of time on this, his "favorite work," it has never been examined systematically.[2] Scholars who have looked at parts of it have either used it to show Grégoire's support for the world's oppressed or have considered it a purposeless compendium of all the information he had received on marginal groups.[3]

The *Histoire des sectes* had an explicit purpose, however: not to defend the groups discussed but to show their error. Grégoire himself told a Catholic acquaintance that the purpose of the work was to "bring our errant brothers back into the bosom of unity [the Catholic Church], and to prove to what disorder . . . one delivers oneself when one has the misfortune to abandon . . . the Catholic religion." A friend of his referred to the book as the abbé's "history of heresies," while others noted that the work taught them about "bizarre customs" and "the aberrations of the human mind."[4]

In the *Histoire,* Grégoire battled on four fronts to establish Catholicism—albeit a purified one—as the one true faith. First, mirroring the efforts of conservative Christians and building on his attack on Barlow's *Columbiad,* he aimed to combat the impiety of the philosophes. Second, he wanted to show the errors of misguided Christian sects, from Protestants to corrupted Catholics. Third, he focused on efforts to reintegrate non-Christians (like Jews and Muslims) into the universal human family and into Christianity. Finally, he worked to exclude women from religious leadership.

THE DANGER OF IRRELIGION, FROM VOLTAIRE TO KANT

Though the primary concern of the *Histoire des sectes* was organized religion, Grégoire spent a good portion of the 1810 edition's introductory discourse and its second volume attacking the "so-called philosophes." His attitude toward Enlightenment writers had indeed hardened since his SPS days; though he still bore the influences of his encounter with Enlightenment ideas, the postrevolutionary years had led him to speak against the philosophes. For him, irreligion had harmed the church far more than any sect: "The sect of Unbelievers is that which, in the last century and until today, has most afflicted religion." While he was willing to grant that the philosophes had helped bring about many positive reforms in French society (such as overturning feudalism), he argued that they frequently had done no more than echo things Christians had said previously.[5] Moreover, while the former bishop continued to concede that the philosophes had had legitimate objections to church corruption, he felt that their positive contributions were dwarfed by the consequences of their irreligion and libertinism. He objected not only to sworn enemies of the church like Voltaire and d'Holbach, but also to self-professed Christians like Rousseau and Kant.

Kantism was a prime target of his hostility. Despite his earlier attraction to Kant's ideas, Grégoire now believed that they were dangerous for religion. He deemed it folly to try to create a purely ethical morality apart from Christian morality. More offensively, Kant's ideas masqueraded as supporting Christianity and thus led many sincere believers astray. Grégoire complained that Kant had dismissed existing proofs of God's existence without substituting new ones, leading only to atheism.[6]

Grégoire also attacked other philosophes, even ones he had often praised and cited. He argued that Voltaire had reigned over the Académie française through a Robespierre-like terror, relentlessly attacking Christians; furthermore, rather than being a man of tolerance, he had been Jews' constant enemy. Echoing themes popular among polemicists on the right, Grégoire charged that d'Holbach's atheism had "demoralized Europe and degraded human dignity," while most of the other so-called philosophes (including Bayle, Diderot, Rousseau, and Mirabeau) had published obscene works alongside their "philosophical" treatises. Grégoire also rejected his old friend Thomas Paine. He complained that the Anglo-American republican had once, in a private letter between them, called Moses "a terrorist, just like Robespierre"; he also criticized Paine for attacking the New Testament while admitting that he had never read it.[7]

The philosophes' ideas, Grégoire contended, had been exposed as a disaster during the Revolution. Sounding strangely like the refractory priests and their descendants, the former bishop suggested that enlightened ideals had led to suicide, guillotining, libertinage, divorce, and a reviling of paternal authority during the "terrible and dismal experiment" of the Terror. He reminded his readers that Rousseau had fathered children out of wedlock and dumped them in an orphanage. Grégoire also attacked the revolutionary cult of the Supreme Being and the Directory-era religion of Theophilanthropy; he accused the latter of copying moral teachings from Christianity, even while trying to destroy it.[8]

To Grégoire, the answer to the world's problems could only come from Christianity itself. Theophilanthropism, deism, and atheism were dead ends; their adherents needed to be shown the error of their ways and reintegrated into the church. "We will always open the arms of charity to our errant brothers," he noted, "while repelling their error." Grégoire reinforced the arguments he was making about the Enlightenment in his own life; by the time he published the second edition of the *Histoire des sectes,* he had sold off a large collection of his Enlightenment books.[9]

REBUILDING THE CHRISTIAN FAMILY

For Grégoire, as we have seen, Christianity was far preferable to the secular philosophy of the eighteenth century. Nevertheless, he was not indiscriminate about what kind of Christianity was needed; for him, Catholicism remained the one true faith. The eighteenth century, he lamented, had witnessed an explosion of Christian sects, some more bizarre than others. He focused on groups that had broken from the Catholic Church, from "Shaking Quakers" to Anabaptists to the Greek Orthodox; his subjects ranged from groups he considered ecstatic and fantastical to those that were merely overzealous or overly austere. With some of his subjects (like figurists or millenialists), he shared some beliefs and therefore adopted a more sympathetic tone. Still, Grégoire generally included a group in the *Histoire* because he saw it as deluded. By using the word *secte*, which, as he himself noted, had an unfavorable connotation, Grégoire sought to locate these groups outside the bounds of legitimate Christian thought and practice. Indeed, the former bishop recognized that those he portrayed would be angered by his description of them. "No work is more capable of making enemies for the author than this one," he admitted. "It will displease sect-members who see nothing but good in their groups."[10]

Grégoire's histories of individual sects were thus value-laden defenses of Catholicism. In his chapter on Universalists (a group who believed that all people would be saved), for example, he argued that their interpretations were not worthy of serious consideration. "*Outside of the Church,*" he told them, "*there is no salvation.*" Grégoire mocked other sects even more. Speaking of "visionary sects" (by which he meant those whose leaders or members claimed communications with the divinity), such as the Swedenborgians, he groaned, "Of what deviations is this poor human reason, of which so much has been claimed, capable!"[11]

Here, Grégoire seemed to renounce the Enlightenment position that men were capable of reasoning about religion on their own. Indeed, during his dispute with Barlow, he had challenged the very foundations of Protestant—and Enlightenment—epistemology. He argued that "a very great number of European Protestants" seemed to be working to destroy Christianity. They were helped, he claimed, by "a fundamental principle of their sect and yours, which, authorizing each individual to interpret the Bible as he pleases, allows them to find in it anything they wish." He noted that Bossuet had predicted that Protestant ideas would lead inevitably to the intermixing into Christianity of "all the absurdities of delirium," and added that his *Histoire des sectes* served to prove that "Bossuet was right." He made similar claims in the *Histoire* itself.[12]

Grégoire's criticisms of Protestantism even extended to his old SPS friends. He was more gentle in his discussions of them than he was in speaking of others; he allowed that some mainstream Protestants held their religious convictions in good faith. Moreover, while he criticized many nominal Protestants for not believing in Jesus' divinity, he noted that there were other Protestants who shared Catholics' belief on this issue. He also made it a point to praise Blessig, Petersen, Hafner, and other Protestant friends for their "distinguished talents" and good character. He added that their efforts, joined with those of well-intentioned Catholics, might lead toward a successful reunion between the main Protestant sects and Catholicism. At the same time, he depicted most

Protestants as unfaithful to Christianity. In a move that was unusual for him, he rebuked his dear friend Blessig by name; he criticized a work in which the latter had praised the theological diversity among Protestants as a healthy means of perfecting human understanding of Christianity. "A body of doctrine that did not offer variations would not allow for progress," Blessig had written. Grégoire judged his friend's reasoning to be both outlandish and dangerous; he countered that either revealed religion was already perfect and the innovations made by Protestants useless, or Blessig believed the earliest Christians to have lacked information necessary for their salvation. Moreover, despite his distancing himself from Enlightenment deists elsewhere in the *Histoire,* Grégoire here invoked Rousseau, who had said that "the Reformists [Lutherans] of our days, or at least their ministers, no longer know or love their religion."[13]

Grégoire was also somewhat more gentle in discussing figurism and millennialism, beliefs with which he had some sympathies, than in treating other sects. He agreed that figurism (a belief linked with Jansenism, which involved the seeing of "figures" of the church's future in the Old Testament) was helpful in understanding the present and predicting the future. At the same time, he felt, some figurists had gone too far. Similarly, his article on millenarians—another idea linked to Jansenists, though not exclusive to them—was perhaps his least critical. Still, the ideas of many millenarians, particularly those who talked of carnal pleasures in the world to come, met with his scorn. Grégoire also did not allot Jansenism its own place in the book as a sect. As he said in a revealing aside in the Theophilanthropy section, "the defenders of the true principles [of Christianity] were from the school of Port-Royal." Because Jansenism did not appear schismatic to a Grégoire who had come to identify with it, it did not merit its own section. Moreover, in sections devoted to particular beliefs to which many Jansenists subscribed, Grégoire distinguished between the correct positions taken on them by noted Jansenists and the wrong-headed views of others.[14]

Theological error on the part of others was not the only obstacle to Christian unity, however; Grégoire also blamed corruption within the Catholic Church. It was difficult to convince unbelievers to join the Church, he argued, when it was full of duplicity. He suggested that "reasonable people will never confuse the court of Rome and the holy Roman [Catholic] Church." Until the Church began to "strike out without mercy against abuses," moreover, it could never win converts. Grégoire attacked the privilege and sycophancy of the Old Regime church (and its post-Concordat successors), and declared that the scandalous behavior of church officials had given ammunition to the philosophes. Furthermore, he charged that irrational hatred on the part of some in the Church had driven away other Christians. For example, the Greek Orthodox were not doctrinally schismatic, yet Catholic leaders, through "negligence and bad faith," had driven them from "the bosom of unity." He hoped that Catholics would work harder to bring the Orthodox "back" to the Church.[15]

JEWS AND MUSLIMS

Grégoire's attentions in the *Histoire* were not limited to wayward Christians; he also wanted to bring Jews and Muslims into the Church. Notwithstanding his having greater sympathy for Jews than many of his contemporaries did, he continued to scorn Jewish religious practices, as he had in the days of his *Essai*. His depiction of their errors thus paralleled that of other misguided groups—with extra bitterness added over their refusal to adopt Christianity in any form. His discussions of Jews thus served not to defend them, but rather (1) to criticize their supposed exclusivity; (2) to prove that the Church had been their most constant defender, notwithstanding their betrayal of Jesus; and (3) to urge Jews to move toward Christianity, if not convert outright.

Grégoire's attacks on what he called Rabbinism (by which he meant mainstream Judaism, which he defined as a tyranny of the rabbis with little connection to scripture) were hardly a new part of his literary arsenal. After the Revolution, he had maintained friendships with individual French Jews, visited foreign Jews on his travels around Europe, and continued to feel that Jews were in many ways treated unfairly by Gentiles. The frustration with them he had evinced in 1791 (*"it is their fault"*) had not diminished, however; on the contrary, he grew increasingly frustrated that, despite French Jews' emancipation—and his efforts of their behalf—they had not succeeded in regenerating themselves. Even as he blasted "persecutors of all ranks and of all nations," he argued that Jews' own prejudices accounted for much of their failure to integrate, and he often made offhand gibes at Judaism. Mystified that Jews were still attached to the Talmud (a collection "that recalls what Horace said about a few pearls stuck in Eunius's excrement"), Grégoire strongly denounced the "despotism" of French rabbis and community leaders in two essays published in 1806–7, at the time of Napoleon's convening of the Sanhedrin. The former bishop encouraged Jews to "courageously escape the yoke of Rabbinism," attacked the "reveries of the Misna [sic]," and insisted that Jews' continuing usury "perpetuates the hate directed against them." He also embraced the Sanhedrin in letters to friends.[16]

While some scholars, such as Hermon-Belot, have suggested that Grégoire's comments appear negative only in retrospect, Grégoire's contemporaries—Jewish and gentile—also read them as harsh. Grégoire's old SPS comrade Frédéric-Rodolphe Saltzmann, even less optimistic about Jews' possibility for regeneration than the abbé himself, told him: "You do not flatter the Jews of our country. But what you say about them is very true." Similarly, some Jews who read Grégoire's essays also recognized the critical nature of his comments. Just as Zalkind Hourwitz had bristled in 1788 at Grégoire's suggestion that the Jews needed correction, Berr-Isaac-Berr, the longtime leader of the Nancy community, was disturbed by Grégoire's new writings. Having worked with Grégoire on the citizenship campaign during the Revolution, Berr emphasized his "gratitude and profound esteem" for the priest. Yet he could barely restrain his anger over Grégoire's latest words. He protested that to attack sacred books "is to attack the very religion to which they belong. . . . It would be extremely easy to throw ridicule on the majority of books that the various Christian sects admit as sacred." But, he asked, "what would be the point, *M. le Sénateur?*" He complained that, when "invitations to renounce totally the yoke of Rabbinism are repeated to the Jews by respectable men like you, *Monsieur,* soon confusion will ensue. These individuals, forgetting the religion of their ancestors, will be neither Jews nor Catholics nor Protestants. They will only augment the number of atheists or men without solid moral principles." Berr's response demonstrated the Jewish community's quandary in dealing with Grégoire. Despite their resentment of his sarcastic assessments of Judaism, few other prominent Christians could be considered Jews' allies in any way. Although they were grateful for Grégoire's attacks on violence against Jews—and even brandished the slogan of regeneration to insist that they could overcome the legacy of past discrimination and be made equal to other citizens—they did not agree with Grégoire's belief in the bankruptcy of their religion.[17]

Despite Berr's critique, Grégoire did not alter his negative statements on Jews; instead, he expanded them in the *Histoire des sectes.* Whatever faith he had once had in Jews' desire to integrate now seemed lost. Sounding just like his impossibilist opponents during the Revolution, Grégoire now depicted a nation deliberately setting itself apart from all others: "The Jew has his eyes constantly turned toward Jerusalem, *desiring only it for his patrie*. . . . All nations have tried in vain to annihilate this people who exist among them, without resembling any or identifying themselves with any." He also continued to criticize the Talmud and the Parnassim (lay leaders of Jewish communities). He derided the former as written in "Babylonian patois, with no taste, no method, no accuracy," and said it "interprets the Holy Scripture absurdly [and] is filled with puerile fables, obscure precepts, explicit obscenities, and even blasphemies." He also dismissed it with the Orientalist remark that it was "born in Asia." As for the Parnassim, Grégoire called them aristocratic "tyrants," from whom average Jews needed Christian protection.[18]

Grégoire also portrayed contemporary Jews' misery as stemming from "their" treatment of Jesus. The Jew's fate of unhappily wandering the earth only confirmed the predictions of Christianity, "a religion he abhors." Jews had betrayed Jesus and had received their just deserts; sounding much like Hell had in 1779, Grégoire wrote: "The blood of Jesus Christ has fallen back on the Jews just as they wished; since the bloody day of Calvary, they are a spectacle all over the earth they wander, longing for a Messiah that they have looked for everywhere, even in Cromwell."[19]

Adding to these comments, Grégoire ridiculed other currents in modern Jewry. Like many contemporaries, he mocked the Jews who had followed the self-proclaimed seventeenth-century messiah Shabbatai Zvi even after the latter had converted to Islam. Citing an account by German-Jewish *maskilim* (Enlightenment-influenced reformers), he also gave a disparaging portrayal of Hasidism. Though Grégoire admitted that the facts were probably exaggerated by its opponents, he noted that Hasidism "would be the most abominable sect if all the facts enumerated against its adherents were true."[20]

Underlying these attacks was Grégoire's refusal to see rabbinic Judaism as normative; for him, the true principles of Judaism should have led Jews to embrace Jesus. He was fascinated by Karaites and Samaritans, both of whom rejected oral tradition and followed only the Pentateuch. Rabbinists, he contended, were only one kind of Jew; it was Karaites, Samaritans, and Rabbinists together who would, through their conversion, "console the Church for the ingratitude and the apostasy of the Gentiles."[21]

Though Grégoire continued to acknowledge, as he had before the Revolution, that Christians were responsible for Jews' sufferings, he made a distinction between nominal and *real* Christians. Whereas the former had oppressed Jews, the latter had magnanimously protected them: "People accuse the clergy of being persecutors. This is so easy to say, and so many people are so comfortable repeating it! Nevertheless, when the Jews were tormented by a rapacious government policy, by an unrestrained populace, they have always found asylum with pastors, and especially the Roman pontiffs." Grégoire's discussion of the Jews became a recounting of the heroism and virtue of the Christian saints who had protected them. Moreover, he commented, even if some false Christians had persecuted Jews, Muslims had treated them worse. He claimed that in Syria Muslims could murder up to seven Jews with impunity.[22]

Meanwhile, Grégoire remained hopeful that trends in rabbinic Judaism might lead Jews "back" to Christianity. He noted that "the prejudices of rabbis against Christianity are diminishing," and enthusiastically informed his readers that Jews were beginning to admire "the morality of the Gospels." He was particularly thrilled to hear reports that a group of Jews in Podolia had declared their hatred for the Talmud in 1756. The "Talmudists" (mainstream Jews) had insulted and excommunicated them, he told his readers, and called them followers of Shabbatai Zvi (a charge that Grégoire considered a baseless lie). Catholic leaders, however, had stepped in to protect them, Grégoire noted, after which the "anti-Talmudists" were so grateful that they "declared to the archbishop of Lemberg that they recognized Jesus-Christ as the Messiah and wanted to be baptized." Apparently, Grégoire did not know the full story of this group, for these particular Jews, members of a sect led by Jacob Frank, were in fact followers of Shabbatai Zvi—and also believed in salvation through orgies and sexual ecstasy. Grégoire, however, chose to see in them a ray of hope for an anti-Talmudist future that could lead to full conversion if Catholics like him reached out to them.[23]

Even if Grégoire hoped that he himself could achieve the same "success" as the archbishop of Lemberg, however, he remained committed only to sincere conversions; any others would desecrate Christianity. As long as Jews were ostracized legally and socially, some of them would convert for social gain, without embracing the Gospels. Grégoire denounced these conversions as "acts of hypocrisy"; he declared that, unlike Muslims, whose "stupidity applauds itself for conquests achieved through terror," Christians should never try to achieve conversion through force.[24]

As Grégoire continued to reexamine his belief in perfectibility, his assessment of the possibilities for Jewish improvement grew more pessimistic. In a comment buried in a footnote in his *Mémoires* (first drafted in 1808), he acknowledged that his hopes for a social regeneration of the Jews had been premised on a Rousseauian view of man as essentially good. This belief now yielded to a more orthodox one. Grégoire chastened himself, "It is an error to say *man is good*, because original sin corrupted him. I must correct this error [which I made] in my work on the Jews."[25] Between Jewish "obstinacy" and his growing disillusionment with Enlightenment ideas, Grégoire seemed to retreat from his previous declarations that Jews could quickly become like others.

If Grégoire was skeptical about Jews' ability to change, he was even more dubious about that of Muslims. His references to Islam, like those of many contemporaries, were generally filled with contempt for "Muslim stupidity."[26] His prejudices were probably a combination of contemporary Orientalism, abiding European resentment for the Islamic occupation of Europe, and the chronological differences between Jews and Muslims. Judaism, after all, had preceded Christianity, and Christians still venerated the Jews' Torah. Muslims, on the other hand, had created their religion in a world where Christianity already existed, implying that it was insufficient.

Nevertheless, Grégoire still wanted to monitor changes in Islam. He discussed "new sects among the Muslims," and was particularly interested in the Wahabis, some of whose beliefs he perceived as approaching Christianity. Grégoire nevertheless remained immensely suspicious of them, describing them as an "immense horde" ready to kill civil authorities if sect leaders commanded. Indeed, he wrote that the Greeks should be grateful to Christianity for keeping them separate from "the stupid horde" of the Islamic world. Although Grégoire spoke of the universal human family, he still saw some groups as not yet suitable to join.[27]

Still, as a believer in the prophecies, Grégoire tried to maintain his faith that the theological regeneration of both groups would be achieved one day. God would choose the time for converting the Jews, but with human help: "He directs events according to his supreme views, and perhaps he reserves for us the glory of preparing, through good deeds, the revolution that must regenerate this people. . . . Through our prayers, wishes, and kindness, let us hasten the moment when our fellow citizens, reunited under the standard of the cross, returned to the same fold, will mix their adoration with ours at the feet of the same altars." In the last decades of his life, Grégoire would read and make extensive notes on works that spoke of Jews' eventual conversion. He confidently predicted in 1824, "The Jews will return to Him whom their ancestors *pierced*."[28]

LIMITING THE INFLUENCE OF WOMEN IN RELIGION

Though much of the *Histoire* aimed to draw more people into the Church, one crucial aspect of it concerned a group whom Grégoire felt had infiltrated it too much. For him, women's attempts to be spiritual leaders only caused harm to religion, just as their attempts to intervene in politics had caused harm to the state. Generalizing about differences between men and women, Grégoire declared that women, motivated by pleasure or power, perverted religion when they attempted to exercise spiritual leadership. In the *Histoire*'s 1810 edition, he proclaimed that women were more devoted to pleasure-seeking than to religious truth; he argued that the religious groups led by women were "almost all founded on the basis of visions and ecstasies" and "yield a more or less marked tendency toward libertinage." Similarly, in the 1828 edition, he asserted that women were "naturally inclined to dominate" and that "their most energetic passion is often to exert a real or ideological authority over others." He charged that the typical woman had vain hopes of "being the founder of a group to which she can give her name, with the hope of attracting to it members of the other sex, or at least of attracting their eyes."[29]

In addition to his generalizations about women's love of pleasure and power, he also asserted that men were wiser and more virtuous. These writings contrasted with the praise for women's specific talents in his Haitian correspondence, suggesting that he saw European women as far more corrupted than their Caribbean sisters: "The devotion of women . . . stems more from the heart, while that of men stems from the mind. Men are directed by conviction, the daughter of reasoning; women, by persuasion, daughter of sentiment. This difference is so inherent in the respective sexes that it perpetuates itself as mental derangement." Grégoire attributed women's inferiority to physical factors, particularly their "exquisitely sensitive" nervous system, which often "inflames them to the point of impairing their intellectual faculties." While he conceded that women sometimes seemed more devout than men, too often they were motivated by "earthly attachments."[30]

Women's participation in religion had long been a disaster for the church and for France, according to the former bishop of Loir-et-Cher. Saint Paul had banned women from "usurping the right" of teaching religion, Grégoire asserted, no doubt in response to existing problems. Even when women only followed men, they still posed dangers because of their susceptibility to manipulation: "From its birth, the church has had to combat fanatics who, with the silly little women *[femmelettes]* they had led astray, tried to thwart the ministry and corrupt the truths of the Gospels." Women had also been one of the chief pawns used by Jews, Grégoire alleged, in their battles against the early Christians. Similarly, in modern times, royal mistresses like Mmes Dubarry and Maintenon had exerted a calamitous influence in ecclesiastical affairs. He also harkened back to the Revolution, when fanatical women had supported refractory priests and fomented attacks on the constitutional clergy. Denouncing the attempted independence of female sect leaders and even many nuns, he made exceptions only for the virtuous nuns of Port-Royal, especially Mother-Superior Angélique Arnaud.[31]

CHRISTIANITY AND DIFFERENCE: THE *DE L'INFLUENCE* CORPUS

The *Histoire des sectes religieuses* makes abundantly clear Grégoire's belief that, for world regeneration to continue, unbelievers would need to yield to the one true faith. Alongside the *Histoire des sectes,* which discussed those whose religious ideas placed them on society's margins, Grégoire prepared a major series of essays during this period on the influence of Christianity on groups oppressed because of their race or presumed origin. Using a formula employed in a handful of other Christian apologetics in the previous few decades, most of these works had titles beginning with the phrase "De l'influence du christianisme sur la condition [or sur l'état] des. . . ."[32] This corpus covered nearly every conceivable oppressed group: from blacks to women, Jews to Indians (South Asian and American), unborn children to animals, and pariahs within and outside of Europe. While some of these essays were read out loud in the Institut national in the 1810s, and two were published in the 1820s, they were mostly still in progress when Grégoire died. Unknown to most scholars of Grégoire, these essays have received almost no attention or analysis.[33]

What were the purposes of these essays? Unlike the groups chronicled in the *Histoire,* Grégoire felt that the groups discussed in these works were unjustly persecuted. He therefore made pleas for greater inclusion of them into the universal human family and urged that persecution end. Like the *Histoire,* though, the essays had a larger goal: proving that Christianity was the most progressive religion the world had ever known. The best hint of the corpus's overall goal comes from a comment he made in 1820 that he soon hoped to publish a work called "L'influence du Christianisme sur la liberté politique et civile," whose purpose would be to prove that "Jesus Christ is the only legislator who

promulgated a plan applicable to all men, in all countries, in all centuries, and in all circumstances." Grégoire's discussion of oppressed
groups *(malheureux)* always returned to his main theme: the essential
generosity of Catholicism and its superiority over their backward views.
The essays thus belong squarely in what William Everdell has called the
"utilitarian apologetic" tradition, an effort to defend Christianity by
showing its many social benefits.[34]

Grégoire began the corpus by arguing that Christianity had dramat-
ically improved the ancient world. "The revolution effected by Christianity is the greatest, and its establishment the strongest institution, that
was ever known," he declared. Long before natural historians had
argued that humankind had but one type descended from a common
source, Genesis had said the same thing. Early Christians had been true
social revolutionaries, who had worked tirelessly to "conserve men's
lives, to make their manners more gentle, to comfort the poor and the
sick, to free captives, and to liberate slaves." They had also been kind
and hospitable to strangers rather than rejecting those who were different. In their concern for future generations (who, Grégoire wrote, "are
also part of the grand [human] family"), Christians had also begun to
combat the abortion practices of the Romans and thereby protect
fetuses. So strong was the Church's stand against injustice, Grégoire
argued, that slavery would have been wiped out if the barbarians had
not defeated the Christians.[35]

When he turned to modern *malheureux* (such as African slaves,
Native Americans, Hindus, Jews, and women), Grégoire similarly aimed
to disprove the Enlightenment idea that the Church was a source of
oppression. In his "Influence du christianisme sur l'affranchissement des
Nègres," he insisted that slavery violated the core values of Christianity.
Similarly, in "Influence du christianisme sur l'état des Juifs," even as he
continued to insist on the essential bankruptcy of Judaism, he decried
persecution of Jews and argued for their reintegration into the universal
human family. "In the final analysis," he commented, "their wrongs are
those of the nations who have humiliated them."[36]

Grégoire was no less interested in European outcasts than in non-
European ones. Detached from the *De l'influence* essays, Grégoire wrote
a separate essay called "Recherches sur les oiseliers, les coliberts, les
cagous, les gahets, les cagots et d'autres classes d'hommes avilies par
l'opinion publique et par les lois," which he read to the Institut in 1810
and which was presumed lost by the only modern scholar to be aware
of it. This essay centered around groups deemed to be vile because of

their occupation, such as executioners or butchers, or because they were considered to have descended centuries earlier from Jews. Some were prohibited from marrying, eating, trading, or living in the same neighborhoods as others, or were "reduced to the most vile labors to earn a skimpy amount of food." Grégoire lamented that discrimination against these groups continued into the nineteenth century in parts of Europe. If these groups seemed debased, Grégoire insisted, it was only because others had reviled them. As he had in his 1788 *Essai,* Grégoire suggested that reviled people (the "avilies") found themselves in a hopeless situation and that their degradation was a consequence of their oppression.[37]

But if the *avilies* had been oppressed, who had done so? Grégoire knew he had a major obstacle to overcome: in most cases, Christians had been their persecutors. As in the discussion of Jews in the *Histoire des sectes,* Grégoire struggled to distinguish true Christians from false ones. His logic was self-reinforcing: if someone protected or tried to civilize the *malheureux,* he counted as a true Christian; if he did not, Grégoire denounced him as a degenerate European. Such logic allowed Grégoire to maintain that "Christians" had been the greatest defenders of humanity on the margins. In his essay on the Jews, for example, he insisted that the Inquisition was actually an anti-Christian institution, not the standard by which the Church's treatment of Jews should be judged. On the contrary, he noted, "rarely did Jews find protectors other than among the clergy." In his essay on "Des indiens protégés par le christianisme," the former bishop of Blois drew a distinction between true Catholics and false ones, and denounced the latter's treatment of Native Americans. While the Spanish and other Europeans had treated the Amerindians with brutality, he maintained, the majority of churchmen had been their greatest friends. Grégoire also suggested that Christians were the great protectors of Asian Indians of mixed race (for whom he used the English term "half cast" *[sic]*); again praising the promise of interracial marriage, he noted that he had high hopes for their potential to bring civilization to Asia.[38]

Grégoire also used these essays to vaunt the successes of Catholic missionaries, who, he gloated, had won more converts than Protestant ones. Indeed, Grégoire often spent more time in his essays exalting missionaries' courage than he did discussing the groups who were ostensibly the essays' subjects. In the essay on outcast Hindus, for example, Grégoire moved his focus away from their suffering to the self-sacrifice and heroism of missionaries who brought the Gospels to them. He praised missionaries' courage in "tearing themselves away from their family and their *patrie,* to which they nearly always bid a final adieu, crossing the

seas, sacrificing themselves to all kinds of dangers, to all kinds of privations, in order to carry to idolatrous or savage peoples the light of the
Gospels and the benefits of civilization."[39]

While defending Catholics, however, Grégoire was forced to admit
that even "true" ones were not always as charitable toward the *malheureux* as Protestants. Grégoire would have liked to provide a long list
of Catholics who had helped African slaves, yet his task was complicated
by the absence of anyone other than Las Casas. Although Grégoire continually claimed that Catholicism was the most benevolent form of
Christianity, Catholics had been virtually absent from the antislavery
movement. He was thus forced to cite Protestants as the movement's
leading lights, even attributing his own activities to their inspiration.
More painfully, Grégoire was forced to admit that the medieval Church
had sometimes supported the persecution of the oppressed. He insisted
that it had done so, however, only "in order not to offend the opinion
of the earthly powers."[40]

It was also a struggle for Grégoire to find evidence for the kindness of
Catholics toward the *malheureux*. When he vaunted the generosity of the
Church toward Native Americans, how did he define this? Grégoire
exulted that after the weakened Indians had converted, Church leaders
had shown special indulgence toward them in their application of religious law: "The calamities which these little tribes *[peuplades]* suffered,
the gentleness of their character and the weakness of their physical constitution constantly attracted for them the commiseration of the leaders
of the Church, who gave baptized Indians numerous privileges. They
were allowed to marry relatives at the third degree of consanguinity without special dispensation, and they were able to obtain it easily for closer
relations." Another of his strongest arguments for Christian kindness
came from the Council of Lima; it had written a book that aimed to bring
Indians "civilization, in habituating them to decency in their deportment,
to order, and to cleanliness in their clothes and abodes." Grégoire did not
discuss the Church's participation in forced labor programs in the New
World, nor the harsh treatment meted out to Indian neophytes.[41]

As in the *Histoire,* Grégoire knew that his argument about Christians-
as-defenders would be controversial among his secular circle of friends.
Indeed, when he had read an early draft of "De l'influence du christianisme sur l'abolition de l'esclavage" to the Institut, his colleagues had
been skeptical. Nevertheless, Grégoire insisted that clerics had been
more tolerant than philosophes: "The Jews, protected by pontiffs and
defended by priests, were spit upon by Horace, by Luther, and especially

by Voltaire." According to him, the clergy—the same clergy who had taught their flock that Jews bore the responsibility for killing Jesus—had been Jews' greatest friends. Grégoire made a similar argument regarding European pariahs.[42]

Grégoire did not simply argue, however, that Christianity had helped the *malheureux*. He went farther, claiming that they were backward and *needed* Christianity. While Christianity had much to offer everyone, he suggested, it was especially good for persecuted people around the world: "Though Christianity is suited to all centuries, regions and conditions, it is especially suited to the needs of the *malheureux,* because it offers consolations for all types of calamities." Without it, he claimed, the *malheureux* would forever remain powerless and uncivilized. Grégoire particularly denounced the caste system in India as akin to a hereditary aristocracy. Maintaining such a caste system kept the Indian nation in its infancy, preventing it from attaining the maturity of civilized nations. Only Christianity would help Indians empower themselves, escape the caste system, and throw off British imperialism: "Christianity would allow Indians to take advantage of the secret of their powers and their rights. It would allow them to develop their intellectual faculties."[43]

That Grégoire used these essays to depict non-Christians as backward can best be seen in *De l'influence du christianisme sur la condition des femmes*. This essay, one of only two in the *De l'influence* corpus to be published,[44] set out to compare how Christian and non-Christian civilizations had treated women; it proved so popular that it went through three editions. Since, as we have seen, Grégoire was hardly an egalitarian when it came to women, why did he write such a book? In Europe, discussions of the treatment of women had long served as the measure of a culture's civilization, implying a belief in gallantry but not in egalitarianism.[45] While Grégoire certainly respected individual women like Mme Dubois, the book therefore had the same purpose as the other essays in the corpus: discussing the status of women was a means to demonstrate Christianity's superiority over other religions.

In the text, Grégoire maintained that Christians had treated women measurably better than non-Christians, whether ancient or modern. Judaism, he charged, had had too little regard for women, while ancient peoples had placed obscenity and prostitution at the heart of their faiths. Meanwhile, in the modern world, women's lot was particularly bad "in the regions of East Asia that profess Shamanism and where inhabitants consider women to be merchandise that can be sold off when it becomes distasteful." He argued that Koreans "treat their women almost like slaves." Among the "little tribes of Negroes in Africa, women cannot even eat with their husbands," he reported. Among savage groups (meaning Native Americans and other "indigenous peoples"), Grégoire informed his readers, "the condition of women is even more deplorable." Citing a history of the voyage of Lewis and Clark, he declared that "among savages, modesty and conjugal fidelity are violated without reservation. Women are to them nothing more than a piece of furniture." Though the *Jesuit Relations* had offered a different picture of gender relations in the New World, Grégoire scorned any evidence to the contrary.[46]

Only Christianity, he insisted, had begun to change women's status, by treating women courteously and substituting "moral power for physical force," something that greatly protected the weaker sex. Yet, again, Grégoire did not consider all Europeans more enlightened on women's issues than the rest of the world—only true Christians. He reminded his readers that his irreligious fellow revolutionaries had legalized divorce, creating "multiple scandals." The barbarous Europeans of the Middle Ages had regarded women as badly as non-Europeans, treating them like merchandise or slaves. Any prejudice currently existing against women in Christian Europe, Grégoire insisted, was the result not of Christianity but of medieval barbarism.[47]

We can therefore see that Grégoire's life and legacy cannot be understood without reference to these two neglected corpuses. Even as we examine his lifelong efforts to defend oppressed groups against prejudice, we must remember that, especially in the years after the Revolution's failure, the former bishop's first priority was to defend his vision of Catholicism. He still held universalist beliefs (though he remained an essentialist with regard to gender), and he had certainly not joined the ranks of slaveholders or more conservative Catholics. Nevertheless, his faith in secular regeneration and in enlightened religion had faded, and he argued emphatically that salvation could come only from the Church. No matter which group he was discussing, his primary concern was to show that it needed to adopt Catholicism, and that a purified Catholicism was the answer for the world's problems. Whether his opponents were philosophes, Protestants, conservative Catholics, Jews, or women—and whether his subjects were Hindus or Native Americans— his interest remained in defending and cleansing the Church, extending its global reach, and recreating the universal human family within it. If a universalist republican Church could not find success in his lifetime, he hoped his words could help bring it to life in the future.

Epilogue

Icon of Universalism:
Grégoire's Life after Death

With the Revolution of 1830, the fortunes of the aging Grégoire changed once more. A new "citizen-king," Louis-Philippe, replaced the ultraconservative Bourbon Charles X, and Grégoire seemed hopeful that his persona non grata status would change. He seemed busier than ever, writing an acquaintance that "since the events of July, the accumulation of work, visitors, and letters does not leave me a free moment."[1]

In what would be his last pamphlet, Grégoire tried to offer conciliatory words to the new regime. While he continued to believe in republicanism, he was pleased by the relative calm of this Revolution. He said he would give the benefit of the doubt to the new regime:

> One may believe that a monarchical base is not the most solid one on which to build the social edifice. But anarchy . . . would be an even more terrible plague than a defective government. In keeping a republican [political] theory, in grieving over the obstacles that prevent it from being implemented, one must yield to the national will. . . . Reconciling royalty with liberty is an attempt whose success I would applaud. . . . As we are promised a *democratic monarchy,* let us hasten to erase the contradictions in this expression and to rectify its imperfections.

Grégoire noted that he would nevertheless watch the new regime carefully. Paralleling his earlier criticism of the Haitian monarchy, Grégoire complained that royal governments tended to be enormously wasteful, sucking the lifeblood of the people: "Fireworks, or a ball destined for the amusement of a few lazy people, consume in a few moments the taxes of twenty communes." He argued that "republican regimes are incontestably the least expensive."[2]

Grégoire's hopes for the new regime were dashed, however, when the same men seemed to stay in power. He complained to a Portuguese acquaintance in August 1830 that many of the conservative priests and nobles who had reigned during the Restoration had retained their influence under Louis-Philippe. He was further puzzled by the new generation of radicals. As Ruth Necheles has noted, a number of them formed a "coterie of young admirers" around him, the most notorious republican elder in France. He claimed to admire the "courage and talents" of this generation. At the same time, he felt that most of the young republicans were "little concerned with the men who preceded them in political life, confine them to what they call the *gerontocracy,* and mark them with a taint of ridicule." He promised that he would stay out of politics: "I am not going to cooperate in this business. . . . A veteran of age and of experience, I am suspending my judgment."[3]

Grégoire was also frustrated with the rise of Saint-Simonianism, an early utopian socialist movement. He admired the Saint-Simonians' efforts to achieve the kind of world he had long desired, particularly by creating a social and political system based on merit. He was disturbed, however, that the Saint-Simonians saw Christianity as needing revision and that "they place St. Simon in the same league as J. Christ."[4] Grégoire felt bitterly disappointed that, like dechristianizing Jacobins before them, the new generation of republicans believed in a secular morality.

This frustration built on the former bishop's more general depression about humankind. Grégoire had told friends during Napoleon's reign that he viewed most men as weak; he had complained about "this lower [earthly] world bombarded with the spectacle of iniquity and meanness," and even referred to himself as a misanthrope. In 1808, he had told a friend: "There was a time when I felt I exercised an important influence . . . , but that time is no more." These feelings deepened and worsened in the twilight of his life. Domestic troubles also seemed to be taking their toll on Grégoire. Though he had been complaining of old age and ill health for thirty years, he now seemed particularly convinced that he would die soon. In 1829, Mme Dubois (whom Grégoire often described in his letters as "suffering") became ill again. Moreover, he grumbled that their servants had become particularly troublesome: "Among the evils of life, one must count the perversity of servants; they will have shortened Mme Dubois's days and mine too" (fig. 8).[5]

FIGURE 8. Bust of Grégoire by David d'Angers (1829). One of the only representations of Grégoire as an older man. Courtesy of the Musée des Beaux-Arts de Nancy.

Grégoire's troubles worsened as he lay close to death in May 1831. Because of Grégoire's support for the Civil Constitution of the Clergy, the archbishop of Paris refused to allow his subordinates to give the former bishop of Loir-et-Cher his final sacraments. A controversy sprouted around his deathbed, as Grégoire refused to retract his oath. "Young man," he reportedly told a young *vicaire* who was sent to his house, "it was not without serious examination that I took the oath that you ask me to renounce. Similarly, it was with no less serious reflection at the foot of the cross that I accepted the episcopacy. . . . All of this, I did before you were even in this world." The former bishop yearned to die with the sacraments he had so frequently given others, but he could find no one with the authority to administer them to him. He found himself forced to justify his entire career in letters to the archbishop, as he pleaded for someone to give him last rites. Meanwhile, his difficulties became the talk of the day in Paris, and his house filled with curious hangers-on. Mme Dubois, who had spent so many hours in quiet conversation with her friend, was horrified by the throngs of people preventing him from dying peacefully; the situation would become even more stressful for her when two of these men tried to wrestle away her control of Grégoire's papers.[6]

Finally an abbé named Marie-Nicolas-Sylvestre Guillon, who differed with Grégoire on theological matters, nonetheless decided that he could not refuse the dying priest the final consolations of religion. Grégoire told Guillon how deeply touched he was by the latter's actions; observers reported that a state of tranquility descended over the dying priest, who was thus relieved of his worry of dying without the final sacrament. On May 28, shortly after Guillon's intervention, the prodigy from Vého stopped fighting for survival and took his last breath. Guillon's act of charity set off a scandal within the Church, however, which did not want the former *conventionnel* to be buried in hallowed ground. Finally, King Louis-Philippe himself, who did not want anticlerical Liberals to have a new martyr, ordered that a funeral be held in Grégoire's neighborhood church. In addition, he arranged for a priest not under the archbishop's jurisdiction to perform the service.[7]

If Grégoire believed himself to have become irrelevant in French society, the scene at his funeral suggested otherwise. Like that of Benjamin Constant a year earlier, the abbé's funeral became an opportunity for the republican (and, ironically, for the anticlerical) faithful to demonstrate their strength. Though they may not have known all of the things for which Grégoire stood, an estimated 25,000 people turned out to accompany his cortège to Montparnasse cemetery. Eulogies included those by Antoine-Claire Thibadeau, a former colleague in the Convention; Cyrille Bissette, a former deputy from Martinique whom Grégoire had helped; and Adolphe Crémieux, a young Jew beginning an important political career. When the news reached Haiti, Boyer ordered solemn prayers and had cannons fired every fifteen minutes.[8]

After his death, Grégoire would continue to have an important impact on French political life and on the development of political ideas globally. In the short term, his most direct contributions came from the six essay contests he funded and authorized in his will; these contests promoted causes ranging from encouraging morality in society to wiping out racial prejudice. The contest on race would become particularly well known; as Anne Girollet has argued, it represented a "decisive link in the long chain" of French abolitionism, tying together the Amis des Noirs of the 1780s with men like Victor Schoelcher who would obtain the final abolition of slavery in 1848. The abbé was able to endow these because of his Senate pension and simple lifestyle, and Mme Dubois's careful management of his finances; when she died in 1836, she indicated that Grégoire's fortune had climbed to 437,503 francs (including the property in the Yonne, valued at 148,472 francs), even after the many charitable donations he had made during his life. Following his instructions, she left the remaining monies not only to fund the essay contests, but also for the poor, elderly, and infirm in Lorraine, Blois, and the Yonne.[9]

Grégoire's bequests to his *patrie* would not be only financial, however. With his repeated reminders to French citizens about the republic they had won and lost, the abbé had done a great deal to preserve the legacy of the French Revolution and to ensure that republicanism remained viable in the eyes of the public. Many of his ideas became part of republican ideology in the nineteenth century, and he would become particularly identified with revolutionary universalism. Despite his disillusionment with enlightened religion at the end of his life, he would also remain a symbol in France of liberal Catholicism.[10]

The legacy of the Revolution and its universalism was never uncontested, however; Grégoire would remain a lightning rod for revolutionary ideas—a veritable "lieu de mémoire," in Pierre Nora's terms—for two hundred years to come.[11] Just as contests between republicans and monarchists had been played out around his person in 1814, 1818–20, and 1831, debate would ignite around his memory at several other key moments in French history. The abbé would also be invoked in other parts of the world when his arguments were deemed useful interventions in contemporary disputes.

In the early years of the Third Republic, for example, the fiftieth anniversary of his death sparked a number of publications and events.

In those times of bitter church-state confrontation, the organizers of these commemorations used Grégoire's republicanism against the Church, arguing that the Republic would celebrate him even if the Church (still bitter over his support for the Civil Constitution and his supposedly having been a regicide) did not. The city of Blois commissioned a copy of his bust and placed it in the municipal museum; a street along the Loire was also named for him. In Lunéville, the Jewish community and local republicans raised funds for a statue of the abbé, which they erected downtown. Contrasting him with contemporary clergy, the Statue Committee praised Grégoire for being a "Catholic priest with ardent convictions, but exempt from fanaticism, [who] assigned religion an inviolable domain while allowing the state its rightful authority." In Grégoire's old neighborhood in Paris, the *rue des Missions* was rebaptized *rue de l'abbé Grégoire.*[12]

Remembrances of Grégoire would be particularly important for nineteenth-century French Jews, who often found themselves having to prove their loyalty to the *patrie* despite their emancipation and decades of patriotic service. The formal Jewish communities all over France *(consistoires)* donated money to the Lunéville statue campaign, and the Jewish newspaper *Univers Israélite* reported with pride on the sums raised by Jews for this purpose: "If ecclesiastical history has its *Grégoire le Grand,* the history of France—and, we can say, of Israel—has its own. Ours is no less—and perhaps even more—grand, because he included in his love all of humanity; because he was the defender of the weak, the oppressed, and the disadvantaged; and because it is to him above all that the French Revolution owes its *human* character. Others made the Revolution heroic and militant; he made it fraternal, merciful, emancipating." Similarly, the Council of Presidents of Israelite Welfare Societies declared that "it is primarily to the abbé Grégoire that we owe the emancipation of the Israelites of France and the great example of tolerance given by our country to all civilized nations. . . . In the National Assembly, he did not let an occasion pass for advocating the rights of Israelites."[13]

West Indian leaders also joined in the late-nineteenth-century campaigns to praise Grégoire. Alexandre Isaac, a senator from Guadeloupe, made it a point to attend the Lunéville statue ceremony and praise Grégoire for his role in emancipating slaves. Haiti, meanwhile, continued its long tradition of venerating Grégoire.[14]

There would also be a new wave of Grégoire celebrations in the 1930s, as fascism and racial politics began to gain strength in Europe. In 1931, the centennial of Grégoire's death became an occasion for republicans and socialists to rise to the defense of universalism. A ceremony was held at Grégoire's birthplace in Vého, attended by Senegalese and Franco-Jewish World War I veterans. In Lorraine, Paris, Blois, Nice, Haiti, and French Morocco, lectures were held in and articles published by public institutions, synagogues, schools, and even a few churches. A Société des Amis de l'abbé Grégoire was formed and began to visit Grégoire's tomb annually. In 1939, the 150th anniversary of the French Revolution, more celebrations of Grégoire, seen as the great emancipator of Jews, were held; moreover, a new Masonic lodge, called Loge Abbé Grégoire, was created by a group consisting primarily of leftist Jews. The same year, the city of Blois moved Grégoire's bust out of the municipal museum and into a prominent place on the *Quai de l'abbé Grégoire*. Alfred Yvonneau, a mayoral aide in Blois, noted that "in this time of heightened racism, displaying this monument to . . . *the friend of men of all colors* shows that democracies, by the breadth and loftiness of their principles, know how to unite all the inhabitants of our globe in equal fraternity." Similarly, the lawyer and scholar Paul Grunebaum-Ballin, who had helped found the Société des Amis de l'abbé Grégoire, invoked Grégoire's defiant patriotic stands during the Revolution to inspire his countrymen to fight against the "perils that menaced" Frenchmen.[15]

The interest in an antiracist Grégoire in the 1930s was anticipated on the other side of the Atlantic, particularly by African-American intellectuals. Despite Grégoire's occasional frustrations over his transatlantic dealings, his *De la littérature des nègres* helped inspire a new generation of American abolitionists after his death. The abbé would also have been delighted to learn that he became an icon of the early-twentieth-century Negro history movement: the self-educated Harlem Renaissance figure Arturo Schomburg built his private library (which would become the New York Public Library's Schomburg Center for Research in Black Culture) around *De la littérature*'s footnotes. Similarly, Guichard Parris, a young Caribbean-American friend of Schomburg, would write a master's thesis on Grégoire in 1932 at Columbia and begin work on a doctoral thesis, before leaving graduate school to become a leader in the nascent civil rights movement; on the basis of *De la littérature*, he saw Grégoire as the "father of Negro literary and biographical history." Grégoire has also been given credit for helping inspire the nationalist West African Students Union in the 1920s.[16]

Grégoire would also become useful in American antifascism and New York City municipal politics. Rabbi Stephen Wise, a leader of Reform Judaism, an early opponent of Nazism, and a liberal involved in the

NAACP and ACLU, gave a sermon on Grégoire in 1931 linked to that year's Paris tributes. He used his sermon both to criticize the corrupt rule of New York Mayor Jimmy Walker (whose resignation Wise ultimately helped force) and to highlight antisemitism among contemporary Catholics. A *New York Times* report on Wise's sermon occasioned a response from a Catholic subscriber and pulp fiction author named Hamilton Craigie, who derided Wise and insisted that Grégoire had cared only incidentally about Jews.[17]

After World War II and the victory of the Allies, Grégoire would continue to be championed by French Jews, people of African descent, and others opposed to colonialism worldwide. He received further attention during the centennial of France's second abolition of slavery in 1948, and as movements for decolonization spread through Asia and Africa. The Vietnamese Communist leader Ho Chi Minh called him "the apostle of the liberty of peoples" in 1946; the celebrated Martiniquan poet and statesman Aimé Césaire praised him in 1950 as "the first *scientific refuter of racism*" and "the first anticolonial militant," whilst baptizing a *Place de l'abbé Grégoire* in Fort-de-France.[18] Césaire's friend Léopold Senghor, the Senegalese poet and president, depicted the abbé as a father of *négritude,* and other African politicians and writers also praised him. In 1956, in the wake of the landmark Bandung Conference of the previous year (a gathering in Indonesia of twenty-nine newly independent African and Asian nations), a group of leftist Frenchmen and foreign ambassadors produced an entire issue of the journal *Europe* in Grégoire's memory; they saw the conference as fulfillment of the abbé's lifework. In the United States, the 1960s witnessed a surge of interest in Grégoire from scholars interested in civil rights and the struggle against racism.[19]

Attention to Grégoire also exploded during the 1989 bicentennial, when the French government decided to place him, along with Condorcet and the scientist Monge, in the Pantheon. In thus elevating the abbé, the government hoped to do three things. First, at a time when many people argued that the Revolution had been bloodthirsty and was not worth celebrating, Grégoire represented a peaceable, nonregicidal alternative to the Revolution of Robespierre. Second, after decades of blows to French national identity from revelations about Vichy and from debilitating losses in France's empire, Grégoire could help vindicate France by depicting it as the source of universalistic ideas that had liberated oppressed peoples throughout the world. To illustrate this point, Grégoire's remains were accompanied along the rue Soufflot by traditionally clad women from the Senegalese island of Gorée, representing with their emancipated bodies the fruit of Grégoire's antislavery campaigns. The government also had a third goal in pantheonizing Grégoire, the first priest to be accorded this honor: that he could, at long last, reconcile Church and Republic.[20]

The pantheonization of Grégoire found wide echoes in the public. In addition to the reprints of his *Essai* on the Jews and of his *Mémoires*, several popular works on him were published, extolling his virtue as a liberal priest and antiracist and as the founder of institutions such as CNAM (the Conservatoire nationale des arts et métiers).[21] A torrent of articles appeared in national and regional newspapers explaining who Grégoire was to a population for whom he had not been a household name. A major exposition was mounted in Nancy and Blois, and new associations modeled after the Société des Amis de l'abbé Grégoire were formed in Blois and Lunéville.[22] Prominent French Jews such as Robert Badinter, a former justice minister, continued to praise Grégoire as the emancipator of the Jews, while an African community organization held a special service in memory of the abbé. Even some critics of the Revolution, such as Henri, count of Paris and pretender to the French throne, tried to claim the former bishop as their own; Count Henri suggested that Grégoire's universalist actions had been inspired by Louis XVI's own Edict of Tolerance.[23]

Grégoire also appeared several times on television—in everything from evening news segments to documentaries. One channel also aired a roundtable discussion of his legacy, which included excerpts from a film dramatizing the history of Jews in the Revolution. This film featured an invented conversation in bucolic Emberménil between its famous curé (played by an earnest-faced young actor) and an equally young Berr-Isaac-Berr. Possibly confusing Berr with Isaïah Berr-Bing, the film imaginatively portrayed Grégoire telling Berr that he was considering entering the Metz contest because of how much he respected the traveling Jewish peddlers who came to his parish, and asking for Berr's input; it certainly did not mention Grégoire's complaints about Jewish usurers exploiting his parishioners, nor Berr's reservations about Grégoire's writings. The most elaborate documentary was coproduced by Hermon-Belot and featured interviews with scientists, priests, and scholars in France and Guadeloupe on Grégoire's legacy. Twentieth-century technology also brought Grégoire to life in another way; the bicentennial spectacle at the Tuileries included a Grégoire android.[24]

The publicity abated only slightly when the bicentennial ended. Grégoire was immortalized the next year on a French postage stamp; within a few years his portrait had been placed in two different metro stations (fig. 9).[25] Planning also began on permanent projects in his honor. Jack Lang, the French culture minister who also served as mayor of Blois, worked to build a new library in that city to be named for the abbé; in 1997, it came into being as the Bibliothèque Abbé-Grégoire (BAG), which launched an ambitious program of collecting rare Grégoire materials while still being a full-service public library (fig. 10). Meanwhile, in Lorraine, the Association Lorraine des Amis de l'abbé Grégoire began to organize festivities for the 250th anniversary of Grégoire's birth. These included building a small museum in Emberménil with stained glass windows depicting the stages of Grégoire's life, and holding a contest for Lorraine schoolchildren on the enduring applicability of his civic ideals. One winning class talked about how Grégoire's ideals helped them learn to play together more harmoniously, while another theorized that, if Grégoire were alive in the twenty-first century, he would lead a campaign against child labor in China.[26]

Since 1989, Grégoire has continued to receive regular mention in newspapers as the founder of numerous ideas and institutions. He is invoked often in discussions of universalism; referring both to the new wave of anti-Jewish attacks in 2002 and to Muslims' increased sense of exclusion from French society, the chief rabbi of Paris's main synagogue exclaimed "Abbé Grégoire, wake up!" The publicity has contributed to making "abbé Grégoire" a slang term of sorts denoting an inclusive multiculturalist.[27]

Acclaim for the abbé has never been universal, however. At the very moments when he was fêted by some French people because of his views, others attacked him on the same grounds. After his death, royalists and conservative Catholics continued to view him as a hothead, regicide, and impious traitor. Anyone praising him was left open to the charge of wanting to revive bloody Jacobinism; those who wished to celebrate him had to fight against the idea that he was a regicide in order to establish him as a suitably moderate national hero.[28]

In the early twentieth century, Grégoire also underwent reassessment from certain French Jews. Early French Zionists, embittered by the Dreyfus Affair and continuing antisemitism in universalist France, began to view the cult of Grégoire as epitomizing Jews' blind embrace of assimilationism. In 1928, André Spire suggested that Grégoire and others had "tried to denationalize us," and he criticized his fellow Jews for having consented. During the centennial of Grégoire's death, a young Zionist named Méïr Leviah sounded a discordant note when he wrote

FIGURE 9. Grégoire in the métro, Arts et Métiers. One of two portraits of Grégoire in the Paris metro system (the other is at Réamur-Sebastopol). Installed during the 1994 remodeling of the Arts et Métiers station celebrating the bicentennial of the nearby Conservatoire national des arts et métiers. Photographs by Brian W. Ogilvie.

FIGURE 10. Bibliothèque Abbé-Grégoire, Blois. New municipal library named for Grégoire and completed in 1997. Photograph by author.

that "Grégoire brought to the Jews the love of a *missionary*, who, in order to better regenerate and save individual souls, combats foreign entities and collectivities. Missionarism is a psychological disposition *sui generis* which involves *hateful contempt for the entire heritage of the 'disadvantaged' group . . . and loving pity for the individuals composing it*" (emphasis his). In the wake of the Holocaust and debates about whether emancipation had liberated Jews or only made them more vulnerable to antisemitism, Grégoire underwent special scrutiny. The American Jewish historian Arthur Hertzberg, for example, grouped him among the so-called friends of the Jews who secretly wanted Jews to "give up their old ways" and convert to Christianity. For Hertzberg, the antisemitism of the twentieth century had been produced not by a reaction against revolutionary universalism but from "within the Enlightenment and Revolution themselves."[29]

More contestation over Grégoire's memory erupted during the bicentennial; once again, the abbé became a contested terrain on which battles about French national identity were played out. Many conservatives, who refused to celebrate 1789 altogether, were predictably aghast. One Blois writer published a work purporting to reveal the "real" Grégoire—someone who had ignored his diocese and turned his back on the Church. A cultural official in Nancy acknowledged that, until 1989, Grégoire had been "poorly viewed and not well liked in this region." One of Monge's descendants decried the linkage of his ancestor with Grégoire, whom he called a "dubious character."[30]

The Church, moreover, despite the liberalization of the post–Vatican II years, opted to absent itself from the pantheonization ceremony. Despite pleas from French president François Mitterrand, the archbishop of Paris (Jean-Marie Lustiger) decided he could not attend; while acknowledging that "certain positive values of the Revolution were Christian values" and praising Grégoire for the purity of his religious convictions, Lustiger made clear that the Church still viewed Grégoire as a turncoat for his support of the Revolution's clerical policies. Only a single bishop—the outspoken leftist Mgr. Jacques Gaillot from Evreux—decided to attend, and he himself would be removed from his bishopric by the pope in 1995 because of his heterodoxy. Meanwhile, Lustiger's decision was strongly criticized by liberal lay Catholics and by scholars like Plongeron. A group calling itself "Appel des 25,000" called for 25,000 lay Catholics and parish priests to attend the ceremony in the bishops' stead, modeling themselves after the 25,000 demonstrators who had accompanied Grégoire's body to its first burial. Nevertheless,

Lustiger's absence made clear that, even after two hundred years, the
Jacobin curé of Emberménil could not be reintegrated into France's post-
Concordat Church; his actions were still seen as injurious to the faith.[31]

Regionalists long resentful of Parisian attempts to impose a central-
ized culture on the rest of the country also proclaimed Grégoire's legacy
to be nefarious. They viewed Grégoire as responsible for inspiring the
Third Republic's largely successful campaign to replace patois with
French (though some regional languages are now experiencing revivals).
The president of the Regional Council of Provence-Alpes-Côte d'Azur,
for example, urged rescinding the decision to place Grégoire in the Pantheon: "With an obstinate will, this man led a virulent campaign against
one of the Rights of Man most dear to France's regions: the right to speak
one's own language on one's natural territory. The abbé Grégoire was the
origin of the severe measures adopted when the Revolution radicalized,
which, discriminating against local languages, annihilated any hope of
bilingualism. . . . Whatever may be the merits of the abbé Grégoire, he
was the instigator of a veritable cultural genocide, which France must not
appear to support at this time." Criticism of Grégoire's language initiatives continues to appear regularly in French newspapers and scholarly
works, with even Jack Lang (a great admirer of Grégoire) acknowledging that, on this issue at least, Grégoire perhaps went too far.[32]

Perhaps the greatest criticism, however, came from French Jewish circles. Jews who had known only Grégoire's general reputation as the
friend of the Jews suddenly gained easy access to the *Essai sur la
régénération* when two inexpensive editions were published in 1988.
Many Jews were shocked by the text's language. Echoing the earlier critiques made by Spire and Leviah, writers such as Shmuel Trigano and
Annie Kriegel pointed to passages in which the abbé had spoken of the
"spirit of greed that universally dominates [Jews]," their "acquired ignorance," their being "perverse," and their having "no idols other than
money"; they argued that Grégoire was hardly a hero for Jews. Pierre
Birnbaum made an analogy between Grégoire and the notorious anti-
semite Edouard Drumont, calling them indistinguishable in many ways.
Though many Jews continued to venerate the abbé, the sentiment of
many younger Jews turned against him; the Centre Rachi, a Jewish cultural association in Paris, voted against Badinter's proposal to name
their auditorium after him.[33] Meanwhile, according to Hermon-Belot,
the Jewish community of Lunéville felt especially betrayed by the discov-
ery of Grégoire's words. Françoise Job (a historian who married into
the family that had led the statue campaigns) was shocked by finding

"a cavalcade of commonplace anti-Jewish expressions" in the text. There was also an uprising against Grégoire in the Nancy community, which was somewhat minimized when Hermon-Belot and others began to give speeches defending him.[34] Grégoire had nevertheless lost his unchallenged place of glory in the Franco-Jewish pantheon.

Disputes over Grégoire also extended to cyberspace. By 2004, he was discussed on thousands of web pages, with differences of opinion about him paralleling those in the physical world. Many pages celebrated Grégoire the abolitionist, the Gallican bishop, the founder of CNAM, the anticolonialist, or the father of the idea of cultural preservation; there were many others, however, that denounced his stance on patois.[35]

In a scholarly work using archival sources to reconstruct Grégoire's life, why conclude with everything from newspaper columns to television programs to web pages? While such materials are often seen as not serious enough to merit analysis in scholarly biography, contemporary and posthumous representations of a historical figure are often key to understanding that figure's influence and legacy. Indeed, the very lack of public consensus about how to see Grégoire—and the fact that only portions of his worldview are today remembered and celebrated—lets us see a key truth. The crucial question of Grégoire's life (and the central problem of the French Revolution)—how to build a coherent and egalitarian national community out of a diverse people—is as yet unresolved.

To understand this, we need only reflect on which aspects of Grégoire's life and writings have been celebrated, and to what end. As we have seen, Grégoire had a rich and varied career, in which his outlook on life underwent many modifications. Those championing Grégoire, however, have generally staked a claim only to certain slices of his life. Liberal Catholics have selected Grégoire the Christian republican or champion of the poor. They have not discussed, in contrast, the great difficulties he had in reconciling his Christianity with a republicanism others wanted to be secular, nor his vocal distaste for the beliefs of non-Catholics.

Another common representation of Grégoire has been that of the emancipator of the Jews, he who was never silent on their behalf. As we have seen, though, such a statement oversimplifies his activities with regard to the Jews. Though he attacked anti-Jewish prejudice at a time when many contemporaries were unwilling to do so, he did opt to remain silent during the Ashkenazi Jews' protracted campaign for citizenship in 1789–91. Lest the reasons for his silence remain in doubt, let us recall the letter in which he told a friend that the Ashkenazim's failure to win citizenship right away was "their fault" for clinging too strongly to their community traditions. Jews who have championed Grégoire have also not cited his two pamphlets on Jews from 1806–7 or his *Histoire des sectes religieuses*—works that are far less well known today but that display openly his distaste for normative Judaism and his frustration with Jews who continued to practice it even after being emancipated.

Similarly, people of African descent who celebrate Grégoire have emphasized the antiracism of his *De la littérature des nègres* and his support for Haitian independence rather than his support of republican colonialism. Certainly, not all West Indians share Isaac's and Price-Mars's interest in Grégoire—or any other European revolutionary or abolitionist. Where many European historians have interpreted the Haitian Revolution in terms of blacks imitating whites after learning of French ideals of liberty and equality, many Haitians and historians of Haiti have insisted on the primacy of internal causes; to them, the Haitian Revolution marked the culmination of decades of slave resistance that had nothing to do with 1789. Many residents of Martinique and Guadeloupe have similarly regarded foreign figures like Grégoire as external to their own hard-fought struggles.[36] Even those who champion Grégoire, though, do not mention his explicit support for certain kinds of colonialism and his contributions toward the idea of a republican civilizing mission. Grégoire's negative views of women have not been discussed at all.

Noting that members of the public have been selective about *which* Grégoire to champion does not require dismissing them for not having a more complete understanding of him. Indeed, nonhistorians can hardly be expected to pore over documents before discussing historical figures. It is worth reflecting, however, on why particular selections have been made. Why Grégoire the emancipator and not Grégoire the mocker of the Talmud and of women? Why Grégoire the abolitionist instead of Grégoire the proponent of new colonization? Why Grégoire the enlightened republican Catholic instead of Grégoire who derided women's influence in the church or attacked Protestantism? Why Grégoire the patriot and eternal optimist instead of the self-proclaimed misanthrope?

One answer is that the first Grégoire of each pairing has had contemporary uses, while the second has not (or there are better heroes to choose for those who wish to make those points). In the 1880s, a Grégoire who could be employed to tell priests to support the Republic was an extremely useful icon. For French Jews and people of African descent facing enduring prejudice, a conditionalist Grégoire has had no contemporary value, whereas one who criticized the prejudices of white Catholics has. At least until the Holocaust sparked more open critiques of European culture, it seemed of little use for most Jews to extol someone who criticized Jews' supposed faults or said their religion was ridiculous; telling Gentiles about Grégoire's attacks on Christian prejudice was a wiser choice. Similarly, what appealed to Guichard Parris, living at a time of lynchings and unconcealed prejudice, was the idea that a white Frenchman had condemned the evils of racism and slavery more than a century earlier, which suggested to partisans of Jim Crow that their views were outdated. The same was true for Price-Mars and for other proponents of *négritude*. Price-Mars celebrated the African traditions that Europhilic Haitian elites (inspired by Grégoire and others) had long sought to squelch; he specifically rejected the idea that Haitians had "no history, no religion, and no morals and that their only hope was to acquire these things from Europeans." For him, Senghor, and others, it was therefore of no use to note that Grégoire had seen Haitians in precisely this way; the abbé's antiracism, by contrast, was far more valuable.[37]

Grégoire has also remained appealing as a symbol because of how few of his contemporaries opposed racial or religious prejudice and because of how forcefully he denounced it. Of course, some Jews and people of color who lived at the same time as the abbé viewed his model of regeneration as problematic, just as some patois-speakers challenged his language projects. We have seen for instance Berr-Isaac-Berr's argument that it was dangerous for someone reputed to be Jews' greatest friend to decry Judaism, and Julien Raimond's insistence that free people of color did not need special regeneration. Both men nevertheless understood that, outside their communities and in a hostile world, they had few other allies.[38] While many posthumous defenders of Grégoire do not even know about such critiques, those aware of them have done the same thing as Grégoire's contemporary defenders: embracing the most inclusive aspects of his writings, regardless of reservations about other parts of his work.

For indeed, we must not forget another reason for the currency of Grégoire as a cherished symbol of French universalism: whatever critiques may be made of him by unconditionalists, impossibilists have hardly disappeared from the world. For them, too, Grégoire has been a symbol, if a despised one. Indeed, the Nazis used Grégoire's body to proclaim their own murderous intentions in 1942, when they destroyed his statue during their occupation of Lunéville (something the residents of that city tried to reverse in 1955 by erecting a new statue, along with a

memorial to local Jews who had perished in the war). In their hatred of
Grégoire, the Nazis drew upon Gallic sources of antisemitism; in 1939,
Lucien Rebautet had condemned the abbé's efforts to help Jews, arguing that antisemitism was a traditional French value. Similarly, Charles
Maurras, founder of the far-right Action française, considered Grégoire
to exemplify all that was wrong with postrevolutionary France, from the
abbé's arguments for the emancipation of the Jews to his "voting for"
the king's death.[39]

The Front National of Jean-Marie Le Pen, who has openly proclaimed his belief in the inequality of races, has similarly seen Grégoire
as an emblem of all of France's ills. At the turn of the twenty-first century, the Front National's newspaper, the National hebdo, put Grégoire
on its cover and ran a brief biography of him. For the FN, what was at
issue was not what kind of friend Grégoire had been to Jews and blacks
but that he had been their friend at all; the newspaper used the terms
"friend of Jews" and "friend of blacks" as damning epithets.[40]

Le Pen's startling finish in the 2002 presidential elections, in which he
finished second on the first ballot with 16.9 percent (behind Jacques
Chirac with 19.9 percent and just ahead of Lionel Jospin with 16.2 percent), spurred a torrent of self-scrutiny in France, with many asking if
French values of universalism were in danger. Commentators fiercely
debated the reasons for Le Pen's success, and many French people insisted
that Le Pen's ideas were still fringe ones, with the nearly five million votes
cast for him merely representing a protest against the incumbents instead
of actual racism. Others noted, however, that Le Pen won even more
votes on the runoff ballot, after an appeal for national unity in the name
of French universalism from the mainstream parties; following that ballot, in which Le Pen received 17.8 percent of votes cast (including an
additional 700,000 votes), there could be no denying that, at the very
least, nearly one in five voters felt comfortable expressing their dissatis-
faction with government policies by voting for a party with a racialist
view of France. Nevertheless, the huge demonstrations held against Le
Pen after the first round of elections—and the 82 percent of runoff voters who cast their ballots for Chirac, regardless of their feelings about his
particular policies—helped show that, for a huge portion of the population, universalism has remained an essential part of French identity.[41]

Even if universalism remains central to French identity in most citizens' eyes, however, there is a noticeable lack of consensus about what
it means. How the persistence and periodic reassertion of old regional,
religious, cultural, racial, and gender differences—and the introduction

of new ones—will fit into French national identity remains undecided. A perfect illustration of this is the recurring controversy over Muslim girls wearing headscarves to school. Is covering one's head an acceptable manifestation of sincere religious beliefs or an offense against the secular universalism of the Republic? To what extent does being French still require regenerating oneself—that is, giving up one's cultural particularities in order to fit with a certain notion of Frenchness (in this case, more secular than Grégoire's ideal but unitary all the same)? It is especially unclear how comfortable the French are with integrating today's immigrants, particularly North Africans, who are often viewed as too different—even when their difference is defined not as one of race but of national origin and culture.[42]

During the French Revolution, as this study has suggested, regeneration was seen as the ideal solution to the challenge of creating equality in a diverse society. It did not succeed in solving it, as battles over what France should become helped torpedo the Revolution's prospects. Regeneration became part of the Revolution's enduring legacy, however, and remains the dominant framework for dealing with difference in numerous societies around the world. Though it still bears the promise of inclusion and liberation, it has also helped to legitimate colonialism. Even when the word itself is not used, much of modern discourse on difference still depends on a regeneratory framework.

The legacy of regeneration is manifested for example in the ubiquitous belief that "Third World" nations need to "join the modern world" or "raise themselves to the level of the West" by adopting the latter's technical know-how and cultural values.[43] Without using the word *regeneration,* Akhil Gupta has shown how, in postcolonial global interactions, the concept of development has largely assumed the function regeneration once served. In his analysis, the mandate of development has perversely kept "undeveloped" nations economically and culturally subservient to "developed" ones, even after decolonization ended the latter's political and military rule.[44] By setting a single path for world progress and viewing nations that do not conform to it as backward, development has thus assumed the mantle once held by regeneration. Grégoire and other abolitionists called for a world in which regenerated nations would instruct others in becoming civilized, yet the former retained their head start. Two hundred years later, they still do not view most other nations as having caught up.

Regeneration has had a similarly paradoxical effect on an individual level. It has allowed for the possibility of ending racism and creating a global society in which all humans have the potential to be seen as equal. The universalism it supports, however, still depends on the expectation that others will become "more like us"— which never quite seems to work, at least not in the way that would-be regenerators expect. On one hand, no matter how much they are encouraged by well-intentioned Europeans or Americans, many subaltern peoples do not wish to ape the values and practices of people who were once their oppressors politically and may still dominate them economically. As Homi Bhabha has noted, however, those who do try to mimic more powerful peoples or at least adopt parts of their culture rarely succeed fully, but instead are seen as creating copies that are "almost the same, but not quite."[45] As with Grégoire in the nineteenth century, idealistic regenerators thus often become irritated when those whom they have worked so hard to improve remain exasperatingly different. Meanwhile, for the would-be regenerees, failure to be fully accepted often leaves them with greater disillusionment, as they end up suspended between two worlds. Vivid examples are the Zionist movement, which arose among Jews in Europe out of a feeling of continual rejection and persecution despite emancipation and attempts at regeneration, and the colonial independence movements led by the African *évolués* [evolved ones], who imbibed French values of liberty and equality yet became frustrated by France's failure to extend these ideals to their colonies. The endpoint at which regeneration aims— an egalitarian world in which all difference is erased—has thus remained scarcely attainable.

Within modern democratic societies, the legacy of regeneration can also be felt. From Eastern Europe to Africa to Latin America, societies have enthusiastically adopted the democratic and nationalist ideas expounded by the French Revolution. Yet, in adopting the idea of the nation as the basis for political society, they have unwittingly inherited the Revolution's unfinished challenge: how to build such a unified nation out of a people with multiple differences. Societies that define themselves as universalist still have not found a way to reconcile equality with diversity.

Even if it were true, as some commentators have maintained, that the era of the nation-state is reaching an end,[46] this problem will not go away. Indeed, the perceived onset of a culturally homogenizing global society has struck many in the world—from Islamic fundamentalists to American militia groups—as a danger to their particular beliefs or practices. This issue is therefore not an academic one, since these anxieties can have bloody manifestations, as the cycle of terrorism and war of the

early twenty-first century attests. The challenge of incorporating difference in the nation and managing it in an increasingly interconnected
world thus remains as vital as ever. Though we do not need to adopt all
of Grégoire's solutions, we must recognize that regeneration is part of
the conceptual baggage of modern life. If we retain Grégoire's passionate belief in human equality—even while working to extend it to those
he did not consider fully equal, such as women—we still need to figure
out ways to create sustainable human communities, without requiring a
cultural homogenization that can lead both to cultural impoverishment
and to deadly resentments.[47] Until we can resolve this difficult issue,
invocations—and denunciations—of Grégoire are likely to continue for
generations to come.

Acknowledgments

Some biographers revere their subjects; others end up exasperated by them. After years of work on this study, and moments of both sentiments, I have fallen somewhere in between. This book would not have been completed, however, if the abbé did not have qualities that I could embrace unconditionally. Just as Grégoire's modern-day admirers often focus on a portion of his life, my Grégoire (the one I have kept always in my mind's eye) is the book-loving student turned engaged scholar—someone who was passionate about learning, who eagerly sought mentoring, who reveled in stimulating conversation, and who, above all, hoped his writings could help create a better future. Another of his admirable qualities was his generosity in acknowledging others; indeed, when he published *De la littérature des nègres,* he thanked so many abolitionists that reviewers rebuked him for the length of his Dedication. As I enumerate my debt to at least some of those who have aided me in the preparation of this book, I hope my readers will prove more forgiving than his.

At Stanford University, I was fortunate to find a cadre of scholars who made my studies both challenging and enjoyable. Keith Michael Baker was a model dissertation advisor, intellectually demanding yet also kind and supportive. Any contribution made here to revolutionary historiography has grown directly from his teaching and good counsel. Aron Rodrigue's role in sparking this study is alluded to in the Prologue; I will add only that, without his scholarship and ongoing mentoring, this book would not have come to fruition. This study also could not have been written without the inspiration of Mary Louise Roberts; my effort to think about biography, rather than just to write one, is one of her myriad influences on this text. I am also grateful for what I learned from the rest of the Stanford faculty in European, British, and Jewish history, and especially to Richard Roberts and the members of the Empires and Cultures Workshop, who turned a French intellectual historian into someone who could think transnationally.

Other scholars who made crucial contributions to this work's early development include Dena Goodman, Colin Jones, Dale Van Kley, and Joe Zizek. Three historians who read the entire manuscript at various stages offered invaluable suggestions: David A. Bell, who deserves special mention for his enduring generosity and for urging me to tackle some of the most contested questions in modern history; Frances Malino, who inspired and encouraged my earliest work on regeneration; and Jeremy Popkin, under whose auspices (and those of his father, Richard Popkin), a new network of Grégoire scholarship has arisen. Marcel Dorigny and Yves Bénot warmly welcomed me into their circle and gave me an audience in France for my work. Jennifer Heuer has been an ideal friend and reader, and her kindness exceeds even her erudition and critical eye.

Of the numerous other scholars who have offered me input, I must thank Andrew Aisenberg, Allan Arkush, Lawrence Baron, Jason Bell, Avner Ben-Amos, Pierre Boulle, Gregory S. Brown, Timothy Brown, Joseph Byrne, Carolyn Lougee Chappell, Paul Cohen, Richie (Yerachmiel) Cohen, Dan Colman, Elizabeth Colwill, James Chokey, Denise Davidson, François Furet, Nina Gelbart, Malick Ghachem, Nancy Green, Jeff Horn, Lynn Hunt, Margaret Jacob, Dominique Julia, Gary Kates, Stewart King, Alan C. Kors (who first inspired my love for history), Hans-Jürgen Lüsebrink, Nadia Malinovich, Darrin McMahon, Lara Moore, Brian Ogilvie, Sarah Pearsall, Sue Peabody, Annie Quinney, Jack Rakove, Katherine Royer, David Ruderman, Peter Sahlins, Jenny Sartori, Ron Schechter, Stephen Schloesser, J. B. Shank, David Sorkin, Martin Staum, Anthony Steinhoff, Sarah Sussman, Adam Sutcliffe, David Troyansky, and Joellyn Zollman. Virginie Mundeteguy, Dominique Rogers, the Hochner clan, and Michelle Bubenicek-Garcia and the entire Bubenicek family offered me the gift of their friendship and hospitality during my stays in France. Without the work of those who studied Grégoire previously, particularly Ruth Necheles, Rita Hermon-Belot, Solomon Posener, the editors of Grégoire's *Oeuvres,*

Guichard Parris, and Bernard Plongeron, it would have been infinitely more difficult to write about the abbé. My heartfelt gratitude also goes to the staff at the University of California Press, especially Stan Holwitz (who spotted this book's potential at an early stage) and Elizabeth Berg, copyeditor extraordinaire.

This book was also shaped by suggestions I received at the Stanford Empires and Cultures Colloquium, European History Workshop, and French Culture Workshop; the Clark Library Conference on the Abbé Grégoire; the Western Society for Eighteenth-Century Studies; the Society for French Historical Studies; the International Workshop on Imperialism and Identity at Berkeley; the Western Society for French History; the Johns Hopkins European History Seminar; the San Diego State University History Seminar; the World History Association; the Harvard International Seminar on the History of the Atlantic World; and especially from my colleagues in the 1998–99 Haskalah seminar at the University of Pennsylvania's Center for Advanced Judaic Studies (CAJS). My research was also facilitated by generous financial assistance from Stanford University, the Mellon Foundation, CAJS, and California State University—San Marcos.

As the abbé Grégoire himself recognized, historical research would be impossible without librarians and archivists. My personal pantheon includes the entire staffs of Stanford's Green Library (especially Roger Kohn, Sonia Moss, and Mary Jane Parrine), the CSUSM Library (especially Teri Roudenbush), the Bibliothèque nationale de France, the CAJS Library and the life-sustaining San Diego Circuit. Among the numerous librarians who assisted me elsewhere, special thanks are owed to Valérie Guittienne-Mürger and Fabien Vandermarcq of the Bibliothèque de la Société de Port-Royal (and their predecessor Hélène Grizot); Martine Mathias and the staff at the Musée lorrain; Thierry Leclair of the Bibliothèque Abbé-Grégoire; Philippe Landau at the Consistoire central des Israélites de France; Mlle François at the Bibliothèque municipale de Nancy; Jean-Yves Mariotte at the Archives municipales de Strasbourg; Monique Rabault of the Archives départementales de Loir-et-Cher; Diana Lachatanere and André Elizée of the Schomburg Center for Research in Black Culture; Roy Goodman of the American Philosophical Society; and librarians at Cornell, Howard, Indiana, and Yale Universities who enabled me to consult materials from their collections from a distance.

At Cal State San Marcos, my colleagues in the History Department have provided a congenial haven for my multiple interests. I could not ask for a more thoughtful, engaged, and kind group of colleagues. This book has also benefited from the insights and energy of my students at CSUSM, whose enthusiasm for learning about Grégoire and the other issues discussed here has been a constant source of inspiration. Outside my department, further thanks go to Kim Knowles-Yanez, Liliana Ross-mann, Veronica Anover, and Vicki Golich. My deepest gratitude extends to my siblings Stacy and Alan Sepinwall, to my parents-in-law Marilyn and Harvey Goldstein, to Meredith Goldsmith, Nicole Carter, and Ofer Matan, as well as to the rest of my extended family and dear friends. I am sure they have grown tired of hearing about the abbé, but their enduring support has meant the world to me.

During the development of this book, I lost two people I treasured: Hyman Resnick, who kept happy memories of France even after seeing it at its worst, and my beloved father, Dr. Jerry Sepinwall. My father was my hero and best friend; he and my mother, Prof. Harriet Lipman Sepin-wall, instilled in me a love for learning and social justice from my earli-est years. I owe them both more than I can say. I am also grateful to my mother for her unremitting enthusiasm for this project, her thoughtful comments on several chapters, and her repeated reminders to make my writing clear enough that even nonhistorians could understand it. The last words of this book, however, go to my husband, Steve Goldstein, who has been my own Madame Dubois—and yet much more. The joy of seeing him each day—or at least speaking to him long-distance from my journeys in the abbé's footsteps—has sustained me through many years of study and writing, and I remain in awe of his intelligence, patience, and unfailing good humor. May this book be but one entry in our collective life oeuvre.

Chapter list of the manuscript labeled "Doctrine du christianisme," BSPR-G, Rév. 177

The following table converts the lettering system used in chapters 8 and 9 to the full title of the chapter drafts in BSPR-G, Rév. 177. Grégoire's spelling has been conserved.

The letters at left show the symbols used in chapters 8 and 9, and the text at right shows Grégoire's chapter titles.

A   Ch. 1: Doctrine du christianisme sur les devoirs de l'homme envers ses semblables, application de cette doctrine aux premiers siecles de l'ere Chrétienne [revised version of D and E].

B   Ch. 2: Reproches faits au christianisme de ne pas compter au nombre des vertus l'amitié ni le patriotisme, réfutation de ces reproches [published version in *Chronique religieuse* VI (janvier 1821): 217—226].

C   Ch. [blank]: L'opposition de la morale chrétienne au despotisme, cause principale des persécutions dirigées contre les chrétiens.

D   Ch. 4: De l'influence du christianisme sur l'abolition de l'esclavage [first version of A].

E   Ch. 1: Doctrine du christianisme sur les devoirs de l'homme envers ses semblables, application de cette doctrine aux premiers siecles de l'ere Chrétienne [second version of A, revising D].

F   Ch. 2: Delivrance des prisonniers et rachat des captifs.

G   Ch. 5: Influence du christianisme sur l'affranchissement des Négres [early version of I].

H   Ch. 6: Des indiens proteges par le christianisme [early version of J].

I   Ch. 7 ou 8: Influence du christianisme sur l'affranchissement des négres [later version of G].

J   Ch. 8. 10: Des indiens protégés par le christianisme [later version of H].

K   Ch. 9. 11: De l'influence du Christianisme sur l'etat des Indous, ~~des Juifs &&c.~~ des *pariahs* & [early version of M].

L   Ch. 10. 12: Influence du christianisme sur l'etat des Juifs.

M   Ch. ~~15~~. 13: Influence du Christianisme sur l'etat des Indous, des pariahs & et d'autres classes d'hommes fletris par les lois ou l'opinion [later version of K].

M-2   Untitled and unnumbered chapter fragment following the previous one, and focusing on Christianity, theater, popular culture, and animals.

N   Chapitre [blank]: Doctrine politique de conciles et d'autres assemblées auxquels le clergé concourent [may signal start of a new book].

O   Ch. 2: Etablissement de la royauté chez les Hébreux.

P   Ch. 3: Abolition de l'esclavage ancien, congregation des parabolains, etablissement des hopitaux [parts revised by R and S].

Q   Ch. ~~3.~~ 4: Abolition de l'esclavage ancien. ~~Congrégation des parabolains établissement des hopitaux~~ [short chapter fragment, rewritten and expanded in R].

R   Ch. 4: Abolition de l'esclavage ancien [revises Q and parts of P].

S   Ch. 5: Etablissement des parabolains, création des hopitaux [revises parts of P].

T   Ch. 5: Abolition du servage feodal, mariage des esclaves consacré par l'Eglise [revised and split into U and V].

U   Ch. 6: Abolition du servage feodal[,] mariage des esclaves consacré par l'Eglise. Etablissement de la treve de Dieu [revised version of parts of T, continued by V].

V   Ch. 7: Continuation du même sujet [revision of parts of T, continuation of U].

W   [Unnumbered chapter]: De la puissance souveraine dans les tems autodiluviens. ~~Doctrine de l'ancien testament sur la puissance souveraine.~~ République des Israëlites sous les juges.

X   Notes on books.

Y   Unnumbered, unnamed chapter, on Christianity, abortion and children.

Z   Unnamed chapter, continuation of Y.

Z-2   Notes on books.

Notes

1. See A. Lloyd Moote, "Introduction: New Bottles and New Wine: The Current State of Early Modernist Biographical Writing," *French Historical Studies* 19 (1996): 911–26; Lloyd Kramer, *Lafayette in Two Worlds: Public Cultures and Personal Identities in an Age of Revolutions* (Chapel Hill: University of North Carolina Press, 1996), 1–2; and Jo Burr Margadant, "Introduction: Constructing Selves in Historical Perspective," in *The New Biography: Performing Femininity in Nineteenth-Century France*, ed. Jo Burr Margadant (Berkeley: University of California Press, 2000), 1–32.

2. See the popular biographies of Grégoire published for the bicentennial (Maurice Ezran, *L'Abbé Grégoire, défenseur des Juifs et des Noirs: Révolution et tolérance* [Paris: Harmattan, 1992]; Pierre Fauchon, *L'Abbé Grégoire: Le prêtre-citoyen* [Paris: Nouvelle république, 1989]; and Georges Hourdin, *L'abbé Grégoire: Evêque et démocrate* [Paris: Descle de Brouver, 1989]); the essay collection on Grégoire by the renowned religious historian Bernard Plongeron (*L'abbé Grégoire, ou, l'arche de la fraternité* [Paris: Letouzey et Ané, 1989]; henceforth "Plongeron, *L'abbé Grégoire*"); Ruth Necheles's study of Grégoire's ideas about Jews and blacks (*The Abbé Grégoire 1787–1831: The Odyssey of an Egalitarian* [Westport, CT: Greenwood, 1971]); and the other older sources cited in this study. Reprints of his works published by the mid 1990s included *Oeuvres de l'Abbé Grégoire* (Nendeln, Liechtenstein: Kraus-Thomson Organization, 1977); two versions of Grégoire's 1788 *Essai sur la régénération physique, morale et politique des Juifs* (one edited by Rita Hermon-Belot [Paris: Flammarion, 1988]; and the other by Robert Badinter [Paris: Stock, 1988]); and *Mémoires de l'abbé Grégoire*, ed. J. M. Leniaud and preface by J. N. Jeanneney (Paris: Editions de Santé, 1989). I later discovered that other scholars who had done unpublished work on Grégoire had left records of their efforts. The best of

these are the annotated bibliography by S. Posener held by the Bibliothèque de l'Arsenal ("Essai d'une bibliographie critique des oeuvres de l'abbé Grégoire" [1946], ms. 14045); and the files left at the New York Public Library's Schomburg Center for Research in Black Culture by Guichard Parris (MG 31), which led me to a number of pre-1940 studies I might otherwise have overlooked. Once I was well into my work on Grégoire, still more studies appeared. See *The Abbé Grégoire and His World* (Archives internationales d'histoire des idées/International Archives of the History of Ideas 169), ed. Jeremy D. Popkin and Richard H. Popkin (Dordrecht, Neth.: Kluwer Academic Publishers, 2000); *Grégoire et la cause des noirs (1789–1831), combats et projets,* ed. Yves Bénot and Marcel Dorigny (Paris: Société française d'histoire d'outre-mer/Association pour l'étude de la colonisation européene, 2000); Rita Hermon-Belot, *L'abbé Grégoire, la politique, et la vérité* (Paris: Seuil, 2000); Plongeron, *L'abbé Grégoire et la république des savants* (Paris: CTHS, 2001; henceforth "Plongeron, *Grégoire et la RS*"); *L'ami des hommes de toutes les couleurs, l'abbé Grégoire 1750–1831: Exposition Bibliothèque Abbé-Grégoire, Ville de Blois, 7 mai–7 juillet 1999* (Blois: Bibliothèque Abbé-Grégoire, 1999); Hans W. Debrunner, *Grégoire l'Européen: Kontinentale Beziehungen eines französischen Patrioten, Henri Grégoire 1750–1831* (Anif/Salzburg: Verlag Müller-Speiser, 1997); along with other reprints of Grégoire's works published recently in France.

3. Linda Wagner-Martin, *Telling Women's Lives: The New Biography* (New Brunswick, NJ: Rutgers University Press, 1994), 1. The author also notes, "Biography of a male subject, then, has usually been a relatively uncomplicated presentation of the persona, shaped by the pattern of the personal success story. That narrative pleases readers, who probably chose to read the book in the first place because of what they already knew about the man" (6). See also the critiques of biography made by Claude Arnaud, "Le retour de la biographie: D'un tabou à l'autre," *Le Débat,* no. 54 (1989): 40–47. It is nevertheless true that certain strains of literary biography (such as the "modern biography" popularized by Lytton Strachey) aimed explicitly to debunk the worldview of their subjects.

4. David Brion Davis, "Some Recent Directions in American Cultural History," *American Historical Review* 73 (1968): 704–705; and, for example, Nick Salvatore, *Eugene V. Debs: Citizen and Socialist* (Urbana: University of Illinois Press, 1982); Jill Watts, *God, Harlem U.S.A.: The Father Divine Story* (Berkeley: University of California Press, 1992); and Estelle Freedman, *Maternal Justice: Miriam Van Waters and the Female Reform Tradition* (Chicago: University of Chicago Press, 1996).

5. Mary Louise Roberts, "Acting Up: The Feminist Theatrics of Marguerite Durand," *French Historical Studies* 19 (1996): 1103–38, and other essays in this special issue on biography; and Bernard Guenée, *Between Church and State: The Lives of Four French Prelates in the Late Middle Ages,* trans. Arthur Goldhammer (Chicago: University of Chicago Press, 1991; French edition published 1987), 7. See also Jacques Revel, "Microanalysis and the Construction of the Social," in *Histories: French Constructions of the Past,* ed. Jacques Revel and Lynn Hunt (New York: New Press, 1995), 492–502; essays in Margadant, *The New Biography*; Jacques Le Goff, "Comment écrire une biographie historique aujourd'hui?" *Le Débat,* no. 54 (1989): 48–53; Gary Kates, *Monsieur D'Eon Is*

a Woman: A Tale of Political Intrigue and Sexual Masquerade (New York: Basic Books, 1995); and Nina Rattner Gelbart, *The King's Midwife: A History and Mystery of Madame du Coudray* (Berkeley: University of California Press, 1998).

6. Joan Wallach Scott, *Only Paradoxes to Offer: French Feminists and the Rights of Man* (Cambridge, MA: Harvard University Press, 1996), esp. 15–16; Keith Michael Baker, *Condorcet: From Natural Philosophy to Social Mathematics* (Chicago: University of Chicago Press, 1975), vii. See also Kathryn Kish Sklar, "Coming to Terms with Florence Kelley: The Tale of a Reluctant Biographer," in *The Challenge of Feminist Biography: Writing the Lives of Modern American Women*, ed. Sara Alpern, Joyce Antler, Elisabeth Israels Perry, and Ingrid Winther Scobie (Urbana: University of Illinois Press, 1992), 17–33; and Kramer, *Lafayette in Two Worlds*, 1–16.

7. Wagner-Martin, *Telling Women's Lives*, 4.

INTRODUCTION TO PART ONE

1. Roger Chartier, *Cultural Origins of the French Revolution*, trans. Lydia G. Cochrane (Durham, NC: Duke University Press, 1991), 5. As Chartier notes, it is somewhat anachronistic to use the singular term *Enlightenment* to describe such a multifaceted and porous movement. Nevertheless, many of the philosophes did see themselves as working on a common project, many of the movement's opponents viewed them as a unit, and much of modern scholarship has continued to rely upon this term. I have therefore retained it, while being careful to distinguish between various strains of Enlightenment where relevant (on this topic, see also Darrin M. McMahon, *Enemies of the Enlightenment: The French Counter-Enlightenment and the Making of Modernity* [New York: Oxford University Press, 2001], esp. 208n34).

2. Notable exceptions are Antoine Sutter, *Les années de jeunesse de l'abbé Grégoire: Son itinéraire jusqu'au début de la Révolution* (Sarreguemines: Editions Pierron, 1992); Louis Edmond Henri Maggiolo, "L'abbé Grégoire, 1750–1789," *Mémoires de l'Académie de Stanislas*, 4th ser., vol. 5 (1873): xxx–cii; and Maggiolo, "La vie et les oeuvres de l'abbé Grégoire, 1750 à 1789," *Revue des travaux de l'Académie des sciences morales et politiques et compte rendus de ses séances*, n.s., 25 (1886): 224–65. Hermon-Belot discusses Grégoire's early years briefly in ch. 1 of her *L'abbé Grégoire*.

CHAPTER 1: FROM TAILOR'S SON TO ENLIGHTENED ABBÉ

1. See Grégoire's certificate of baptism, cited in Sutter, *Les années de jeunesse*, 15; Grégoire's father was also referred to as Sébastien (see Maggiolo [1886], 247–48).

2. On Grégoire's "compulsive sociability," see Plongeron, *Grégoire et la RS*, 74.

3. *Mémoires*, 49, 113.

4. Sutter, *Les années de jeunesse*, 16; and René Taveneaux, *Le Jansénisme en Lorraine, 1640–1789* (Paris: J. Vrin, 1960), 7. For more on the Jansenist-Jesuit quarrels, see Dale Van Kley, *The Jansenists and the Expulsion of the Jesuits from*

France, 1757–1765 (New Haven, Conn.: Yale University Press, 1975); *The Damiens Affair and the Unraveling of the Ancien Régime, 1750–1770* (Princeton, N.J.: Princeton University Press, 1984); and *The Religious Origins of the French Revolution: From Calvin to the Civil Constitution, 1560–1791* (New Haven, Conn.: Yale University Press, 1996).

5. Maggiolo (1873), xxxiii–xxxiv; Sutter, *Les années de jeunesse,* 17.

6. Maggiolo (1873), xxxiv, liii; and Dom Augustin Calmet, *Histoire de l'ancien et du nouveau testament, et des Juifs . . . Nouvelle édition, revue & corrigée . . .* (Paris: Chez les libraires associés, 1770), 1: iii, iv, 121–22. It has been suggested that Grégoire went to hear Calmet lecture at Senones (Hermon-Belot, "Préface," in *Essai sur la régénération,* 21), but Calmet died when Grégoire was seven. On Grégoire's later plan to update Calmet's history of Lorraine, see BM Nancy Mss. 957 (533), 958 (534), fol. 55 and 2074 (936).

7. Plongeron, *L'abbé Grégoire,* 38 and passim.

8. Maggiolo (1873), lxv, lxxii. As his tone suggests, Maggiolo was not an admirer of Grégoire's revolutionary actions. On the friendship between Grégoire and Jennat, see BM Nancy Ms. 1688 letters, reprinted in Henri Cosson, "Lettres de l'abbé Grégoire à l'abbé Jennat," *Révolution française,* nos. 1/3 (1935): 70–89, 247–77.

9. Cf. Maggiolo (1873), xxxiv; and Sutter, *Les années de jeunesse,* 18–19.

10. *Mémoires,* 50.

11. *Archives parlementaires de 1787 à 1860, première série (1787 à 1799),* ed. M. J. Mavidal and M. E. Laurent (Paris: Librairie administrative de Paul Dupont, 1862–), vol. 11 (Feb. 19, 1790): 647 (henceforth *"AP"*). See also Maggiolo (1873), xxxvi, lxiiin15.

12. Sutter and Maggiolo provide slightly different chronologies for these years (Maggiolo [1873], lx; Sutter, *Les années de jeunesse,* 22–23). Though a supporter of the Revolution like Grégoire, Lamourette would have a different fate; when the people of Lyon decided to resist the revolutionary armies, Lamourette sided with his flock and was executed. For more on Lamourette, see Norman Ravitch, "Catholicism in Crisis: The Impact of the French Revolution on the Thought of the Abbé Adrien Lamourette," *Cahiers internationaux d'histoire économique et sociale* 9 (1978): 354–85.

13. Léon-Noël Berthe, "Deux illustres correspondants de l'Académie d'Arras: Lamourette et Grégoire," in *Arras à la veille de la Révolution: Traditions et lumières* (Mémoires de l'Académie des Sciences, Lettres et Arts d'Arras, 6e sér., T. 1) (Arras: Imprimerie Mordacq, 1990), 204. Cf. Lamourette's suggestions that Grégoire had inspired him on this matter, in his 1790 *Observations sur l'état civil des Juifs* (Paris: Chez Belin). See also the respectful letter Lamourette wrote to his former pupil in 1789: "Would you be kind enough to receive, Monsieur, from the hand of your former teacher a small work that might offer you some insights that would be to your liking? . . . I have seen your work on the Restoration of the Jews, and I recognized there the maturity of talent whose first flowering I saw at Metz. I would be thrilled if this portion of our brothers who have been so humiliated would feel all the effects of the zeal that animates you to reintegrate them into the human species" (Lamourette to Grégoire, Sept. 9, 1789, in Bibliothèque de la Société de Port-Royal, Collection Grégoire [henceforth "BSPR-G"], dossier

"Rhône") [NOTE: In the late 1990s, the BSPR began assigning call numbers to individual documents as it constructed a database of its holdings. Except in those cases where my primary work with a document occurred after the recataloguing, all references to dossiers here reflect the previous system, in which documents were classified only by the geographical or thematic folder in which they were stored. BSPR-G call numbers beginning with "Rév.," however, have not changed since the reorganization.]

14. See Grégoire's expression of his "feelings of gratitude, esteem, and veneration" toward Sanguiné and Lamourette in his *Défense de l'ouvrage intitulé: Légitimité du serment civique . . .* (Paris: Imprimerie nationale, 1791), 13–15.

15. "Lettre d'un curé lorrain, émigré, sur l'abbé Grégoire," reprinted in *La Revue lorraine populaire* (Dec. 1989), 21–25. Cf. Sutter, *Les années de jeunesse,* 26–27. Grégoire also used the title *Professeur à Pont-à-Mousson* in his Nancy contest essay.

16. Sutter, *Les années de jeunesse,* 28–29; Grégoire, *Histoire des confesseurs des empereurs, des rois, et d'autres princes* (Paris: Baudouin Frères, 1824), 28 (also cited in Sutter); Grégoire, *Opinion de M. Grégoire . . . sur la gabelle, à la séance du 19 Septembre au soir* (Versailles: Chez Baudouin, [1789]).

17. "Lettre d'un curé lorrain," 22; Maggiolo (1873), xiii.

18. See, for instance, his eventual praise for Grégoire's essay on the Jews, cited in Sutter, *Les années de jeunesse,* 49.

19. Sutter, *Les années de jeunesse,* 40. This annual salary can be understood by comparing it to that of the average curé elected to the National Assembly (1,000–3,000 livres) and the average Third Estate deputy (7,000 livres). Timothy Tackett, *Becoming a Revolutionary: The Deputies of the French National Assembly and the Emergence of a Revolutionary Culture (1789–1790)* (Princeton, N.J.: Princeton University Press, 1996), 27, 40.

20. *Mémoires,* 51; Maggiolo (1873), lxvii; and "L'abbé Grégoire vu par l'abbé Laurent Chatrian," 22. Grégoire did not give dates for his acquaintance with these two men, but they died in 1773 and 1776, respectively.

21. *Mémoires,* 51. On Grégoire's love for books as an adult, see for instance his correspondence with Antoine-Alexandre Barbier (BN, nouvelles acquisitions françaises [henceforth "NAF"], Ms. 1391, fols. 231–344); and chs. 5 and 6.

22. *Mémoires,* 51; and Grégoire, *Rapport sur la bibliographie, séance du 22 Germinal, l'an 2 . . .* (Paris: Imprimerie de Quiber-Pallissaux, 1794), 6. Though Grégoire, like most people of his time, named Languet as the author of the *Vindiciae,* the work is now generally attributed to Philippe Duplessis-Mornay, Henri IV's minister of state.

23. Plongeron, *Théologie et politique au siècle des Lumières (1770–1820)* (Geneva: Droz, 1973), 110. Van Kley has noted that Boucher borrowed in particular from the *Vindiciae (Religious Origins,* 30). See also Hermon-Belot, *L'abbé Grégoire,* 183–88.

24. *Mémoires,* 51.

25. Grégoire, *Eloge de la Poésie, discours qui a remporté le prix . . . de la Société royale des Sciences et Belles-lettres de Nancy . . .* (Nancy: Chez les Frères Leseure, 1773), 29–30. Grégoire would return to the subject of David and Hebrew poetry in "Sur la Littérature des Juifs," in *Correspondance sur les*

affaires du tems, ou Lettres sur divers sujets de Politique, d'Histoire, de Littérature, d'Arts et Sciences, etc. (Paris: Imprimerie Polémique, 1797), 3: 90–91. On the place of essay contests in the provincial Englightenment, see Daniel Roche, *Le siècle des lumières en province* (Paris: Mouton, 1978).

26. Grégoire, *Eloge de la Poésie*, 3, 56–58; and Maggiolo (1873), lxxvi. See Hermon-Belot for an alternate reading of the *Eloge* focusing on Grégoire's celebration of virtue in poetry (*L'abbé Grégoire*, 115–18).

27. Grégoire, *Eloge de la Poésie*, 56–58.

28. *Mémoires*, 113.

29. See Leniaud, "Introduction," in *Mémoires*, 23; Auguste Pouget, *Les idées religieuses et réformatrices de l'évêque constitutionnel Grégoire* (Paris: Société nouvelle de librairie et d'édition, 1905), 68; Claude Jolly, "La bibliothèque de l'abbé Grégoire," *Livre et Révolution: Mélanges de la bibliothèque de la Sorbonne* 9 (1989): 209–20; Plongeron, *L'abbé Grégoire*, 9; and Taveneaux, "L'abbé Grégoire et la démocratie cléricale," 155. Jolly also relied on examining Grégoire's "Catalogue de ma bibliothèque" (BSPR-G, Rév. 254), but the abbé had several other inventories of his private collection (see BSPR-G, Rév. 166 and 167; "Catalogue de livres de l'abbé Henri Grégoire," Bibliothèque de l'Arsenal [henceforth "Ars."], Ms. 6573; "Catalogue des livres légués à la Bibliothèque du Roi par M. Grégoire" [1831], Ars. Fol. Z-1013; and *Catalogue des livres de la Bibliothèque de M.*** [Grégoire], dont la vente se fera le Jeudi 20 Septembre 1821* . . . [Paris: Silvestre/Gallimard, 1821] [BN Delta-14098]). Moreover, these catalogues only list the books Grégoire owned; they do not refer to books he borrowed from others or even all of the works he cited in his writings. Though Grégoire's relationship to the Enlightenment was not wholly hostile, neither was he only a product of the Enlightenment, as is suggested in casual references to him that underemphasize his religiosity.

30. *Mémoires*, 113. [Grégoire], "Lettre XIII [on the Vosges]," in *Correspondance sur les affaires du tems*, 1: 159. On this essay's having been written earlier, see ch. 2, note 14. Grégoire's profession that reason had led him to faith was similar to that of other enlightened Christians (see Plongeron, *L'abbé Grégoire*, 40).

31. *Mémoires*, 51. Despite Grégoire's claim to have burned all his early poems, Maggiolo claimed to have seen some of them (Maggiolo [1873], lxxvii). Though Grégoire omitted mention of the 1774 contest in his *Mémoires*, Christian Pfister has convincingly attributed a "bizarre" entry to Grégoire (Pfister, "Histoire de l'Académie de Stanislas," in *Table alphabétique des publications de l'Académie de Stanislas [1750–1900]*, ed. Justin Favier [Nancy: Imprimerie Berger-Levrault & Cie, 1902], 25).

32. Franklin L. Ford, *Strasbourg in Transition, 1648–1789* (New York: W. W. Norton, 1966), 196, 102–30, 179. See also David G. Troyansky, "Alsatian Knowledge and European Culture: Jérémie-Jacques Oberlin, Language and the Protestant *Gymnase* in Revolutionary Strasbourg," *Francia* 27, no. 2 (2001): 119–38; David A. Bell, "Nation Building and Cultural Particularism in Eighteenth-Century France: The Case of Alsace," *Eighteenth-Century Studies* 21, no. 4 (1988): 472–90; and Bernard Vogler, *Histoire culturelle de l'Alsace : Du Moyen Age à nos jours . . .* , 3d ed. (Strasbourg: La Nuée Bleue, 1994).

33. See brief discussions in Sutter, *Les années de jeunesse,* 37–40; Maggiolo (1886), 243; and Hermon-Belot, *L'abbé Grégoire,* 43–44.

34. Société des Philantropes, *Statuts généraux de la Société des Philantropes, rédigés dans les comices de 1776* ([Strasbourg]: n.p., 1776) (1932 facsimile edition with signatures, including Grégoire's, conserved at Hollins University, South Carolina); Grégoire, *Motion en faveur des juifs* (Paris: Chez Belin, 1789), iii; and Grégoire's manuscript note in the BN's copy of *Mémoires de la Société des Philantropes* (Berne: Chez la société typographique, 1778) [BN Z-28454]. Grégoire's entry does not appear in this volume, and seems lost to history. Jean Tild referred to it as *Mémoire sur les moyens de recréer le peuple juif et, partant, de l'amener à la vertu et au bonheur* (Tild, *L'abbé Grégoire d'après ses Mémoires recueillis par Hyppolyte Carnot* [Paris: Nouvelles éditions latines, 1946], 11), but he seems to have created this title based on Grégoire's description of it in his 1789 *Motion en faveur des juifs.*

35. See letters in M. Ginsburger, "Zwei unveröffentlichte Briefe von Abbé Grégoire," in *Festschrift zu Simon Dubnows siebzigstem Geburtstag (2. Tischri 5691),* ed. Ismar Elbogen, Josef Meisl, and Mark Wischnitzer (Berlin: Jüdischer Verlag, 1930), 201–6. Though Ginsburger did not know how Grégoire knew these Strasbourg figures, he clearly met them through the SPS. On Grégoire's continued friendship with them, see letters in BSPR-G, dossier "Bas-Rhin"; letters to Blessig, Ars. Ms. 14635, fols. 2–4; the 1827 letter cited in Rodolphe Peter, "Le pasteur Oberlin et l'abbé Grégoire," *Bulletin de l'histoire du Protestantisme français* 126 (Jul.–Sept. 1980); and Necheles, *Abbé Grégoire,* 256.

36. Although Grégoire claimed in the nineteenth century to be "a complete outsider with respect to Freemasonry" (Grégoire, *Histoire des sectes religieuses qui sont nées, se sont modifiées, se sont éteintes dans les différentes contrées du globe, depuis le commencement du siècle dernier jusqu'à l'époque actuelle. Nouvelle édition, corrigée et considérablement augmentée* [Paris: Baudouin, 1828], 2: 17), unsupported rumors linking Grégoire to the Masons persist. Much of the evidence is, however, contradictory. Sutter cites an exhibition in Vého "that indicated that Grégoire was also a member of the 'Harmony' Masonic lodge in Nancy, explaining however that 'sources are rare'" (Sutter, *Les années de jeunesse,* 55). In contrast, the journalist and Masonic historian Jean Bossu argued that Grégoire was not listed among the ranks of any of the known lodges in Nancy or elsewhere in Lorraine, though he noted that a few lodges had lost their records (Bossu, "Réponse: Henri Grégoire évêque et franc-maçon," *L'intermédiaire des chercheurs et des curieux* 4 [1954]: 63). Bossu suggested that Grégoire might have belonged during the First Empire (along with his episcopal comrades Mauviel and Saurine) to the neo-Masonic Ordre du Temple "without considering himself a Mason." He noted that the Masonic historian André Bouton had told him definitively that Grégoire was a Mason but "without giving me a precise reference" (Bossu, "Réponse: Henri Grégoire évêque et franc-maçon," *L'intermédiaire des chercheurs et des curieux* 6 [1956]: 170). Bouton himself wrote in 1958, however, that Grégoire was a "profane," a non-Mason (Bouton, *Les francs-maçons manceaux et la révolution française, 1741–1815* [Le Mans: Imprimerie Monnoyer, 1958], 150).

Dictionaries of Freemasonry are no less definitive. The *Dictionnaire de la franc-maçonnerie* (ed. Daniel Ligou [Paris: PUF, 1987], 550) includes Grégoire with the following notation: "The famous constitutional bishop of Blois is considered to have been a Mason by many authors who, without giving precise proof, name him as a member of the Loge L'Harmonie, Orient de Paris," while the *Dictionnaire des francs-maçons français,* ed. Michel Gaudart de Soulages and Hubert Lamant (Paris: Editions Albatros, 1980), names Grégoire as a member of the same lodge without providing clear-cut evidence. Another recent dictionary of Freemasonry (Jean-André Faucher, *Dictionnaire historique des francs-maçons: Du XVIIIe siècle à nos jours* [Paris: Librairie Académique Perrin, 1988], 46), names Grégoire as a Mason by citing him on the 1788 roster of a different Paris lodge, Le Comité Secret des Amis Réunis. This information seems suspect, however, for two reasons: first, if the roster does in fact date from 1788, it was likely a different Henri Grégoire, since our priest did not arrive in Paris until 1789. Second, in an earlier work on Freemasonry, Faucher made only one mention of Grégoire: he noted that the *conventionnel* Antoine-François Sergent-Marceau had included Grégoire among several colleagues who were members in 1790 of the Loge des Amis Réunis. Faucher commented, however, that "this list, cited by several historians, remains suspect." (Jean-André Faucher and Achielle Ricker, *Histoire de la franc-maçonnerie en France* [Paris: Nouvelles éditions latines, 1968], 199). Allegations that Grégoire was a Mason persist on the internet. See, for example, the article claiming Grégoire as an illustrious Mason: Claude Wauthier, "Africa's Freemasons: A Strange Inheritance," *Le monde diplomatique,* English edition (Aug./Sept. 1997) (http://www.monde-diplomatique.fr/md/en/1997/08–09/masons.html, accessed August 2002).

37. Bossu, "Réponse: Henri Grégoire évêque et franc-maçon," *L'intermédiaire des chercheurs et des curieux* 5 (1955): 204–5.

38. Margaret C. Jacob, *Living the Enlightenment: Freemasonry and Politics in Eighteenth-Century Europe* (New York: Oxford University Press, 1994), 186–87; and Bertrand Diringer, "Franc-maçonnerie et société à Strasbourg au XVIIIème siècle" (Mémoire de maîtrise, Université de Strasbourg, 1980), 197 and passim. See also Pierre Chevallier, *Histoire de la franc-maçonnerie française,* vol. 1, *La Maçonnerie: Ecole de l'Egalité, 1725–1799* (Paris: Fayard, 1974), 327: "Even if [the SPS] had a President, Vice-President, Secretary and Treasurer instead of reception ceremonies and a formal hierarchy, the Masonic origin of the society betrays itself through the use of certain expressions. The meeting place was a 'sanctuary,' the unit called a 'maison' (analogous to the usage in Masonic temples), and as with all Masons, the Philanthropes were required to 'aid each other mutually in their maladies and afflictions.' "

39. Diringer, "Franc-maçonnerie et société," 201–208, 195. Though Chatrian called the SPS an actual Masonic lodge, this seems to contradict available evidence, particularly since his claim is not duplicated by others and he often used *Mason* as an epithet ("L'abbé Grégoire vu par l'abbé Laurent Chatrian," 22). Bossu has suggested that the Nancy SPS affiliate (to which Grégoire belonged) competed with Masonic lodges for members rather than being one itself (Bossu [1955], 204).

40. Bell, "Nation Building and Cultural Particularism," 477; F. Ford, chs. 8 and 9; and also Tackett, *Becoming a Revolutionary,* 44, 52, 53.

41. Jacob, *Living the Enlightenment,* 222, building on the work of Aram Vartanian. Because of the Masonic and philosophic influences in the SPS, it would be difficult to trace which ideas came from which portion of the Enlightenment. See Jacob on commonalities between philosophic and Masonic discourse (esp. intro. and ch. 1).

42. *Précis instructif sur la Société des Philantropes* ([Strasbourg]: n.p., n.d.), 3–7; *Statuts de la Société des Philantropes* ([Strasbourg]: n.p., [1777]), 3–5.

43. *Précis instructif,* 20, 21, 13; *Statuts de la Société,* Art. 6.

44. *Précis instructif,* 16–18; *Programmes de la Société des Philantropes* ([Strasbourg]: n.p., n.d.), 3.

45. *Précis instructif,* 18; *Statuts de la Société,* 15.

46. *Précis instructif,* 7–9. On enlightenment sociability and the limits of its egalitarianism, see Jürgen Habermas, *The Structural Transformation of the Public Sphere: An Inquiry into a Category of Bourgeois Society,* trans. Thomas Burger (Cambridge, MA: MIT Press, 1991); Daniel Gordon, *Citizens without Sovereignty: Equality and Sociability in French Thought, 1670–1789* (Princeton, N.J.: Princeton University Press, 1994), esp. ch. 1; and Dena Goodman, *The Republic of Letters: A Cultural History of the French Enlightenment* (Ithaca, N.Y.: Cornell University Press, 1994), 111–22 and passim. On Masonic sociability, see Jacob, *Living the Enlightenment,* 5, 20, and passim.

47. "L'abbé Grégoire vu par l'abbé Laurent Chatrian," 22.

48. *Précis instructif,* 21; and Voss, "Die Strassburger 'Société des Philantropes' und ihre mitglieder im Jahre 1777," *Revue d'Alsace* 108 (1982): 74–75. Citing Grégoire's letter to Ehrmann (reprinted in Ginsburger, "Zwei unveröffentlichte Briefe"), Necheles claimed that the Société had Jewish members (*Abbé Grégoire,* 15n20), but there is no evidence of this. Though Grégoire indicated in the letter that one of Ehrmann's grandfathers had been Jewish, Ehrmann himself was a Protestant minister. Moreover, though Ehrmann was a student of Blessig's and would be associated with several of the members, his name does not appear on the 1777 list reprinted in Voss, "Die Strassburger 'Société des Philantropes.'"

49. See Arthur Hertzberg, *The French Enlightenment and the Jews* (New York: Columbia University Press, 1968); Zosa Szajkowski, "Growth of the Jewish Population in France," in *Jews and the French Revolutions of 1789, 1830 and 1848* (New York: Ktav Publishing, 1970), 76–79; Paula Hyman, *The Jews of Modern France* (Berkeley: University of California Press, 1998), ch. 1; and Esther Benbassa, *The Jews of France: A History From Antiquity to the Present* (Princeton, N.J.: Princeton University Press, 1999), 41–57. Yiddish and Ladino varied from place to place in Europe, but I have used these terms instead of the more technical *Judeo-German* and *Judeo-Spanish* because they are more familiar to most readers.

50. Hertzberg, *The French Enlightenment,* 118; Hyman, *Jews of Modern France,* ch. 1; Benbassa, *Jews of France,* 58–72.

51. See Hertzberg, *The French Enlightenment*; and the vast literature on Voltaire's relation to Jews and Judaism (including Allan Arkush, "Voltaire on

Judaism and Christianity," *AJS Review* 18, no. 2 [1993]: 223–43; and Adam
Sutcliffe, "Myth, Origins, Identity: Voltaire, the Jews and the Enlightenment
Notion of Toleration," *Eighteenth Century* 39, no. 2 [1998]: 107–26). Despite
Rousseau's largely positive reputation with regard to Jews, he did display anti-
Jewish stereotypes in a 1772 essay (Sutcliffe, *Judaism and Enlightenment* [New
York: Cambridge University Press, 2003], 248).

52. On Luther and the Jews, see Martin Luther, "On the Jews and Their
Lies," in *Luther's Works*, vol. 47, *The Christian in Society IV*, ed. Franklin Sherman, trans. Martin H. Bertram (Philadelphia: Fortress Press, 1971), 137–306
(and introduction by Sherman, 123–36); and Léon Poliakov, *The History of
Anti-Semitism*, trans. Richard Howard (New York: Vanguard Press, 1965), 1:
216–26.

53. Hertzberg, *The French Enlightenment*, 120–21, 287–88; and Robert
Liberles, "Dohm's Treatise on the Jews: A Defence of the Enlightenment," *Leo
Baeck Institute Year Book* 33 (1988): 33–34.

54. *Programmes de la Société des Philantropes,* at BSPR-G, Rév. 86/6, 1–2.

55. Ibid.

56. *Mémoires de la Société des Philantropes,* which Grégoire indicated was
the only volume of transactions (ms. note, BN Z-28454). Chatrian later recalled
the volume vividly; he noted that it contained an anonymous article on ecclesiastical greed that he attributed "for certain" to Grégoire ("L'abbé Grégoire vu
par l'abbé Laurent Chatrian," 22). Voss was unable to find the society's
Mémoires anywhere in Europe and was also unsure how many volumes were
published; indeed, the BN copy seems to have surfaced only after its move to the
Tolbiac site and changes in the BN's computer catalog. A second copy has long
resided, however, at the Schomburg Center for Research in Black Culture in New
York (call number F306-S), where it was acquired presumably on the basis of an
abolitionist essay in the volume. Chatrian's attribution appears reliable based on
the content of the anonymous article on the Church, which closely parallels later
writings by Grégoire. For a more detailed discussion of this article, see ch. 2.

57. *Précis instructif,* 22.

58. Jean-Jacques Rousseau, *The Creed of a Priest of Savoy,* trans. Arthur H.
Beattie (New York: Frederick Ungar Publishing Co., 1957); Rousseau, *Observations de Jean-Jacques Rousseau, de Genève, Sur la réponse qui a été faite à
son Discours* (Paris: n.p., 1751), esp. 27; and John Lough, *The Encyclopédie*
(New York: D. McKay Co., 1971), 208–11.

59. McMahon, *Enemies of the Enlightenment*; and R. R. Palmer, *Catholics
and Unbelievers in Eighteenth-Century France* (New York: Cooper Square Publishers, 1939). See also Harvey Chisick, *The Limits of Reform in the Enlightenment: Attitudes towards the Education of the Lower Classes in
Eighteenth-Century France* (Princeton, N.J.: Princeton University Press, 1981),
117; Monique Cottret, "Les jansénistes juges de Jean-Jacques," in *Jansénisme et
Révolution,* ed. Catherine Maire (Paris: Chroniques de Port-Royal/Bibliothèque
Mazarine, 1990), 81–102; Mona Ozouf, "De-Christianization," in *A Critical
Dictionary of the French Revolution,* ed. François Furet and Mona Ozouf (Cam-
bridge, MA: Belknap Press of Harvard University Press, 1989), 23–24; Dale Van
Kley, "The Abbé Grégoire and the Quest for a Catholic Republic," in Popkin

and Popkin, *Abbé Grégoire and His World,* 79; and Nigel Aston, *Religion and Revolution in France, 1780–1804* (Washington, D.C.: Catholic University of America Press, 2000), 87–88. Palmer believed that the idea of enlightened religion was dead by 1759, though this is earlier than the existence of the SPS suggests. He nevertheless pointed out that many abbés were "favorably inclined to the sensationalist metaphysics formulated by Locke and Condillac" and that revelation was sometimes the "only issue" on which Catholics and unbelievers disagreed (125, 124, 221). See also his discussion of Rousseau's religious views (98, 193) and his argument that many Enlightenment ideas were anticipated by orthodox Christians (221 and passim).

60. Jacob, *Living the Enlightenment,* 87, 153, 145. The referenced document is the codified 1723 *Constitutions* of English masonry.

61. See ms. note in BN Z-28454; and Grégoire, *Motion en faveur des juifs,* iii.

62. On enlightened religion in other countries, see Roy Porter and Mikulas Teich, *The Enlightenment in National Context* (Cambridge: Cambridge University Press, 1981); Mark A. Noll, *Princeton and the Republic, 1768–1822: The Search for a Christian Enlightenment in the Era of Samuel Stanhope Smith* (Princeton, N.J.: Princeton University Press, 1989); David Sorkin, *The Berlin Haskalah and German Religious Thought: Orphans of Knowledge* (London: Vallentine Mitchell, 2000); and Joseph P. Chinnici, *The English Catholic Enlightenment: John Lingard and the Cisalpine Movement, 1780–1850* (Shepherdstown, W. Va.: Patmos Press, 1980).

63. Plongeron, "Recherches sur l'Aufklärung catholique en Europe occidentale (1770–1830)," *Revue d'histoire moderne et contemporaine* 16 (1969): 555–605.

CHAPTER 2: THE "BON CURÉ" OF EMBERMÉNIL

1. Grégoire destroyed nearly all of his prerevolutionary personal papers during the Terror (see Paul Pisani, "Henri Grégoire," in *Dictionnaire de théologie catholique,* ed. E. Mangenot, A. Vacant, and Mgr. E. Amann [Paris: Letouzey et Ané, 1947], col. 1854–63), and only two of his prerevolutionary writings (his 1773 poetry essay and his 1788 essay on the Jews) have been previously known to scholars. See, however, discussion in ch. 1 and below of two anonymous essays from this period likely written by him.

2. Sutter, *Les années de jeunesse,* 40.

3. Philip T. Hoffman, *Church and Community in the Diocese of Lyon, 1500–1789* (New Haven, Conn.: Yale University Press, 1984), 2, 84–85, 94, and passim; and Keith P. Luria, *Territories of Grace: Cultural Change in the Seventeenth-Century Diocese of Grenoble* (Berkeley: University of California Press, 1991), 4–5 and passim.

4. Timothy Tackett, *Priest and Parish in Eighteenth-Century France: A Social and Political Study of the Curés in a Diocese of Dauphiné, 1750–1791* (Princeton, N.J.: Princeton University Press, 1977), 169; and Tackett, *Becoming a Revolutionary,* 129. See also Suzanne Desan, *Reclaiming the Sacred: Lay Religion and Popular Politics in Revolutionary France* (Ithaca, N.Y.: Cornell University Press, 1990), 77–78.

5. *Mémoires,* 118; Peter Gay, *The Enlightenment, an Interpretation,* vol. 2, *The Science of Freedom* (New York: Knopf, 1966–69), 517–22; and Chisick, *The Limits of Reform,* 278 and passim.

6. *Mémoires,* 117–18.

7. Ibid, 118; and Grégoire, *Compte rendu aux évêques réunis à Paris de la visite de son diocèse (Paris, le 8 décembre 1796)* (Paris: Imprimerie-librairie chrétienne, 1796), 30–31.

8. See Pierre Bernadau to Grégoire (1791), reprinted in Michel de Certeau, Dominique Julia, and Jacques Revel, *Une politique de la langue: La Révolution française et les patois: L'enquête de Grégoire* (Paris: Gallimard, 1975), 193; and Hermon-Belot, *L'abbé Grégoire,* 352.

9. Grégoire to Dubois de Fosseux, Dec. 8, 1788, in Berthe, "Grégoire, élève," 39–40.

10. [Louis Philipon de la Madelaine], *Vues patriotiques sur l'éducation du peuple . . .* [Lyon: P. Bruyset-Ponthus, 1783], 24 and passim. See also Chisick, *The Limits of Reform,* 133–34 and passim.

11. Grégoire to Dubois de Fosseux, in Berthe, "Grégoire, élève," 40. On Grégoire's continued admiration of Philipon during the Revolution, see Chisick, *The Limits of Reform,* 17.

12. De Certeau, Julia, and Revel, *Une politique de la langue,* 140, 149.

13. Maggiolo (1873), xlii; *Mémoires,* 118; "Lettres des habitants d'Ember-ménil à M. Grégoire du 7 mars 1791," in *Mémoires,* 182–83; and BM Nancy, Ms. 958 (534), fols. 46 and 222.

14. Maggiolo (1873), xli; [Grégoire], "Lettre XXX [on the Vosges and Switzerland]," in *Correspondance sur les affaires du tems,* 2: 168; Grégoire, "Promenade dans les Vosges," 146, 157–58, 170–71; Sutter, *Les années de jeunesse,* 41–42; and Debrunner, *Grégoire l'Européen,* 58, 262, and passim. According to Arthur Benoît, the travel essay that Grégoire included in *Correspondance sur les affaires du tems* was based primarily on notes from the 1784–87 trips, with some minor updating (A. Benoît, "Description des Vosges, par l'abbé Grégoire, publiée pour la première fois et annotée," *Annales de la Société d'émulation du département des Vosges* 71 [1895]: 223–24). Sutter indicates that Grégoire met the famed Swiss agricultural educator Philipp Emanuel von Fellenberg during the 1784 trip, but Fellenberg was born in 1771 and did not set up his model school until 1799, so it is likely that their acquaintance began later.

15. Grégoire refers to these men as "nos amis" in his letters to J.-J. Oberlin in BN, fonds allemands (henceforth "All."), Ms. 195 (reprinted in Christian Pfister, "Lettres de Grégoire à Jérémie-Jacques Oberlin," *Mémoires de la Société d'archéologie lorraine et du Musée historique lorrain* 42 [3d ser., vol. 20] [1892]: 333–73). On SPS involvement with the newspaper, see Diringer, "Franc-maçonnerie et société," 206; and Nicole Sourdive, "Un périodique stras-bourgeois à la fin du XVIIIème siècle: *Le Bürgerfreund* (1776–1777)," in *Les lettres en Alsace* (Strasbourg: Librairie Istra, 1962), 269–75. For more on J.-J. Oberlin, see Troyansky, "Alsatian Knowledge and European Culture."

16. Jérémie-Jacques Oberlin, *Essai sur le patois lorrain des environs du comté du Ban de la Roche, fief Royal d'Alsace* (Strasbourg: Jean Fréd. Stein, 1775), 2, 84.

17. Grégoire, "Catalogue de ma bibliothèque," BSPR-G, Rév. 254; and Grégoire to J.-J. Oberlin, 26 vendémiaire an 7 [Oct. 17, 1798], BN All. Ms. 195, fol. 161v. Despite Grégoire's praise, Jérémie-Jacques himself saw Grégoire as the pioneer for having made eradication of patois a part of government policy (J.-J. Oberlin to Grégoire, 21 prairial an II [June 9, 1794], BN NAF Ms. 2798, fol. 95).

18. See BN All. Ms. 195, especially Grégoire to J.-J. Oberlin, 1 frimaire an III [Nov. 21, 1794] and Nov. 4, 1802, fols. 152 and 178. Grégoire would also help obtain pensions for Jean-Frédéric Oberlin and for his Strasbourg friends Jean Hermann and Jean-Chrétien Ehrmann (ibid.; and J.-F. Oberlin to Grégoire, 9 vendémiaire an III [Sept. 30, 1794], in Archives nationales [henceforth "AN"] 510 AP 2 [Grégoire Papers].

19. M. Grucker, "Le pasteur Oberlin," *Mémoires de l'Académie de Stanislas,* 5th ser., vols. 4–6 (1888): xxxi–lvi; Malou Schneider and Marie-Jeanne Geyer, *Jean-Frédéric Oberlin: Le divin ordre du monde, 1740–1826* (Strasbourg/Mulhouse: Les Musées de la ville de Strasbourg/Editions du Rhin, 1991); and John F. Kurtz, *John Frederic Oberlin* (Boulder: Westview Press, 1976), 149–50, 283.

20. Grégoire to François de Neufchâteau, Mar. 1, 1818, and "Extrait d'un voyage dans les Vosges en 1787," both in Archives municipales de Strasbourg, Fonds Oberlin (15 NA) (henceforth "AMS-O"), no. 172, fols. 87, 89; also Kurtz, *John Frederic Oberlin,* 17, 277.

21. Peter, "Le pasteur Oberlin et l'abbé Grégoire," 301; Anne-Louise Salomon, *Frédéric-Rodolphe Saltzmann, 1749–1820: Son rôle dans l'histoire de la pensée religieuse à Strasbourg* (Paris: Editions Berger-Levrault, 1932), 64; John Graham, *Lavater's Essays on Physiognomy: A Study in the History of Ideas* (Berne/Las Vegas: Peter Lang, 1979), 61–62; Bernard Keller, "Relations et rayonnement: Les contacts de J.-F. Oberlin avec l'Europe de la culture," and Geyer, "La pédagogie du portrait," both in Schneider and Geyer, *Jean-Frédéric Oberlin,* 21–22, 183–94. Though this visit is their earliest confirmed meeting, Grégoire nevertheless seems to have known Jean-Frédéric from the late 1770s; see Grégoire to François de Neufchâteau, Mar. 1, 1818, in AMS-O, no. 172, fol. 89.

22. [Grégoire], "Lettre XXX," in *Correspondance sur les affaires du tems,* 2: 170–71.

23. AMS-O, no. 428-III (reprinted in Peter, "Le pasteur Oberlin et l'abbé Grégoire," 305–8).

24. "Extrait d'un voyage dans les Vosges en 1787," AMS-O, no. 172, fol. 87. On Grégoire's attitudes toward Christian sects, see ch. 9.

25. Ibid., fol. 88.

26. M. Grucker, "Le pasteur Oberlin," *Mémoires de l'Académie de Stanislas,* 5th ser., 4–6 (1888): xxxi–lvi, xxxi–lvi, xlii; and Edmond Stussi, "Oberlin pédagogue," and Schneider, "Le Ban-de-la-Roche," in Schneider and Geyer, *Jean-Frédéric Oberlin,* 75, 55; Kurtz, *John Frederic Oberlin,* 56, 77.

27. Kurtz, *John Frederic Oberlin,* 12–15, 122, 277; Grégoire to François de Neufchâteau, Mar. 1, 1818, AMS-O, no. 172; and Louis Rauscher (Oberlin's grandson) to Daniel-Ehrenfried Stoeber, May 3, 1827, in Peter, "Le pasteur Oberlin et l'abbé Grégoire," 321–24.

28. Grégoire to J.-J. Oberlin, Mar. 30, 1795, BN All. 195, fol. 156; Grégoire to François de Neufchâteau, Mar. 1, 1818, AMS-O, no. 172; and Rauscher to Stoeber, May 3, 1827, in Peter, "Le pasteur Oberlin et l'abbé Grégoire," 321–24.

29. Sutter, *Les années de jeunesse*, 43; de Certeau, Julia, and Revel, *Une politique de la langue*, 21; C. Maire, "La Rosière de Réchicourt," *La Revue lorraine populaire*, no. 52 (1983): 174–76. See his comments about the Lunéville sermon in ch. 3, note 11.

30. Cardinal François-Désiré Mathieu, *L'ancien régime en Lorraine et Barrois, d'après des documents inédits (1698–1789),* 3d ed. (Paris: Librairie Honoré Champion, 1907), 357; "Lettre d'un curé lorrain, émigré, sur l'abbé Grégoire," 22; and Taveneaux, "L'abbé Grégoire et la démocratie cléricale," 142.

31. Taveneaux, "L'abbé Grégoire et la démocratie cléricale," 137–38, 144; Van Kley, *Religious Origins,* 68 and passim; and idem, "The Abbé Grégoire and the Quest for a Catholic Republic," 81–82.

32. [Grégoire], "Considérations sur les abus de la sécularisation des biens ecclésiastiques," in *Mémoires de la Société des Philantropes*; see also ch. 1, note 56.

33. Ibid., 163, 167, 170, 171.

34. Ibid., 174.

35. Ibid., 175, 188–89, 181, 184–85.

36. Ibid., 188–89.

37. Chatrian, "L'abbé Grégoire vu par l'abbé Laurent Chatrian," 22.

38. Grégoire to Dubois de Fosseux, Dec. 8, 1788, in Berthe, "Grégoire, élève," 40–41.

39. See *Plan d'études pour les jeunes ecclésiastiques* (Metz: Claude Lamort, 1790).

40. Ibid., 6–8. Cf. Alan Charles Kors, *Atheism in France, 1650–1729* (Princeton, N.J.: Princeton University Press, 1990).

41. *Plan d'études,* 4, 8, 9, 15, 20–21. The author added that one of his own teachers had confusingly mixed the ideas of Voltaire, Rousseau, and other philosophes into theological discussions, and "I myself witnessed the consequences I am talking about" (14n1).

42. Ibid., 1, 4, 16–19.

43. E. Duvernoy, "Le cahier d'Embermenil, paroisse de l'abbé Grégoire en 1789," *Annales de l'Est* 12 (1898): 577–83; L. Jérome, *Les élections et les cahiers du clergé lorrain aux Etats généraux de 1789 (Bailliages de Nancy, Lunéville, Blâmont, Rosières, Vézelise et Nomeny)* (Nancy: Berger-Levrault et Cie., 1899); Taveneaux, "L'abbé Grégoire et la démocratie cléricale," 142–44; and idem, *Le Jansénisme en Lorraine,* 721.

44. Grégoire, Valentin (curé de Leyr), Didry (curé de Farroy), *A MM. les curés lorrains et autres ecclésiastiques séculiers du diocèse de Metz* (Nancy: n.p., 1789), 2.

45. Excerpt from the "Procès-Verbal de l'assemblée des trois ordres, tenues en l'hôtel de ville," Archives de la Meurthe, c. 514 and 520, reprinted in Maggiolo (1886), 257–60.

46. L. Jérome, *Les élections et les cahiers du clergé lorrain,* 107–109, 144–49; Chatrian, "L'abbé Grégoire vu par l'abbé Laurent Chatrian," 22; letters between Grégoire and Guilbert, Grand Séminaire de Nancy, MB 17, fols. 5,

289, 294, reprinted in Jérome, "Centenaire de l'abbé Grégoire: Quelques lettres de l'abbé et de l'évêque constitutionnel," *Académie de Stanislas: Mémoires,* ser. 6, no. 29 (1932): 55–66; and procès-verbal of the Nancy election, Archives départementales de Meurthe-et-Moselle (Nancy), 57 B 3 [copy provided by the BM Nancy]. La Fare's support of Grégoire (which, according to the abbé Chatrian, stemmed from the bishop's frustration with his local Richerist curés along with some shrewd flattery by the curé of Emberménil) is a great irony given later events. La Fare, a conservative who opposed the Revolution and especially citizenship for Jews, was horrified by what he had done once Grégoire's true convictions began to emerge (see Chatrian, 22).

47. See the works of Van Kley, cited in ch. 1.

48. Hermon-Belot, "Introduction," in Grégoire, *Les Ruines de Port-Royal des Champs* (Paris: Réunion des musées nationaux, 1995), 14 (see also ch. 14 of her *L'abbé Grégoire*); Paul Grunebaum-Ballin, "Grégoire convertisseur? ou la croyance au 'Retour d'Israël,' " *Revue des Etudes Juives,* 4th ser., vol. 1 (labeled vol. 121), nos. 1/2 (1962): 388; Leniaud, "Introduction," in *Mémoires,* 22; Gazier, *Etudes sur l'histoire religieuse de la Révolution française d'après des documents originaux et inédits* (Paris: Armand Colin, 1887), 4. Bell wrote of the Jansenist origins of Grégoire's early thought in his "Lingua Populi, Lingua Dei: Language, Religion and the Origins of French Revolutionary Nationalism," *American Historical Review* (1995), 1403–37, but has since moved toward the perspective of multiple influences outlined here; see Bell, *Cult of the Nation,* 190–95, citing an early version of this chapter. See also Gazier's backing away from calling Grégoire a Jansenist in his *Etudes sur l'histoire religieuse,* 261; and *Histoire générale du mouvement janséniste depuis ses origines jusqu'à nos jours* (Paris: Edouard Champion, 1922), 2: 147–48.

49. See Hermon-Belot, "Introduction," in *Les Ruines de Port-Royal,* 7–25; idem, "Préface," in *Essai sur la régénération,* 7–39; idem, *L'abbé Grégoire,* ch. 14 and passim; Maggiolo (1873), lxxxiii; Leniaud, "Introduction," 22n12; Grunebaum-Ballin, "Grégoire convertisseur?" 389; and Mathieu, 357n1. The possibility of Grégoire's late identification with Jansenism was first suggested to me by Dominique Julia. On Grégoire's later Jansenist sympathies, see ch. 6.

50. Grunebaum-Ballin, "Grégoire convertisseur?" 383–98; and Hermon-Belot, "Préface," in *Essai sur la régénération,* esp. 29–30.

51. See letters in BSPR-G, dossier "Bas-Rhin"; Oberlin, "Judaei: Conversion finale des Juifs," 1767 and 1770, AMS-O, no. 314, fols. 69–77; and Christopher M. Clark, *The Politics of Conversion: Missionary Protestantism and the Jews in Prussia, 1728–1941* (Oxford: Clarendon Press, 1995). On pietism and the Oberlins, see Kurtz, *John Frederic Oberlin,* 122–23.

52. Necheles, *Abbé Grégoire,* 10; Plongeron, *L'abbé Grégoire,* 39; also Ravitch, "Catholicism in Crisis," 363.

53. See Van Kley's review of Plongeron's *L'abbé Grégoire, Catholic Historical Review* 78 (1992): 669; Leniaud, "Introduction," 22; and Van Kley, "The Abbé Grégoire and the Quest for a Catholic Republic," 80–81. Van Kley nevertheless detected sympathies with Gallicanism in Grégoire's writing, and argues that, "whether [Grégoire] knew it or not," these were part of Jansenism's legacy in the eighteenth century. On Maire, see ch. 6.

54. Hermon-Belot, *L'abbé Grégoire*, 352; and Taveneaux, *Le Jansénisme en Lorraine*, 718.

55. See Tackett, *Priest and Parish*, 243; Taveneaux, "L'abbé Grégoire et la démocratie cléricale," 137; Aston, *Religion and Revolution*, 30; and the writings of Van Kley, including *The Damiens Affair* and "The Religious Origins of the Patriot and Ministerial Parties in the Maupeou Revolution: Controversy over the Chancellor's Constitutional Coup, 1771–1775," *Historical Reflections/Réflexions historiques* 18, no. 2 (1992): 17–63. Van Kley has opted to refer to Grégoire as a Jansenist nonetheless (see his "Abbé Grégoire and the Quest for a Catholic Republic," 83, 104–105; and *The Jansenists and the Expulsion of the Jesuits*, 234n13).

CHAPTER 3: A PHYSICAL, MORAL, AND POLITICAL
REGENERATION OF THE JEWS

1. See François Manchuelle, "The 'Regeneration of Africa': An Important and Ambiguous Concept in 18th and 19th Century French Thinking about Africa," *Cahiers d'Etudes Africaines* 144, no. 36–4 (1996): 559–88; Jean-Loup Amselle, *Vers un multiculturalisme français: L'empire de la coutume* (Paris: Aubier, 1996); Aron Rodrigue, *French Jews, Turkish Jews: The Alliance Israélite Universelle and the Politics of Jewish Schooling in Turkey, 1860–1925* (Bloomington: Indiana University Press, 1990); and Jay R. Berkovitz, *The Shaping of Jewish Identity in Nineteenth-Century France* (Detroit, Mich.: Wayne State University Press, 1989).

2. On Dohm's motivations, see Liberles, "Dohm's Treatise on the Jews: A Defence of the Enlightenment," *Leo Baeck Institute Year Book* 33 (1988): 37, 39.

3. Ozouf, "Regeneration" in *Critical Dictionary*; Antoine de Baecque, "L'homme nouveau est arrivé: La 'régénération' du français en 1789," *Dix-huitième siècle*, no. 20 (1988): 193–208; and idem, *Le corps de l'histoire: Métaphores et politique (1770—1800)* (Paris: Calmann-Lévy, 1993), esp. 166–71.

4. The following linguistic history is based largely on searches of the ARTFL database, a joint project of the University of Chicago and the CNRS, conducted in October 1996 (the URL for this database has changed frequently and was http://www.lib.uchicago.edu/efts/ARTFL/databases/TLF/ as of April 2004). Because this database is selective (and focuses heavily on classic Enlightenment texts), it cannot be stated definitively that any text in the database that appears to be the first to use *regeneration* in a new way actually was. Writers often signal, though, when they are using a word in a way that may be unfamiliar to readers. It thus seems likely that the *Encyclopédie*, discussed below, did mark an important shift in usage. As Van Kley has suggested, however, it is possible that there may be an alternate history of *regeneration* to be written out of Jansenist-Jesuit debates *(Religious Origins, 325)*.

5. On regeneration as baptism, see *Dictionnaire universel d'Antoine Furetière* (1690; reprint, Paris: SNL-Le Robert, 1978), and its updated eighteenth-century edition, *Dictionnaire universel françois et latin, vulgairement*

appellé Dictionnaire de Trévoux . . . nouvelle édition corrigée et considérablement augmentée (Paris: La Veuve Delaune, 1743), 5: 858. On *regeneration* as baptism but also resurrection, see M. l'abbé Bergier, *Encyclopédie Méthodique: Théologie* (Paris: Panckoucke, 1790), 3: 335. On medical definitions, see *Dictionnaire historique de la langue française* (Paris: Dictionnaires le Robert, 1992), 2: 1747; and *Grand Larousse de la langue française* (Paris: Librairie Larousse, 1971–78), 6: 4993. See also ARTFL.

6. Jean Le Rond d'Alembert, *Discours préliminaire de l'Encyclopédie* (1751; reprint, Stuttgart: Friedrich Fromann, 1966), 1: xix–xx; letter from Bouchetière to Crutély, 1778, in François Joseph Grille, *Lettres, mémoires et documents publiés avec des notes sur la formation, le personnel, l'esprit du 1er bataillon des volontaires de Maine et Loire . . .* (Paris: Amyot, 1850), 1: 123–25.

7. Marquis de Mirabeau, *L'ami des hommes, ou traité de la population* (The Hague: Benjamin Gibert, 1758). See also Robert John Morrissey, *L'empereur à la barbe fleurie: Charlemagne dans la mythologie et l'histoire de France* (Paris: Gallimard, 1997), 268. Mirabeau has also been credited with coining the term *civilization*; see Joachim Moras, *Ursprung und Entwicklung des Begriffs der Zivilisation in Frankreich (1756–1830)* (Hamburg: Seminar für Romanische Sprachen und Kultur, 1930), 5, citing the *Dictionnaire de Trévoux*. I am grateful to David Bell for these references.

8. Charles Bonnet, *La palingénésie philosophique . . .* (Geneva: Philibert et Chirol, 1769), 234; Grégoire, *Essai sur la régénération*, ch. 7, n.14, citing Buffon's "Des Epoques de la nature," in *Histoire naturelle* (Paris: Imprimerie Royale, 1778), vol. 5. See also Sean Quinlan, "Colonial Bodies, Hygiene and Abolitionist Politics in Eighteenth-Century France," *History Workshop* 42 (1996): 106–25.

9. Mona Ozouf, "La Révolution française et la formation de l'homme nouveau," in *L'homme régénéré: Essais sur la Révolution française* (Paris: Editions Gallimard, 1989), 128; de Baecque, "L'homme nouveau est arrivé"; and Van Kley, *Religious Origins*, 325.

10. Cf. Necheles, *Abbé Grégoire*, 5.

11. See letters from Blessig, Saltzmann, and others to Grégoire in BSPR-G, dossier "Bas-Rhin"; and Grégoire, *Histoire des sectes religieuses* (1828), 3: 390. Though the contents of this sermon are lost, he gave another sermon a year or two later in Lunéville, in which he spoke of the "hope that the Catholic Church preserves of one day seeing the Jewish nation enter its bosom" (see Grégoire to Ehrmann, Sept. 1, 1788, reprinted in Ginsburger, "Zwei unveröffentlichte Briefe," 206).

12. Abraham Cahen, "L'émancipation des Juifs devant la Société royale des sciences et des arts de Metz en 1787 et M. Roederer," *Revue des études juives* 1, no. 1 (1880): 83–104; Henri Tribout de Morembert, "Est-il des moyens de rendre les Juifs plus utiles et plus heureux? Considérations sur les concours de l'Académie Royale de Metz de 1787 et 1788," *Mémoires de l'Académie nationale de Metz* 154 (6e sér., t. 1) (1974): 179–265; David Feuerwerker, *L'émancipation des Juifs en France: De l'ancien régime à la fin du Second Empire* (Paris: A. Michel, 1976), 49–142; and Frances Malino, *A Jew in the French Revolution: The Life of Zalkind Hourwitz* (Cambridge, MA: Blackwell, 1996), 14–59.

13. Christian Wilhelm Dohm, *De la réforme politique des Juifs,* preface and notes by Dominique Bourel (1782; reprint, Paris: Stock, 1984), 78.

14. On censorship in eighteenth-century France, see Daniel Roche, "Censorship and the Publishing Industry," in *Revolution in Print: The Press in France, 1775–1800,* ed. Robert Darnton and Daniel Roche (Berkeley: University of California Press, 1989), 3–26.

15. [P.-L. Roederer], *Prix proposés, en 1788, par la Société royale des sciences et des arts de Metz, pour les concours de 1789 et 1790* (Metz: Veuve Antoine & fils, 1788), AN 29 AP 6 (Roederer Papers); and Roederer's manuscript notes on the entries, AN 29 AP 101.

16. The reference to "Turkheim" *(sic)* and their "other friends" is in ch. 8, n. 7 of the *Essai.* In order to better understand the goals of Grégoire's intervention in debates on Jews, the following discussion focuses on texts that he himself read and cited. For fuller discussions of other positions on Jews, see Hertzberg, *The French Enlightenment*; also Sutcliffe, *Judaism and Enlightenment*; and Ronald Schechter, *Obstinate Hebrews: Representations of Jews in France, 1715–1815* (Berkeley: University of California Press, 2003).

17. For a slightly different, but also tripartite, model of discourses on Jews around the time of the French Revolution, see Lawrence Scott Lerner, "Beyond Grégoire: A Third Discourse on Jews and the French," *Modern Judaism* 21, no. 3 (2001): 199–215.

18. John Toland, *Reasons for Naturalizing the Jews in Great Britain and Ireland, On the same foot with all other Nations. Containing also, a Defence of the Jews against All vulgar Prejudices in all Countries* (1714; reprint, Jerusalem: Hebrew University, 1963), 10–11, 52; and Grégoire, *Essai sur la régénération,* ed. Hermon-Belot, 195 (all further references to the published *Essai* are from this edition, unless otherwise noted). In other texts, Toland's ideas about Jews and Judaism were more ambiguous (see Sutcliffe, *Judaism and Enlightenment,* 197–205).

19. Pierre-Louis Lacretelle, *Plaidoyer pour Moyse May, Godechaux & Abraham Lévy, Juifs de Metz* (1775; reprint, Paris: Lipschutz, 1928), 4, 16, 35, and passim. Some commentators have suggested that Lacretelle (whose work contained the phrase *arrêt de régénération*) preceded Grégoire in urging a civic regeneration of the Jews (see Hermon-Belot, "Préface," in *Essai sur la régénération,* 25). In using this phrase, however, Lacretelle was not urging the passage of an actual law to regenerate the Jews but distinguishing between juridical and theological questions. Using *regeneration* in its theological sense, he conceded that civic inclusion, which Jews deserved, would of course not regenerate them spiritually: "Yet we must not believe that they can thus receive an *arrêt de grace,* an *arrêt de régénération* [a divine decree of grace and of spiritual resurrection]" (Lacretelle, *Plaidoyer pour Moyse May,* 35). Malino has shown that by 1787 (when he himself entered the Metz contest), Lacretelle focused more on how to reform Jewish moral corruption than on their right to unconditional inclusion in the polity (Malino, *A Jew in the French Revolution,* 16). Lacretelle's entry was not available, though, to Grégoire as he drafted his *Essai,* so he responded only to the *Plaidoyer.*

20. J.B.D.V.S.J.D.R. [Israël Bernard Valabrègue], *Lettre, ou Réflexions d'un milord à son correspondant à Paris* . . . (London: n.p., 1767), 42, 63, and passim. On the authorship of the pamphlet, see Malino, *A Jew in the French Revolution*, 63; and Hertzberg, *The French Enlightenment*, 62.

21. Basnage, *Histoire des Juifs, depuis Jésus-Christ jusqu'à présent pour servir de continuation à l'histoire de Joseph. Nouvelle édition augmentée* (The Hague: Henri Scheurleer, 1716), 1: v, xxi; 8: 210–14; and 9: esp. 1121–37. Grégoire's summary of Toland in ch. 16, n. 2 of the *Essai*, for example, is virtually identical to that of Basnage, 9: 1141–42.

22. Grégoire, *Essai sur la régénération*, 117 and passim; Blessig to Oberlin, Mar. 6, 1775, in BN All. Ms. 192; and Grégoire, *Histoire des sectes religieuses* . . . (Paris: Potey, 1810), 2: 217.

23. Dohm, *De la réforme politique des Juifs*, 33, 38, 62, 49, 66, 77–97; and Liberles, "Dohm's Treatise on the Jews," 34–35.

24. Feuerwerker, *L'émancipation des Juifs*, 127, 137.

25. This passage, from the first two pages of the manuscript version of Grégoire's first contest entry, does not appear in the published version of the *Essai*. Grégoire would also delete at least one footnote referring to Dohm, even as he preserved the material to which the footnote alluded (first entry ms. 46n3 v. *Essai sur la régénération*, 128). On this manuscript, see below; on Dohm's SPS membership, see Voss, "Die Strassburger 'Société des Philantropes.' " It is unknown whether Dohm was present when Grégoire read his entry to the SPS.

26. See Malino, *A Jew in the French Revolution*, 25, 216n6; Feuerwerker, *L'émancipation des Juifs*, 86–87; Roederer, *Prix proposés, en 1788*; and Maggiolo (1886), 252–53.

27. See *L'abbé Grégoire, révolutionnaire de la tolérance: Exposition Nancy 1989/Exposition Blois 1989* . . . , 19; Tribout de Morembert, "Est-il des moyens," 199; Sutter, *Les années de jeunesse*, 56; and Hermon-Belot, *L'abbé Grégoire*, 475.

28. Grégoire, manuscript labeled on binding as *Mémoire sur les juifs*, collection of the Musée lorrain, ex libris Lucien Wiener (the volume does not have a call number). I am extremely grateful to Mlle Martine Mathias and her staff for granting me access to the manuscript. On the publishing history of the *Essai*, see below; on the typographical errors in the *Essai*, see Feuerwerker, *L'émancipation des Juifs*, 134n2.

29. Compare pp. 54v and 57 of the manuscript to *Essai sur la régénération*, 161, 165. The manuscript itself did not bear a title other than its inscription, a line from Psalm 43: "Dedisti nos tanquam oves escarum et en gentibus dispersisti nos" (Thou hast given us up as sheep to be eaten, and among the nations hast Thou scattered us). He did, however, refer to it as "Mémoire sur les juifs" (the same title used on the binding) in his cover letter for this contest (quoted in Tribout de Morembert, "Est-il des moyens," 197–98), so I use this title to refer to it. Because Grégoire's pagination was not consistent throughout the manuscript, the page numbers cited here are those added at the bottom by another hand, probably that of Jean Le Payen, the perpetual secretary of the academy.

30. "Mémoire sur les juifs," 30, 31, 61; cf. Comte de Mirabeau, *Sur Moses Mendelssohn, sur la Réforme politique des Juifs* (London, 1787), 76.

31. Fritz Heymann, *Der Chevalier von Geldern: Eine Chronik vom Abenteuer der Juden* (Amsterdam: Querido Verlag N.V., 1937), 110–15; Ludwig Rosenthal, *Heinrich Heines Grossoheim Simon von Geldern: Ein historischer Bericht mit dem bisher meist unveröffentlichten Quellenmaterial* (Kastellaun: Aloys Henn Verlag, 1978), 24, 65–66, and passim; "Simon von Geldern" in *Encyclopaedia Judaica* (New York: Macmillan, 1971–72), 7: 364–65; Sutter, *Les années de jeunesse*, 47 (and 27, citing Hermon-Belot); Hertzberg, *The French Enlightenment*, 175; and Michel Berr, *Appel à la justice des nations et des rois . . . au nom de tous les habitans de l'Europe qui professent la Religion juive* (Strasbourg: Levrault, 1801), 59.

32. For a fuller discussion of the passages Grégoire added after discussions with these men and behind-the-scenes tensions between them, see Sepinwall, "Strategic Friendships: Jewish Intellectuals, the Abbé Grégoire, and the French Revolution," in *Renewing the Past, Reconfiguring Jewish Culture: From Al-Andalus to the Haskalah,* ed. Ross Brann and Adam Sutcliffe (Philadelphia: University of Pennsylvania Press, 2004), 189–212. Grégoire's seeking out these Jews only before submitting the second entry is further intimated by other factors. First, a biographical essay, probably written by Grégoire himself, states that Bing met the abbé only after 1787, when Bing wrote a pamphlet that brought him public attention (see "Isaïe-Beer Bing," in *Biographie de la Moselle . . . ,* ed. Emile Auguste Nicolas Jules Bégin [Metz: Verronnais, 1829–1832], 90–94). Another factor that makes it unlikely that they befriended each other in the 1770s is that Bing was a preteen or young teenager for most of the decade, having been born in 1759. Moreover, the evidence cited in the case of von Geldern shows only that Grégoire sought some information from him after the contest was over, not that von Geldern had cowritten the *Essai* from its inception; indeed, the one story Grégoire included from von Geldern was absent from the first entry (see Ginsburger, "Zwei unveröffentlichte Briefe," 201–6; and *Essai sur la régénération,* 65–66, 186n9, absent from "Mémoire sur les juifs"). For more on Bing and Ensheim, see Jonathan Helfand, "The Symbiotic Relationship between French and Germany Jewry in the Age of Emancipation," *Leo Baeck Year Book* 29 (1984): 331–50; and Ronald B. Schechter, "Translating the Marseillaise: Biblical Republicanism and the Emancipation of Jews in Revolutionary France," *Past & Present,* no. 143 (May 1994): 108–35.

33. Cf. the highly sympathetic treatment by Hermon-Belot and Badinter in their reeditions of the *Essai,* with the critical appraisals of writers such as Pierre Birnbaum, "Sur l'étatisation révolutionnaire: L'abbé Grégoire et le destin de l'identité juive," *Le Débat,* no. 53 (1989): 157–73; Shmuel Trigano, "The French Revolution and the Jews," *Modern Judaism* 10 (1990): 171–90; and Gil Tzarefaty, "Une relecture de l'Essai de l'abbé Grégoire," in *Juifs en France au XVIIIe siècle,* ed. Bernhard Blumenkranz (Paris: Collection Franco-judaïca, 1994), 213–21. See also the thoughtful essay by Yerachmiel (Richard) Cohen in the Hebrew translation of Grégoire's *Essai* (*Masa al ha-tehiya ha-fisit, ha-mosrit, v'ha-m'dinit shel ha-yehudim* [Jerusalem: Mercaz Dinur, 1989]).

34. *Essai sur la régénération,* 67, 94, 117, 177.

35. Ibid., 131.

36. Basnage, *Histoire des Juifs,* 8: 210–14; "Mémoire sur les juifs," 4–4v; and *Essai sur la régénération,* 45–46, 179n8.

37. *Essai sur la régénération,* 96, also 48.

38. Ibid., 58, 61. See also Hermon-Belot's discussion about the presence of Jews posing "a real intellectual problem" for Grégoire and other Christians, in her "L'abbé Grégoire et la conversion des Juifs," in *Les Juifs et la Révolution française: Histoire et mentalités . . . ,* ed. Evelyne Oliel-Grausz and Mireille Hadas-Lebel (Louvain: E. Peeters, 1992), 22. Turckheim (the framer of the SPS contest) may himself have been heavily influenced by Basnage. The Turckheim family owned a copy of Basnage's work, and the SPS contest proposal mirrored Basnage's depiction of the issue (see Turckheim family copy at Stanford University Libraries, Taube-Baron Collection).

39. Grégoire contested Dohm on this count even more strongly in his first entry, asserting that Jews are "obligated to believe a rabbi even when he says his right hand is his left." See *Essai sur la régénération,* 87, 161; and "Mémoire sur les juifs," 29. On Dohm's religious beliefs, see Liberles, "Dohm's Treatise on the Jews," 32, 37.

40. *Essai sur la régénération,* 164, 201n6–7, 167–68; the new footnote on "great men" among the Jews, a sarcastic joke about the absurdity of rabbis (*Essai sur la régénération,* 200n4; absent from "Mémoire sur les juifs," 55v); and Sepinwall, "Strategic Friendships."

41. *Essai sur la régénération,* 189n8, 83, 85; and "Observations sur l'Etablissement et la Population des Juifs, à Metz," in original edition of *Essai* (Metz: Claude Lamort, 1789), 257–62.

42. *Essai sur la régénération,* 95, 192n8; compare to "Mémoire sur les juifs," 26v. Cf. Hermon-Belot, *L'abbé Grégoire,* 258–59; Plongeron, *L'abbé Grégoire,* 18; and Dohm, who had denounced Hell in his essay, *De la réforme politique des Juifs,* 150. On Grégoire's backing away from some of his harsher statements in the *Essai*'s notes, see also Michael Alpert, "The French Enlightenment and the Jews: An Essay by the Abbé Grégoire," *Patterns of Prejudice* 31, no. 1 (1997): 31–41, esp. 36.

43. *Essai sur la régénération,* 55.

44. Ibid., 62, 134, 138, 148–49.

45. Ibid., 168.

46. "Mémoire sur les juifs," 28v; and Grégoire to Malesherbes, Sept. 6, 1788, in AN, 154 AP II 136 (Chartrier de Tocqueville Papers), fol. 1.

47. *Essai sur la régénération,* 75, 65, 72; Grégoire to Mme de Chatenay, Aug. 22, 1789, collection of André Spire, reprinted in Spire, "Autour d'un autographe de l'abbé Grégoire," *Europe* 34, nos. 128–29 (1956): 78–84. See also "Mémoire sur les juifs," 14v.

48. *Essai sur la régénération,* 75, 157, 140, 155. See also Amselle, *Vers un multiculturalisme français,* 57 and passim.

49. On this point, see also de Baecque, *Le corps de l'histoire,* 171.

50. See John Caspar Lavater, *Essays on Physiognomy,* ed. and trans. Thomas Holcroft (London: William Tegg & Co., 1848), 349, 353; and Amselle, *Vers un multiculturalisme français,* 13, 16–17.

51. *Monthly Review* (1791), 174.

52. *Essai sur la régénération*, 96–97, 191, 192, 195; Zalkind-Hourwitz, *Apologie des juifs en réponse à la question; Est-il des moyens de rendre les Juifs plus heureux & plus utiles en France?* . . . (Paris: Gattey/Royer, 1789), 1, 2, 61, 75, 78–79, 85–86; Isaïah Berr Bing, *Mémoire particulier pour la Communauté des Juifs établis à Metz, rédigé par Isaac Ber-Bing* [sic] (n.p.: [1789]), 2, 13; and also Martine Lemalet, "L'émancipation des Juifs de Lorraine à travers l'oeuvre de Berr Isaac Berr," in *Politique et religion dans le judaïsme moderne* . . . , ed. Daniel Tollet (Paris: Presses de l'Université de Paris-Sorbonne, 1987), 63–83. For a fuller discussion of these men and their complicated relationships with Grégoire, see Sepinwall, "Strategic Friendships." Cf. Hermon-Belot ("The Abbé Grégoire's Program for the Jews: Social Reform and Spiritual Project," trans. J. Popkin, in Popkin and Popkin, *Abbé Grégoire and His World,* 13–14; and *L'abbé Grégoire,* 255), who argues that contemporary Jews did not object to Grégoire's *Essai* and that objections to it among Jews are a modern phenomenon.

53. Feuerwerker, *L'émancipation des Juifs,* 135–38.

54. Ibid., 90, 122, 127; and Claude-Antoine Thiéry, *Dissertation sur cette question: Est-il quelques moyens de rendre les Juifs plus heureux et plus utiles en France?* (Paris: Knapen Fils, 1788). On Berr's frustration with Grégoire's fashion of discussing Jews, see also ch. 9.

55. Grégoire to Malesherbes, Sept. 6, 1788 and Feb. 28, 1789, in Chartrier de Tocqueville Papers, fols. 1 and 5; and Feuerwerker, *L'émancipation des Juifs,* 117–19.

56. Grégoire to Malesherbes, Sept. 6, 1788; Gregory S. Brown, "Dramatic Authorship and the Honor of Men of Letters in Eighteenth-Century France," *Studies on Eighteenth-Century Culture* 27 (1998): 257–81, quote from 261; and idem, *A Field of Honor: Writers, Court Culture and Public Theater in French Literary Life from Racine to the Revolution* (New York: Columbia University Press, 2002; available at http://www.gutenberg-e.org/brg01).

57. Feuerwerker, *L'émancipation des Juifs,* ch. 3; Malesherbes to Grégoire, undated draft response, in Chartrier de Tocqueville Papers, fol. 2; and Grégoire to Ehrmann, Sept. 1, 1788, in Ginsburger, "Zwei unveröffentlichte Briefe," 205.

58. Feuerwerker, *L'émancipation des Juifs,* 102, 126; and Grégoire to "Docteur de Gueldres" [Simon von Geldern], Sept. 1, 1788, in Ginsburger, "Zwei unveröffentlichte Briefe," 204–5.

59. Grégoire to Dubois de Fosseux, Dec. 8, 1788, in Berthe, "Grégoire, élève," 39–40. See also *Mémoires,* 53.

60. Grégoire to Bing, Feb. 23, 1789, reprinted in "Lettres de Grégoire à I. B. Bing, 23 février 1789 et 20 août 1789," *Archives israélites* 5 (1844): 417.

INTRODUCTION TO PART TWO

1. For fuller chronologies of this crisis, see William Doyle, *Oxford History of the French Revolution* (Oxford: Oxford University Press, 1989); and Jeremy D. Popkin, *A History of Modern France,* 2d ed. (Upper Saddle River, N.J.: Prentice Hall, 2001), 35–40.

2. Tackett, *Becoming a Revolutionary*, 23; Edna Hindie Lemay, *La vie quotidienne des députés aux Etats généraux: 1789* (Paris: Hachette, 1987), 205; Jacques Antoine Creuzé-Latouche, *Journal des Etats généraux et du début de l'Assemblée nationale, 18 mai–29 juillet 1789*, ed. Jean Marchand (Paris: H. Didier, 1947), 195; and Dubois de Crancé, "L'abbé Grégoire," in *Le Véritable portrait de nos législateurs, ou galerie des tableaux exposés à la vue du Public . . .* (Paris: 1792), 118–19. The poems include *L'auteur et la fortune, satyre patriotique, dialoguée en vers et en prose . . . par un Citoyen passif de la Cité de Nancy* (A Démocratopolis: Aux dépens de l'Aristocratie Moderne, 1790); Ignace Kolly, *Epître a M. l'abbé Grégoire, . . . pour le remercier d'avoir embrassé la défense de deux Fribourgeois . . .* (Paris: Imprimerie de Millet, 1790); and many others.

3. Blessig to Grégoire, May 29, 1791, in BSPR-G, dossier "Bas-Rhin."

4. Adrien Duquesnoy, *Journal d'Adrien Duquesnoy* (Paris: Alphonse Picard et fils, 1894), 1: 88, 91, 127, 192; abbé Laurent Chatrian, "Calendrier historique et ecclésiastique de Diocèse de Nancy, pour l'année 1789," entry for Jul. 14, 1789, Bibliothèque du Grand Séminaire—Nancy, Ms. MC 121; and Pierre Dubois, "Diatribes, l'abbé Grégoire jugé par l'abbé Laurent Chatrian," *La Revue lorraine populaire* (October 1987): 298–302.

5. Grégoire to Guilbert, Apr. 8, 1789, and Guilbert to Grégoire, June 29, 1789, reprinted in Jérome, "Centenaire de l'abbé Grégoire," 62–65; and [Grégoire], *Nouvelle lettre d'un curé, à ses confrères, députés aux Etats-Généraux* (n.p., [1789]). Because of its content, this pamphlet was published quasi-anonymously ("M. G***, Curé d'I**** en Lorraine"), but its authorship was widely known. For more on the revolt of the curés, see Ruth Necheles, "The Curés in the Estates-General of 1789," *Journal of Modern History* 46 (1974): 425–44.

6. Grégoire to Guilbert, July 6, 1789, and letters between Guilbert and Verdet (another Lorraine cleric), in ibid., 66–70, 81–84.

7. For a brief sketch of Grégoire's activities during the Constituent, see Lemay, *Dictionnaire des Constituants, 1789–1791* (Paris: Universitas, 1991), 426–29. The Reports Committee was particularly swamped with work (*AP* 11 [Feb. 5, 1790]: 436; *AP* 12 [Mar. 14 and 30, 1790]: 162, 443; and AN, series D 29).

8. Lemay, *La vie quotidienne*; Mercier to Grégoire, Jan. 8, 1790, and Cabanis to Grégoire, Mar. 19, 1790, both in AN 510 AP 2, dossiers "M" and "C/D"; and Dorigny, "The Abbé Grégoire and the *Société des Amis des Noirs*," in Popkin and Popkin, *Abbé Grégoire and His World*, 27–39.

9. On a trip Grégoire took to Le Havre, see Grégoire to officiers municipaux du Havre, Nov. 26, 1790, in Archives municipales du Havre (AMH), P 24, no. 3, first discovered by Sylvie Barot, "L'abbé Grégoire et le Havre sous la monarchie constitutionnelle: L'histoire d'une brève alliance," in *Révolution et mouvements révolutionnaires en Normandie* (Le Havre: Centre havrais de recherche historique, 1990), 27–33. Barot, the conservateur of the AMH, was not sure when the trip took place, but a letter in the BSPR-G, dossier "Seine Inférieure" (new côte GR 1591 ms), along with a reference in Grégoire's *Mémoires* (78), confirms that the trip was earlier in 1790.

10. Ezran, *L'Abbé Grégoire*, 169; Grégoire to Jennat, Apr. 10, 1791, in Cosson, "Lettres de l'abbé Grégoire," 73.

11. My periodization here emphasizes Directory- and Consulate-era efforts to preserve the Revolution, even if a more moderate version of it, as well as the initial hopes many had that Napoleon would also try to maintain revolutionary ideals. Though Grégoire and other Thermidorians sometimes referred to the Revolution in the past tense after 1794, by this they meant only the turbulence of the Terror, and they remained committed to republican principles. The use of 1801 as a dividing point rather than other years between 1799 and 1804 is based on the symbolic importance of Napoleon's Concordat with the pope; for Grégoire and other patriotic priests, that agreement signaled the definitive end of revolutionary Christianity. Some of the material in ch. 7, however, begins earlier than 1801.

CHAPTER 4: CREATING A FRENCH NATION

1. François Furet, *Interpreting the French Revolution,* trans. Elborg Forster (Cambridge: Cambridge University Press, 1981), 26.

2. Grégoire, *Discours prononcé le jour de Toussaint 1789,* 5.

3. Antoine de Baecque, "Le choc des opinions: Le débat des droits de l'homme, juillet–août 1789," in *L'an I des droits de l'homme,* ed. de Baecque, Wolfgang Schwale, and Michel Vovelle (Paris: Presses de CNRS, 1988), 7–37; Keith Michael Baker, *Inventing the French Revolution* (Cambridge: Cambridge University Press, 1990), esp. "Fixing the French Constitution," 301–305; Tackett, *Becoming a Revolutionary,* 120; also Chartier, *Cultural Origins of the French Revolution,* 5. On the language and political culture of the Revolution, see also Lynn Avery Hunt, *Politics, Culture, and Class in the French Revolution* (Berkeley: University of California Press, 1984).

4. Marcel Gauchet, *La Révolution des droits de l'homme* (Paris: NRF/Editions Gallimard, 1989); idem, "Rights of Man," in Furet and Ozouf, *Critical Dictionary,* 818–28; de Baecque, "Le choc des opinions"; and Baker, "The Idea of a Declaration of Rights," in *The French Idea of Freedom: The Old Regime and the Declaration of Rights of 1789,* ed. Dale Van Kley (Stanford, CA: Stanford University Press, 1994), 154–96.

5. Cf. discussion of Rabaut Saint-Etienne in Raymond Birn, "Religious Toleration and Freedom of Expression," in Van Kley, *The French Idea of Freedom,* 265–300, esp. 267–72.

6. David A. Bell, *The Cult of the Nation in France: Inventing Nationalism, 1680–1800* (Cambridge, Mass.: Harvard University Press, 2001), 75.

7. De Baecque, *Le corps de l'histoire,* 171.

8. Grégoire, *Motion en faveur des Juifs,* xvi, 25, and passim; Necheles, *Abbé Grégoire,* 29; *AP* 8 (Aug. 3, 1789): 336, and *AP* 9 (Sept. 29, 1789): 201. On the topic of Jews and the French Revolution more generally, see the classic studies by Zosa Szajkowski, *Jews and the French Revolutions of 1789, 1830, and 1848* (New York: Ktav Publishing House, 1970); *Les Juifs et la Révolution Française: Problèmes et aspirations,* ed. Bernhard Blumenkranz and Albert Soboul (Toulouse: Edouard Privat, 1976); and Frances Malino, *The Sephardic Jews of Bordeaux* (University: University of Alabama Press, 1978). Newer works include Schechter, *Obstinate Hebrews*; and Frederic Cople Jaher, *The Jews and*

the Nation: Revolution, Emancipation, State Formation, and the Liberal Paradigm in America and France (Princeton, N.J.: Princeton University Press, 2002) (on the latter, see my review in the *Historian,* Winter 2004).

9. Grégoire, *Essai sur la régénération,* 131; and Necheles, *Abbé Grégoire,* 59–60. On the situation in Saint-Domingue on the eve of the Revolution, see Carolyn E. Fick, *The Making of Haiti: The Saint Domingue Revolution from Below* (Knoxville: University of Tennessee Press, 1990), 15–75. Grégoire's *Motion* shows a change in his position in the fall. While its text included the same critical comment about far-away blacks that had appeared in the *Essai,* its foreword, which must have been completed later, urged that defenders of the Jews also speak "in favor of the *gens de couleur* . . . and in favor of the Negroes, whose name alone draws to mind the feeling of suffering" (*Motion en faveur des Juifs,* xv–xvi, 43).

10. *AP* 10 (Dec. 3, 1789): 362; *AP* 12 (Mar. 28, 1790): 383; *AP* 26 (May 14, 1791): 70; Grégoire, *Lettre aux philantropes,* 9; idem, *Mémoire en faveur des gens de couleur ou sang-mêlés de St.-Domingue & des autres Isles françoises de l'Amérique, adressé à l'Assemblée Nationale* (Paris: Chez Belin, 1789), 6–8, 21, 46; G. Legal, *Observations sur tout ce qui concerne les colonies . . . Réponse à un mémoire de M. Grégoire en faveur des gens de couleur . . .* (Paris: [1790]), 19; *AP* 27 (June 14, 1791): 231; and Michael L. Kennedy, *The Jacobin Clubs in the French Revolution: The First Years* (Princeton, N.J.: Princeton University Press, 1982), 205–208. There is a sizable literature on the debates on citizenship for people of mixed race and blacks. For overviews, see Geggus, "Racial Equality, Slavery and Colonial Secession during the Constituent Assembly," *American Historical Review* 94 (1989): 1290–1308; and Dorigny, "Grégoire et le combat contre l'esclavage pendant la Révolution," in Bénot and Dorigny, *Grégoire et la cause des noirs,* 51–68. On the nuances of the various terms for people of mixed racial heritage, see Dominique Rogers, "Les libres de couleur dans les capitales de Saint-Domingue: Fortune, mentalités, et intégration à la fin de l'ancien régime (1776–1789)" (Ph.D. diss., Université de Bordeaux-III, 1999), 7. Rogers notes that *gens de couleur* could embrace free blacks as well as people of mixed race, though many contemporaries used the term only for the latter.

11. *Le patriote françois,* no. 78 (Oct. 24, 1789): 1; *AP* 9 (Oct. 22, 1789): 479; *AP* 25 (May 10, 1791): 687; *AP* 29 (Aug. 12, 1791): 384; and Kennedy, *Jacobin Clubs,* 245.

12. Necheles, *Abbé Grégoire,* 27–33. He does seem to have allowed the issue to be raised in the Assembly during his presidency (*AP* 22 [Jan. 17, 1791]: 318), only to have his colleagues defer it again.

13. Grégoire to J. A. Balthasar, Jul. 2, 1791, Lucerne, Zentralbibliothek, Abt. Bürgerbibliothek, Nachlass Balthasar, no. 70, reprinted in Debrunner, *Grégoire l'Européen,* 27–30. Though Debrunner published this letter, he did not comment on this passage.

14. On the different time frames through which revolutionaries envisioned regeneration at different moments of the Revolution, see Ozouf, "Regeneration"; and de Baecque, "L'homme nouveau est arrivé." On the unitary character of French universalism, see Bell, *Cult of the Nation,* 201, 205; and Pierre Birnbaum, *The Idea of France* (New York: Hill and Wang, 2001), 54 and passim.

15. Grégoire, *Mémoire en faveur des gens de couleur*, 13, 19, 26–27, 38–39. For an alternate account of family life among the *gens de couleur*, see Stewart R. King, *Blue Coat or Powdered Wig: Free People of Color in Pre-Revolutionary Saint Domingue* (Athens: University of Georgia Press, 2001), ch. 9.

16. Grégoire, *Lettre aux philantropes*, 4; Geggus, "Racial Equality," 1299.

17. *AP* 25 (May 11, 1791): 737–42; Grégoire, *Mémoire en faveur des gens de couleur*, 38, 51n24.

18. Grégoire, *Lettre aux citoyens de couleur et nègres libres de Saint-Domingue, et des autres isles françoises de l'Amérique* (Paris: Imprimerie du Patriote françois, 1791), 11–14. Outside the Assembly, he tried to push for an end to the slave trade but could not even persuade the Société des Amis des Noirs to support such a radical move (see Dorigny, "L'abbé Grégoire et la Société des Amis des Noirs").

19. Grégoire, *Observations sur une nouvelle circonscription des Paroisses*, 14; idem, *Essai sur la régénération*, 154; patois survey at ADLC, F 1273, fol. 5 (also in *Le patriote françois* [Aug. 23, 1790]: 2); also de Certeau, Julia, and Revel, *Une politique de la langue*; and Bell, "Lingua Populi, Lingua Dei."

20. Bell, *Cult of the Nation*, 179.

21. Important works on women and the Revolution include Joan B. Landes, *Women and the Public Sphere in the Age of the French Revolution* (Ithaca, N.Y.: Cornell University Press, 1988); Lynn Hunt, *The Family Romance of the French Revolution* (Berkeley: University of California Press, 1992); Sara E. Melzer and Leslie W. Rabine, *Rebel Daughters: Women and the French Revolution* (New York: Oxford University Press, 1992); and Dominique Godineau, *The Women of Paris and Their French Revolution* (Berkeley: University of California Press, 1998). On the later period, see also Elizabeth Colwill, "Women's Empire and the Sovereignty of Man in *La Décade philosophique*, 1794–1807," *Eighteenth-Century Studies* 29, no. 3 (1996): 265–89; and Jennifer Heuer, "Hats on for the Nation! Women, Citizens, Soldiers, and the 'Sign of the French,' " *French History* 16, no. 1 (2002): 28–52.

22. Hippolyte Carnot, "Notice historique sur Grégoire," in *Mémoires de Grégoire* (Paris: A. Dupont, 1837); reprinted in *Mémoires* (1989 edition), 215, 256–63 (all further references to Carnot are to the 1989 edition); Pierre Dufay, [Testament of Mme Dubois], *Blois et le Loire-et-Cher*, no. 1 (March 1937): 5–10; Plongeron, *L'abbé Grégoire*, 24; Cosson, "Lettres de l'abbé Grégoire"; Grégoire to [Pougens], June 5, 1819, Ars. Ms. 14694/7; *Mémoires*, 128; and "Memoire pour M. l'abbé Baradère . . . contre Mme. V[euve] Dubois," Ars. Ms. 15049, fol. 206, p. 12.

23. A. Mathiez, "Une lettre de Grégoire [22 septembre 1792]," *La Révolution française* 47 (1904): 371; and Maggiolo (1884), 68.

24. See for example *Lettre au C.en Grégoire, ci-devant évêque constitutionnel du département de Loir & Cher, à l'occasion d'un prétendu synode qu'il annonce pour la foire de Blois, an 8* (Orléans: n.p., 1800), 23–24; and Grégoire to Trognon, Jan. 11, 1829, Archives départementales de Loir-et-Cher (henceforth "ADLC"), F 592, fol. 87.

25. See Benoît, "Description des Vosges," 223; letter from Oersner to Grégoire, Jan. 27, 1819, in AN 510 AP 2, dossier "N-R"; and Grégoire's will reprinted in Carnot, "Notice historique sur Grégoire," 326–28.

26. On Rousseau and women, see for example Landes, *Women and the Public Sphere*; Hunt, *Family Romance*, ch. 4; and Goodman, *The Republic of Letters*, 54–56 and passim.

27. Grégoire, *Lettre aux philantropes*, 19. On this controversy, see Jean-Daniel Piquet, "La prétendue belle-soeur de couleur de l'abbé Grégoire: Une homonymie, cause de la bourde du Club Massiac?" *Etudes théologiques et religieuses* 74, no. 4 (1999): 463–75.

28. See for example his *De la noblesse de la peau ou de préjugé des blancs contre la couleur des Africains et celle de leurs descendans noirs et sang-mêlés* (Paris: Baudouin, 1826), 20.

29. Grégoire to Brissot, n.d. [spring 1791], AN 446 AP 7 (Brissot Papers), transcription courtesy of Jeremy Popkin.

30. Grégoire, *Discours sur la fédération du 14 juillet 1792*, 9.

31. Grégoire, *Discours prononcé pour les citoyens morts à Paris le 10 août 1792*, 17; and F.-A. Aulard, *La Société des Jacobins: Recueil de documents pour l'histoire du club des Jacobins à Paris* (Paris: Librairie Jouaust, 1889), 3: 179. Grégoire may have been influenced in this regard by J.-F. Oberlin, a pioneer in the field; see Kurtz, *John Frederic Oberlin*, 238, 279. Grégoire also seemed to advocate at least some measure of equality for women when, in 1788, he attacked Jews for their treatment of women (*Essai sur la régénération*, 166–67). Nevertheless, when Grégoire had an opportunity to create schools for girls during the Revolution, he declined to do so. Though the Committee of Public Instruction instructed him twice to report on this subject, it appears that he let the idea fall by the wayside (see Guillaume, *Procès-verbaux du Comité d'instruction publique de la Convention nationale* [Paris: Imprimerie nationale, 1891–1907] 2: 746; 4: 313, 371). The abbé did, however, fulfill his promise to visit a school where women learned to do typography, and he reported back that women's learning to do such mechanical tasks would free men to do more important work in agriculture and the arts (ibid., 4: 493, 502).

32. Grégoire, *Discours prononcé dans l'église cathédrale de Blois au service célébré pour Jacques-Guillaume Simonneau, maire d'Etampes, assassiné le 3 mars 1792, pour avoir défendu la loi* (Blois: Imprimerie de Jean-François Billault, 1792), 7.

33. *Extrait du registre des délibérations du directoire du département de Loir et Cher, séance du 7 avril 1791* (Blois: J. P. J. Masson, 1791), conserved by Grégoire in BSPR-G, Rév. 159/4; Gazier, *Etudes sur l'histoire religieuse*, 54, 62; Michel de Sachy de Foudrinoy, *La Révolution en Loir-et-Cher: Acteurs et victimes* (Blois: Editions Lignages, 1989), n.p. I owe the observation about the post-Tridentine church to Timothy Tackett.

34. Compare esp. Landes, *Women and the Public Sphere*, 7, 204, with Hunt, *Family Romance*, esp. 203–4; Hunt, "Introduction: The Revolutionary Origins of Human Rights," in *The French Revolution and Human Rights: A Brief Documentary History* (Boston: Bedford Books, 1996), 11, 18, 29; and Carla Hesse, *The Other Enlightenment: How French Women Became Modern* (Princeton, N.J.: Princeton University Press, 2001), esp. xiv–xv. Alternate positions are offered by Dena Goodman, "Difference: An Enlightenment Concept," in *What's*

Left of Enlightenment? A Postmodern Question, ed. Keith Michael Baker and
Peter Hanns Reill (Stanford, CA: Stanford University Press, 2001), 129–47; and
Scott, *Only Paradoxes to Offer.*

35. *AP* X (Dec. 23 and 24, 1789): 757–58, 778, 780. A later alternative was
the half-serious comment by the doctor-*conventionnel* Marc Antoine Baudot
that, because of Jews' continued practice of their "ridiculous superstitions . . . I
wonder if it wouldn't be worthwhile to think about regenerating them through
the guillotine" (1794, cited in Patrice Higonnet, *Goodness beyond Virtue:
Jacobins during the French Revolution* [Cambridge, MA: Harvard University
Press, 1998], 236–37).

36. De Laissac, *Lettre à M. Chapelier* (Paris: n.p., 1790), 3, 21 [at Jewish
Theological Seminary Library, New York]; petition by the municipality of Col-
mar, French Jewish Communities Collection, Jewish Theological Seminary,
Archives, Box 6/11b, folder "Colmar, 1790 & 1793"; also *Les Juifs d'Alsace:
Doivent-ils être citoyens* (n.p., 1790), 35 and passim.

37. Geggus, "Racial Equality"; Legal, *Observations,* 51, 53; and Charles de
Chabanon, *Dénonciation de M. l'abbé Grégoire et de sa lettre du 8 juin 1791
adressée aux citoyens de couleur et nègres libres de Saint-Domingue* (Paris:
Imprimerie de la Feuille du Jour, 1791), 8, 26, 42.

38. [M. L. E. Moreau de Saint-Méry], *Observations d'un habitant des
colonies, sur le mémoire en faveur des gens de couleur, ou sang-mêlés . . . par M.
Grégoire . . .* (n.p.: [1789]), 49–51, 66–67, and passim. For more on Moreau,
see Malick Ghachem, "Montesquieu in the Caribbean: The Colonial Enlightenment Between *Code Noir* and *Code Civil,*" in *Postmodernism and the Enlightenment: New Perspectives in Eighteenth-Century French Intellectual History,*
ed. Daniel Gordon (New York: Routledge, 2001), 7–30.

39. Geggus, "Racial Equality," 1294–95, 1300; and Grégoire, *Notice sur la
Sierra-Leona . . .* (n.p.: 1796), 11. The idea that the Revolution in Saint-
Domingue was Grégoire's fault recurred through the nineteenth century. See for
example [F. R. de Tussac], *Cri des Colons contre un ouvrage de M. L'Evêque et
Sénateur Grégoire, ayant pour titre De la littérature des Nègres, ou Réfutation
des inculpations calomnieuses faites aux colons par l'auteur . . .* (Paris: Delau-
nay, 1810), 14.

40. Raimond, *Réclamations adressées à l'Assemblée nationale* (1789) and
Observations adressées à l'Assemblée nationale (1789), cited in and translated
by Mercer Cook, "Julien Raimond," *Journal of Negro History* 26, no. 2 (1941):
142, 144; and Rogers, "Les libres de couleur," esp. 589–93. Despite his discomfort with the idea of specialized regeneration for freedmen, Raimond was nevertheless extremely grateful for Grégoire's efforts to help freedmen gain rights
(see Raimond to Grégoire, le 28 ventôse IV [Feb. 10, 1796] in BSPR-G, dossier
"Charente-Inférieure").

41. Abraham Furtado, Azevedo, David Gradis, and Salomon Lopes du Bec,
*Lettre adressée à M. Grégoire . . . par les Députés de la Nation Juive Portugaise
de Bordeaux* (Versailles: Baudouin, 1789), 2–3. Cf. *Mémoires,* 53, 171; and
Hermon-Belot, *L'abbé Grégoire,* 255–56 (which uses Grégoire's excerpted version of the letter, describing it only as a "thank-you letter," to support the
author's argument that contemporary Jews did not object to Grégoire's ideas).

42. Jean-Claude-Antoine de Bourge, *Lettre au Comité de Constitution sur l'affaire des Juifs* (Paris: Imprimerie du Patriote français, 1790), 43, 7; Brissot, *Rapport sur la lettre de M. de Bourge . . . à l'Assemblée Générale des Représentans de la Commune* ([Paris]: Lottin, [1790]), 3; *Arrêté de l'Assemblée Générale des Représentans de la Commune* (Paris: Lottin, 1790), 1; and comments of Duport, *AP* 31 (Sept. 27, 1791): 372.

43. Gazier, *Lettres à Grégoire sur les patois de France, 1790–1794. Documents inédits sur la langue, les moeurs et l'état des esprits dans les diverses régions de la France, au début de la Révolution* (1880; reprint, Geneva: Slatkine Reprints, 1969), 81. The responses to Grégoire are conserved primarily in BSPR-G, Rév. 222, and BN NAF Ms. 2798 (some of which are reprinted in Gazier, *Lettres à Grégoire*; and in de Certeau, Julia, and Revel, *Une politique de la langue*).

44. "Opinion sur la nécessité des deux langues, françoise et allemande, dans les officiers de justice et les Greffiers de la province d'Alsace," in BSPR-G, Rév. 222/279 (unsigned, [1790]).

45. Etta Palm d'Aelders, "Adresse des citoyens françoises à l'Assemblée nationale" (1791), translated by Darline Gay Levy, Harriet Branson Applewhite, and Mary Durham Johnson, in *Women in Revolutionary Paris, 1789–1795* (Urbana: University of Illinois Press, 1979), 75; and Olympe de Gouges, "Les droits de la femme" (1791), in *Ecrits politiques, 1788–1791* (Paris: Côté-femmes, 1993), 204–15; see also Scott, *Only Paradoxes to Offer*, 19–56.

46. Especially good overviews of the vast literature on citizenship and difference during the Revolution can be found in Shanti Marie Singham, "Betwixt Cattle and Men: Jews, Blacks, and Women, and the Declaration of the Rights of Man," in *The French Idea of Freedom: The Old Regime and the Declaration of Rights of 1789*, ed. Van Kley, 114–53; and Hunt, "Introduction," in *The French Revolution and Human Rights*, 1–32. See also Sylvie Chevalley, "La civilisation des comédiens," *Revue de la société d'histoire du théâtre* 41, no. 1 (1989): 49–55.

47. See especially Rodrigue, *French Jews, Turkish Jews*; Berkovitz, *Shaping of Jewish Identity*; references to *régénération* in Consistoire central des israélites de France (Paris), Registre du correspondance, 1810–1813, 1 C 2, pp. 5, 18v, 26v-27, 50v-51, 105v, 127v, 141, 205v; and Procès-verbaux, Nov. 10, 1808–Sept. 28, 1815, 1 B 1, pp. 51, 80, 87, 120; and discussion of Haitians and regeneration in ch. 8.

48. For a fuller discussion of the institution of citizenship and of legal decisions governing its application, see Jennifer Heuer's forthcoming monograph on nationality, gender, and citizenship in the Revolution (Cornell University Press). Heuer distinguishes between the political aspects of citizenship (such as voting rights) and the nationality components of citizenship, which women were deemed to possess at various stages of the Revolution.

49. Scott, *Only Paradoxes to Offer*, 13. This was also true to a lesser extent of the other groups who were seen as needing special regeneration; though regeneration provided a mechanism for their inclusion, they were required to speak as Jews or as *gens de couleur* in order to assert that they were capable of it and to deny their difference from other Frenchmen.

50. Cited in de Baecque, "L'homme nouveau est arrivé," 204.

CHAPTER 5: A RELIGIOUS REVOLUTION?

1. On the transfer of sacrality, see Ozouf, *Festivals and the French Revolution,* trans. Alan Sheridan (Cambridge, MA: Harvard University Press, 1988), ch. 10.

2. Van Kley, *Religious Origins,* 2, 7; see also Bell, *Cult of the Nation,* esp. 160–68.

3. *AP* 8 (Aug. 18, 1789): 452; Grégoire, *Nouvelles réflexions . . . sur la Déclaration des Droits de l'Homme & du Citoyen, à la séance du 18 Août* (Versailles: Baudouin, 1789), 1, 2; *Motion en faveur des Juifs,* 17; *Discours prononcé le jour de la Toussaint 1789, en l'église de l'Abbaye de St.-Germain-des-Prés, pour la Bénédiction des quatre Flammes de la Milice-Nationale de ce District* (Paris: Cl. Simon, 1789), 6–7; *Observations sur le décret de l'Assemblée nationale qui ordonne une nouvelle circonscription des Paroisses* (Paris: Belin, 1790), 10.

4. *AP* 8 (Aug. 10, 1789): 385; *AP* 9 (Nov. 9, 1789): 729; *AP* 11 (Dec. 31, 1789, Feb. 12, 1790): 55, 575; Grégoire, *Mémoire sur la dotation des curés en fonds territoriaux* (Paris: Baudouin, 1790); also Taveneaux, "L'abbé Grégoire et la démocratie cléricale," esp. 145–48.

5. *Moniteur,* Dec. 27, 1790, 1493; Grégoire, *Légitimité du serment civique, exigé des fonctionnaires ecclésiastiques* (Paris: Imprimerie nationale, 1791), 33.

6. Many people nevertheless called him *l'abbé* or *le conventionnel,* or by his postrevolutionary titles *le comte* and *le sénateur.* Technically, Grégoire had never been the *évêque de Blois* (the title approved by Rome before and after the Revolution) but rather the *évêque de Loir-et-Cher,* the equivalent position in the Constitutional Church. See the anonymous taunts on this subject in *Lettre au C.en Grégoire à l'occasion d'un prétendu synode,* 5. For more on Grégoire's tenure in Blois, see Nathalie Bercet, Catherine Bony, et al., *L'abbé Grégoire et Blois* (Blois: Les amis de la bibliothèque de Blois, 1999).

7. Grégoire, *Lettre pastorale de M. l'évêque du département de Loir et Cher (24 mars 1791)* (Blois: Imprimerie de J. P. J. Masson, 1791), 5; "Lettre de M. Grégoire à l'Assemblée électorale du département de Loir & Cher, 16 février 1791," conserved in ADLC, F 1273; Grégoire's speech to the Conseil général of Loir-et-Cher, Dec. 15, 1791 (ms. copy at ADLC, L 103/5). Grégoire was also elected bishop by the department of Mans, which he declined. Interestingly, Grégoire was elected bishop of Loir-et-Cher only after three ballots (see ADLC, L 862).

8. *Lettre circulaire de M. Grégoire, Evêque du Département de Loir et Cher, à ses diocésains, pour la convocation des Elèves au Séminaire de Blois (7 juillet 1791)* (n.p., 1791), 2–3. See also Grégoire to electors of Loir-et-Cher, Feb. 26, 1791, reprinted in Gazier, *Etudes sur l'histoire religieuse,* 39–40.

9. Gazier, *Etudes sur l'histoire religieuse,* 178n3; Grégoire, *Lettre pastorale . . . aux pasteurs et aux fidèles de son diocèse, sur la confirmation (le 25 février 1792)* (Blois: Imprimerie de Jean-François Billault, 1792), 1–2, 5, 9 (and "Observations à MM. les curés et desservans," bound with it at the BN, p. 2); *Mémoires,* 123; and Ezran, *L'Abbé Grégoire,* 34.

10. Grégoire, *Lettre pastorale de 24 mars 1791,* 22; *Discours prononcé dans l'église cathédrale de Blois . . . au service célébré pour les citoyens morts à Paris*

le 10 août 1792 (Blois: Imprimerie de Jean-François Billault, 1792), 10; and *Discours pour Jacques-Guillaume Simonneau, 13.*

11. On the men listed here and others interested in a religious Revolution, see Gary Kates, *The Cercle Social, the Girondins and the French Revolution* (Princeton, N.J.: Princeton University Press, 1985); Norman Ravitch, "The Abbé Fauchet: Romantic Religion During the French Revolution," *Journal of the American Academy of Religion* 42 (1974): 247–62; Plongeron, *L'abbé Grégoire,* 52–53; Hermon-Belot, *L'abbé Grégoire,* ch. 2 ("Une révolution française catholique"); Aston, *Religion and Revolution,* 196–97; AP 10: 761–63; Kennedy, *Jacobin Clubs,* 152, 304, and the chart on 371, which indicates that 10 percent of the members of many local clubs were priests; and Ruth Graham, "The Revolutionary Bishops and the *Philosophes,*" *Eighteenth-Century Studies* 16, no. 2 (1982–83): 117–40. Lamourette was less enthusiastic than the others, however, with regard to the philosophes (see McMahon, *Enemies of the Enlightenment,* 46).

12. Ozouf, "Revolutionary Religion," in Furet and Ozouf, *Critical Dictionary,* 562; *Couplets chantés dans un dîner donné par les Amis de la Constitution de Rouen, à M. l'abbé Grégoire, Député de l'Assemblée Nationale, le lundi 6 Septembre 1790* (Rouen: P. Seyer & Behourt, 1790); and Desan, *Reclaiming the Sacred.*

13. Tackett, *Religion, Revolution, and Regional Culture in Eighteenth-Century France: The Ecclesiastical Oath of 1791* (Princeton, N.J.: Princeton University Press, 1986), 300 and passim; Van Kley, *Religious Origins,* 351, 371; and Ravitch, "The Abbé Fauchet," 251.

14. *Mémoires,* 121, 123; *M. Grégoire . . . dénoncé à la nation, comme ennemi de la constitution, infidèle à son serment, perturbateur de repos public, . . . par les habitans dudit département, ci-devant diocèse de Blois* (Paris: Imprimerie de Crapart, [1791]), 6; Gazier, *Etudes sur l'histoire religieuse,* 52–53, 77–78; and letters welcoming Grégoire and excerpt titled *Souvenirs de la Terreur à Blois,* 1877, in BSPR-G, carton "Loir & Cher. Documents Divers—Blois." In his *Mémoires,* Grégoire claimed that the anonymous pamphlet found a hostile reception in Blois, where it was burned in a kind of "autodafé" (123).

15. See Ozouf's two models of regeneration in her *Critical Dictionary* entry "Regeneration."

16. Grégoire, *Lettre pastorale de 24 mars 1791,* 6, 4, 7, 14; *Discours sur la fédération du 14 juillet 1792,* 5; and *Lettre circulaire pour la convocation des Elèves,* 2.

17. Grégoire, *Lettre pastorale de 24 mars 1791,* 16–20; *Discours pour Jacques-Guillaume Simonneau,* 22.

18. Grégoire, *Adresse aux députés de la seconde législature, lue à la Société des Amis de la Constitution, séante aux Jacobins de Paris . . .* (Paris: Imprimerie du Patriote François, 1791), 25; *Discours sur la fédération du 14 juillet 1792, . . . dont la Société des Amis de la Constitution de Blois a voté l'impression* (Orléans: Jacob l'aîné, [1792]), 5; and *Mémoires,* 89.

19. Grégoire, *Lettre pastorale . . . aux pasteurs et aux fidèles de son diocèse, sur le payement des contributions publiques (le premier février 1792)* (Blois: Imprimerie de Jean-François Billault, 1792), 13.

20. Grégoire, *Discours pour Jacques-Guillaume Simonneau,* 19–20.

21. Grégoire, Camereau, and other administrators of the Conseil-Général, *Adresse de l'Assemblée administrative du département de Loir et Cher, réunis en Conseil général, à ses concitoyens, le 1 août 1792* (Blois: J. F. Billault, 1792), ADLC, F 1275, which was inspired by Grégoire's motion to increase the number of volunteers (see ADLC, L 109, July 24, 1792).

22. See the lumping of Grégoire with the most radical dechristianizers as an "enemy of God" in Litda, Militaire Provençal, *L'Apêchêmie, ou Discordance entre les principes de l'Eglise & ceux qu'établissent les évêques constitutionnels . . . dans leurs pastorales* (Mons: n.p., 1792), 45; Hunt, *Family Romance*; and Grégoire, *Discours pour Jacques-Guillaume Simonneau,* 15. On the shifting balance between patriotism and universalism in Grégoire's life, see chs. 4 and 5 of Sepinwall, "Regenerating France." On this tension more generally in the Revolution, see Michael Rapport, "Robespierre and the Universal Rights of Man, 1789–1794," *French History* 10, no. 3 (Sept. 1996): 305, and Higonnet, *Goodness beyond Virtue.*

23. *AP* 28 (July 15, 1791): 318–20; Grégoire, *Adresse aux députés de la seconde législature,* 14. Critiques of this famous pamphlet include *La contre-révolution démontrée nécessaire par . . . le Testament politique de la Souveraineté expirante de M. l'abbé Grégoire . . .* (n.p.: n.d.). See also the sentiments expressed in Grégoire, *Opinion . . . sur la sanction royale, à la séance du 4 Sptembre* [sic] (n.p.: [1789]). On the longer-term origins of Grégoire's hatred for the monarchy, see also the interpretation of Hermon-Belot, *L'abbé Grégoire,* 138–40, 165, and 183–227.

24. *Mémoires,* 89; and Aulard, *La Société des Jacobins* 4: 234.

25. Grégoire, *Discours prononcé dans l'église cathédrale de Blois . . . au service célébré pour les citoyens morts à Paris le 10 août 1792* (Blois: Imprimerie de Jean-François Billault, 1792), 2–4, 14–15.

26. *AP* 52 (Sept. 21, 1792): 73. Grégoire later noted that he had wanted to propose his motion on the first day, but colleagues had advised him to wait (*Mémoires,* 90).

27. Mathiez, "Une lettre de Grégoire," 371; see also *Mémoires,* 90.

28. Grégoire, *Discours pour les citoyens morts à Paris le 10 août 1792,* 1; *Discours sur la fédération du 14 juillet 1792 . . .* (Orléans: Jacob l'aîné, [1792]), 6; *Convention nationale. Système* [sic] *de dénominations topographiques pour les places, rues, quais, etc. de toutes les communes de la République . . .* (Paris: Imprimerie nationale, 1794), 16; and *Rapport sur la bibliographie,* 6.

29. Grégoire, *Discours sur la fédération du 14 juillet 1792,* 6; Mercure Daniel Conway, *The Life of Thomas Paine, with a History of His Literary, Political, and Religious Career in America, France and England* (London: Watts & Co., 1909), 145; and Mathiez, "Une lettre de Grégoire," 371. Although it is not clear when he acquired them, Grégoire owned two 1776 editions of Paine's *Common Sense* ("Catalogue de ma bibliothèque," BSPR-G, Rév. 254).

30. See for instance Antoine Claire Thibaudeau, *Mémoires sur la Convention, et le Directoire* (Paris: Baudouin frères, 1824), 1: 74.

31. Grégoire, *Discours pour les citoyens morts à Paris le 10 août 1792,* 17; *Opinion . . . concernant le jugement de Louis XVI, séance du 15 Novembre*

1792, l'an premier de la République française (Paris: Imprimerie nationale, 1792), 10; *Moniteur,* Nov. 21, 1792, 541; and Grégoire, *Rapport sur la réunion de la Savoie à la France, fait au nom des Comités Diplomatique et de Constitution . . .* (Paris: Imprimerie nationale, 1792), 2.

32. *Moniteur,* Nov. 29, 1792, 1415; *AP* 53 (Nov. 30, 1792): 674; Grégoire, *Rapport sur la réunion de la Savoie,* 6–7; and *AP* 53 (Nov. 7, 1792): 273. See also his "Déclaration du droit des gens [1793]," in *Choix de rapports, opinions et discours prononcés à la tribune nationale, depuis 1789 jusqu'à ce jour,* ed. Guillaume N. Lallement (Paris: A. Eymery, 1820), 397–98; and "Déclaration du droit des gens (1795)," *Réimpression de l'ancien moniteur* 24 (1795): 294–96.

33. Grégoire, *Rapport sur la réunion de la Savoie,* 6–7.

34. Simond, Grégoire, Hérault, and Jagot to Danton, Chambéry, Feb. 3, 1793, in Bibliothèque historique de la Ville de Paris (henceforth "BHVP"), Ms. 791, fol. 286. This letter was recently published by Jean-Daniel Piquet, "Lettre secrète de l'abbé Grégoire, et de ses trois collègues en mission dans le Mont-Blanc, à Danton," *Cahiers d'histoire* 46, nos. 3/4 (2001): 397–415. Grégoire later attempted to discredit reports of friction *en mission,* however, and Carnot claimed that the inhabitants of Savoy, including its clerics, loved Grégoire and hoped he would remain there permanently (Carnot, "Notice historique sur Grégoire," 224).

35. Henri Moris, *Organisation du département des Alpes-Maritimes formé du ci-devant comté de Nice et de la ci-devant principauté de Monaco. Mars–Avril 1793. Lettres des représentants du peuple Grégoire et Jagot . . .* (Paris: Librairie Plon, 1915), vi; Grégoire, *Convention nationale. Rapport présenté à la Convention nationale, au nom des Commissaires envoyés par elle, pour organiser les départemens du Mont-Blanc & des Alpes maritimes . . .* (Paris: Imprimerie nationale, 1793), 33; and article in *La Justice,* June 6, 1887 (clipping conserved in Augustin Gazier's notes on Grégoire in BSPR-G, carton "Loir & Cher II. Diverses lettres—Grégoire etc.," dossier "Notes diverses, S. Augustin Gazier, relatives à Grégoire").

36. Grégoire, *Adresse aux citoyens des campagnes du département du Mont-Blanc* (n.p.: [1793?]) 1, 3–4, 7, 8–9; *Adresse aux habitans du Valais . . .* (Chambéry: Imprimerie de Gorrin père & fils, [1793]), 3, 5. On biological metaphors employed against the nobility, see de Baecque, *Le corps de l'histoire.*

37. Grégoire and Jagot to the Provisional Administration of Monaco, Mar. 15, 1793, and to the mayor and municipal officers of Menton, Mar. 20, 1793, both in Moris, *Organisation du département des Alpes-Maritimes,* 12, 20 (reprinted from AN D §1.25, dossier 1). Moris has argued that Grégoire authored the entire collection of letters (xxiv). See also Grégoire, *Rapport présenté au nom des Commissaires,* 36.

38. Grégoire and Jagot to the Popular Society of Monaco, Mar. 21, 1793, to the mayor and municipal officers of Menton, Mar. 28, 1793, and to the Provisional Administration of Monaco, Apr. 13, 1793, all in Moris, *Organisation du département des Alpes-Maritimes,* 22, 29, 51. See also *Mémoires,* 95. On Jacobin ambivalence about the "people" more generally, see Higonnet, *Goodness beyond Virtue,* 54–57.

39. Gazier, *Etudes sur l'histoire religieuse,* 184.

40. Grégoire, *Adresse aux citoyens . . . du Mont-Blanc* (n.p.: [1793?]), 24; *Adresse aux habitans du Valais*, 2–3.

41. Grégoire, *Adresse aux citoyens du Mont-Blanc*, 24.

42. Ibid., 12, 23; Bell, *Cult of the Nation*, 146–54; see also *AP* 78 (Oct. 30, 1793/9 brumaire an II): 48–51; Hunt, *Family Romance*, esp. ch. 4; and Godineau, *The Women of Paris*, esp. ch. 7.

43. Grégoire, *Adresse aux habitans du Valais*, 96.

44. *Mémoires*, 79, 96.

45. On other aspects of Grégoire's self-portrayal in this work, see J. Popkin's excellent essay "Grégoire as Autobiographer," in Popkin and Popkin, *Abbé Grégoire and His World*, 167–81.

46. *AP* 65 (May 31, 1793): 654.

47. *AP* 65 (June 1 and 2, 1793): 687–90, 706; *AP* 66 (June 4, 1793): 23; Maggiolo (1883), 133; and Hermon-Belot, *L'abbé Grégoire*, 280–84, 286–89. While Hermon-Belot has acknowledged Grégoire's centrality in the Girondin Affair, she has sought to defend him on the grounds that he was never a Girondin and therefore his actions bear no hint of contradiction. Cf. Sepinwall, "Regenerating France," 132–33, 145–46, 154.

48. Graham, "Revolutionary Bishops," 135–36.

49. Grégoire, *Opinion concernant le jugement de Louis XVI*, 10.

50. Piquet, "L'abbé Grégoire et ses trois collègues en mission dans le Mont-Blanc furent 'régicides.' Article et documents inédits," *Annales historiques de la Révolution française*, no. 303 (1996): 113–17; and the fuller argumentation contained in idem, "L'abbé Grégoire, un régicide panthéonisé," *Cahiers d'histoire: Espaces Marx*, no. 63 (1996): 61–77. In these articles and his "L'abbé Grégoire ou l'universalisme jacobin d'une déclaration des droits et des devoirs des hommes de toutes les couleurs," *Annales de l'Est*, no. 1 (2002): 269–91, Piquet has asserted the persistence of radical Jacobinism in Grégoire's activities during this period, despite the abbé's later claims.

51. Plongeron, "Sur Grégoire 'régicide' d'après des documents pris pour 'sources,' " *Annales historiques de la Révolution française*, no. 305 (1996): 535–36; and Hermon-Belot, *L'abbé Grégoire*, 275–79.

52. See article by Moïse (bishop of Saint-Claude) in *Annales de la Religion* 14 (1801): 35–41.

53. Grégoire, *Rapport présenté au nom des Commissaires*, 37–38; Grégoire to J.-F. Oberlin, Aug. 21, 1793, reprinted in Peter, "Le pasteur Oberlin et l'abbé Grégoire," 309; and *Mémoires*, 96.

54. Grégoire, *Essai historique et patriotique sur les arbres de la liberté*, 47, 50, 55; *Discours sur la fédération du 14 juillet 1792*, 11.

55. Norman Ravitch, "Liberalism, Catholicism, and the Abbé Grégoire," *Church History* 36 (1967): 424n21; see also Ozouf, "Préface," in Hermon-Belot, *L'abbé Grégoire*, 14–16. Even while disagreeing with Piquet, Hermon-Belot offers another interesting alternative, that Grégoire opposed the king's death before it happened, but that "the death of Louis XVI liberated . . . his truly obsessive fear of the monarchy." She has therefore also rejected the idea that Grégoire's statement in the Alps report was a fabrication (*L'abbé Grégoire*, 275–77).

56. Grégoire, Simond, Hérault, and Jagot, "Egalité, Liberté. Proclamation sur la liberté de la presse. Les commissaires de la Convention Nationale, aux Citoyens du Département du Mont-Blanc . . . fait à Chambéry, ce 25 janvier 1793" (Chambéry: C. F. Lullin, 1793; reprinted in *Oeuvres*, 3: 61); Grégoire, *Rapport présenté au nom des Commissaires*, 34; *Rapport sur les inscriptions des monumens publics, séance du 22 Nivôse, l'an 2* . . . (Paris: Imprimerie nationale, 1794), 5; *Discours sur la liberté des cultes* (n.p.: 1794), 4; *Convention nationale. Rapport à la séance du 8 août 1793*, 4, 6; *Convention nationale. Instruction publique. Rapport sur l'établissement d'un conservatoire des arts et métiers, séance du 8 vendémiaire, l'an 3* . . . (Paris: Imprimerie nationale, 1794), 6. See also the reference to the "genius of J.-J. Rousseau" even as Grégoire challenged his disinterest in educating the poor, in *Convention nationale. Discours sur l'éducation commune . . . séance du 30 juillet* (Paris: Imprimerie nationale, 1793), 3, 5.

57. Grégoire, *Rapport sur l'ouverture d'un concours*, 6; Palmer; and ch. 9.

58. Grégoire, *Mémoires*, 114; *Légitimité du serment civique*, 30; *Lettre pastorale du 24 mars 1791*, 4; and Graham, "Revolutionary Bishops." On Rousseau's being seen differently from other philosophes by Catholic writers, at least before the Terror, see also McMahon, *Enemies of the Enlightenment*, 35 and passim; and Ravitch, "Catholicism in Crisis," 359–60.

59. *Mémoires*, 47, 113, 135; and Ravitch, "Liberalism, Catholicism, and the Abbé Grégoire," 427.

60. Grégoire, *Rapport sur les inscriptions*, 7; *Système de dénominations topographiques*, 11; *Convention nationale. Instruction publique. Rapport sur l'établissement du Bureau des longitudes, séance du 7 Messidor, l'an 3* . . . (Paris: Imprimerie nationale, 1795), 6; *Discours sur la liberté des cultes*, 1, 8, 10; *Convention nationale. Rapport à la séance du 8 août 1793*, 4, 8, 10; and *Catalogue des livres de la Bibliothèque de M.*** [Grégoire]* . . . (1821) [BN Delta-14098], 5, 6 and passim. The attribution is the BN's.

61. Guillaume, *Procès-verbaux*, 4 (6 ventôse an II/Feb. 24, 1794): 9; Grégoire, *Système de dénominations topographiques*, 2.

62. *AP* 53 (Nov. 30, 1792): 674; Grégoire, *Rapport [sur les jardins botaniques]*, 4.

63. There is a vast and contentious literature on dechristianization. See for example F. A. Aulard, *Christianity and the French Revolution*, trans. Lady Frazer (New York: H. Fertig, 1966), ch. 3; John McManners, *The French Revolution and the Church* (New York: Harper Torchbooks, 1970), esp. ch. 10; Michel Vovelle, *The Revolution against the Church: From Reason to the Supreme Being*, trans. Alan José (Columbus: Ohio State University Press, 1991); and Aston, *Religion and Revolution*, ch. 10.

64. Grégoire to the bishop of Côte d'Or [Jean-Baptiste Volfius], 26 vendémiaire an II [Oct. 17, 1793], in BHVP, ms. 3064, T. 46, f. 48.

65. [Grégoire], *Première et dernière réponse aux libellistes* (Paris: A. Egron, [1814]), 14–16; *Mémoires*, 128. Cf. Necheles, who found differing accounts on the degree to which Grégoire defended Christianity that day ("The Abbé Grégoire and the Constitutional Church: 1794–1802" [Ph.D. diss., University of Chicago, 1963], 12–14).

66. Hermon-Belot, *L'abbé Grégoire,* ch. 9. Hermon-Belot does not acknowledge enough, however, Grégoire's having shaped the very policies to which he
now wished to provide an alternative.

67. Grégoire, *Mémoires,* 57; Guillaume, *Procès-verbaux,* 4: liii; and Grégoire to Cassini, Oct. 1, 1793, reprinted in Guillaume, *Procès-verbaux,* 2: 478.
For more on Grégoire's cultural politics, see Sepinwall, "Regenerating France,"
182–96.

68. Grégoire, *Convention nationale. Instruction publique. Rapport sur la
nécessité & les moyens d'anéantir le patois, & d'universaliser l'usage de la
langue française, séance du 16 prairial, l'an deuxième* . . . (Paris: Imprimerie
nationale, 1794), 6; *Convention nationale. Discours sur l'éducation commune* . . . *séance du 30 juillet 1793* (Paris: Imprimerie nationale, 1793), 5; *Convention nationale. Instruction publique. Rapport sur l'ouverture d'un concours
pour les livres élémentaires de la première éducation, séance du 3 pluviôse, l'an
second* . . . (Paris: Imprimerie nationale, 1794), 2; *Convention nationale. Nouveaux développemens sur l'amélioration de l'agriculture, par l'établissement de
maisons d'économie rurale* . . . , *séance du 16 brumaire, l'an deuxième* . . . (Paris:
Imprimerie nationale, 1793); *Convention nationale. Instruction sur les semailles
d'automne adressée aux citoyens cultivateurs, lue à la séance du 2e primdi* [sic]
de Brumaire, l'an 2e . . . (Paris: Imprimerie nationale, 1793).

69. Guillaume, *Procès-verbaux,* 2 (Aug. 22, Oct. 7, 1793): 334, 595; 3 (23
frimaire an II/Dec. 13, 1793): xii and passim; Grégoire, *Rapport sur la bibliographie,* 4, 5, 13, 14; *Convention nationale. Rapport et projet de décret présenté au
nom du Comité d'Instruction publique, à la séance du 8 août* . . . (Paris:
Imprimerie nationale, 1793), 3–5, 8. See also his earlier comments at *AP* 18
(Aug. 20, 1790): 175.

70. Grégoire, *Rapport sur l'ouverture d'un concours,* 9; *Rapport sur la
nécessité & les moyens d'anéantir le patois,* 4, 5, 12, 16; see also *Rapport
présenté au nom des Commissaires,* 37. On language and national identity in
Grégoire's thought, see Bell, "Lingua Populi, Lingua Dei." On the influence of
riots in the southwest in 1790 on Grégoire's interest in suppressing patois, see
Bell, *Cult of the Nation,* 173 and 278n31, citing *Moniteur,* Dec. 27, 1790,
1493.

71. Grégoire, *Rapport sur la nécessité & les moyens d'anéantir le patois,*
6–9; [Grégoire], *Adresse de la Convention nationale au peuple français, du 16
prairial, l'an second de la République* . . . (Paris: Imprimerie nationale, 1794),
2. Grégoire's authorship of the latter is suggested in *AP* 91 (16 prairial an II/June
4, 1794): 326.

72. Grégoire, *Rapport sur les inscriptions,* 7, 8; *Rapport sur la nécessité &
les moyens d'anéantir le patois,* 5.

73. Grégoire, *Rapport sur les inscriptions,* 4, 9, 10, 14.

74. Grégoire, *Système de dénominations topographiques,* 15 and passim;
Essai historique et patriotique sur les arbres de la liberté (Paris: Desenne, 1794),
54 and passim. On the history of this phenomenon, see Daniel Milo, "Street
Names," in *Realms of Memory: Rethinking the French Past,* ed. Pierre Nora and
Lawrence D. Kritzman, trans. Arthur Goldhammer (New York: Columbia Uni-
versity Press, 1996), 2: 362–89.

75. Grégoire, *Système de dénominations topographiques,* 4; John Markoff, *The Abolition of Feudalism: Peasants, Lords, and Legislators in the French Revolution* (University Park: Pennsylvania State University Press, 1996), 418–19.

76. Grégoire, *Rapport sur l'ouverture d'un concours,* 4, 6; *Convention nationale. Rapport fait au nom des comités des finances, des domaines et d'instruction publique, séance du 11 prairial, l'an deuxième . . . [sur les jardins botaniques]* (Paris: Imprimerie nationale, 1794), 5. On eighteenth-century views of breastfeeding, see Londa Schiebinger, "Why Mammals Are Called Mammals: Gender Politics in Eighteenth-Century Natural History," *American Historical Review* 98, no. 2 (1993): 382–411; and Mary Jacobus, "Incorruptible Milk: Breast-Feeding and the French Revolution," in Melzer and Rabine, *Rebel Daughters,* 54–75.

77. Vovelle, *The Revolution against the Church,* 58–61; McMahon, *Enemies of the Enlightenment,* 13–14 and passim; and Tackett, "Interpreting the Terror," *French Historical Studies* 24, no. 4 (2001): 569–78.

78. For a stronger critique of the idea of regeneration than that given here, see Ozouf, "La Révolution française et la formation de l'homme nouveau," 120 and passim.

79. The idea of a connection between 1789 and 1793–94 has been argued most notably by Baker (*Inventing the French Revolution,* particularly "Fixing the French Constitution") and has attracted much controversy. Though a case might be made that the Revolution could have developed in a less repressive manner, Baker's position, which is not the same as that of Furet, has often been misunderstood and consequently not convincingly refuted. See Bell's incisive analyses in the following book reviews: on Barry Shapiro, *Revolutionary Justice in Paris, 1789–1790,* in *Journal of Modern History* 68 (March 1996): 199–201; on P. M. Jones, *Reform and Revolution in France: The Politics of Transition, 1774–1791,* H-Net Reviews, H-France, February 1997 [URL: http://www.h-net. msu.edu/reviews/showrev.cgi?path=28082865515017]; and on Arno Mayer, *The Furies,* in *French Historical Studies* 24, no. 4 (2001): 559–67.

80. Lord Ashbourne [Mac Giolla Bríde], *Grégoire and the French Revolution* (London: Sands & Co., 1932), 80.

CHAPTER 6: OVERCOMING THE TERROR, REBUILDING THE EMPIRE

Epigraphs taken from: Grégoire, *Convention nationale. Instruction publique. Rapport sur les encouragemens, récompenses et pensions à accorder aux Savans, aux Gens de Lettres & aux Artistes, séance du 17 vendémiaire, l'an 3 . . .* (1794; reconstituted in *Oeuvres de l'abbé Grégoire,* 2: 305) (all subsequent references are to this edition); Grégoire to Scipione de' Ricci, May 31, 1796, reprinted in Maurice Vaussard, *Correspondance, Scipione de' Ricci, Henri Grégoire (1796–1807)* (Florence: Edizioni Sansoni Antiquariato, 1963), 11–12; and Grégoire, *Traite de l'uniformité et de l'amélioration de la liturgie, présenté au Concile national de 1801* (Paris: Imprimerie-librairie chrétienne, 1801), 57.

1. On Thermidorian ideals, see Bronislaw Baczko, *Comment sortir de la Terreur: Thermidor et la Révolution* (Paris: Gallimard, 1989).

2. On the use of history in eighteenth-century French political quarrels, see Baker, "Memory and Practice: Politics and the Representation of the Past in Eighteenth-Century France," in *Inventing the French Revolution,* 32. A fuller discussion of Grégoire's historical consciousness can be found in Sepinwall, "Regenerating France," 205–10, much of which is inspired by Joseph John Zizek's "The Politics and Poetics of History in the French Revolution, 1787–1794" (Ph.D. diss., University of California at Berkeley, 1995).

3. Grégoire, *Convention nationale. Instruction publique. Rapport sur les destructions opérées par le Vandalisme, et sur les moyens de le réprimer . . .* (Paris: Imprimerie nationale, 1794); reconstituted in *Oeuvres,* 2: 268.

4. Ibid.; *Convention nationale. Instruction publique. Second rapport sur le Vandalisme, séance du 8 brumaire, l'an III . . .* (Paris: Imprimerie nationale, 1794); and *Convention nationale. Instruction publique. Troisième rapport sur le Vandalisme, séance du 24 Frimaire, l'an IIIe . . .* (Paris: Imprimerie nationale, 1794). For a recent analysis, see Anthony Vidler, "The Paradoxes of Vandalism: Henri Grégoire and the Thermidorian Discourse on Historical Monuments," in Popkin and Popkin, *Abbé Grégoire and His World,* 129–56. See also comments of Serge Bianchi, cited in Birnbaum, *The Idea of France,* 55, 300n31.

5. See Hennebert to Grégoire, St. Omer, 19 frimaire an III [Dec. 9, 1794], in BSPR-G, Rév. 222, fol. 515, along with the many letters on this subject in the same volume and throughout the BSPR-G; and the letters in AN 510 AP 2, dossier "A-B" (including de Beauharnais's poem). For a sample response, see Grégoire to unnamed, 17 nivôse an III [Jan. 6, 1795], Ars. Ms. 14642, fol. 29. Though Grégoire has been widely credited with inventing the term *vandalism,* François Souchal argues that Grégoire was not the first to use it but only the loudest (Souchal, *Le vandalisme de la Révolution* [Paris: Nouvelles Editions Latines, 1993], 14, 115).

6. See the essays in *The Terror,* ed. Baker, particularly those of Baczko and Françoise Brunel; and Daniel Hollander Colman, "The Foundation of the French Liberal Republic: Politics, Culture and Economy after the Terror" [Ph.D. diss., Stanford University, 1997]).

7. Baker, *Condorcet: From Natural Philosophy to Social Mathematics,* 197, 214–15, 294, 303–304.

8. Ibid., 343. For more on the Class and Thermidorian political culture, see Martin Staum, *Minerva's Message: Stabilizing the French Revolution* (Montreal/Kingston: McGill-Queen's University Press, 1996); on Grégoire's involvement, see p. 12 and passim. See also Giovanna Procacci, *Gouverner la misère: La question sociale en France, 1789–1848* (Paris: Editions du Seuil, 1993).

9. Grégoire, *Rapport sur les encouragemens,* 312, 309, 304–305.

10. Grégoire, "Réflexions extraites d'un ouvrage du citoyen Grégoire sur les moyens de perfectionner les sciences politiques," *Mémoires de l'Institut national des sciences et des arts: Sciences morales et politiques* 1 (1798), 554.

11. See the blueprint for a faculty of political science, adopted in the CPI based on Grégoire's report, in Guillaume, *Procès-verbaux,* 6: 732; and Grégoire, "Réflexions . . . sur les moyens de perfectionner les sciences politiques." On eighteenth-century models of social science, see Staum, *Minerva's Message,*

esp. ch. 2. For a fuller discussion of Grégoire's vision of the social sciences, see Sepinwall, "Regenerating France," 211–25.

12. Grégoire, "Réflexions . . . sur les moyens de perfectionner les sciences politiques," 555–57, 563; see also "Extrait fait d'un rapport fait à la société d'agriculture du département de la Seine . . . sur les plantations de Malesherbes," *Décade philosophique, littéraire et politique, 30 nivôse an VII* (1800), 110–25; Plongeron, *Grégoire et la RS*, 86–100; and Colman, "Foundation of the French Liberal Republic," 157–58. On this institution (now called CNAM), see Grégoire, *Rapport sur l'établissement d'un conservatoire des arts et métiers*; *Corps législatif. Conseil des Cinq-Cents. Rapport fait au nom d'une commission spéciale, sur le Conservatoire des arts et métiers, séance du 17 floréal an 6* (Paris: Imprimerie nationale, 1798); Alain Mercier, *1794. L'abbé Grégoire et la création du Conservatoire national des Arts et Métiers* (Paris: Musée national des techniques/CNAM, 1989); and the manuscripts by or about Grégoire in the CNAM library (incl. Bibl. ms. 91 and 396). Grégoire's efforts in this domain nevertheless proved occasionally frustrating; see Maurice P. Crosland, ed., *Science in France in the Revolutionary Era, Described by Thomas Bugge, Danish Astronomer Royal . . .* (Cambridge, Mass.: Society for the History of Technology, 1969), 148.

13. Grégoire, "Réflexions . . . sur les moyens de perfectionner les sciences politiques," 554; and *Rapport sur les encouragemens*, 309.

14. Grégoire, *Rapport sur les encouragemens*, 314; *Mémoires*, 72; "Réflexions . . . sur les moyens de perfectionner les sciences politiques," 564–65; "Rapport sur la Bibliothèque nationale fait à la commission d'instruction publique de la Convention nationale en 1794–1795," ed. H. Omont, *Revue des Bibliothèques* 15 (avril 1905): 67–98; and *Rapport inédit de Grégoire sur l'état de l'instruction publique, des bibliothèques, des archives, et des monuments dans les départements de l'Est*, ed. Ulysse Robert (Paris: H. Menu, 1876).

15. Grégoire, *Convention nationale. Rapport et projet de décret présentés au nom du Comité d'Instruction publique, sur les costumes des législateurs et des autres fonctionnaires publics . . .* (Paris: Imprimerie nationale, 1795), 2; and *Corps législatif. Rapport fait au Conseil des Cinq-Cents, sur les sceaux de la République . . .* (Paris: Imprimerie nationale, 1795), 3. On Grégoire's role in revolutionary debates about images, see Joan B. Landes, *Visualizing the Nation: Gender, Representation, and Revolution in Eighteenth-Century France* (Ithaca, N.Y.: Cornell University Press, 2001), 24–30.

16. Grégoire, "Réflexions . . . sur les moyens de perfectionner les sciences politiques," 556–57, 552, 566; also Staum, *Minerva's Message*, 172–73, 214. See Grégoire's later comments on this speech in *Mémoires*, 99.

17. Staum, *Minerva's Message*, 216–17, 224 and passim; cf. Colman, "Foundation of the French Liberal Republic," 217, 251.

18. Though Staum counted Grégoire among the non-Ideologues in the Class, the abbé had been linked to the Auteuil circle since the early years of the Revolution; he also met at Mme Helvétius's house with Cabanis, Tracy, and others to organize opposition to Napoleon throughout the Empire (J. Lavaud, *Notice sur Henri Grégoire, ancien curé d'Emberménil, etc.* [Paris: Corréard, 1819], 62; see

also Antoine Guillois, *Le salon de Madame Helvétius* [Paris: Calmann Lévy, 1894], 185, 188).

19. Grégoire, *Compte rendu aux évêques réunis à Paris . . . de la visite de son diocèse (Paris, le 8 décembre 1796)* (Paris: Imprimerie-librairie chrétienne, 1796), 36–37. On Grégoire's opposition to Theophilanthropy, see ch. 9; also Mathiez, *La Théophilanthropie et le culte décadaire, 1796–1801* (Paris: Félix Alcan, 1904).

20. See references to Kant in Blessig and Müller letters, BSPR-G, dossier "Bas-Rhin," some of which are reprinted in François Azouvi and Dominique Bourel, *De Königsberg à Paris: La réception de Kant en France (1788–1804)* (Paris: J. Vrin, 1991) (see also discussion of Grégoire therein at 66–68, 70, 81, 103).

21. Aulard, *Christianity and the French Revolution,* 138; Hermon-Belot, *L'abbé Grégoire,* 380; and Grégoire, *Discours sur la liberté des cultes.*

22. Grégoire, *Corps législatif. Conseil des Cinq-Cents. Discours sur la liberté des cultes . . . , séance du 25 frimaire an 6* (Paris: Imprimerie nationale, 1797); *Moniteur,* no. 105, 15 nivôse an VI/Jan. 4, 1798; *Journal du Citoyen,* no. 50, 9 nivôse an VI/Dec. 27, 1797; Louis-Antoine-Esprit Rallier, *Lettres de Rallier, membre au Conseil des anciens, au Citoyen Grégoire, membre du Conseil des Cinq-Cents* (Paris: Desenne, an IV), 12–14; and Aston, *Religion and Revolution,* 282, 298.

23. See especially Gazier, *Etudes sur l'histoire religieuse*; Pouget, *Les idées religieuses*; Necheles, "Grégoire and the Constitutional Church"; Plongeron, *L'abbé Grégoire,* esp. 65–80; and Hermon-Belot, *L'abbé Grégoire,* ch. 12.

24. On French Gallicanism, see especially Van Kley, *Religious Origins.*

25. Pouget, *Les idées religieuses,* esp. 31, 122, 124; and Eléonore-Marie Desbois, Claude-François-Marie Primat, H. Grégoire, Jean-Baptiste Royer, and Jean-Pierre Saurine, *Seconde lettre encyclique de plusieurs évêques de France, à leurs frères les autres évêques et aux églises vacantes* (Paris: Imprimerie-librairie chrétienne, 1795), 9–10.

26. Sutter, *Les années de jeunesse,* 24; Grégoire, *Lettre pastorale . . . (le 12 mars 1795/le 22 ventôse, l'an 3)* (Blois/Paris: Maradan/Leclerc, 1795), 7.

27. Grégoire, *Lettre pastorale . . . le 12 mars 1795,* 11.

28. J. B. Gratien, H. Grégoire, Jean-Baptiste Royer, and Jean-Pierre Saurine, *Lettre encyclique de plusieurs évêques de France, à leurs frères les autres évêques et aux églises vacantes* (Paris: Imprimerie-librairie chrétienne, 1795), 11.

29. Grégoire, *Histoire du mariage des prêtres en France particulièrement depuis 1789* (Paris: Baudouin, 1826), 88, 111–12. The BSPR-G contains many letters to Grégoire from priests who had contracted marriages during the Revolution and now wished to renounce them and reenter the ministry. See for example Gasson to Grégoire, 8 nivôse an IV [Dec. 28, 1795], dossier "Lot et Garonne"; and Castres to Grégoire, 24 germinal an III [Apr. 13, 1795], dossier "Tarn." See also petitions to the 1797 Concile, like that from "un grand nombre de prêtres mariés aux Citoyens Evêques & curés du Concile National de France," BSPR-G, carton "Concile 1797," dossier "sur le mariage." See also Grégoire's compilations on this subject at BSPR-G, Rév. 44 and 45.

30. Sanadon to Grégoire, 5 floréal an III [Apr. 24, 1795], BSPR-G, dossier "Basses-Pyrénées"; Blessig to Grégoire, 27 germinal an IV [Apr. 16, 1796], BSPR-G, dossier "Bas-Rhin"; *Journal du Bon-Homme Richard*, no. 209 (22 pluviôse an IV/Feb. 11, 1796) [BSPR-G, Rév. 60/19]; and *Lettre au C.en Grégoire . . . à l'occasion d'un prétendu synode*, 10, 23–24. See also Plongeron, *L'abbé Grégoire*, 30; and Pouget, *Les idées religieuses*, 98–99.

31. Gratien et al., *Lettre encyclique*, 4; Grégoire, *Lettre pastorale . . . sur la réorganisation du Culte dans les Diocèses de Bourges, Guéret et Moulins* (Paris: Imprimerie-librairie chrétienne, 1796), 1.

32. Gratien et al., *Lettre encyclique*, 4–5; and Paul Pisani, *Répertoire biographique de l'Episcopat constitutionnel (1791–1802)* (Paris: Alphonse Picard et fils, 1907), 61, 113–14. See also Pouget, *Les idées religieuses*, 54; and Desan, *Reclaiming the Sacred*, ch. 3. Cf. Aston, *Religion and Revolution*, 300.

33. McMahon, *Enemies of the Enlightenment*, ch. 3; Graham, "The Revolutionary Bishops"; and Grégoire to K. E. Oelsner, 28 nivôse an II [Jan. 17, 1795], reprinted in Debrunner, *Grégoire l'Européen*, 58.

34. "Extrait du Journal historique (ou plutôt procès-verbal des séances) de la Société libre et littéraire de Philosophie chrétienne," AN 510 AP 1, dossier 6, fol. 42, séance du 5 août; Marc Antoine Berdolet to Grégoire, May 4, 1797 and 22 prairial an VI (June 10, 1798), BSPR-G, dossier "Haut-Rhin," reprinted in Ingold, *Grégoire et l'Eglise*, 93–94; and Grégoire to Scipione de' Ricci, 12 prairial an IV (May 31, 1796), reprinted in Vaussard, *Correspondance*, 14, 47. For more on these two institutions, see Virginie Munduteguy, "Recherche sur l'église constitutionnelle post-Thermidorienne à travers une société et un périodique (An III–An VI)," mémoire de maîtrise, Institut d'histoire de la Révolution française, Université de Paris-I, 1996, directed by Catherine Duprat; Sepinwall, "Regenerating France," 234–37; Plongeron, *Grégoire et la RS*, 100–15, and recurring references to the *Annales* in BSPR-G department dossiers.

35. See undated "Tableau des citoyens composant la Société littéraire de philosophie chrétienne," ms. in BSPR-G, Rév. 181/76; Maire, "Port-Royal," 508; Grégoire, *Les Ruines de Port-Royal en 1801* (Paris: Imprimerie-librairie chrétienne, 1801), 22; *Les Ruines de Port-Royal des Champs en 1809 . . . Nouvelle édition, considérablement augmentée* (Paris: Levacher, 1809), 88 (and Hermon-Belot's introduction to its 1995 reedition); and Necheles, *Abbé Grégoire*, 49n33.

36. Gazier, *Etudes sur l'histoire religieuse*, 261; Obino, "Rapport in promtu de l'état de l'Eglise de Sardaigne lu dans la séance de Germinal an X, à la Société de Philosophie chrétienne à Paris" (1802), ms. in BSPR-G, Rév. 180/31; questionnaire in *Annales de la religion* 2 (Jan. 1796): 250–55; Vaussard, "Avant-Propos"; Leniaud, "Introduction," in *Mémoires*, 22n12; and Debrunner, *Grégoire l'Européen*. On the Jansenist network, see Van Kley, "Piety and Politics in the Century of Lights" (forthcoming in the *Cambridge History of Eighteenth-Century Political Thought*).

37. Catherine Maire, *De la cause de Dieu à la cause de la Nation: Le jansénisme au XVIIIe siècle* (Paris: Gallimard, 1998), 586, 587; and idem, "Port-Royal," 505, 507, 508. A similar argument is made by Leniaud, "Introduction," 22n12.

38. Others who have discussed the SANC include Necheles, *Abbé Grégoire,* 157–69; Manchuelle, "The 'Regeneration of Africa' "; and Marcel Dorigny and Bernard Gainot, *La société des amis des noirs 1788–1799: Contribution à l'histoire de l'abolition de l'esclavage* (Paris: Editions UNESCO, 1998). My conclusions about it parallel in some respects those made by Manchuelle, Dorigny and Gainot, and Yves Bénot, *La démence coloniale sous Napoléon* (Paris: Le Découverte, 1991), though my own purpose is to situate the SANC within the context of Thermidorian reconstruction.

39. Documents explaining the founding of the SANC include draft of letter from Lanthenas to the Directoire exécutif, 20 pluviôse an IV (Feb. 8, 1796), BSPR-G, dossier "Colonies"; and the "esquisse des règlements" of the society (undated), BSPR-G, Rév. 171/38. On the composition of the society, see "Liste générale des Membres de la Société des Amis des Noirs et des Colonies, au vingt Brumaire, an Sept . . .", BSPR-G, dossier "Colonies"; and "Noms des membres de la Société des Amis des Noirs et des Colonies formant la première liste arrêtée le 20 prairial an VI," BSPR-G, carton "Loir & Cher II. Diverses lettres—Grégoire etc.," dossier "Documents prêtés aux Archives nationales pour l'Exposition (novembre 1951)."

40. Ms. "Réglemens de la Société des Amis des Noirs et des Colonies," and minutes of SANC meetings from 20 frimaire and 30 pluviôse an VII (Dec. 10, 1798, Feb. 18, 1799), all in BSPR-G, dossier "Colonies"; BSPR-G Rév. 171/20, 171/39, 171/40, and 171/41; and *Lettre de la Société des Amis des Noirs et des Colonies, aux Auteurs de la Décade philosophique* [BSPR-G, Rév. 171/21], 1.

41. *Décade philosophique,* 30 pluviôse an IV (Feb. 19, 1796): 374. Cf. Abbé Guillaume Thomas Raynal, *Histoire des deux Indes* (1783 English translation of 1770 French edition, bk. 11), reprinted in Hunt, ed., *The French Revolution and Human Rights,* 54. For an excellent discussion of ideas about the colonies in the late 1790s and anxieties about trade, see Bénot, *La démence coloniale,* esp. ch. 8.

42. *Décade philosophique,* 20 pluviôse an IV (Feb. 9, 1796): 311, and 30 pluviôse an IV (Feb. 19, 1796): 375.

43. *Réglement de la Société des Amis des Noirs et des Colonies, adopté à la Séance tenue à Paris le 30 Frimaire an VII* (Paris: Imprimerie des Sciences et Arts, an VII), 5 [BSPR-G, Rév. 171/37]; and ms. "Réglemens de la Société des Amis des Noirs et des Colonies," BSPR-G, dossier "Colonies."

44. On earlier British efforts to rethink empire, but within a monarchical, Christian context, see esp. Christopher L. Brown, "Empire Without Slaves: British Concepts of Emancipation in the Age of the American Revolution," *William and Mary Quarterly,* 3d ser., 56, no. 2 (1999): 273–306. Though some of the writings Brown discusses were unknown to SANC members, other authors (such as Granville Sharp and James Ramsay) maintained regular contact with French abolitionists. On Raynal's support for monarchy and Diderot's authorship of the more radical parts of the *Histoire des deux Indes,* see *Lectures de Raynal: L'Histoire des deux Indes en Europe et en Amérique au XVIIIe siècle* (Oxford: Voltaire Foundation, 1991), ed. Hans-Jürgen Lüsebrink and Manfred Tietz, esp. Lüsebrink's introduction; J. H. M. Salmon, "The Abbé Raynal, 1713–1796: An Intellectual Odyssey," *History Today* 26 (1976): 109–17; and

John Mason, "Materialism and History: Diderot and the *Histoire des deux Indes*," *European Review of History* 3, no. 2 (1996): 151–60.

45. *Lettre . . . aux Auteurs de la Décade philosophique*, 1; and "Rapport fait à la Société des Amis des Noirs par sa commission de Rédaction, composée des Citoyens Lasteyrie, Théremin, & J. B. Say," BSPR-G, dossier "Colonies."

46. "Rapport de la Commission des Colonies anciennes sur l'ordre de ses Travaux," BSPR-G, carton "Presbytère de Paris."

47. See for example *Lettre . . . aux Auteurs de la Décade philosophique*, 2–8; and minutes for 10, 20, and 30 nivôse; 10 pluviôse; and 25 and 29 germinal an VI (Dec. 30, 1797; Jan. 9, 19, and 29; and Apr. 14 and 18, 1798), in BSPR-G, dossier "Colonies."

48. "Discours prononcé à la Société des Amis des Noirs à Paris, dans la séance du 30 Messidor, an 6, par le C^{en} Dupuch" and "Rapport fait . . . [par] Lasteyrie, Théremin, & J. B. Say," both in BSPR-G, dossier "Colonies."

49. Bénot, *La démence coloniale*, 307 and passim; discourses cited in previous note; SANC minutes from 30 floréal and 20 fructidor an VI (May 19 and Sept. 6, 1798) in BSPR-G, dossier "Colonies"; and Dorigny, "La Société des Amis des Noirs et les projets de colonisation en Afrique," in *Révolutions aux colonies* (Paris: Publication des Annales historiques de la Révolution française/Société des Etudes Robespierristes, 1993), 85–93. See also Christopher L. Miller, "Unfinished Business: Colonialism in Sub-Saharan Africa and the Ideals of the French Revolution," in *The Global Ramifications of the French Revolution*, ed. Joseph Klaits and Michael H. Haltzel (New York: Woodrow Wilson Center and Cambridge University Press, 1994), 105–26. On the connections between abolitionism and imperialism in the British context, see C. Brown, "Empire Without Slaves."

50. Necheles, *Abbé Grégoire*, 157–67.

51. See minutes of the SANC from 29 germinal an VI (Apr. 18, 1798) in BSPR-G, dossier "Colonies"; and Dorigny, "Intégration républicaine des colonies et projets de colonisation de l'Afrique: Civiliser pour émanciper?" in Bénot and Dorigny, *Grégoire et la cause des noirs*, 89–105.

52. Grégoire, *Notice sur la Sierra-Leona*, 1, 3, 5, 6.

53. Grégoire, "Rapport fait . . . [sur] des questions dont l'Institut de Caïre serait invité à procurer la solution," 6. On the expedition's place in the development of French colonial ideology, see Amselle, *Vers un multiculturalisme français*, 55–84. See also Grégoire's praise for the wealth that could come from trading with the Orient in Grégoire, *Rapport sur les encouragemens*, 307–8.

54. On spreading Gallican Christianity abroad, see Grégoire, *Compte rendu . . . au Concile national . . .* (Paris: Imprimerie-librairie chrétienne, 1797), 29–53, 58–74; H. Grégoire, J.-S. Saurine, E.-M. Desbois, and N. Jacquemin, *Observations sur ce qu'on appelle reservas, en Espagne; par les évêques réunis à Paris* (Paris: Imprimerie-librairie chrétienne, 1799); and Plongeron, *L'abbé Grégoire*, 81–101.

55. Louis Marin, "Le rôle de l'Abbé Grégoire dans la fondation de l'Institut et de l'Académie des Sciences Morales et Politiques," *Revue des travaux de l'Académie des sciences morales et politiques et comptes rendus de ses séances* 109, 4è série, 2è semestre 1956 (1956): 38–64.

56. On earlier ideas of a civilizing mission in early modern Europe, which were explicitly tied to Christian evangelization, see Anthony Pagden, *Lords of All the World: Ideologies of Empire in Spain, Britain and France c. 1500–c. 1800* (New Haven, Conn.: Yale University Press, 1995).

INTRODUCTION TO PART THREE

1. Cf. discussion of Léonard Bourdon, who lived only until 1807, in M. J. Sydenham, *Léonard Bourdon: The Career of a Revolutionary, 1754–1807* (Waterloo, Ontario: Wilfrid Laurier University Press, 1999), xiv–xv.

2. Grunebaum-Ballin, "L'abbé Grégoire, bibliothécaire," *Archives et Bibliothèques* 3, no. 2 (1937/38): 76–81; and Maggiolo (1884), 46. His new salary, 4,000 francs per year, remained his major source of income until he was elected to the Napoleonic Senate. On Grégoire's financial worries even before he lost his Council seat, see Necheles, "Grégoire and the Constitutional Church," 142–43.

3. Lavaud, *Notice sur Henri Grégoire,* 62; Grégoire, "Mémoire sur la manière de négocier avec la cour de Rome pour faire cesser les troubles religieux de la France" [1800], BN NAF Ms. 22737, fol. 60–67, pp. 1–2; Grégoire to unidentified, July 30, 1821, Ars. Ms. 14126/1; and Guillois, *Le salon de Madame Helvétius.*

4. Grégoire to de' Ricci, July 25, 1801, in Vaussard, *Correspondance,* 99; Hermon-Belot, *L'abbé Grégoire,* 406–11; and Aston, *Religion and Revolution,* 322. Grégoire would later report, however, that he had opposed the Concordat in conversations with Napoleon (see Carnot, "Notice," 242).

5. Bordes to Grégoire, 30 floréal an IX [May 19, 1801], BSPR-G, dossier "Ariège"; Carnot, "Notice," 238, 314; "Grégoire et le chapeau de Cardinal" (clipping at Alliance Israélite Universelle, R 1474 [24]); Plongeron, *L'abbé Grégoire,* 31; P[al] Crouzet, *A M. J[h] de Villèle, sur ses Observations à Messieurs les députés au Corps législatif* ([Toulouse]: n.p., [1814]), 6; and *Mémoires,* 141. Carnot's dating differs slightly from the other pieces in placing Grégoire's near-elevation in the Directory years. See also Grégoire, *Homélie du cardinal Chiaramonti, évêque d'Imola, actuellement souverain pontife Pie VII . . . (1797)* (Paris: Baudouin, 1818); and Aston, *Religion and Revolution,* 319.

6. François Furet, *Revolutionary France, 1770–1880,* trans. Antonia Nevill (Oxford: Blackwell, 1992), 226; and Grégoire to Lambert, 30 fructidor an IX (Sept. 16, 1801), in Ars. Ms. 15049/115. Cf. the view of the Concordat in Aston, *Religion and Revolution,* ch. 12.

7. On Napoleon and the Jews, see esp. Robert Anchel, *Napoléon et les Juifs* (Paris: Presses universitaires de France, 1928); Simon Schwarzfuchs, *Napoleon, the Jews, and the Sanhedrin* (London: Routledge/Littman Library of Jewish Civilization, 1979); and Albert Soboul and Bernhard Blumenkranz, *Le Grand Sanhédrin de Napoléon* (Toulouse: E. Privat, 1979). On Grégoire and the Sanhedrin, see ch. 9.

8. Ezran, *L'Abbé Grégoire,* 152; Guillois, *Le salon de Madame Helvétius,* 158n1, 214; and Carnot, "Notice," 254–55. On the narrow margin of Grégoire's election to the Senate, see BAG ms. 859.

9. Pierre Rosanvallon, *La monarchie impossible: Les Chartes de 1814 et de 1830* (Paris: Fayard, 1994), chs. 1 and 2.

10. [Grégoire], *Réponse à quelques pamphlets contre la Constitution, par M. G . . .* (Paris: 1814), 4–5, 7, 8 (attributed to Grégoire in Posener, #295, though the Bibliothèque nationale recently began cataloguing it as the work of a young liberal named Charles Denoyer); and [Grégoire], *De la constitution française de l'an 1814,* 1st ed. (Paris: Le Normant/Delaunay, 1814), 19–20 and passim. The latter pamphlet bore Grégoire's name after its first edition.

11. Lavaud, *Notice sur Henri Grégoire,* 67; Crouzét, *A M. Jᵇ de Villèle,* 6; also D.L., *Epître amicale à M. l'abbé Barruel, sur sa brochure au Sénateur Grégoire* (n.p., [1814]), 11; and [Fanny Raoul], *Réponse à l'écrit de M. l'abbé Barruel . . . par une française* (n.p., [1814]).

12. M. Auguste D***, *Le Philanthrope dévoilé, ou, Réponse aux observations de l'abbé Grégoire, sur la Constitution de 1814* (Paris: n.p., 1814), 4–6, 15, 17; also Abbé Barruel, *Du principe et de l'obstination des Jacobins, en réponse au Sénateur Grégoire* ([Paris: n.p., 1814]).

13. On attacks on Grégoire, see his ostensibly anonymous *Première et dernière réponse aux libellistes* (Paris: A. Egron, [1814]). On his removal from the Institut, see P. Barthélemy, *Pétition à la Chambre des députés . . . à l'effet d'obtenir la réintégration à l'Institut de MM. Grégoire, Arnault et Etienne* (Paris: Chez les marchans de nouveautés, 1822); and "L'Institut crée par une loi, démembré par une ordonnance," *La Révolution de 1830,* no. 100 (Nov. 15, 1830). On the Restoration, compare Furet, *Revolutionary France*; Rosanvallon, *La monarchie impossible*; and Pamela M. Pilbeam, *The Constitutional Monarchy in France, 1814–48* (New York: Longman, 2000).

14. Maggiolo (1884), 86–87; Grégoire to F. Münter, Feb. 18, 1817, reprinted in Debrunner, *Grégoire l'Européen,* 288.

15. See for example Jean Siffrein Maury, *Lettre de M. l'abbé Maury, au régicide Comte Grégoire* (Montpellier: J.-G. Tournel, [1818?]); *Aux électeurs de l'Isère. Notice historique, tirée des Moniteurs du temps* (n.p.: [1819?]); *Observations sur un article de M. Castelbajac . . . relatif au Régicide Grégoire et à la Convention Nationale* (n.p.: Imprimerie de P. Gueffier, [1819?]).

16. Grégoire, "Aux bons citoyens du département de la Meurthe. Paris, 6 août 1790," *Le patriote françois* (Paris: 1790), 3; and Grégoire to Jennat, Mar. 20, 1817, reprinted in Cosson, "Lettres de l'abbé Grégoire," 255. On other forms of popular protest during the Restoration, see Sheryl Kroen, *Politics and Theater: The Crisis of Legitimacy in Restoration France, 1815–1830* (Berkeley: University of California Press, 2000).

17. Carnot, "Notice," 279; Grégoire to Jennat, Mar. 2, 1818, reprinted in Cosson, "Lettres de l'abbé Grégoire," 258; and Maggiolo (1884), 79, 92, 98, 137. Because the Grégoire papers conserved in Parisian libraries cover political and philosophical issues almost exclusively, the details of his daily life have remained mostly hidden to scholars. Maggiolo's mention of the property bought in 1807 matches the information in an intriguing and heretofore unknown letter that lies between the pages of Grégoire's original Metz contest entry ms. (Grégoire to M. Moreau, Dec. 13, 1814, unnumbered sheet inserted in "Mémoire sur les juifs," at the Musée lorrain, probably as a result of Lucien Wiener's having bought it from an autograph dealer). In this rare piece of evidence, Grégoire complained to his notary about his tenants' ingratitude in continually asking for

rent reductions or extensions, and he indicated that he was no longer inclined to behave leniently toward them.

18. Grégoire, *De la littérature des nègres, ou Recherches sur leurs facultés intellectuelles, leurs qualités morales et leur littérature, suivies de Notices sur la vie et les ouvrages des nègres qui sont distingués dans les sciences, les lettres, et les arts* (Paris: Maradan, 1808); *Essai historique sur les libertés de l'Église gallicane*; and "Notes biographique sur les personnages lorrains, par l'abbé Grégoire," BM Nancy, 957 (533). On Grégoire's involvement with the *Chronique religieuse,* see Posener, "Essai d'une bibliographie critique." On heroic collective biography, see Bell, *Cult of the Nation,* ch. 4.

19. Exceptions include Necheles's and Hermon-Belot's biographies, and Maggiolo's 1884 essay. Necheles focuses mostly on Grégoire's abolitionist activities, however, while Hermon-Belot's treats Grégoire's political theology to a far greater extent than his other postrevolutionary interests and activities. Maggiolo's essay contains many invaluable nuggets of information, but it is more useful as a chronology than as an analysis.

20. See for example the usage in *Le Memento des Vivans et des Morts . . . par un desservant du diocèse de Bayeux, membre d'un des Comités d'Instruction public* (Caen: F. Poisson, 1817), 107 ("Robespierre was the first pope of this *shameful, puerile* and *ridiculous* heresy . . . , of our *regeneration*"). Cf. however Katia Sainson's discussion of regeneration used in an authoritarian sense during the Empire (Sainson, " 'Le Régénérateur de la France': Literary Accounts of Napoleonic Regeneration 1799–1805," *Nineteenth-Century French Studies* 30, nos. 1–2 (2001–2002): 9–25.

CHAPTER 7: THE JOYS AND FRUSTRATIONS OF
THE ATLANTIC REPUBLICAN NETWORK

1. On his hopes to build such a network, see Grégoire, *Plan d'association générale entre les savans, gens de lettres, et artistes . . .* (n.p.: 1817); *Essai sur la solidarité littéraire entre les savants de tous les pays . . .* (Paris: Les principaux libraires, 1824); and Plongeron, *Grégoire et la RS.*

2. Grégoire, *Apologie,* 10, 29; Grégoire to Usteri and to Abrahamson, reprinted in Debrunner, *Grégoire l'Européen,* 303–4, 307; [idem], "Notice critique sur l'ouvrage: La Bibliotheca columbiana," *Revue encyclopédique* 18 (Apr. 1823): 107–108; [idem], "Notice critique sur deux écrits mexicains au sujet de la Lettre encyclique du Pape Léon XII aux archevêques et évêques d'Amérique," *Revue encyclopédique* 30 (May 1826): 399–401; and Grégoire to [Trognon], Sept. 30, 1825, BAG ms. 870. On Grégoire's authorship of these unsigned reviews, see Posener, "Essai d'une bibliographie critique."

3. Grégoire to Verplanck, May 17, 1823, in New-York Historical Society (hereafter NYHS), Gulian Verplanck Papers, Box #4, Folder G, fol. 69, p. 2; Grégoire to Clarkson, May 13, 1823, in Henry Huntington Library (San Marino, CA), Thomas Clarkson Papers, CN 103; and Grégoire to unnamed, Aug. 12, 1821, BAG ms. 714 (copy of original in the collection of B. Fillon)

4. D. A. Brading, *The First America: The Spanish Monarchy, Creole Patriots, and the Liberal State, 1492–1867* (New York: Cambridge University Press,

1991), 585–90; and letters between Servando and Grégoire, in Ars. Ms. 6339, fol. 26–33, and in *Escritos inéditos de fray Servando Teresa de Mier,* ed. J. M. Miquel i Vergés and Hugo Díaz-Thomé (México: El Colegio de México—Centro de estudios históricos, 1944), 507–12.

5. See the works collected in *Coleccion de las Obras del venerable obispo de Chiapa, don Bartolomé de Las Casas, Defensor de la libertad de los Americanos* . . . (Paris: En casa de Rosa, 1822); and Plongeron, "Apologie de Barthélémy de Las Casas . . . ," in Bénot and Dorigny, *Grégoire et la cause des noirs,* 37–50. Recent research has revealed that Grégoire's efforts were somewhat misguided, as Las Casas did support the enslavement of Africans early in his life and only renounced it later. See Laurie Barbara Gunst, "Bartolomé de las Casas and the Question of Negro Slavery in the Early Spanish Indies" (Ph.D. diss., Harvard University, 1982); and Henry Raup Wagner and Helen Rand Parish, *The Life and Writings of Bartolomé de Las Casas* (Albuquerque: University of New Mexico Press, 1967), 246 and passim.

6. His donations included his edition of Olivier de Serres's *Essai historique sur l'état de l'agriculture en Europe au seizième siècle,* APS Pam. v. 1097, no. 8, donated July 18, 1806 (also sent by him to Thomas Jefferson and John Milnor; see Grégoire to Joel and Ruth Barlow, Dec. 21, 1805, in Houghton Library, Harvard University [Cambridge, MA], Barlow Papers, bMS AM 1448 [henceforth "Houghton—Barlow Papers"], fol. 603, cited by permission of the Houghton Library); Société d'agriculture du Département de la Haute-Marne, *Rapport fait à la société . . . par 3 commissaires qu'elle a nommés . . .* (Paris: Marchant, 1808), APS, 630 Pam. v. 2, no. 8, donated Dec. 2, 1808; and Société nationale d'agriculture, *Séance publique . . . 15 juillet 1810* (Paris: Imprimerie de Mme. Huzard, 1810), APS, Pam. v. 1102, no. 3, donated Jan. 18, 1811. Information about Grégoire's gifts comes from the APS Association File Card Catalog and the APS Transactions (APS Library, Philadelphia, PA).

7. *De la constitution de l'an 1814,* 4th ed. (Paris: Egron, 1814), APS, Pam. v. 43, no. 10, donated Apr. 1816; Jean-Denis Lanjuinais, *Notice d'un discours prononcé par M. Jamme, directeur de l'école spéciale de droit de Toulouse, le 2 novembre 1807 . . .* (n.p., n.d.), APS, Pam. v. 43, no. 4, donation undated.

8. *Observations nouvelles sur les juifs . . . d'Allemagne* (n.p.: 1806), APS Pam. v. 43, no. 11, and *Observations nouvelles sur les juifs . . . d'Amsterdam* (n.p.: 1807), APS Pam. v. 43, no. 12, both of which were likely donated on Feb. 5, 1808; and "Articles recommandés à la bienveillance de Mr. Michaux . . . (From Mon. Le Sénateur Grégoire au palais du Senât, Paris, to his friend B. Vaughan)," APS, Benjamin Vaughan Papers, B V46p. On Grégoire and Noah, see Richard H. Popkin, "Mordecai Noah, the Abbé Grégoire and the Paris Sanhedrin," *Modern Judaism* 2 (1982): 131–48; and Jonathan Sarna, *Jacksonian Jew: The Two Worlds of Mordecai Noah* (New York: Holmes & Meier, 1981), 21.

9. Hannah Adams, *The History of the Jews from the Destruction of Jerusalem to the Nineteenth Century* (Boston: John Eliot, 1812), 2: 152; Grégoire, "Articles recommandés à la bienveillance de Mr. Michaux"; the pamphlet he conserved on converting the Oneidas (BSPR-G, Rév. 147/20); and ch. 9.

10. See Jacques M. Gres-Gayer, "Four Letters from Henri Grégoire to John Carroll, 1809–1814," *Catholic Historical Review* 79, no. 4 (1993): 681–703

(originals in Archives of the Archdiocese of Baltimore); and Jay P. Dolan, *The American Catholic Experience: A History from Colonial Times to the Present* (Notre Dame, Ind.: University of Notre Dame Press, 1992), 101–24. Carroll did, however, praise Grégoire's criticism of Barlow's *Columbiad*.

11. Grégoire, *Discours sur la liberté des cultes* (1794), 7; Richard H. Popkin, "An Aspect of the Problem of Religious Freedom in the French and American Revolutions," *Freedom: Proceedings of the American Catholic Philosophical Association* 50 (1976): 146–61; Grégoire, *De la liberté de conscience et de culte à Haïti* (Paris: Baudouin Frères, 1824), 16; and R. Popkin, "Mordecai Noah," 132. Cf. Sarna, *Jacksonian Jew*, 26–33.

12. These included his own works *Apologie de Barthélemy de Las-Casas* (Paris: Baudouin, 1800), APS, Pam. v. 1094, no. 19, given Aug. 20, 1802; *De la littérature des nègres* (Paris: Maradan, 1808), APS 326.92 G86, donated Dec. 2, 1808; and *De la traite et de l'esclavage des noirs et des blancs* (Paris: Egron, 1815), APS Pam. v. 718, no. 5, donated July 21, 1815; along with several books by others.

13. Pennsylvania Abolition Society Papers, Committee of Correspondence letter book, 1794–1809, pp. 71–73, 78–80, 83–85, 87–89, Historical Society of Pennsylvania (Philadelphia, PA), AmS 081; and Grégoire to Verplanck, May 17, 1823.

14. Grégoire, *De la littérature des nègres*, 14, 44–45, 35.

15. Ibid., 36, 150, 255–56, 260.

16. Gulian C. Verplanck, *An Anniversary Discourse, Delivered before the New-York Historical Society, December 7, 1818* (New York: James Eastburn & Co., 1818), 15; and Livingston to Grégoire, 12 germinal an X/Apr. 2, 1802, in NYHS, Robert Livingston Papers.

17. The Library Company has Grégoire's 1790 *Lettre aux philantropes* and a 1791 English translation of his *Essai sur la régénération*. Both were owned by the time the library printed its 1807 catalog, and, according to Chief Reference Librarian Phil Lapsansky, were probably acquired soon after publication. It is not clear when the Library Company acquired its two French copies of *De la littérature*.

18. R. Popkin, "Mordecai Noah," 132, 136; Channing to Vaughan, May 13, 1822, in APS, Benjamin Vaughan Papers, B V46p; and [George Ticknor], *Life, Letters, and Journals* (Boston: J. R. Osgood, 1876), 1: 130.

19. *Critical Observations on the Poem of Mr. Joel Barlow, The Columbiad* (Washington City: Roger Chew Weightman, 1809); *An Enquiry Concerning the Intellectual and Moral Faculties, and Literature of Negroes . . .* trans. D. B. Warden (Brooklyn: Printed by Thomas Kirk, 1810); and *Report on the Means of Compleating and Distributing the National Library . . .* (Philadelphia: Market Street, 1794).

20. [John Hurford Stone], *Copies of Original Letters Recently Written by Persons in Paris to Dr. Priestley in America . . .* (Philadelphia: James Humphreys, 1798), 19; and Ticknor, *Life, Letters, and Journals*, 1: 142–43. On Grégoire and Vaughan, see Craig C. Murray, *Benjamin Vaughan (1751–1835): The Life of an Anglo-American Intellectual* (New York: Arno Press, 1982), 276–77, 343, 362n35, 388, 417, and passim; and *Mémoires*, 66–67.

21. Grégoire to Joel Barlow, Dec. 21, 1805, June 3, 1806, and Sept. 1, 1806, and to Ruth Barlow, Aug. 17, 1806, all in Houghton—Barlow Papers, fol. 603—

606. It is not clear why the PAS stopped writing to Grégoire, though it possibly related to Haitian independence; most Americans, including members of the PAS, were horrified by Haitian violence and fearful of its potentially contagious effects on American slaves (see Richard S. Newman, *The Transformation of American Abolitionism: Fighting Slavery in the Early Republic* [Chapel Hill: University of North Carolina Press, 2002], 26; and Sepinwall, "La révolution haïtienne et les Etats-Unis: Etude historiographique," in *1802: Rétablissement de l'esclavage dans les colonies françaises: Aux origines de Haïti,* ed. Bénot and Dorigny [Paris: Maisonneuve et Larose, 2003], 387–401).

22. Jefferson to Grégoire, Feb. 25, 1809; and Jefferson to Barlow, Oct. 8, 1809, both in *Writings of Thomas Jefferson,* ed. Paul L. Ford (New York: Putnam, 1892–99), 9: 246, 261.

23. Grégoire, *De la noblesse de la peau,* 23–24.

24. *Mémoires,* 95.

25. M. Dubois's chronic illness continued until his death in 1812, and he thus did not socialize with the married couples whom Grégoire and Mme Dubois often visited. While Mme Dubois continued to take care of her husband, Grégoire's letters generally refer only to her (see however Grégoire to Dom Grappin, Jan. 28, 1813, passing along Mme Dubois' gratitude for Grappin's condolences about M. Dubois' death, reprinted in Plongeron, *Dom Grappin, correspondant de l'abbé Grégoire (1796–1830)* [Paris: Les belles lettres, 1969], 73).

26. Grégoire to Joel and Ruth Barlow, Dec. 21, 1805; Grégoire to Barlow, June 3, 1806; Grégoire to R. Barlow, Aug. 17, 1806; Grégoire to Barlow, Sept. 1, 1806; and Parise to R. Barlow, Sept. 1, 1806 (all in Houghton—Barlow Papers, fols. 603–6, 687). See also Grégoire to R. Barlow, 23 Messidor (July 16) 1803, in French Revolution Collection, Cornell University, Rare and Manuscript Collections, University Library, Accession #4606, Box 8. It is not clear how long Parise continued to work for Grégoire and Mme Dubois.

27. Ibid., fols. 603–4 and fol. 602 (Grégoire to Barlow, Oct. 26 [1807]).

28. Barlow, *The Columbiad* (London: Printed for Richard Phillips, 1809), 340 (Book 10, lines 599–610) [edition available online through the Making of America project, http://moa.umdl.umich.edu/cgi/sgml/moa-idx?notisid=APT9199, accessed July 2002].

29. Grégoire, *Observations critiques sur le poème de M. Joël Barlow, The Colombiad* (Paris: Maradan, 1809), 3; translated into English as *Critical Observations on the Poem of Mr. Joel Barlow,* as noted above.

30. Ibid., 3–4. In fact, the poem was received less enthusiastically than Grégoire imagined. See James Woodress, *A Yankee's Odyssey: The Life of Joel Barlow* (Philadelphia: J. B. Lippincott Company, 1958), esp. 266–71; and John Bidwell, "The Publication of Joel Barlow's The Columbiad," *Proceedings of the American Antiquarian Society* 93, no. 2 (1984): 337–80.

31. Barlow to Grégoire, Mar. 15, 1809, in Archives nationales (Paris), 510 AP 2, dossier "A-B."

32. Barlow, *Letter to Henry Gregoire . . . in Reply to His Letter on The Columbiad* (Washington: Roger Chew Weightman, 1809), 4–8; Woodress, *A Yankee's Odyssey,* 270.

33. Barlow, *Letter to Henry Gregoire,* 6, 9–10.

34. Stephen Jacob to Barlow, Windsor, Vermont, Dec. 7, 1809; William Little to Barlow, Boston, Oct. 12, 1809; Henry Dearborn to Barlow, Boston, Jan. 22, 1810; Jonathan Law to Barlow, Hartford, Oct. 14, 1809; and T. Law to Barlow, Philadelphia, Oct. 16, 1809, all in Beinecke Rare Book and Manuscript Library, Yale University, Pequot Papers (henceforth "Beinecke—Pequot Papers"), respectively M995, M1001, M970, M998 and M999; and *Correspondence, Critical and Literary, On the Subject of The Columbiad, An American Epic Poem of Joel Barlow, Esq.* (Ballston-Spa, N.Y.: Printed by Brown and Miller, 1810), 2.

35. Grégoire to Barlow, [1810], in Beinecke—Pequot Papers, M 981.

36. Ibid.

37. Jefferson to Barlow, Oct. 8, 1809, in *Writings of Thomas Jefferson,* 9: 261.

38. On antislavery as a core element in French republican festivals, see Jeff Horn, "Representations of the Other under the Terror in Provincial France," *Proceedings of the Annual Meeting of the Western Society for French History: Selected Papers,* ed. Barry Rothaus 26 (2000): 234–42; and Elizabeth Colwill, "Lactating Liberty: Festivals of Emancipation in Revolutionary France," presented at the meeting of the International Society for Eighteenth Century Studies, Los Angeles, Calif., Aug. 7, 2003. This text will appear in Colwill's forthcoming book on ritual, gender, and emancipation in revolutionary France and Saint-Domingue. After Napoleon's reimposition of slavery in 1802, slavery would be permanently abolished during the Revolution of 1848.

CHAPTER 8: EXPORTING THE REVOLUTION

The epigraph is taken from: Grégoire to Servando de Mier, Sept. 30, 1825, reprinted in *Escritos inéditos de fray Servando Teresa de Mier,* 511 (emphasis in original).

1. Grégoire to Usteri, July 12, 1814, and Grégoire to Goethe, Aug. 12, 1829, reprinted in Debrunner, *Grégoire l'Européen,* 276–77 and 313; Necheles, *Abbé Grégoire,* esp. chs. 10 and 13; and Lawrence C. Jennings, *French Anti-Slavery: The Movement for the Abolition of Slavery in France, 1802–1848* (New York: Cambridge University Press, 2000), esp. 6–8. On Grégoire's travels and European contacts, see Debrunner; and Plongeron, *Grégoire et la RS,* esp. chs. 4 and 5.

2. Grégoire to N. von Rosenthal, Sept. 28, 1821, cited in Nelly Schmidt, *Victor Schoelcher et l'abolition de l'esclavage* (Paris: Fayard, 1994), 281n8.

3. Grégoire, *De la liberté de conscience et de culte à Haïti . . .* (Paris: Baudouin Frères, 1824), 42. This involvement has been little analyzed in the literature on Grégoire, with the exception of Necheles, *Abbé Grégoire,* ch. 12; Duraciné Vaval, "L'abbé Henri Grégoire dans ses rapports avec Saint-Domingue et Haïti. Conférence prononcée le 31 mai 1931," *Revue de la Société d'histoire et de géographie d'Haïti* 2, no. 4 (1931); and a few of the articles in *La révolution française et Haïti: Filiations, ruptures, nouvelles dimensions,* ed. Michel Hector ([Port-au-Prince]: Société Haïtienne d'histoire et de géographie/Editions Henri Deschamps, [1995]), particularly those of Hans-Jürgen Lüsebrink and Pierre Buteau. See also Geggus, "Haiti and the Abolitionists:

Opinion, Propaganda and International Politics in Britain and France, 1804–1838," in *Abolition and Its Aftermath: The Historical Context, 1790–1916,* ed. David Richardson (Totowa, N.J.: F. Cass, 1985), 113–40.

4. Grégoire to unidentified, Apr. 15, 1815, BN NAF Ms. 24910, fol. 288.

5. The color difference between north and south was not absolute but one of degree. Like leaders in the south, most of Christophe's top assistants were of mixed race. Still, many of them had sided with the *nouveaux libres* (former black slaves) during the earlier civil war. Moreover, while the majority of southern army chiefs were of mixed race, the majority of officers in the north were black (see David Nicholls, *From Dessalines to Duvalier: Race, Colour and National Independence in Haiti* [Cambridge: Cambridge University Press, 1979], 55 and passim).

6. Comte de Limonade to Grégoire, June 10, 1814, Ars. Ms. 6339/44v-47.

7. Nicholls, *From Dessalines to Duvalier,* 59; Earl Leslie Griggs and Clifford H. Prator, *Henry Christophe and Thomas Clarkson: A Correspondence* (New York: Greenwood Press, 1968); and Vaval, "L'abbé Henri Grégoire."

8. Grégoire, "Observations sur la constitution du Nord d'Haïti et sur les opinions qu'on s'est formées en France de ce gouvernement," 1818 [?], Ars. Ms. 15049/204, 1–3, 5, 7; reprinted and analyzed recently by Bénot in Bénot and Dorigny, *Grégoire et la cause des noirs,* 142–52.

9. The collection in which this document is found (Ms. 15049) was acquired by the Arsenal only in the 1970s. Two letters in the collection, however, had been reprinted in nineteenth-century histories of Haiti by Haitians (Thomas Madiou, *Histoire d'Haïti* [1848; reprint, Port-au-Prince: Editions Henri Deschamps, 1988], 6: 215–19; B. Ardouin, *Etudes sur l'histoire d'Haïti suivies de la vie du général J.-M. Borgella: Deuxième édition conforme au texte original . . .* [Port-au-Prince: Chez l'Editeur, 1958], 9: 17–19).

10. Vastey to Thomas Clarkson, Nov. 29, 1819, reprinted in Griggs and Prator, *Henry Christophe and Thomas Clarkson,* 179–80.

11. Vastey, *Réflexions sur une lettre de Mazères, ex-colon français . . .* (Cap-Henry: P. Roux, 1816), 19; and Nicholls, *From Dessalines to Duvalier,* esp. 5, 41, 43–46.

12. Clarkson to Christophe, Sept. 7, 1819, in Griggs and Prator, *Henry Christophe and Thomas Clarkson,* 154–56.

13. Clarkson to Christophe, Sept. 7, 1819; Christophe to Clarkson, Nov. 20, 1819; and Clarkson to Christophe, Apr. 28, 1820; all reprinted in Griggs and Prator, *Henry Christophe and Thomas Clarkson,* 154–56, 168–70, and 196–99. Haiti's eventual recognition agreement with France, reached in 1825, did include a staggering indemnity payment. For details on this agreement, see esp. François Blancpain, "L'ordonnance de 1825 et la question de l'indemnité," and Gusti Klara Gaillard-Pourchet, "Aspects politiques et commerciaux de l'indemnisation haïtienne," both in *Rétablissement de l'esclavage dans les colonies françaises,* ed. Bénot and Dorigny, 221–30, 231–37.

14. Clarkson to Boyer, May 25, 182[1], reprinted in Griggs and Prator, *Henry Christophe and Thomas Clarkson,* 224–25.

15. Griggs and Prator, *Henry Christophe and Thomas Clarkson,* 229–30 (letter of Boyer to Clarkson, July 30, 1821), 237–40 (letter of Clarkson to Zachary Macaulay, Nov. 19, 1821), and 246.

16. "Copie d'une lettre du grand juge d'Hayti daté du 25 7bre 1818 an 15 de l'indépendance . . . ," Ars. Ms. 6339/60; letter from Colombel to Grégoire, Nov. 9, 1819, Ars. Ms. 6339/73; and Inginac to Grégoire, Apr. 1, 1820, Ars. Ms. 6339/81.

17. See Ars. Ms. 15049.

18. Buteau, "L'abbé Grégoire: Evolution et traitement du mythe à Saint-Domingue et en Haïti," in Hector, *La révolution française et Haïti*, 1: 335–52. Negative depictions of Haiti in France, even after the indemnity agreement of 1825, are discussed in greater detail in Sepinwall, "The Specter of Saint-Domingue: American and French Reactions to the Haitian Revolution," presented at the John Carter Brown Library, Brown University, conference on "The Haitian Revolution: Two Hundred Years After," June 20, 2004.

19. See letter of Jean-Louis-Antoine in *La concorde*, no. 34 (Dec. 30, 1821), 136; J. B. Romane, "Intérieur," *Le phare*, no. 34 (Mar. 24, 1831), 151; [Grégoire], "Notice critique sur l'ouvrage: 'Considérations diverses sur Haïti,' par Desrivières-Chanlatte," *Revue encyclopédique* 17 (Feb. 1823): 272; and Buteau, "L'abbé Grégoire," 347. On government uses, see for example Jean-Pierre Boyer, "République d'Hayti: Proclamation au peuple et à l'armée de l'artibonite et du Nord, 16 octobre 1820," in BSPR-G, dossier "Colonies."

20. Grégoire to Boyer, June 22, 1821, Ars. Ms. 15049/169. See also Grégoire to unnamed, Aug. 12, 1821, BAG ms. 714.

21. Grégoire to Boyer, June 22, 1821; and Grégoire, *Histoire des confesseurs*.

22. Grégoire, *De la liberté de conscience*, 10, 33; Grégoire to Boyer, Nov. 5, 1824, Ars. Ms. 15049/194; and *AP* 9 (Nov. 9, 1789): 729.

23. Grégoire to Boyer, June 22, 1821, Ars. Ms. 15049/194.

24. Ibid.; Grégoire, *Manuel de piété*, 103; and *Considérations sur le mariage et le divorce adressés aux citoyens d'Haïti* (Paris: Baudouin, 1823), 61.

25. Grégoire, *De la noblesse de la peau*, 18; *Considérations sur le mariage*, 1, 45.

26. See for example Grégoire to Colombel, Aug. 22, 1821, Ars. Ms. 15049/195; and BSPR-G, Rév. 171/51.

27. Grégoire to Inginac, Apr. 26, 1825, Ars. Ms. 15049/185; and Grégoire, *Considérations sur le mariage*, 42–43.

28. Grégoire, *Considérations sur le mariage*.

29. On mixed-race women in late colonial Saint-Domingue, see John D. Garrigus, " 'Sons of the Same Father': Gender, Race and Citizenship in French Saint-Domingue, 1760–1792," in *Visions and Revisions of Eighteenth-Century France*, ed. Christine Adams, Jack R. Censer, and Lisa Jane Graham (University Park: Pennsylvania State University Press, 1997); Rogers, "Les libres de couleur dans les capitales de Saint-Domingue"; and King, *Blue Coat or Powdered Wig*, ch. 9.

30. Cited in Hufton, "Femmes, religion, et contre-révolution: L'expérience de sept diocèses," in *Les femmes et la révolution française: Modes d'action et d'expression*, ed. Marie-France Brive (Toulouse: Presses universitaires du Mirail, 1989), 2:231.

31. See Grégoire, *Les Ruines de Port-Royal* (1801), 17 and passim; references to "Mylady Moncashel" in Grégoire to Fabroni, 22 fructidor an X (Sept. 9, 1802), APS, B F113, no. 1; the women included on the Committee of Public Instruction's list of grants, which Grégoire was responsible for preparing (Guillaume, *Procès-verbaux,* 6: 426–27, 447–48); and Grégoire's letter to Mme Dubois regarding Erasmus, in which he nevertheless defended the Dutch writer's critical comments on women (reprinted in *Mémoires,* 260).

32. "Doctrine du christianisme," BSPR-G, Rév. 177: A, 7 (see appendix); and *Essai sur la régénération,* 167. The former quote combined Corinthians 12:13, Galatians 3:28, and Colossians 3:11. Las Casas had also brandished the Colossians passage as an argument for equality; see Las Casas, *In Defense of the Indians . . . ,* trans. Stafford Poole (DeKalb: Northern Illinois University Press, 1992), 39. Given that Grégoire's version incorporated all the categories listed in Colossians but added to it the male/female distinction of Galatians, his listing gender difference as an arbitrary one was deliberate. Grégoire would also direct Haitians to recite the Galatians passage in his *Manuel de piété,* 24–25.

33. Wollstonecraft's closest associates when she lived in Paris were also close friends or colleagues of Grégoire, such as the Barlows, Helen Maria Williams, and the Girondin circle around Condorcet and the Rolands. On Grégoire's reading Wollstonecraft's *Vindication,* see reference to her in his *De l'influence du christianisme sur la condition des femmes,* 3d ed. (Paris: Baudouin, 1829), 106n1. Grégoire himself owned a copy of this book at his death ("Catalogue des livres légués à la Bibliothèque du Roi par M. Grégoire" [1831], Ars. Fol. Z-1013, section "Sciences et Arts").

34. On the *Histoire des sectes,* see ch. 9.

35. See Grégoire to Mme Inginac, Apr. 26, 1825, Ars. Ms. 15049/192; Grégoire to Clarisse Descloches, Sept. 8, 1821, Ars. Ms. 15049/174; and his other letters to them in the same collection. See also Grégoire, *Manuel de piété,* 15.

36. Grégoire, *De l'influence du christianisme sur la condition des femmes,* 122–25; Grégoire to Mme Inginac, Oct. 21, 1825, Ars. Ms. 15049/191; and the letters cited in the previous note.

37. See especially Grégoire, *De l'influence du christianisme sur la condition des femmes*; Grégoire to Descloches, Oct. 22, 1822, Ars. Ms. 15049/200; and other letters to her and Mme Inginac.

38. Goodman, "Difference: An Enlightenment Concept," 135, building upon Sylvana Tomaselli, "The Enlightenment Debate on Women," *History Workshop Journal* 20 (1985), 101–24.

39. Grégoire, *Manuel de piété,* 6, 15; *De la noblesse de la peau,* 20, 22.

40. Scott notes that, in the wake of the abolition of slavery, during the Convention session when citizenship was granted to former male slaves, the deputies publicly recognized and applauded a black woman in the gallery who was crying with happiness. She argues that "it was no accident . . . to make a black woman the sign of the entry of black men into the ranks of citizenship. The men's difference from women served to eradicate differences of skin color and race among men" (Scott, *Only Paradoxes to Offer,* 9).

41. Grégoire, *Considérations sur le mariage*, 14; ADLC, F592, fol. 4; "Questions religieuses," Ars. Ms. 15049/140; and "Doctrine du christianisme," BSPR-G, Rév. 177: K, 6, 8 (see appendix). During this period, Grégoire was also involved in promoting Greek independence (see especially Stamati Theodore Lascaris, "L'abbé Grégoire et la Grèce," *Révolution française* 85 [1932]: 220–31).

42. Necheles, *Abbé Grégoire,* 243.

43. Grégoire, *Epître aux Haïtiens* (Port-au-Prince: Imprimerie du gouvernement, 1827), 14, 15; Carnot, "Notice," 321.

44. Grégoire, *Epître aux Haïtiens,* 9n; Jean Price-Mars, *Silhouettes de Nègres et de Négrophiles* (Paris: Présence Africaine, 1960), 198; Nicholls, *From Dessalines to Duvalier,* 155, 231. For more on the memory of Grégoire in Haiti, see Vaval, *Histoire de la littérature haïtienne, ou 'L'âme noire'* [Port-au-Prince: Imprimerie A. Heraux, 1933]), dedication to Grégoire; Buteau, "L'abbé Grégoire"; also epilogue.

45. See David Brion Davis, *The Problem of Slavery in the Age of Revolution, 1770–1823* (Ithaca, N.Y.: Cornell University Press, 1975); the essays in John Ashworth, David Brion Davis, and Thomas L. Haskell, *The Antislavery Debate: Capitalism and Abolitionism as a Problem in Historical Interpretation,* ed. Thomas Bender (Berkeley: University of California Press, 1992); also Jean Comaroff and John Comaroff, *Of Revelation and Revolution: Christianity, Colonialism and Consciousness in South Africa, Volume One* (Chicago: University of Chicago Press, 1991).

46. See for example his *De l'influence du christianisme sur la condition des femmes,* 127–29.

47. Grégoire to Inginac, Aug. 20, 1821, Ars. Ms. 15049/171. On Grégoire's paternalism, see also Lüsebrink, "Grégoire et Haïti: Dimensions politiques, culturelles et anthropologiques d'une relation intellectuelle (1789–1831)," in Hector, *La révolution française et Haïti,* 1: 306–22.

48. Vaval, "L'abbé Henri Grégoire," 27–28. Many modern Haitian historians do criticize Christophe's agricultural policy, however, which kept the rural masses on the farms.

49. See *AP* 27 (June 14, 1791): 231; and Dorigny, "Intégration républicaine."

50. For a more egalitarian model of exchange, see Lafayette-Boyer correspondence, Department of Rare and Manuscript Collections, Cornell University, Ithaca, N.Y., 4611 Boxes 14, 25 and 27; and Lafayette to Boyer, Nov. 1, 1824, Lafayette mss., Manuscripts Department, Lilly Library, Indiana University, Bloomington, Ind.

51. On the connections between regeneration and colonization, see also Manchuelle, "The 'Regeneration of Africa' "; and Amselle, *Vers un multiculturalisme français.*

52. Y. D. Sémach, *L'Abbé Grégoire et l'émancipation des Juifs* (Paris: Librairie Larose, 1931), 11 (conserved at AIU, 8-UBR-1664). For more on the Alliance, see Rodrigue, *French Jews, Turkish Jews.* See also Yves Bénot's discussion of Grégoire's being invoked in contradictory ways in 1946, both by would-be decolonizers and by their opponents (Bénot, *La révolution française et la fin des colonies* [Paris: Editions La Découverte, 1989], 216).

CHAPTER 9: CHRISTIAN APOLOGETICS AND THE UNIVERSAL HUMAN FAMILY

1. See Grégoire Papers, Schomburg Center, MG 243, no. 54; Lafayette correspondence in AN 510 AP 2, dossier "L"; "Visites de Weiss, bibliothécaire de Besançon, à Grégoire, 1822–1828," entry of Oct. 5, 1828, transcribed (possibly by Gazier) in BSPR-G, dossier "Doubs-II"; and Lerouge to Grégoire, Jan. 9, 1830, in AN 510 AP 2, dossier "L."

2. Maggiolo (1884), 115. The copy analyzed here was one of the rare copies smuggled out of the country before the ban and therefore has an 1810 imprint (Paris: Potey, 1810; at Stanford University Libraries, ex-libris University of Vilna). This edition, whose pagination is the same as the two-volume edition with an 1814 title page that was issued after the ban's expiration, is herein referred to as "*Histoire 1810*." "*Histoire 1828*" refers to the six-volume edition (Paris: Baudouin, 1828–1845).

3. See for example Lascaris, "L'abbé Grégoire et la Grèce," 220; and Grunebaum-Ballin, "Grégoire convertisseur?" 385–86.

4. See Grégoire to John Carroll (archbishop of Baltimore), Sept. 10, 1810, and Carroll to Grégoire, June 4, 1811, in Gres-Gayer, "Four Letters from Henri Grégoire," 690, 692; "Visites de Weiss," entry of Oct. 5, 1828, BSPR-G, dossier "Doubs-II"; and review of the *Histoire des sectes,* in *Magasin encyclopédique* (Feb. 1, 1815): 439–40.

5. *Histoire* 1810, 1: lvii, xxix–xxx. All references in this chapter are to works by Grégoire unless otherwise noted.

6. *Histoire* 1810, 1: lv, lvi, iv–viii; and *Histoire* 1828, 6: 181–87.

7. *Histoire* 1810, 1: xxxiv–xxxvi, xxxviii, xlix, 2: 67, 392; and *Histoire* 1828, 6: 237.

8. *Histoire* 1810, 1: lii–liii, liv; and 2: 85, 110–13. Cf. McMahon, chs. 4 and 5.

9. *Histoire* 1810, 2: 116; and *Catalogue des livres de la Bibliothèque de M.*** [Grégoire]* ... (1821) [BN Delta-14098].

10. *Histoire* 1810, 2: 107; and 1: lxxvii.

11. *Histoire* 1810, 2: 78, 81; 1: 107–108, 285, 223, 258.

12. Grégoire to Barlow, [1810], in Beinecke—Pequot Papers, M981; *Histoire* 1810, 2: 237–38, 242–43. For an example of other attempts by him to refute Protestant claims, see his unfinished "Voyage de St-Pierre à Rome," BAG ms. 812, early 19th c.

13. *Histoire* 1810, 2: 186, 189, 266, 236–37, 200 (citing Rousseau's *Lettres de la Montagne*), 268–69; and Blessig's comments in F. V. Reinhard, *De l'influence de la religion protestante sur les relations de la vie civile et domestique.* ... *traduit de l'allemand [par Blessig]* (Strasbourg: König, 1808), 62–64.

14. *Histoire* 1810, 1: 292–93, 207; 2: 63, and passim. For more on Grégoire's nineteenth-century identification with Jansenism, see Hermon-Belot, *L'abbé Grégoire,* esp. ch. 14.

15. *Histoire* 1810, 1: lxxx–lxxxii; 2: 281, 279, 300; *Histoire* 1828, 6: 216.

16. See *Traite de l'uniformité,* 98; *Mémoires,* 53; *Observations nouvelles sur les Juifs ... d'Amsterdam,* 4, 18; *Observations nouvelles sur les Juifs ... d'Allemagne,* 6, 7, 9, and passim; and Grégoire to Barlow, Aug. 17, 1806 and Sept. 1,

1806, in Houghton—Barlow Papers, fols. 605–606. On Jews' adopting the idiom of regeneration but not always meaning the same thing by it as Grégoire, see sources in ch. 4, note 47.

17. Saltzmann to Grégoire, Mar. 21, 1806, BSPR-G, dossier "Bas-Rhin"; Malino, *A Jew in the French Revolution*, 52 et passim; Berr-Isaac-Berr, *Lettre . . . à M. Grégoire*, 5, 6, 9; and Sepinwall, "Strategic Friendships." See also Martine Lemalet, "Berr Isaac Berr: Un bilan contemporain de l'émancipation," in Oliel-Grausz and Hadas-Lebel, *Les Juifs et la Révolution*, 119–38; and Sepinwall, "Regenerating France," 323n40. Cf. Hermon-Belot, who does not discuss Berr at all in her *L'abbé Grégoire*, even while asserting that Jews of Grégoire's time did not criticize him (see ch. 3, note 52).

18. *Histoire* 1810, 2: 349–50, 357, 358, 366–68.

19. *Histoire* 1810, 2: 349–50. Cf. Hell, cited in Hertzberg, *The French Enlightenment and the Jews*, 288.

20. *Histoire* 1810, 2: 309, 338–39, 348.

21. *Histoire* 1828, 3: 302, 303; *Histoire* 1810, 2: 309, 314. See also R. Popkin, "Les Caraïtes et l'émancipation des juifs," *XVIIIe siècle* 13 (1981): 137–47.

22. *Histoire* 1810, 2: 308, 349–52; *Histoire* 1828, 3: 367.

23. *Histoire* 1810, 2: 401, 312; Gershom Scholem, "Jacob Frank and the Frankists," in *Kabbalah* (New York: Quadrangle/New York Times Book Co., 1974), 287–309; and Louis Jacobs, *The Jewish Religion: A Companion* (Oxford: Oxford University Press, 1995), 173.

24. *Histoire* 1810, 2: 398; *Histoire* 1828, 3: 225.

25. *Mémoires*, 110.

26. *Histoire* 1810, 2: 363 and passim.

27. *Histoire* 1810, 2: 426, 432, 278.

28. *Histoire* 1810, 2: 402; *De la liberté de conscience*, 30; Grégoire Papers, Schomburg Center, MG 243, fol. 4 (late 1820s); Howard University, Moorland-Springarn Collection, miscellaneous, Grégoire autograph reading notes (c. 1826).

29. *Histoire* 1810, 1: lxvii; *Histoire* 1828, 2: 21, 24, 26, 28.

30. *Histoire* 1828, 2: 26, 27–28.

31. *Histoire* 1828, 2: 20–22, 23, 24–26.

32. See Charles-César Robin, *De l'influence du christianisme sur le bonheur des peuples . . .* (Paris: Valleyre, [1785]); A.-J.-B. Chapuis, *De l'Influence de la religion sur les moeurs . . .* (Paris: L'auteur, [1796]); J.-J.-L.-G. Monnin, *De l'Influence de la religion sur la gloire et le bonheur des peuples* (Paris: Debray, an X); and Reinhard, *De l'influence de la religion protestante*. Grégoire did not discuss these works in his own version, and his corpus is both more extended and more specifically tied to the condition of peoples worldwide. He did make one reference to the Reinhard text in the 1810 *Histoire*, but only to comments made by its translator (see note 13 above).

33. The largest series remains in manuscript form at the BSPR-G (Rév. 177, labeled "Doctrine du christianisme"). The volume lacks consistent pagination, and its chapter names and numbers sometimes overlap. I therefore have adopted an alphabetic system to refer to various sections of the volume; see appendix for conversion to full section titles and numbering. Further analysis of this corpus

can be found in Sepinwall, "Regenerating France," 333–48. The dating of some of the essays can be gleaned by references in them to recent events and by Grégoire's letters. See also Necheles, *The Abbé Grégoire,* 154 and 186–87 (though she dated the entire corpus to 1813). Necheles's brief mentions of the essay on slavery are the only references to the work in existing scholarship (except for the essay on women, which is more widely known but has not been analyzed in detail). Posener listed a few of the essays in his bibliography (#273, #291) but without having seen them or knowing that they still existed.

34. *Essai historique sur les libertés de l'église gallicane,* 546 (see also Carnot, "Notice," 282); and William R. Everdell, *Christian Apologetics in France, 1730–1790: The Roots of Romantic Religion* (Lewiston, N.Y.: E. Mellen Press, 1987).

35. BSPR-G, Rév. 177: A, 1–3; P, 8, 22, 23; Y, 1–2; and passim.

36. BSPR-G, Rév. 177: G, 2–4; L, 7. The inclusion of the Jews in both this corpus and the *Histoire des sectes* reflected their peculiar status: they had placed themselves on society's margins because of their religious beliefs, yet also suffered excessive prejudice because of their social origins.

37. "Recherches sur les oiseliers . . . ," 12, 13, 59, in Bibliothèque Sainte-Geneviève, ms. 3954, #19, listed as anonymous. The idea that this essay might have been written by Grégoire was first suggested to that library by a Mme Lévy in 1989. I can confirm that the handwriting is that of Grégoire and his secretary. Posener alluded to the work (#273), but without knowing that it had been preserved. For a recent account of dishonorable classes in Europe, see Kathy Stuart, *Defiled Trades and Social Outcasts: Honor and Ritual Pollution in Early Modern Germany* (New York: Cambridge University Press, 1999).

38. BSPR-G, Rév. 177: L, 1–2; H, 1–8, K, 6.

39. He also noted that, while they were winning souls for Catholicism, European missionaries could win commercial advantages for their countries (BSPR-G, Rév. 177: K, 9–10, 13).

40. BSPR-G, Rév. 177: G, 14; "Recherches sur les oiseliers . . . ," 7–8.

41. BSPR-G, Rév. 177: H, 6, 8. Grégoire alternately used the expressions *indigènes de l'Amérique* and *indiens du nouveau monde.* For an alternate view of how native peoples were treated in New World missions, see Ramón A. Gutiérrez and Richard J. Orsi, eds., *Contested Eden: California before the Gold Rush* (Berkeley: University of California Press, 1998); and Auguste Bernard Duhaut-Cilly, *A Voyage to California, the Sandwich Islands & around the World in the Years, 1826–1829,* trans. and ed. August Frugé and Neal Harlow (Berkeley: University of California Press, 1999).

42. BSPR-G, Rév. 177: D, 1; L, 4; "Recherches sur les oiseliers . . . ," 61, 62.

43. BSPR-G, Rév. 177: M-2, 9; K, 1–4; M, 2–3.

44. The only other essay in the corpus that seems to have been published was BSPR-G, Rév. 177, B, "Reproches faits au christianisme de ne pas compter au nombre des vertus l'amitié, ni le patriotisme; réfutation de ces reproches," published anonymously in the *Chronique religieuse* 6 (Jan. 1821): 217–26. This essay reveals another point on which Grégoire tried to convince secular friends: that Christians could be as heroic as others in defending the *patrie.*

45. See Goodman, "Difference: An Enlightenment Concept."

46. *De l'influence du christianisme sur la condition des femmes*, 4, 14, 46, 13, 20–23, 25–26, 27, 28. Cf. Allan Greer, ed., *The Jesuit Relations: Natives and Missionaries in Seventeenth-Century North America* (Boston: Bedford/St. Martin's, 2000).

47. *De l'influence du christianisme sur la condition des femmes*, 31, 46, 71, 92, and passim.

EPILOGUE

1. Note from Grégoire to M. Pappenheimer [1830], ADLC, F 592, fol. 65.

2. Grégoire, *Considérations sur la liste civile* (Paris: Chez les marchands de nouveautés, 1830), 1, 2, 23, 14, 3, 11.

3. Necheles, *Abbé Grégoire*, 273–74; and Grégoire to Constancio, Aug. 6, 1830, reprinted in Carnot, "Notice," 306.

4. See Grégoire's 1830 reading notes in Grégoire Papers, Schomburg Center, MG 243, nos. 27, 39, 28, 21, 23. On Saint-Simonianism, see Robert B. Carlisle, *The Proffered Crown: Saint-Simonianism and the Doctrine of Hope* (Baltimore, Md.: Johns Hopkins University Press, 1987).

5. Grégoire to Delandine, 15 germinal an 12 [Apr. 5, 1804], Apr. 1, 1810, and June 11, 1808, BAG ms. 822 (nos. 5, 11, 7); Grégoire to Servando de Mier, Mar. 17, 1824, in *Escritos inéditos de Fray Servando Teresa de Mier*, 507–9; Grégoire to unidentified, Aug. 12, 1821, BAG ms. 714 (copy of letter in B. Fillon collection), including comments on modern priests; Plongeron, *Grégoire et la RS*, 157; and Grégoire to Jennat, Feb. 17, 1829, reprinted in Cosson, "Lettres de l'abbé Grégoire," 268.

6. Carnot, "Notice," 311; Maggiolo (1884), 127–42; and "Memoire pour M. l'abbé Baradère, chanoine du Diocèse de Tarbes, et Duplès, conseiller à la cour Royale de Paris . . . contre Mad^e Ve Dubois, *légataire universelle* de mon dit sieur Grégoire, aussi *son exécutrice testamentaire* . . . ," in Ars. Ms. 15049, fol. 206. After three years of struggle, Mme Dubois triumphed in 1834 (see Maggiolo [1884], 137).

7. I am following here Carnot's account of Grégoire's final days in "Notice," 22 (which records comments made by Grégoire, Guillon, and others). See also Necheles, *Abbé Grégoire*, 276–77; and the items cited in Sepinwall, "Regenerating France," 354n9.

8. Carnot, "Notice," 323. Crémieux's eulogy is excerpted in Daniel Amson, *Adolphe Crémieux: L'oublié de la gloire* (Paris: Editions du Seuil, 1988), 89–90.

9. Anne Girollet, "L'abbé Grégoire, son legs: Six concours pour la liberté et l'égalité," in Bénot and Dorigny, *Grégoire et la cause des noirs*, 163–75; Pierre Dufay, "31 Août 1833: Testament du Mme Dubois," *Blois et le Loire-et-Cher* (1937): 5–10; Carnot, "Notice," 324–29; and Maggiolo (1884), 136–38. Though Grégoire did not mention them specifically in his own will, that of Mme Dubois refers to two first cousins of his (and the children of another cousin) to whom she had already given funds on his behalf. No other family members were mentioned in either will.

10. Cf. Necheles, *Abbé Grégoire*, 281.

11. Pierre Nora, *Les lieux de mémoire* (Paris: Editions Gallimard, 1992).

12. See for example Antonin Debidour, *L'abbé Grégoire* (Nancy: Imprimerie P. Sordoillet, 1881); Bercet et al., *L'abbé Grégoire et Blois* (though a few dates in the chronology are inaccurate); Françoise Job, "Les deux statues de l'Abbé Grégoire à Lunéville (1885–1955)," *Le Pays Lorrain* 61, no. 1 (1980): 35–41; "Circulaire du Comité de la Statue de l'abbé Grégoire, 10 novembre 1881," reprinted in *Univers israélite* 37, no. 9 (Jan. 16, 1882): 259–60; and http://www.paris-france.org/CARTO/NOMENCLATURE/10.nom.html (accessed July 2002).

13. *Univers israélite* 40, no. 22 (Aug. 1, 1885): 694; and "Circulaire du Comité des Présidents des Sociétés de bienfaisance israélite," reprinted in *Univers israélite* 37, no. 12 (Mar. 1, 1882): 363. On French Jews and the state, see Birnbaum, *Les fous de la République: Histoire politique des juifs d'Etat de Gambetta à Vichy* (Paris: Fayard, 1992). On the term *Israelite*, see Simon Schwarzfuchs, *Du Juif à l'israélite: Histoire d'une mutation (1770–1870)* (Paris: Fayard, 1989). On the influence of Grégoire on Jews elsewhere in Europe, see for example Israel Bartal, "Ha-model ha-mishni: Tsarfat c'mekor hashpa'ah b'tahlichi ha-modernizatziah shel yehudei mizrach (1772–1863)," in *Ha-mahapachah ha-tsarfatit v'rishumah [The French Revolution and Its Impact]*, ed. Yerachmiel (Richard) Cohen (Jerusalem: Mercaz Zalman Shazar l'Toldot Yisrael, 1989), 274.

14. *Univers israélite* 37, no. 9 (Jan. 16, 1882): 260, and 40, no. 22 (Aug. 1, 1885): 695; and Price-Mars, "La participation haïtienne à la commémoration du centenaire de l'abbé Grégoire," *Revue de la Société d'histoire et de géographie d'Haïti* 2, no. 4 (1931): 1–15.

15. Philippe Boukara, "Commémorations juives de la Révolution française: Le cas du cent cinquantenaire (1939) vu par les juifs de Paris—immigrés en particulier," in Oliel-Grausz and Hadas-Lebel, *Les Juifs et la Révolution,* 337; Alfred Yvonneau and Grunebaum-Ballin, *Ville de Blois. 14 juillet 1939. Inauguration d'un buste de l'Abbé Grégoire . . .* (Blois: Editions du Jardin de la France, 1939), 3–4, 9; http://www.abbe-gregoire.com/reconnu.htm (accessed August 2002); Price-Mars, "La participation haïtienne"; idem, *Silhouettes de nègres,* 197–210; and the many 1931 publications on Grégoire, such as Académie des sciences morales et politiques, *Centenaire de l'Abbé Grégoire (1750–1831) célébré à Paris, le 31 mai 1931* (Paris: Firmin-Didot, 1931); "Le Centenaire de l'abbé Grégoire, organisateur en 1793 du département des Alpes-Maritimes," *Nice historique,* no. 4 (July/Aug. 1931): 133–36; Société des Amis de l'abbé Grégoire, "Centenaire de l'abbé Grégoire," invitation conserved at Alliance Israélite Universelle, R 1473 (17); and Sémach, *L'Abbé Grégoire.*

16. Charles Sumner, "The Abbé Grégoire, 1808," in *Prophetic Voices Concerning America* (Boston: Lee, Shephard and Dillingham, 1874), 151–54; Jean-François Brière, "Introduction," in Grégoire, *On the Cultural Achievements of Negroes* [translation of *De la littérature des nègres*], ed. Thomas Cassirer and J.-F. Brière (Amherst: University of Massachusetts Press, 1996), xlv–xlvi; F. Harrison Hough, "Grégoire's Sketch of Angelo Solimann," *Journal of Negro History* 4 (1919): 281–89; Guichard B. Parris, "Abbé Grégoire, 1750–1831: Some Aspects of His Political Credo" (M.A. thesis, Romance Languages, Columbia University, 1932); Parris to Duraciné Vaval, Jan. 12, 1937, in Guichard Parris Papers (MG 31), Schomburg Center, Box 1, folder "Gregoire—Correspondence"; and Amady

Aly Dieng, "L'abbé Grégoire et l'Afrique noire aujourd'hui," in Bénot and Dorigny, *Grégoire et la cause des noirs,* 85 and passim. See also Sepinwall, "French Abolitionism with an American Accent," H-France, H-Net Reviews, Jan. 1998, http://www2.h-net.msu.edu/reviews/showrev.cgi?path=3438887056586.

17. "Warns on Condoning Public Wrongdoing: Rabbi Stephen Wise by Implication Criticizes Walker Speech Before Jewish Guild," *New York Times,* Apr. 20, 1931, 26; and Hamilton Craigie, "Abbé Grégoire's Work for the Jews" (Letter to the Editor), *New York Times,* May 20, 1931, 24 (copies and transcriptions from Parris Papers, Schomburg Center). Craigie, who noted that his knowledge of Grégoire was based mostly on encyclopedias, was particularly upset by what he perceived as Wise's sarcastic comments about Catholics. Though he usually wrote Westerns (see Worldcat database), Craigie dabbled in popular history; see his "Persecution—Then and Now," *Sign Magazine* 3 (Oct. 1923): 120–21 (copy courtesy of the Passionist Historical Archives), on the status of Catholics in the United States and England. On Wise and Walker, see Wise Papers inventory at http://www.huc.edu/aja/SWise.htm (accessed July 2002).

18. Raoul Cenac-Thaly, *Evangile d'outre-mer, hommages à l'abbé Grégoire, Victor Schoelcher, Félix Eboué* (Paris: Pourtout, 1948); Ho Chi Minh to Société des Amis de l'abbé Grégoire, July 6, 1946, reprinted in Gérard Lyon-Caen, "Grégoire et les droits des peuples," *Europe* 34, nos. 128–29 (1956): 84–85; and Aimé Césaire, "Discours d'inauguration de la place de l'abbé Grégoire. Fort-de-France—28 décembre 1950," in *Oeuvres complètes* ([Fort-de-France]: Editions Desormeaux, 1976), 3: 422–23. Dieng notes that Victor Schoelcher received more attention than Grégoire in 1848, however, which he attributes to the Church's long attempt to suppress interest in the abbé ("L'abbé Grégoire et l'Afrique noire," 76–78).

19. Léopold Sédar Senghor, *Négritude et civilisation de l'universel* (Paris: Seuil, 1977), esp. 55, 351; Lüsebrink, "Grégoire et Haïti," esp. 310–12; Dieng, "L'abbé Grégoire et l'Afrique noire"; *Europe* 34, nos. 128–29 (1956); Société des Amis de l'abbé Grégoire, *Résurrection du Souvenir de l'abbé Grégoire, promoteur de la lutte contre l'esclavage et le racisme* (Paris/Lunéville: n.p., 1956); and R. Popkin's very interesting "Afterword—Discovering the Abbé Grégoire," in Popkin and Popkin, *Abbé Grégoire and His World,* 183–86.

20. See esp. Steven Laurence Kaplan, *Farewell, Revolution: Disputed Legacies: France, 1789/1989* (Ithaca, N.Y.: Cornell University Press, 1995), 15–61, 341–42, and passim; also J. Popkin, "Introduction—The Abbé Grégoire: A Hero for Our Times?" in Popkin and Popkin, *Abbé Grégoire and His World,* ix–x, xv. See also full text of Lang speech in Bibliothèque du CNAM, B1659 (copy donated by Lang). Footage of the ceremony was aired on French television and is archived in the Inathèque de France (Paris); see for example "IT1 20h: Cérémonie Panthéon," TF1, aired 12.12.1989, 20:01:00.

21. See for example *L'abbé Grégoire, évêque des Lumières,* ed. Frank Paul Bowman (Paris: Editions France-Empire, 1988); Mercier; and the works cited in prologue, note 2.

22. *L'abbé Grégoire, révolutionnaire de la tolérance: Exposition Nancy 1989/Exposition Blois 1989/L'abbé Grégoire, 1750–1831 . . . Texte biogra-*

phique de Richard Figuier ([Nancy/Blois]: Conseil général de Meurthe-et-Moselle et Conseil général de Loir-et-Cher, 1989); http://www.abbe-gregoire
.com/association.htm, the site of the Société des Amis de l'abbé Grégoire
(accessed August 2002); circular of the ARAG (Actualité et rayonnement de
l'abbé Grégoire), Blois, available from BAG; and 1999 catalogue cited in Prologue. The Lunéville society is the ALAAG (Association lorraine des Amis de
l'abbé Grégoire), information courtesy of BSPR-G.

   23. Robert Badinter, "Eloge de l'abbé Grégoire," *L'Express,* Dec. 15, 1989,
21; "Une célébration pour Grégoire," *Témoignage chrétien,* Dec. 11–17, 1989,
17; Henri, comte de Paris, "Par la bonté du Roi" (1989), reprinted in *Pour ou
contre la Révolution,* ed. Antoine de Baecque (Paris: Bayard, 2002), 902–904.

   24. Jacques Trefouel and Hermon-Belot, "Henri Grégoire, la mémoire
renouée," Fr3, aired 12.12.1989, 11:01:00; Josy Eisenberg, "La source de vie:
Un abbé pour les juifs," A2, aired 10.12.1989, 09:29:03, including clip from
"Les Juifs de France et la Révolution," by Lily Scheer and Pierre Sorlin (all in
Inathèque); and recollection of Claude Arnaud in "Leur 14 Juillet," *Le débat,*
no. 57 (Nov.–Dec. 1989), 50.

   25. Arts & Métiers and Réamur-Sebastopol, both of which relate to his work
with the CNAM.

   26. Michel Caffier and Association Lorraine des Amis de l'Abbé Grégoire,
*Grégoire 2000: Deux cent cinquantième anniversaire du curé-citoyen d'Ember-
ménil, défenseur des Droits de l'homme et humaniste* (Essey-lès-Nancy:
Imprimerie Christmann, 2000), 16–23.

   27. See for example Antoine de Baecque, "Le 14 juillet, la monarchie, c'est
gratis," *Libération,* July 5, 2002, 33; Gilles Bernheim, "Les Juifs de France face
à la 'nouvelle judéophobie' islamo-progressiste; Abbé Grégoire, réveillez-vous!"
Le Figaro, May 30, 2002, 15; and the philosopher Blandine Kriegel on Aimé
Jacquet, the coach of France's World Cup–winning soccer team: "This Catholic
WASP . . . has revealed himself to be an Abbé Grégoire. For having brought
together Brittany and Guadeloupe, the North African neighborhoods of Mar-
seille and the Basque regions of the southwest, for having welcomed . . . the team
of a multiracial France, where Le Pen is absent . . . , he has already earned a place
in the Pantheon" (Kriegel, "Philosophie du ballon rond," *Le Monde,* July 17,
1998, 12).

   28. See for example *Univers israélite* 37, no. 9 (Jan. 16, 1882): 262–63, and
no. 12 (Mar. 1, 1882): 362, citing Debidour; and the ongoing debate over
whether Grégoire voted for the king's death. Cf. discussion of Robespierre, in
Kaplan, *Farewell, Revolution,* 441–69.

   29. Spire, *Quelques juifs et demi-juifs* (Paris: Bernard Grasset, 1928), 2: 215;
Méïr Leviah, "L'abbé Grégoire contre la synagogue," *Chalom: Revue juive men-
suelle* 10, no. 58 (1931): 4–7; Hertzberg, *The French Enlightenment and the
Jews,* 138, 335, 5, and passim. See also Rabi [Wladimir Rabinowitch], *Anatomie
du Judaïsme français* (Paris: Editions du Minuit, 1962), 14, building on Leviah.
Hertzberg seems to have since changed his view of Grégoire, however; see his
"Honoring the Wrong Catholic Priest" (on Cardinal Lustiger), *Jewish Week*
[New York] (Nov. 6, 1998): 33. Hermon-Belot's argument that criticism of Gré-
goire on Jewish issues is a post-Holocaust American import, sparked mostly by

Hertzberg's and Necheles's work (see ch. 3, note 52) fails to take Spire's and Leviah's work into account.

30. Kaplan, *Farewell, Revolution,* 15–173; Michel de Sachy de Foudrinoy, *L'abbé Grégoire: Une autre vision* (Blois: Ed. Lignages, 1989); "La Lorraine découvre l'abbé Grégoire," *Le Monde,* July 16–17, 1989, 8; and "Courrier des lecteurs: Monge," letter of Françoise de Cools, *Le Figaro,* Dec. 13, 1989, 2.

31. See for example *Le Monde,* Dec. 13, 1989, 1a, 14b, 16b (interview with Lustiger); Michel Riquet S. J., "Un hommage mérité," *Le Figaro,* Dec. 12, 1989, 2; "Grégoire: Un évêque de Vatican II" [interview with Plongeron] and "L'appel des 25,000 et l'abbé Grégoire," *Témoignage Chrétien,* Dec. 11–17, 1989, 16–17; also Alan Riding, "French Honor an Abbot the Church Dislikes," *New York Times,* Dec. 13, 1989, A16. As a compromise gesture, Lustiger held an alternate ceremony the previous day in the Church of Saint-Gervais to pray over Grégoire's corpse, which stopped there during its passage between Montparnasse and the Pantheon. In his speech, Lustiger praised Grégoire's actions in favor of blacks and Jews while noting that his actions, though motivated by Christianity and sometimes good, had also sometimes been "in error or for ill" ("Soir 3: Service religieux abbé-Grégoire," Fr3, aired 11.12.1989, 22:43:00, archived in Inathèque; text of speech reprinted in Maurice de Germiny, "Son action comme évêque de Loir-et-Cher," in Bercet et al., *L'abbé Grégoire et Blois,* 12).

32. Jean-Claude Gaudin to Jack Lang, June 20, 1989, AN 900506–1051, transcription courtesy of Avner Ben-Amos; articles such as Béatrice Vallaeys, "La langue de l'Etat est une langue étrangère aux Français," *Libération,* May 11, 2002, 40; Catherine Trautmann, "La France et ses langues," *Le Monde,* July 31, 1999, 14; "Nous sommes des militants de la diversité" [interview with Lang], *Le Monde,* Sept. 15, 2001, III (Supplément Ecole); Birnbaum, *Idea of France,* 48, 242 and passim; and Bell, *Cult of the Nation,* 15.

33. Shmuel Trigano, "The French Revolution and the Jews," *Modern Judaism* 10 (1990): 171–90 (quotes from 171n12, 173n27, 174n35 and 178n68); and Annie Kriegel, "Un hommage critiquable," *Le Figaro,* Dec. 12, 1989, 2. Also Birnbaum, "Sur l'étatisation révolutionnaire"; Dominique Schnapper and Chantal Benayoun, "Citoyenneté républicaine et spécificité juive," *Nouveaux cahiers,* no. 97 (1989): 5–9; and Kaplan, *Farewell, Revolution,* 44.

34. Hermon-Belot, "La politique et la vérité: L'abbé Grégoire et la Révolution française" (Doctorat en histoire, Ecole des hautes études en sciences sociales, 1999), 1: 387.

35. See for example http://www.outremer.com/~sharad/agreg/grego.html; http://www.gallican.org/gregoire.htm; http://www.cnam.agropolis.fr/cnam/gregoire.htm; http://kawann.k1.online.fr/panneau4.htm; http://www.univ-paris1.fr/jeudis/11_2000.HTM; http://membres.lycos.fr/simorre/linha/pasnier.htm; http://www.gwalarn.org/brezhoneg/istor/gregoire.html (links accessed July 2002). I myself created one of the earliest Grégoire web pages (http://www.stanford.edu/~alyssas/gregoire.html) in 1997 as an experimental critical bibliography of other Grégoire-related sites, but gave up as pages mushroomed.

36. See Fick, *The Making of Haiti*; interview with Cherubin Celeste, priest in Cadet St. Rose, Guadeloupe, in Trefouel and Hermon-Belot, "Henri Grégoire, la mémoire renouée"; and comments to me by André Elizée, June 1996.

37. See Nicholls, *From Dessalines to Duvalier,* esp. 155–56, 231.

38. See Sepinwall, "Strategic Friendships"; and Necheles, *Abbé Grégoire,* 286.

39. Job, "Les deux statues"; Lucien Rebatet, "Je suis partout" (1939), and Charles Maurras, "Réflexions sur la Révolution de 1789 [excerpt]" (written c. 1900–1930, self-published by Maurras in 1948), reprinted in *Pour ou contre la Révolution,* ed. de Baecque, 666–70 and 498–500.

40. I owe this information to Virginie Munduteguy, who was disgusted when she spotted the *National Hebdo* cover at the newsstand and did not note its date.

41. See http://www.elysee.fr/actus/elections/ (accessed June 2002). I am grateful to the many friends and colleagues in France who discussed the 2002 election with me, and especially to Julius Lawson-Daku.

42. On these issues, see especially Birnbaum, *The Idea of France,* esp. ch. 6; Bell, *Cult of the Nation,* esp. Conclusion; and the forum in *Le Débat,* no. 58 (Jan./Feb. 1990). The policy adopted by the French government in 1989 did not resolve anxieties over headscarves in schools. In 2004, the Chirac government aimed to strengthen this prohibition by banning all "conspicuous religious symbols," whether veils, beards, yarmulkes, or large crosses. The government's efforts sparked demonstrations by French-born Muslim women chanting, "Mon voile, mon choix" (My veil, my choice) and criticism from both the Bush administration and Arab governments. Meanwhile, school principals worried that the policy would prove unenforceable, since it would require determining whether a young man had a beard, or a woman wore a bandana, for reasons of fashion or faith.

43. As Edward Said has noted, the West is a constructed idea rather than a bounded place (*Orientalism* [New York: Vintage Books, 1978]).

44. Akhil Gupta, *Postcolonial Developments: Agriculture in the Making of Modern India* (Durham, NC: Duke University Press, 1998).

45. Homi K. Bhabha, "Of Mimicry and Man: The Ambivalence of Colonial Discourse," in *The Location of Culture* (New York: Routledge, 1994), 85–92.

46. Arjun Appadurai, *Modernity at Large: Cultural Dimensions of Globalization* (Minneapolis: University of Minnesota Press, 1996); and Manuel Castells, *The Power of Identity* (Oxford: Blackwell, 1997).

47. On alternatives to homogenization in civil society, see also Goodman, "Difference: An Enlightenment Concept."

Selected Bibliography

This work draws upon the enormous amount of archival and printed material by and about Grégoire and a varied historiography on issues related to his activities. What follows is a selection of the most important of these materials. A fuller list of sources can be found in the notes.

ARCHIVAL AND MANUSCRIPT SOURCES

France

Archives départementales de Loir-et-Cher, Blois
F 592. "Lettres et notes de l'abbé Grégoire."
L 862. Documents on election of Grégoire as bishop of Loir-et-Cher.

Archives municipales de Strasbourg—Fonds Jean-Frédéric Oberlin (15 NA)
No. 172. Various Grégoire mss.
No. 428-III. Oberlin, Silhouette of Grégoire, letter to Grégoire.

Archives nationales, Paris
29 AP 101. Pierre-Louis Roederer Papers.
154 AP II 136. Chrétien de Lamoignon de Malesherbes. Chartrier de Tocqueville Papers.
510 AP 1–3. Grégoire Papers.

Bibliothèque de l'Alliance Israélite Universelle, Paris
R 1474. Grégoire materials collected by Paul Grunebaum-Ballin.

Bibliothèque de l'Arsenal, Paris
Fol. Z-1013. "Catalogue des livres légués à la Bibliothèque du Roi par M. Grégoire," 1831.

Mss. 6339, 15049. Grégoire Papers, focusing on slavery.

Ms. 6573. "Catalogues de livres de l'abbé Henri Grégoire."

Ms. 14045. S. Posener. "Essai d'une bibliographie critique des oeuvres de l'abbé Grégoire," 1946. Typescript, with ms. annotations by Paul Grunebaum-Ballin.

Mss. 14126, 14560, 14642, 14694. Autograph collections, including Grégoire letters.

Bibliothèque de la Société de Port-Royal, Paris—Collection Grégoire

Cartons "Concile 1797," "Loir & Cher. Documents Divers—Blois," "Loir & Cher II. Diverses lettres—Grégoire etc.," "Presbytère de Paris."

Dossier "Colonies" and departmental dossiers (e.g., "Bas-Rhin," "Meurthe").

Rév. 1–Rév. 259. Grégoire's bound pamphlet/manuscript collection. Manuscripts cited include:

Rév. 171. Papers of the Société des Amis des Noirs et des Colonies, and Haiti misc.

Rév. 177. Unpublished Grégoire *De l'influence* corpus, labeled "Doctrine du christianisme."

Rév. 222. Letters to Grégoire on the patois.

Rév. 254. "Catalogue de ma bibliothèque."

Bibliothèque de Sainte-Geneviève, Paris

Ms. 3954, #19. Grégoire ms., "Recherches sur les oiseliers, les coliberts, les cagous, les gahets, les cagots et d'autres classes d'homme avilies par l'opinion publique et par les lois."

Bibliothèque du Grand Séminaire de Nancy

Ms. MC 121. Abbé Laurent Chatrian. "Calendrier historique et ecclésiastique de Diocèse de Nancy, pour l'année 1789."

Bibliothèque historique de la ville de Paris

Ms. 791, fol. 286. Letter from représentants en mission in Chambéry to Convention, 1793.

Ms. 3064, T. 46. Grégoire autographs.

Bibliothèque municipale de Blois (Bibliothèque Abbé-Grégoire)

Ms. 677. "Procès verbaux des sociétés populaires, 1791– [1793]."

Mss. 714, 715, 822, 870. Grégoire letters.

Ms. 812. Grégoire ms., "Voyage de St-Pierre à Rome" (c. 1800–1810).

Bibliothèque municipale de Nancy

Ms. 469 (532). Grégoire ms., "Promenades dans les Vosges."

Ms. 957 (533). Grégoire mss., "Notes biographiques sur les personnages lorrains."

Ms. 958 (534). "Recueil des pièces provenant de l'abbé Grégoire."

Ms. 1134 (536). "Titres et diplômes donnés à l'abbé Grégoire, par les diverses sociétés savantes dont il faisait partie."

Ms. 1688a-b. Grégoire letters.

Mss. 2074 (936). Grégoire letter, copy.

Bibliothèque nationale, Paris—Salle des manuscrits
All. Ms. 192, 195. Jérémie-Jacques Oberlin Papers.
NAF Ms. 1391. Antoine-Alexandre Barbier Papers.
NAF Ms. 2798. Responses to Grégoire's language questionnaire.
NAF Ms. 22737. Bixio Collection. Grégoire ms., "Mémoire sur la manière de négocier avec la cour de Rome pour faire cesser les troubles religieux de la France," 1800 [published version available in *La Revue indépendante* 21 (1845): 294–304].
NAF Ms. 24910. Reinach Papers.

Conservatoire national des arts et métiers, Paris—Bibliothèque
Mss. 91 and 396. Letters concerning Grégoire's involvement with CNAM.

Consistoire central des Israélites de France, Paris—Archives
1 B 1. Consistoire central. Procès-verbaux, 10 nov. 1808–28 sept. 1815.
1 C 2. Consistoire central. Registre du correspondance, 1810–1813.

Inathèque de France—Paris
Television programs on Grégoire, 1989.

Musée lorrain—Nancy
Grégoire ms., "Mémoire sur les juifs" (first Metz essay contest entry), ex-libris Lucien Wiener.

United States

American Philosophical Society—Philadelphia, PA
B F113. Fabbroni Papers. Grégoire letters.
B V46 p. Benjamin Vaughan Papers. Grégoire letters.
APS Association File Card Catalog and APS Transactions.

Beinecke Library, Yale University—New Haven, CT
M970, M981, M995, M998, M999, M1001. Pequot Papers. Letters on Columbiad controversy.

Cornell University, Dept. of Rare and Manuscript Collections— Ithaca, NY
4606, Box 8. French Revolution Collection. Grégoire letters.
4611, Boxes 14, 25, and 27. Lafayette Papers. Lafayette-Boyer correspondence.

Henry M. Huntington Library—San Marino, CA
CN101–104. Clarkson Papers. Grégoire letters.
HM30754–30755. Bowring Papers. Grégoire letters.

Houghton Library, Harvard University—Cambridge, MA
bMS AM 1448. Joel Barlow Papers.

Lilly Library (Manuscripts Dept.), Indiana University—Bloomington, IN
Lafayette Papers. Lafayette-Boyer letters.

New-York Historical Society—New York, NY
Gulian Verplanck Papers. Box #4, Folder G. Grégoire letters.
Robert Livingston Papers. Grégoire letters.

Schomburg Center for Research in Black Culture, New York Public
*   Library—New York, NY*
MG 31. Guichard Parris Papers.
Additions—Unaccessioned Papers, Guichard Parris Papers.
MG 243. Grégoire Papers.

PRINTED PRIMARY SOURCES

Works Published by Henri-Baptiste Grégoire

Adresse aux citoyens des campagnes du département du Mont-Blanc. . . . n.p.,
   [1793?].
Adresse aux députés de la seconde législature, lue à la Société des Amis de la
   Constitution, séante aux Jacobins de Paris, et imprimé par son ordre, pour
   être distribuée aux nouveaux députés et envoyée aux sociétés affiliées. Paris:
   Imprimerie du Patriote François, 1791.
Adresse aux habitans du Valais. . . . Chambéry: Imprimerie de Gorrin père &
   fils, [1793].
"Aux bons citoyens du département de la Meurthe (6 août 1790)." *Le patriote*
   françois, 11 août 1790, 3–4.
Compte rendu . . . au Concile national. . . . Paris: Imprimerie-librairie chréti-
   enne, 1797.
Compte rendu aux évêques réunis à Paris . . . de la visite de son diocèse . . . (Paris,
   le 8 décembre 1796). Paris: Imprimerie-librairie chrétienne, 1796.
Considérations sur la liste civile. Paris: Chez les marchands de nouveautés, 1830.
Considérations sur le mariage et le divorce adressés aux citoyens d'Haïti. Paris:
   Baudouin, 1823.
Convention nationale. Discours sur l'éducation commune . . . séance du 30 juil-
   let. . . . Paris: Imprimerie nationale, 1793.
Convention nationale. Instruction publique. Rapport sur l'établissement du
   Bureau des longitudes, séance du 7 Messidor, l'an 3. . . . Paris: Imprimerie
   nationale, 1795.
Convention nationale. Instruction publique. Rapport sur l'établissement d'un
   conservatoire des arts et métiers, séance du 8 vendémiaire, l'an 3. Paris:
   Imprimerie nationale, 1794.
Convention nationale. Instruction publique. Rapport sur l'ouverture d'un con-
   cours pour les livres élémentaires de la première éducation, séance du 3 plu-
   viôse, l'an second. . . . Paris: Imprimerie nationale, 1794.
Convention nationale. Instruction publique. Rapport sur la bibliographie, séance
   du 22 Germinal, l'an 2. . . . Paris: Imprimerie de Quiber-Pallissaux, 1794.
Convention nationale. Instruction publique. Rapport sur la nécessité & les
   moyens d'anéantir le patois, & d'universaliser l'usage de la langue française,
   séance du 16 prairial, l'an deuxième. . . . Paris: Imprimerie nationale, 1794.
Convention nationale. Instruction publique. Rapport sur les destructions
   opérées par le Vandalisme, et sur les moyens de le réprimer, séance du 14
   Fructidor, l'an second. . . . 1794. Reconstituted in *Oeuvres de l'abbé Gré-*
   goire, 2: 257–78. Nendeln, Liechtenstein: KTO Press, 1977.

Convention nationale. Instruction publique. Rapport sur les encouragemens, récompenses et pensions à accorder aux Savans, aux Gens de Lettres & aux Artistes, séance du 17 vendémiaire, l'an 3. . . . 1794. Reconstituted in *Oeuvres de l'abbé Grégoire*, 2: 303–19. Nendeln, Liechtenstein: KTO Press, 1977.

Convention nationale. Instruction publique. Second rapport sur le Vandalisme, séance du 8 brumaire, l'an III. . . . Paris: Imprimerie nationale, 1794.

Convention nationale. Instruction publique. Troisième rapport sur le Vandalisme, séance du 24 Frimaire, l'an IIIe. . . . Paris: Imprimerie nationale, 1794.

Convention nationale. Instruction sur les semailles d'automne adressée aux citoyens cultivateurs, lue à la séance du 2e primdi [sic] de Brumaire, l'an 2e. . . . Paris: Imprimerie nationale, 1793.

Convention nationale. Nouveau développemens sur l'amélioration de l'agriculture, par l'établissement de maisons d'économie rurale. . . . séance du 16 brumaire, l'an deuxième. . . . Paris: Imprimerie nationale, 1793.

Convention nationale. Rapport et projet de décret présenté au nom du Comité d'Instruction publique, à la séance du 8 août. . . . Paris: Imprimerie nationale, 1793.

Convention nationale. Rapport et projet de décret présentés au nom du Comité d'Instruction publique, sur les costumes des législateurs et des autres fonctionnaires publics, séance du vingt-huit fructidor, l'an trois. . . . Paris: Imprimerie nationale, 1795.

Convention nationale. Rapport fait au nom des comités des finances, des domaines et d'instruction publique, séance du 11 prairial, l'an deuxième . . . [sur les jardins botaniques]. Paris: Imprimerie nationale, 1794.

Convention nationale. Rapport présenté à la Convention nationale, au nom des Commissaires envoyés par elle, pour organiser les départemens du Mont-Blanc & des Alpes maritimes. . . . Paris: Imprimerie nationale, 1793.

Convention nationale. Rapport sur les inscriptions des monumens publics, séance du 22 Nivôse, l'an 2. . . . Paris: Imprimerie nationale, 1794.

Convention nationale. Système de dénominations topographiques pour les places, rues, quais, etc. de toutes les communes de la République. . . . Paris: Imprimerie nationale, 1794.

Corps législatif. Conseil des Cinq-Cents. Discours sur la liberté des cultes . . . , séance du 25 frimaire an 6. Paris: Imprimerie nationale, 1797.

Corps législatif. Conseil des Cinq-Cents. Rapport fait au nom d'une commission spéciale, sur le Conservatoire des arts et métiers, séance du 17 floréal an 6. Paris: Imprimerie nationale, 1798.

Corps législatif. Rapport fait au Conseil des Cinq-Cents, sur les sceaux de la République, séance du 11 pluviôse, an IV. Paris: Imprimerie nationale, 1795.

De l'influence du christianisme sur la condition des femmes. 3d ed. Paris: Baudouin, 1829.

De la constitution française de l'an 1814. 1st ed. Paris: Le Normant/Delaunay, 1814.

De la liberté de conscience et de culte à Haïti. . . . Paris: Baudouin Frères, 1824.

De la littérature des nègres, ou Recherches sur leurs facultés intellectuelles, leurs qualités morales et leur littérature, suivies de Notices sur la vie et les ouvrages des nègres qui sont distingués dans les sciences, les lettres, et les arts. Paris: Maradan, 1808.

De la noblesse de la peau ou de préjugé des blancs contre la couleur des Africains et celle de leurs descendans noirs et sang-mêlés. Paris: Baudouin, 1826.

"Déclaration du droit des gens [1795]." In *Réimpression de l'ancien Moniteur.* Paris: H. Plon, 1853–63. 24: 294–96.

Défense de l'ouvrage intitulé: Légitimité du serment civique. . . . Paris: Imprimerie nationale, 1791.

Discours prononcé dans l'église cathédrale de Blois . . . au service célébré pour Jacques-Guillaume Simonneau, maire d'Etampes, assassiné le 3 mars 1792, pour avoir défendu la loi. Blois: Imprimerie de Jean-François Billault, 1792.

Discours prononcé dans l'église cathédrale de Blois . . . au service célébré pour les citoyens morts à Paris le 10 août 1792. Blois: Imprimerie de Jean-François Billault, 1792.

Discours prononcé le jour de la Toussaint 1789, en l'église de l'Abbaye de St.-Germain-des-Prés, pour la Bénédiction des quatre Flammes de la Milice-Nationale de ce District. Paris: Imprimerie de Cl. Simon, 1789.

Discours sur la fédération du 14 juillet 1792, . . . dont la Société des Amis de la Constitution de Blois a voté l'impression. Orléans: Jacob l'aîné, [1792].

Discours sur la liberté des cultes. N.p., 1794.

Eloge de la Poésie, discours qui a remporté le prix des belles lettres, au jugement de MM. de la Société royale des Sciences et Belles-lettres de Nancy. Nancy: Frères Leseure, 1773.

Epître aux Haïtiens. Port-au-Prince: Imprimerie du gouvernement, 1827.

Essai historique et patriotique sur les arbres de la liberté. Paris: Desenne, 1794.

Essai historique sur les libertés de l'Eglise gallicane et des autres églises de la catholicité, pendant les deux derniers siècles. Nouvelle édition, corrigée et augmentée. Paris: Aimé Comte, 1820.

Essai sur la régénération physique, morale et politique des Juifs: Ouvrage couronné par la Société Royale des sciences et des arts de Metz, le 23 août 1788. 1789. Reprint edited by Rita Hermon-Belot, Paris: Flammarion, 1988.

Essai sur la solidarité littéraire entre les savants de tous les pays. . . . Paris: Les principaux libraires, 1824.

"Extrait fait d'un rapport fait à la Société d'agriculture du département de la Seine . . . sur les plantations de Malesherbes." *Décade philosophique, littéraire et politique,* 30 nivôse an VII (19 janvier 1800), 110–25.

Histoire des confesseurs des empereurs, des rois, et d'autres princes. Paris: Baudouin Frères, 1824.

Histoire des sectes religieuses qui, depuis le commencement du siècle dernier jusqu'à l'époque actuelle, sont nées, se sont modifiées, se sont éteintes dans les quatre parties du monde. 2 vols. Paris: Potey, 1810 (copy with annotation by Grégoire's secretary, Rare Books Collection, Stanford University Libraries).

Histoire des sectes religieuses qui sont nées, se sont modifiées, se sont éteintes dans les différentes contrées du globe, depuis le commencement du siècle dernier jusqu'à l'époque actuelle. Nouvelle édition, corrigée et considérablement augmentée. 6 vols. Paris: Baudouin, 1828–45.

Histoire du mariage des prêtres en France particulièrement depuis 1789. Paris: Baudouin, 1826.

Homélie du cardinal Chiaramonti, évêque d'Imola, actuellement souverain pontife Pie VII . . . . Paris: Baudouin, 1818.

Légitimité du serment civique, exigé des fonctionnaires ecclésiastiques. Paris: Imprimerie nationale, 1791.

Lettre aux citoyens de couleur et nègres libres de Saint-Domingue, et des autres isles françoises de l'Amérique. Paris: Imprimerie du Patriote françois, 1791.

Lettre aux philantropes sur les malheurs, les droits et les réclamations des gens de couleur de Saint-Domingue, et des autres îles françoises de l'Amérique. Paris: Belin, 1790.

Lettre circulaire de M. Grégoire, Evêque du Département de Loir et Cher, à ses diocésains, pour la convocation des Elèves au Séminaire de Blois [7 juillet 1791]. n.p., 1791.

Lettre de M. Grégoire . . . à ses diocésains sur le départ du Roi. Paris: Renaudière, 1791.

Lettre pastorale . . . (le 12 mars 1795/le 22 ventôse, l'an 3). Blois/Paris: Maradan/Leclerc, 1795.

Lettre pastorale . . . aux pasteurs et aux fidèles de son diocèse, sur la confirmation (le 25 février 1792). Blois: Imprimerie de Jean-François Billault, 1792.

Lettre pastorale . . . aux pasteurs et aux fidèles de son diocèse, sur le payement des contributions publiques (le premier février 1792). Blois: Imprimerie de Jean-François Billault, 1792.

Lettre pastorale de M. l'évêque du département de Loir et Cher (le 24 mars 1791). Blois: Imprimerie de J. P. J. Masson, 1791.

Lettre pastorale . . . sur la réorganisation du Culte dans les Diocèses de Bourges, Guéret et Moulins. Paris: Imprimerie-librairie chrétienne, 1796.

Manuel de piété à l'usage des hommes de couleur et des noirs. Paris: Baudouin, 1818.

Mémoire en faveur des gens de couleur ou sang-mêlés de St.-Domingue & des autres Isles françoises de l'Amérique, adressé à l'Assemblée Nationale. Paris: Belin, 1789.

Mémoire sur la dotation des curés en fonds territoriaux, lu à séance du 11 Avril 1790. . . . Paris: Baudouin, 1790.

Motion de M. l'abbé Grégoire . . . à la séance du 14 Juillet 1789. Paris: Baudouin, 1789.

Motion en faveur des juifs. Paris: Belin, 1789.

Notice sur la Sierra-Leona. . . . N.p., 1796.

Nouvelles réflexions . . . sur la Déclaration des Droits de l'Homme & du Citoyen, à la séance du 18 Août. Versailles: Baudouin, 1789.

Observations critiques sur le poème de M. Joël Barlow, The Colombiad. Paris: Maradan, 1809.

Observations nouvelles sur les Juifs, et spécialement sur ceux d'Allemagne. N.p, 1806.

Observations nouvelles sur les Juifs, et spécialement sur ceux d'Amsterdam et de Francfort (Extrait de La Revue philosophique, littéraire et politique). N.p., 1807.

Observations sur le décret de l'Assemblée nationale; qui ordonne une nouvelle circonscription des Paroisses. . . . Paris: Belin, 1790.

Opinion de M. Grégoire . . . sur la gabelle, à la séance du 19 Septembre au soir. Versailles: Baudouin, [1789].

Opinion de M. Grégoire . . . sur la sanction royale, à la séance du 4 Sptembre [sic]. N.p., [1789].

Opinion du citoyen Grégoire . . . concernant le jugement de Louis XVI, séance du 15 Novembre 1792, l'an premier de la République française. Paris: Imprimerie nationale, 1792.

Plan d'association générale entre les savans, gens de lettres et artistes. . . . N.p., 1817.

"Rapport fait au nom de la commission chargée de présenter à l'Institut des questions dont l'Institut de Caïre serait invité à procurer la solution." *Mémoires de l'Institut national des sciences et des arts. Sciences morales et politiques [2e classe]* 3 (1801): 5–19.

Rapport sur la réunion de la Savoie à la France, fait au nom des Comités Diplomatique et de Constitution. . . . Paris: Imprimerie nationale, 1792.

"Réflexions extraites d'un ouvrage du citoyen Grégoire sur les moyens de perfectionner les sciences politiques." *Mémoires de l'Institut national des sciences et des arts. Sciences morales et politiques [2e classe]* 1 (1798): 552–66.

Les Ruines de Port-Royal des Champs en 1809, année séculaire de la destruction de Monastère. Nouvelle édition, considérablement augmentée. Paris: Levacher, 1809.

Les Ruines de Port-Royal en 1801. Paris: Imprimerie-librairie chrétienne, 1801.

Traite de l'uniformité et de l'amélioration de la liturgie, présenté au Concile national de 1801. Paris: Imprimerie-librairie chrétienne, 1801.

Works Published Anonymously by Grégoire

Adresse de la Convention nationale au peuple français, du 16 prairial, l'an second de la République. . . . Paris: Imprimerie nationale, 1794.

"Considérations sur les abus de la sécularisation des biens ecclésiastiques." In *Mémoires de la Société des Philantropes,* 163–89. Berne: La société typographique, 1778 [at Schomburg Center for Research in Black Culture, F306-S; also at BN Z-28454].

"Lettre XIII [on the Vosges]" and "Lettre XXX [on the Vosges and Switzerland]." *Correspondance sur les affaires du tems, ou Lettres sur divers sujets de Politique, d'Histoire, de Littérature, d'Arts et Sciences, etc.,* 1: 153–75; 2: 143–73. Paris: Imprimerie Polémique, 1797.

"Notice critique sur l'ouvrage: 'Considérations diverses sur Haïti,' par Desrivières-Chanlatte." *Revue encyclopédique* 17 (février 1823): 267–72.

Nouvelle lettre d'un curé, à ses confrères, députés aux États-Généraux. N.p., [1789].

Plan d'études pour les jeunes ecclésiastiques. Metz: Imprimerie de Claude Lamort, 1790.

Première et dernière réponse aux libellistes. Paris: A. Egron, [1814] [edition at NYPL; BN edition titled *Réponse aux libellistes*].

Réponse à quelques pamphlets contre la Constitution, par M. G. . . . Paris: n.p., 1814 [attributed to Grégoire in Posener, though the BN has begun attributing it to Charles Denoyer].

"Reproches faits au christianisme de ne pas compter au nombre des vertus l'amitié, ni le patriotisme; réfutation de ces reproches." *Chronique religieuse* 6 (janvier 1821): 217–26 (published version of BSPR-G, Rév. 177, ch. "B").

Works Published by Grégoire with Others

Abeille, Bergon, Cels, Chabert, Chassiron, Cadet-de-Vaux, Chaptal, Creuzé-Latouche, Descemet, Depeuty, Fourcroy, Garnier-Deschesnes, Gillet-Laumont, Gossuin, Grégoire, Guerre, Huzard, Lefebvre, Lasteyrie, Molard, Moreau-Saint-Méry, Parmentier, Pepin, Sageret, Silvestre, Tessier, Thouin (André), Thouin (Jean), Valmont-Bomare, and Vilmorin. "Observations de la Société d'agriculture du département de la Seine, sur un Article inséré dans le *Moniteur* relatif au Rapport précédent." *Mémoires d'agriculture, d'économie rurale et domestique, publiés par la Société d'agriculture du département de la Seine* 2 (an IX): 110–25.

Chaptal, Moreau-Saint-Méry, Grégoire, Duquesnoy, and Chassiron. "Rapport fait à la Société d'agriculture du département de la Seine sur la nécessité de conserver l'Établissement rural de l'ancienne Ménagerie de Versailles, par une Commission spéciale . . . [séance du 26 Floréal an VIII]." *Mémoires d'agriculture, d'économie rurale et domestique, publiés par la Société d'agriculture du département de la Seine* 2 (an IX): 97–109.

Desbois, Eléonore-Marie, Claude-François-Marie Primat, H. Grégoire, Jean-Baptiste Royer, and Jean-Pierre Saurine. *Seconde lettre encyclique de plusieurs évêques de France, réunis à Paris, à leurs frères les autres évêques et aux églises vacantes. . . .* Paris: Imprimerie-librairie chrétienne, 1795.

Gratien, J. B., H. Grégoire, Jean-Baptiste Royer, and Jean-Pierre Saurine. *Lettre encyclique de plusieurs évêques de France, à leurs frères les autres évêques et aux églises vacantes.* 1st ed. Paris: Imprimerie-librairie chrétienne, 1795.

Grégoire, Simond, Hérault, and Jagot. "Egalité, Liberté. Proclamation sur la liberté de la presse. Les commissaires de la Convention Nationale, aux Citoyens du Département du Mont-Blanc . . . fait à Chambéry, ce 25 Janvier 1793." 1793. Reprinted in *Oeuvres de l'abbé Grégoire,* 3: 61. Nendeln, Liechtenstein: KTO Press, 1977.

Grégoire, Valentin (Curé de Leyr), and Didry (Curé de Farroy). *Lettre à MM. les curés lorrains et autres ecclésiastiques séculiers du diocèse de Metz.* Nancy: n.p., 1789.

Saurine, J. S., E. M. Desbois, H. Grégoire, and N. Jacquemin. *Observations sur ce qu'on appelle reservas, en Espagne; par les évêques réunis à Paris.* Paris: Imprimerie-librairie chrétienne, 1799.

Other Grégoire Writings Published Posthumously

Benoît, A. "Description des Vosges, par l'abbé Grégoire, publiée pour la pre-mière fois et annotée." *Annales de la Société d'émulation du département des Vosges* 71 (1895): 221–25.

Cosson, Henri. "Lettres de l'abbé Grégoire à l'abbé Jennat." *Révolution française,* nos. 1/3 (1935): 70–89, 247–77.

Duvernoy, E. "Le cahier d'Emberménil, paroisse de l'abbé Grégoire en 1789." *Annales de l'Est* 12 (1898): 577–83.

Ginsburger, M. "Zwei unveröffentlichte Briefe von Abbé Grégoire." In *Festschrift zu Simon Dubnows siebzigstem Geburtstag (2. Tischri 5691),* ed. Ismar Elbo-gen, Josef Meisl, Mark Wischnitzer, 201–6. Berlin: Jüdischer Verlag, 1930.

[Grégoire, Henri]. *Mémoires de l'abbé Grégoire.* Edited by J. M. Leniaud and preface by J. N. Jeanneney. 1837. Reprint, Paris: Editions de Santé, 1989 [original edition edited by Hippolyte Carnot].

[———]. *Rapport inédit de Grégoire sur l'état de l'instruction publique, des bib-liothèques, des archives, et des monuments dans les départements de l'Est.* Edited by Ulysse Robert. Paris: H. Menu, 1876.

[———]. "Rapport sur la Bibliothèque nationale fait à la commission d'instruc-tion publique de la Convention nationale en 1794–1795." Edited by H. Omont. *Revue des Bibliothèques* 15 (1905): 67–98.

Gres-Gayer, Jacques M. "Four Letters from Henri Grégoire to John Carroll, 1809–1814." *Catholic Historical Review* 79, no. 4 (1993): 681–703.

Ingold, A.-M.-P. *Grégoire et l'Eglise constitutionnelle d'Alsace [documents inédits].* Paris: A. Picard & Fils, 1894.

Jérome, L. *Les élections et les cahiers du clergé lorrain aux Etats généraux de 1789 (Bailliages de Nancy, Lunéville, Blâmont, Rosières, Vézelise et Nomeny).* Nancy: Berger-Levrault et Cie., 1899.

Mathiez, A. "Une lettre de Grégoire" [letter of September 22, 1792 from Gré-goire to the Loir-et-Cher departmental administrators]. *La Révolution française* 47 (1904): 370–72.

Moris, Henri. *Organisation du département des Alpes-Maritimes formé du ci-devant comté de Nice et de la ci-devant principauté de Monaco. Mars–Avril 1793. Lettres des représentants du peuple Grégoire et Jagot, chargés de cette organisation.* Paris: Librairie Plon, 1915.

Peter, Rodolphe. "Le pasteur Oberlin et l'abbé Grégoire." *Bulletin de l'histoire du Protestantisme français* 126 (juill/août/sept 1980): 297–326.

Pfister, Christian. "Lettres de Grégoire à Jérémie-Jacques Oberlin." *Mémoires de la Société d'archéologie lorraine et du Musée historique lorrain* 42 (3d ser., vol. 20) (1892): 333–73.

Vaussard, Maurice. *Correspondance, Scipione de' Ricci, Henri Grégoire (1796–1807).* Florence: Edizioni Sansoni Antiquariato, 1963.

Other Primary Sources

Archives parlementaires de 1787 à 1860, première série (1787 à 1799). Edited by M. J. Mavidal and M. E. Laurent. 99 vols. to date. Paris: Librairie admi-nistrative de Paul Dupont, 1862–pres.

Aulard, F.-A. *La Société des Jacobins. Recueil de documents pour l'histoire du club des Jacobins à Paris.* 6 vols. Paris: Librairie Jouaust, 1889.

Barlow, Joel. *The Columbiad.* London: Printed for Richard Phillips, 1809 [available at http://moa.umdl.umich.edu/cgi/sgml/moa-idx?notisid = APT9199].

Barlow, Joel. *Letter to Henry Gregoire, . . . in reply to his letter on The Columbiad.* Washington: Roger Chew Weightman, 1809.

Basnage, Jacques. *Histoire des juifs, depuis Jésus-Christ jusqu'à présent pour servir de continuation à l'histoire de Joseph. Nouvelle édition augmentée.* La Haye: Henri Scheurleer, 1716.

Berr, Berr-Isaac. *Lettre du sieur Berr-Isaac-Berr, manufacturier, membre du Conseil municipal de Nancy, à M. Grégoire, Sénateur, à Paris.* Nancy: Imprimerie de P. Barbier, 1806.

Catalogue des livres de la Bibliothèque de M.*** [Grégoire], dont la vente se fera le Jeudi 20 Septembre 1821. . . . Paris: Silvestre/Gallimard, 1821 [BN Delta-14098].

Chabanon, Charles de. *Dénonciation de M. l'abbé Grégoire et de sa lettre du 8 juin 1791 adressée aux citoyens de couleur et nègres libres de Saint-Domingue.* Paris: Imprimerie de la Feuille du Jour, 1791.

[Chatrian, L.]. "L'abbé Grégoire vu par l'abbé Laurent Chatrian." *La Revue lorraine populaire* (1989): 21–25.

Dohm, Christian Wilhelm. *De la réforme politique des Juifs.* 1782. Edited by Dominique Bourel. Paris: Stock, 1984.

Furtado, Abraham, Azevedo, David Gradis, and Salomon Lopes du Bec. *Lettre adressée à M. Grégoire . . . par les Députés de la Nation Juive Portugaise de Bordeaux.* Versailles: Baudouin, 1789.

Gazier, Augustin. *Lettres à Grégoire sur les patois de France, 1790–1794. Documents inédits sur la langue, les moeurs et l'état des esprits dans les diverses régions de la France, au début de la Révolution.* 1880. Reprint, Geneva: Slatkine Reprints, 1969.

Griggs, Earl Leslie, and Clifford H. Prator. *Henry Christophe and Thomas Clarkson: A Correspondence.* New York: Greenwood Press, 1968.

Guillaume, James, ed. *Procès-verbaux du Comité d'instruction publique de la Convention nationale.* 6 vols. Paris: Imprimerie nationale, 1891–1907.

Lacretelle, Pierre-Louis. *Plaidoyer pour Moyse May, Godechaux & Abraham Lévy, Juifs de Metz.* Brussels, 1775. Reprint, Paris: Lipschutz, 1928.

Laroche, Benjamin. *Lettres de M. Grégoire, ancien évêque de Blois, adressées l'une à tous les journalistes, l'autre à M. de Richelieu. . . . .* 2d ed. Paris: Chez tous les marchands de nouveautés, 1820.

Lettre au C.en Grégoire, ci-devant évêque constitutionnel du département de Loir & Cher, à l'occasion d'un prétendu synode qu'il annonce pour la foire de Blois, an 8. Orléans: n.p., 1800.

Maury, Jean Siffrein. *Lettre de M. l'abbé Maury, au régicide Comte Grégoire.* Montpellier: J.-G. Tournel, [c. 1818].

Miquel i Vergés, J. M., and Hugo Díaz-Thomé. *Escritos inéditos de fray Servando Teresa de Mier.* México: El Colegio de México—Centro de estudios históricos, 1944.

M. Grégoire . . . dénoncé à la nation, comme ennemi de la constitution, infidèle
    à son serment, perturbateur de repos public, rénovateur du despotisme épis-
    copal, tyran de la liberté, etc., etc., etc., et par conséquent criminel de lèze-
    nation, par les habitans dudit département, ci-devant diocèse de Blois. Paris:
    Imprimerie de Crapart, [1791].
Oberlin, Jérémie-Jacques. Essai sur le patois lorrain des environs du comté du
    Ban de la Roche, fief Royal d'Alsace. Strasbourg: Chez Jean Fréd. Stein,
    1775.
[Philipon de la Madelaine, Louis]. Vues patriotiques sur l'éducation du peuple,
    tant des villes que de la campagne; avec beaucoup de Notes intéressantes.
    Ouvrage qui peut être également utile aux autres classes de citoyens. Lyon:
    Chez P. Bruyset-Ponthus, 1783.
Rallier, Louis-Antoine-Esprit. Lettres de Rallier, membre au Conseil des anciens, au
    Citoyen Grégoire, membre du Conseil des Cinq-Cents. Paris: Desenne, an 4.
[Raoul, Fanny]. Réponse à l'écrit de M. l'abbé Barruel, intitulé: Du principe et
    de l'obstination des Jacobins, en réponse au Sénateur Grégoire, par une
    française. N.p., [1814].
[Roederer, Pierre-Louis]. Prix proposés, en 1788, par la Société royale des sci-
    ences et des arts de Metz, pour les concours de 1789 et 1790. Metz: Veuve
    Antoine & fils, 1788 [copy in AN 29 AP 6, Roederer Papers].
Société des Amis des Noirs et des Colonies. Réglement de la Société des Amis
    des Noirs et des Colonies, adopté à la Séance tenue à Paris le 30 Frimaire an
    VII (Paris: Imprimerie des Sciences et Arts, an VII).
Société des Philantropes. Précis instructif sur la Société des Philantropes. [Stras-
    bourg]: n.p., n.d.
Société des Philantropes. Programmes de la Société des Philantropes. [Stras-
    bourg]: n.p., n.d.
Société des Philantropes. Statuts de la Société des Philantropes. [Strasbourg]:
    n.p., [1777].
Toland, John. Reasons for Naturalizing the Jews in Great Britain and Ire-
    land. . . . London: J. Roberts, 1714. Reprint, Jerusalem: Hebrew University,
    1963.
[Tussac, F. R. de]. Cri des Colons contre un ouvrage de M. L'Evêque et Sénateur
    Grégoire, ayant pour titre De la littérature des Nègres, ou Réfutation des
    inculpations calomnieuses faites aux Colons par l'auteur, et par les autres
    philosophes négrophiles, tels que Raynal, Valmont de Bomare, etc. . . . Paris:
    Delaunay, 1810.
[Valabrègue, Israël Bernard]. J. B. D. V. S. J. D. R. Lettre, ou Réflexions d'un
    milord à son correspondant à Paris; au sujet de la requête des marchands des
    six-corps, contre l'admission des Juifs aux Brevets &c. London: n.p., 1767.

SECONDARY SOURCES

Studies of Grégoire

"L'Abbé Grégoire, 'l'ami des hommes de toutes les couleurs.' " Europe: Revue
    Mensuelle. 34, nos. 128–29 (1956) [special issue].

L'abbé Grégoire, révolutionnaire de la tolérance. Exposition Nancy 1989/Exposition Blois 1989 . . . Texte biographique de Richard Figuier. [Nancy/Blois]: Conseil général de Meurthe-et-Moselle et Conseil général de Loir-et-Cher, 1989.

Ashbourne, Lord [Mac Giolla Bríde]. *Grégoire and the French Revolution.* London: Sands & Co., 1932.

Badinter, Robert. "Préface." In *Essai sur la régénération physique, morale et politique des Juifs.* Paris: Stock, 1988.

Bénot, Yves, and Marcel Dorigny, eds. *Grégoire et la cause des noirs (1789–1831), combats et projets.* Paris: Société française d'histoire d'outre-mer/Association pour l'Etude de la Colonisation Européenne, 2000 [including articles by Lucien-René Abénon, Yves Bénot, Amady Aly Dieng, Marcel Dorigny, Anne Girollet, Rita Hermon-Belot, Bernard Plongeron, Alyssa Goldstein Sepinwall, Ann Thomson].

Bercet, Nathalie, Catherine Bony, Francis Clément, Régine Gaillot, Maurice de Germiny, Maurice Gobillon, Jack Lang, Jean-Paul Sauvage, and Daniel Viaud. *L'abbé Grégoire et Blois* [Les cahiers de la Bibliothèque municipale de Blois, no. 15]. Blois: Les amis de la bibliothèque de Blois, 1999.

Berthe, Abbé Léon-Noël. "L'abbé Grégoire, élève de l'abbé Lamourette." *Revue du Nord* 44 (1962): 39–46.

Birnbaum, Pierre. "Sur l'étatisation révolutionnaire. L'abbé Grégoire et le destin de l'identité juive." *Le Débat,* no. 53 (1989): 157–73.

Carnot, Hippolyte. "Notice historique sur Grégoire." 1837. Reprinted in *Mémoires de Grégoire,* 201–30. Paris: Editions de Santé, 1989.

Certeau, Michel de, Dominique Julia, and Jacques Revel. *Une politique de la langue. La Révolution française et les patois: L'enquête de Grégoire.* Paris: Gallimard, 1975.

Debrunner, Hans W. *Grégoire l'Européen. Kontinentale Beziehungen eines französischen Patrioten. Henri Grégoire 1750–1831.* Anif/Salzburg: Verlag Müller-Speiser, 1997.

Ezran, Maurice. *L'Abbé Grégoire, défenseur des Juifs et des Noirs: Révolution et tolérance.* Paris: Harmattan, 1992.

Fauchon, Pierre. *L'Abbé Grégoire: Le prêtre-citoyen.* Paris: Nouvelle république, 1989.

Gazier, Augustin. *Etudes sur l'histoire religieuse de la Révolution française d'après des documents originaux et inédits.* Paris: Armand Colin, 1887.

Grunebaum-Ballin, Paul. "Grégoire convertisseur? ou la croyance au 'Retour d'Israël.' " *Revue des Etudes Juives,* 4th ser., vol. 1 (labeled vol. 121), nos. 1/2 (1962): 383–98.

Hermon-Belot, Rita. *L'abbé Grégoire, la politique, et la vérité.* Paris: Seuil, 2000.

Hourdin, Georges. *L'abbé Grégoire: Evêque et démocrate.* Paris: Descle de Brouver, 1989.

Jolly, Claude. "La bibliothèque de l'abbé Grégoire." *Livre et Révolution: Mélanges de la bibliothèque de la Sorbonne* 9 (1989): 209–20.

Lascaris, M. "L'abbé Grégoire et la Grèce." *Révolution française* 85 (1932): 220–31.

Leviah, Méïr. "L'abbé Grégoire contre la synagogue." *Chalom: Revue juive mensuelle* 10, no. 58 (1931): 4–7.

Lüsebrink, Hans-Jürgen. " 'Negrophilie' und Paternalismus: Die Beziehungen Henri Grégoires zu Haiti (1790–1831)." In *Der Karibische Raum zwischen Selbst- und Fremdbestimmung: Zur Karibischen Litteratur, Kultur und Gesellschaft,* ed. Reinhard Sander, 99–108. Frankfurt am Main: Verlag Peter Lang, 1984.

Maggiolo, Louis Edmond Henri. "L'abbé Grégoire, 1750–1789." *Mémoires de l'Académie de Stanislas,* 4th ser., vol. 5 (1873): xxx–cii.

———. "La vie et les œuvres de l'abbé Grégoire, 1789–1831." *Mémoires de l'Académie de Stanislas,* 5th ser., vol. 1 (1883): 75–147.

———. "La vie et les œuvres de l'abbé Grégoire, 1794–1831." *Mémoires de l'Académie de Stanislas,* 5th ser., vol. 2 (1884): 1–145.

———. "La vie et les oeuvres de l'abbé Grégoire, 1750 à 1789." *Revue des travaux de l'Académie des sciences morales et politiques et compte rendus de ses séances,* nouvelle série, 25 (1886): 224–65.

Mercier, Alain. *1794: L'abbé Grégoire et la création du Conservatoire national des Arts et Métiers.* Paris: Musée national des techniques/CNAM, 1989.

Necheles, Ruth. *The Abbé Grégoire 1787–1831. The Odyssey of an Egalitarian.* Westport, CT: Greenwood, 1971.

———. "The Abbé Grégoire and the Constitutional Church: 1794–1802." Ph.D. diss., University of Chicago, 1963.

Piquet, Jean-Daniel. "L'abbé Grégoire, un régicide panthéonisé." *Cahiers d'histoire: Espaces Marx,* no. 63 (1996): 61–77.

Plongeron, Bernard. *L'abbé Grégoire et la république des savants.* Paris: CTHS, 2001.

———. *L'abbé Grégoire, ou, l'arche de la fraternité.* Paris: Letouzey et Ané, 1989.

Popkin, Jeremy D., and Richard H. Popkin, eds. *The Abbé Grégoire and His World [Archives internationales d'histoire des idées/International Archives of the History of Ideas 169].* Dordrecht, Neth.: Kluwer Academic Publishers, 2000 [including articles by David A. Bell, M. Dorigny, R. Hermon-Belot, H.-J. Lüsebrink, J. Popkin, R. Popkin, A. Sepinwall, Dale Van Kley, Anthony Vidler].

Popkin, Richard H. "Mordecai Noah, the Abbé Grégoire and the Paris Sanhedrin." *Modern Judaism* 2 (1982): 131–48.

Pouget, Auguste. *Les idées religieuses et réformatrices de l'évêque constitutionnel Grégoire.* Paris: Société nouvelle de librairie et d'édition, 1905.

Ravitch, Norman. "Liberalism, Catholicism, and the Abbé Grégoire." *Church History* 36 (1967): 419–39.

Sachy de Foudrinoy, Michel de. *L'abbé Grégoire: Une autre vision.* Blois: Editions Lignages, 1989.

Sepinwall, Alyssa Goldstein. "French Abolitionism with an American Accent." Review of Cassirer/Brière translation of Grégoire's *De la littérature des nègres.* H-France, H-Net Reviews, January 1998 [URL: http://www.h-net.msu.edu/reviews/showrev.cgi?path = 3438887056586].

———. "Regenerating France, Regenerating the World: The Abbé Grégoire and the French Revolution, 1750–1831." Ph.D. diss., Stanford University, 1998.

———. "Strategic Friendships: Jewish Intellectuals, the Abbé Grégoire, and the French Revolution." In *Reconfiguring Jewish Culture from Spinoza to the Haskalah,* 189–212. Edited by Ross Brann and Adam Sutcliffe. Philadelphia: University of Pennsylvania Press, 2004.

Sutter, Antoine. *Les années de jeunesse de l'abbé Grégoire: Son itinéraire jusqu'au début de la Révolution.* Sarreguemines: Editions Pierron, 1992.

Taveneaux, René. "L'abbé Grégoire et la démocratie cléricale." In *Jansénisme et réforme catholique,* 137–57. Nancy: Presses universitaires de Nancy, 1992.

Tild, Jean. *L'abbé Grégoire d'après ses Mémoires recueillis par Hyppolyte Carnot.* Paris: Nouvelles éditions latines, 1946.

Vaval, Duraciné. "L'abbé Henri Grégoire dans ses rapports avec Saint-Domingue et Haïti. Conférence prononcée le 31 mai 1931 à la Société d'histoire et de géographie d'Haïti." *Revue de la Société d'histoire et de géographie d'Haïti* 2, no. 4 (1931): 16–34.

Other Studies

Amselle, Jean-Loup. *Vers un multiculturalisme français: L'empire de la coutume.* Paris: Aubier, 1996.

Aston, Nigel. *Religion and Revolution in France, 1780–1804.* Washington, D.C.: Catholic University of America Press, 2000.

Aulard, F. A. *Christianity and the French Revolution.* Translated by Lady Frazer. New York: H. Fertig, 1966.

Baczko, Bronislaw. *Comment sortir de la Terreur : Thermidor et la Révolution.* Paris: Gallimard, 1989.

Baecque, Antoine de. *Le corps de l'histoire: Métaphores et politique (1770–1800).* Paris: Calmann-Lévy, 1993.

———. "L'homme nouveau est arrivé: La 'régénération' du français en 1789." *Dix-huitième siècle,* no. 20 (1988): 193–208.

Baker, Keith Michael. *Condorcet: From Natural Philosophy to Social Mathematics.* Chicago: University of Chicago Press, 1975.

———. *Inventing the French Revolution.* Cambridge: Cambridge University Press, 1990.

Bell, David A. *The Cult of the Nation in France: Inventing Nationalism, 1680–1800.* Cambridge, Mass.: Harvard University Press, 2001.

———. "Lingua Populi, Lingua Dei: Language, Religion and the Origins of French Revolutionary Nationalism." *American Historical Review* (1995): 1403–37.

———. "Nation Building and Cultural Particularism in Eighteenth-Century France: The Case of Alsace." *Eighteenth-Century Studies* 21, no. 4 (1988): 472–90.

Benbassa, Esther. *The Jews of France: A History from Antiquity to the Present.* Princeton, N.J.: Princeton University Press, 1999.

Bénot, Yves. *La démence coloniale sous Napoléon.* Paris: La Découverte, 1991.

Berkovitz, Jay R. *The Shaping of Jewish Identity in Nineteenth-Century France.* Detroit: Wayne State University Press, 1989.

Bhabha, Homi K. "Of Mimicry and Man: The Ambivalence of Colonial Discourse." In *The Location of Culture,* 85–92. New York: Routledge, 1994.

Chartier, Roger. *Cultural Origins of the French Revolution.* Translated by Lydia G. Cochrane. Bicentennial Reflections on the French Revolution, ed. Keith M. Baker and Steven L. Kaplan. Durham, NC: Duke University Press, 1991.

Chevallier, Pierre. *Histoire de la franc-maçonnerie française, vol. 1: La Maçonnerie: Ecole de l'Egalité, 1725–1799.* Paris: Fayard, 1974.

Chisick, Harvey. *The Limits of Reform in the Enlightenment: Attitudes towards the Education of the Lower Classes in Eighteenth-Century France.* Princeton, N.J.: Princeton University Press, 1981.

Colman, Daniel Hollander. "The Foundation of the French Liberal Republic: Politics, Culture and Economy after the Terror." Ph.D. diss., Stanford University, 1997.

Desan, Suzanne. *Reclaiming the Sacred: Lay Religion and Popular Politics in Revolutionary France.* Ithaca, N.Y.: Cornell University Press, 1990.

Diringer, Bertrand. "Franc-maçonnerie et société à Strasbourg au XVIIIème siècle." Mémoire de maîtrise, Université de Strasbourg, 1980.

Dorigny, Marcel, and Bernard Gainot. *La société des amis des noirs 1788–1799: Contribution à l'histoire de l'abolition de l'esclavage.* Paris: Editions UNESCO, 1998.

Everdell, William R. *Christian Apologetics in France, 1730–1790: The Roots of Romantic Religion.* Lewiston, N.Y.: E. Mellen Press, 1987.

Feuerwerker, David. *L'Emancipation des Juifs en France : De l'Ancien régime à la fin du Second Empire.* Paris: A. Michel, 1976.

Fick, Carolyn E. *The Making of Haiti: The Saint Domingue Revolution from Below.* Knoxville: University of Tennessee Press, 1990.

Ford, Franklin L. *Strasbourg in Transition, 1648–1789.* New York: W. W. Norton, 1966.

Furet, François. *Interpreting the French Revolution.* Translated by Elborg Forster. Cambridge: Cambridge University Press, 1981.

———. *Revolutionary France, 1770–1880.* Translated by Antonia Nevill. Oxford: Blackwell, 1992.

Furet, François, and Mona Ozouf, eds. *A Critical Dictionary of the French Revolution.* Cambridge, MA: Belknap Press of Harvard University Press, 1989.

Garrigus, John D. " 'Sons of the Same Father': Gender, Race and Citizenship in French Saint-Domingue, 1760–1792." In *Visions and Revisions of Eighteenth-Century France.* Edited by Christine Adams, Jack R. Censer, and Lisa Jane Graham, 137–153. University Park: Pennsylvania State University Press, 1997.

Gauchet, Marcel. *La révolution des droits de l'homme.* Paris: NRF/Editions Gallimard, 1989.

Geggus, David. "Racial Equality, Slavery and Colonial Secession during the Constituent Assembly." *American Historical Review* 94, no. 5 (1989): 1290–1308.

Goodman, Dena. "Difference: An Enlightenment Concept." In *What's Left of Enlightenment? A Postmodern Question.* Edited by Keith Michael Baker and

Peter Hanns Reill, 129–147. Stanford, Calif.: Stanford University Press, 2001.

———. *The Republic of Letters: A Cultural History of the French Enlightenment*. Ithaca, N.Y.: Cornell University Press, 1994.

Graham, Ruth. "The Revolutionary Bishops and the *Philosophes*." *Eighteenth-Century Studies* 16, no. 2 (1982–83): 117–40.

Hector, Michel, ed. *La révolution française et Haïti: Filiations, ruptures, nouvelles dimensions*. [Port-au-Prince]: Société Haïtienne d'histoire et de géographie/Editions Henri Deschamps, [1995].

Helfand, Jonathan. "The Symbiotic Relationship between French and Germany Jewry in the Age of Emancipation." *Leo Baeck Year Book* 29 (1984): 331–50.

Hertzberg, Arthur. *The French Enlightenment and the Jews*. New York: Columbia University Press, 1968.

Hesse, Carla Alison. *The Other Enlightenment: How French Women Became Modern*. Princeton, N.J.: Princeton University Press, 2001.

Higonnet, Patrice. *Goodness beyond Virtue: Jacobins during the French Revolution*. Cambridge, Mass.: Harvard University Press, 1998.

Hunt, Lynn. *The Family Romance of the French Revolution*. Berkeley: University of California Press, 1992.

Hyman, Paula. *The Jews of Modern France*. Berkeley: University of California Press, 1998.

Jacob, Margaret C. *Living the Enlightenment: Freemasonry and Politics in Eighteenth-Century Europe*. New York: Oxford University Press, 1994.

Job, Françoise. "Les deux statues de l'Abbé Grégoire à Lunéville (1885–1955)." *Le Pays Lorrain* 61, no. 1 (1980): 35–41.

Kaplan, Steven Laurence. *Farewell, Revolution: Disputed Legacies: France, 1789/1989*. Ithaca, N.Y.: Cornell University Press, 1995.

King, Stewart R. *Blue Coat or Powdered Wig: Free People of Color in Pre-Revolutionary Saint Domingue*. Athens: University of Georgia Press, 2001.

Kurtz, John F. *John Frederic Oberlin*. Boulder: Westview Press, 1976.

Landes, Joan B. *Women and the Public Sphere in the Age of the French Revolution*. Ithaca, NY: Cornell University Press, 1988.

Liberles, Robert. "Dohm's Treatise on the Jews: A Defence of the Enlightenment." *Leo Baeck Institute Year Book* 33 (1988): 29–42.

Madiou, Thomas. *Histoire d'Haïti*. 7 vols. 1848; reprint, Port-au-Prince: Editions Henri Deschamps, 1988.

Maire, Catherine. *De la cause de Dieu à la cause de la Nation: Le jansénisme au XVIIIe siècle*. Paris: Gallimard, 1998.

Malino, Frances. *A Jew in the French Revolution: The Life of Zalkind Hourwitz*. Cambridge, MA: Blackwell, 1996.

Manchuelle, François. "The 'Regeneration of Africa': An Important and Ambiguous Concept in 18th and 19th Century French Thinking about Africa." *Cahiers d'Etudes Africaines* 144, no. 36–4 (1996): 559–88.

Margadant, Jo Burr, ed. *The New Biography: Performing Femininity in Nineteenth-Century France*. Berkeley: University of California Press, 2000.

McMahon, Darrin M. *Enemies of the Enlightenment: The French Counter-Enlightenment and the Making of Modernity.* New York: Oxford University Press, 2001.

Melzer, Sara E., and Leslie W. Rabine, eds. *Rebel Daughters: Women and the French Revolution.* New York: Oxford University Press, 1992.

Moote, A. Lloyd. "Early Modern Biography. Introduction: New Bottles and New Wine: The Current State of Early Modernist Biographical Writing." *French Historical Studies* 19 (1996): 911–26.

Nicholls, David. *From Dessalines to Duvalier: Race, Colour and National Independence in Haiti.* Cambridge: Cambridge University Press, 1979.

Nora, Pierre. *Les lieux de mémoire.* 3 vols. Paris: Editions Gallimard, 1992.

Oliel-Grausz, Evelyne, and Mireille Hadas-Lebel, eds. *Les Juifs et la Révolution française: Histoire et mentalités: Actes du colloque tenu au Collège de France et à l'Ecole normale supérieure, les 16, 17 et 18 mai 1989.* Louvain: E. Peeters, 1992.

Ozouf, Mona. *Festivals and the French Revolution.* Translated by Alan Sheridan. Cambridge, MA: Harvard University Press, 1988.

———. *L'homme régénéré: Essais sur la Révolution française.* Paris: Editions Gallimard, 1989.

Palmer, R. R. *Catholics and Unbelievers in Eighteenth-Century France.* New York: Cooper Square Publishers, 1939.

Plongeron, Bernard. "Recherches sur l'Aufklärung catholique en Europe occidentale (1770–1830)." *Revue d'histoire moderne et contemporaine* 16 (1969): 555–605.

Ravitch, Norman. "Catholicism in Crisis: The Impact of the French Revolution on the Thought of the Abbé Adrien Lamourette." *Cahiers internationaux d'histoire économique et sociale* 9 (1978): 354–85.

Roberts, Mary Louise. "Acting Up: The Feminist Theatrics of Marguerite Durand." *French Historical Studies* 19 (1996): 1103–38.

Rodrigue, Aron. *French Jews, Turkish Jews: The Alliance Israélite Universelle and the Politics of Jewish Schooling in Turkey, 1860–1925.* Bloomington: Indiana University Press, 1990.

Rogers, Dominique. "Les libres de couleur dans les capitales de Saint-Domingue: Fortune, mentalités, et intégration à la fin de l'ancien régime (1776–1789)." Ph.D. diss., Université Michel de Montaigne, Bordeaux III, 1999.

Rosanvallon, Pierre. *La monarchie impossible: Les Chartes de 1814 et de 1830.* Paris: Fayard, 1994.

Schechter, Ronald B. "Translating the Marseillaise: Biblical Republicanism and the Emancipation of Jews in Revolutionary France." *Past & Present* no. 143 (1994): 108–35.

Schneider, Malou, and Marie-Jeanne Geyer. *Jean-Frédéric Oberlin: Le divin ordre du monde, 1740–1826.* Strasbourg/Mulhouse: Les Musées de la ville de Strasbourg/Editions du Rhin, 1991.

Scott, Joan Wallach. *Only Paradoxes to Offer: French Feminists and the Rights of Man.* Cambridge, MA: Harvard University Press, 1996.

Staum, Martin. *Minerva's Message: Stabilizing the French Revolution.* Montreal/Kingston: McGill-Queen's University Press, 1996.

Tackett, Timothy. *Becoming a Revolutionary: The Deputies of the French National Assembly and the Emergence of a Revolutionary Culture (1789–1790)*. Princeton, N.J.: Princeton University Press, 1996.

———. *Priest and Parish in Eighteenth-Century France: A Social and Political Study of the Curés in a Diocese of Dauphiné, 1750–1791*. Princeton, N.J.: Princeton University Press, 1977.

———. *Religion, Revolution, and Regional Culture in Eighteenth-Century France: The Ecclesiastical Oath of 1791*. Princeton, N.J.: Princeton University Press, 1986.

Taveneaux, René. *Le Jansénisme en Lorraine, 1640–1789*. Paris: J. Vrin, 1960.

Troyansky, David G. "Alsatian Knowledge and European Culture: Jérémie-Jacques Oberlin, Language and the Protestant *Gymnase* in Revolutionary Strasbourg." *Francia* 27, no. 2 (2001): 119–38.

Van Kley, Dale, ed. *The French Idea of Freedom: The Old Regime and the Declaration of Rights of 1789*. Stanford, Ca.: Stanford University Press, 1994.

———. *The Jansenists and the Expulsion of the Jesuits from France, 1757–1765*. New Haven, Conn.: Yale University Press, 1975.

———. *The Religious Origins of the French Revolution: From Calvin to the Civil Constitution, 1560–1791*. New Haven, Conn.: Yale University Press, 1996.

Wagner-Martin, Linda. *Telling Women's Lives: The New Biography*. New Brunswick, NJ: Rutgers University Press, 1994.

Woodress, James. *A Yankee's Odyssey: The Life of Joel Barlow*. Philadelphia: J. B. Lippincott Company, 1958.

Zizek, Joseph John. "The Politics and Poetics of History in the French Revolution, 1787–1794." Ph.D. diss., University of California at Berkeley, 1995.

Index

Page numbers in italics refer to illustrations.

abolitionism: in Britain, 93, 185–86; Grégoire as exponent of, 93, 150, 155, 164, 169, 171–74, 179, 182, 195, 221, 223; and Haiti (Saint-Domingue) emancipation struggle, 93, 150, 181, 182, 185, 195; in Latin America, 169, 179; and Société des Amis des Noirs et des Colonies (SANC), 150, 151, 155; in United States, 171–74, 179. *See also* slavery

abortion, 212

academies, 12, 15, 22, 128, 129–30, 132–33, 140. *See also* Nancy: academy of; Metz: academy of; scholarly activity, importance of

action française, 234

Actualité et rayonnement de l'abbé Grégoire, 305n22

Adams, Hannah, 170

Adams, John Quincy, 174

Africa, 152, 154, 182, 184, 186, 188, 189, 193, 195, 196, *197, 198,* 216, 223, 224, 225, 233, 236

Agier, Pierre-Jean, 148

agriculture, 38, 81, 111, 132, 141, 152, 153–54, 170, 193

Alembert, Jean Le Rond d', 27, 39, 58, 73

Alexander I (emperor of Russia), 162

Alliance Israélite Universelle, 197

Alpes-Maritimes. *See* Nice, Grégoire's mission to; Monaco, Grégoire's mission to

Alsace, 25–27, 30, 31, 36, 40–41, 53, 60, 81. *See also* Strasbourg

American Philosophical Society (APS), 170, 171

American Revolution. *See* Revolution, American

Amerindians, 169, 170, 211, 212, 213, 214, 216

Angers, Pierre David d', *197, 198, 199,* 219

Annales de la religion, 148

Annales school, 1

antimonarchism: biblical sources of, 118; and Boucher's writings, 23, 118; and Enlightenment, 118; Grégoire as exponent of, 23, 116–19, 125–28, 162–63, 183–85; and Protestantism, 23

antisemitism, 30–31, 224, 226, 229, 230, 234

aristocracy, 17–18, 27, 35, 120, 130, 215

Arnauld, Angélique, 211

Arnauld, Antoine, 17, 50

Arras, academy of, 49

ARTFL database, 57, 260n4

Ashkenazim, 30, 94, 95, 231. *See also* Jews

Asia, 1, 119, 207, 213, 215, 281n53. *See also* India

Assembly, National. *See* National Assembly

Assembly of Notables, 81

36, 39, 43, 49, 55, 56–57, 59–60, 62–77, 83; Grégoire as student in, 19; Grégoire ordained in, 20; Jewish community in, 60, 67

Mexico, 168, 169

Michaelis, Johann David, 60, 62, 64, 67, 68

militarism, 96, 115–16, 119, 123. *See also* wars, French revolutionary; patriotism

millennialism, 53, 148, 202, 204

Milton, John, 118

Mirabeau, Victor Requetti, marquis de, 58, 67, 202

missionaries, 188, 189, 213, 229

Mitterrand, François, 229

mixed-race persons, 93, 95–96, 99, 102, 107, 183, 184, 188, 190, 193, 195, 295n5. *See also gens de couleur*

Monaco, Grégoire's mission to, 120

Monge, Gaspard, 224, 229

Monroe, James, 171

Mont-Blanc. *See* Savoy

Montesquieu, Charles de Secondat, baron de, 11, 50, 140

monuments, 133–34

morality: Grégoire's views on, 38, 43, 45, 46, 55, 188, 201; and Haitian politics, 188; and intermarriage, 95; of Jews, 62–63, 70, 72; and Lavater's ideas on physiognomy, 36; of peasantry, 28, 37, 38, 43, 45, 46; of women, 99, 100, 190, 192, 216

moral science, 140, 143, 149

Moreau de Saint-Méry, Médéric-Louis-Elie, 104

Moris, Henry, 120

Morocco, 197, 223

motherhood, 134–35, 190, 193

mulattos. *See métis; gens de couleur;* mixed-race persons

Mulot, François, 113

multiculturalism, 226

Musée lorrain manuscript ("Mémoire sur les juifs"), 66–67, 263nn28,29, 264n32, 265nn39,40,42,46,47

Muslims, 138, 201, 205, 208, 209, 226, 235, 307n42

mysticism, 43, 71

Nancy: academy of, 12, 22, 23, 25; Grégoire as student in, 18–19, 22–23; Grégoire's election to Estates-General in, 51–52, 76; Grégoire's literary activity in, 22–25, 74; library of, 22–23

Napoleon. *See* Bonaparte, Napoleon

nation, idea of the: during Old Regime, 28, 191; applied to Jews, 31, 63, 76, 103, 206–7; during the Revolution, 6, 7, 90–1, 94, 95, 96, 97, 102–3, 105, 107–8, 109, 115, 116, 121, 134; and gender, 97, 100–2, 106–8, 122–23, 134

National Assembly, 3, 19, 82, 86, 89–94, 102–4, 1068, 111, 112, 113, 114, 116, 129, 149

National Convention, 4, 87, 107, 110, 117–21, 123–25, 127, 128, 130, 131, 132, 134, 136, 149, 159, 160, 193

national identity, 133, 234–35

national liberation, 166, 198

national unity, 90–91, 97, 107–8, 133

nation-state, modern: 8, 87, 236–37

Native Americans. *See* Amerindians

natural history, 22, 59, 72, 73, 184, 189

Nazis, 6, 223, 233, 234

Necheles, Ruth, 53, 94, 148, 153, 218, 253n48, 290n19, 301n33

négritude, 102, 194, 224, 233

Neufchâteau, François de, 159

Nice, Grégoire's mission to, 120, 121, 123

Noah, Mordecai, 170, 171, 173

noblesse de peau, 188, 191

Nora, Pierre, 221

Notre-Dame de Paris, 144

nuns, 48, 101, 114, 122, 190, 211

Oberlin, Jean-Frédéric, 26, 40–43, 45, 53, 54, 257n18

Oberlin, Jérémie-Jacques, 26, 40–42, 45, 54, 257n17

Oberlin College, 42

Old Regime: corruption of, 87, 91, 204; injustices of, 20, 94; and women, 122–23

oppressed groups, Grégoire's defense of, 95, 109, 144, 166, 199, 200, 211–16

Orientalism, 64, 138, 207, 209. *See also* Asia

original sin, 28, 129, 166, 209

Ottomans, 154, 193

Ozouf, Mona, 57, 113

Paine, Thomas, 118, 119, 202

Palm d'Aelders, Etta, 106, 107

Palmer, R. R., 33, 129, 255n59

Pantheon, 224–25, 230

Paris municipality, 105

Parris, Guichard, 223, 233, 246n2

passive citizenship, 94, 107

Compositor:	IBT Global
Indexer:	Andrew Joron
Text:	10/13 Sabon
Display:	Sabon

Milton Keynes UK
Ingram Content Group UK Ltd.
UKHW041014011024
449095UK00005B/102